En la Lucha

Praise for the first edition—

"*En la Lucha* is the charter document of *mujerista* theology, a theology shaped by the experience of Hispanic/Latina women living in the United States. . . . The book is a delight to read. It is more than just another academic text. . . . It is also a sign of the increasingly active role of Hispanic women in North American society and church."

—*Toronto Journal of Theology*

"She has both feet firmly on the ground and her theology draws its inspiration from her knowledge of and communication with the Hispanic women/Latinas on whose behalf she takes up the theological cudgels."

—*Theological Book Review*

En la ucha

In the Struggle

Elaborating a *Mujerista* Theology

Ada María Isasi-Díaz

FORTRESS PRESS
MINNEAPOLIS

EN LA LUCHA / IN THE STRUGGLE
Elaborating a *Mujerista* Theology

Scripture quotations from the Revised Standard Version are copyright © 1946, 1952, and 1971 by the Division of Christian Education of the National Council of Churches.

Cover art: Woman, 1915–1917. Juan Gris (1887–1927). Private Collection, Switzerland. © 2003 Erich Lessing / Art Resource, N.Y. Used by permission.
Cover design: Ann Delgehausen
Book design: Michelle L. N. Cook

The Library of Congress has catalogued the first edition as follows:
Isasi-Díaz, Ada María.
   En la lucha-In the struggle: a Hispanic Women's liberation theology / Ada María Isasi-Díaz.
   p. cm.
English text with chapter summaries in Spanish.
Includes bibliographical references and index.
ISBN 0-8006-3599-X (alk. paper)
1. Theology—Hispanic American Women. 2. Liberation theology. 3. Women's Studies. 4. Christian and culture. I. Title. II. Title: En la lucha-In the struggle.
BR563.H57I82 1993
230'.082—dc20

The paper used in this publication meets the minimum requirements of American National Standard for Information Services-Permanence of Paper for Printed Library Materials, ANSI Z329.48-1984.

Manufactured in the U.S.A.

08   07   06   05   04   1   2   3   4   5   6   7   8   9   10

Pero Nueva York no fue la ciudad de mi infancia,
no fue aquí que adquirí las primeras certidumbres,
no está aquí el rincón de mi primera caída
ni el silbido lacerante que marcaba las noches.
Por eso siempre permaneceré al margen,
una extraña entre las piedras,
aún bajo el sol amable de este día de verano,
como ya para siempre permaneceré extranjera,
aún cuando regrese a la ciudad de mi infancia.
Cargo esta marginalidad inmune a todos los retornos,
demasiado newyorkina para ser,
—aún volver a ser—
cualquier otra cosa.

Lourdes Casal, Para Ana Velford[*]

But New York was not the city of my infancy,
nor was it here that I grasped truth for the first time,
not here the corner of my first fall,
or where I heard the whistle that cuts the night.
That is why I will always remain marginalized
a stranger among the stones,
even under the kindly sun of this summer day,
just as I will always remain a foreigner,
even when I return to the city of my infancy,
I carry this marginality immune to all returns,
too much a New Yorker to be
—even to once again be—
anything else.

[*] Originally this poem was published in a literary magazine called *Areíto* (New York) 3, no. 1 (verano 1976): 52. Later it was included in the posthumous volume, *Palabras juntan revolución* (La Habana: Casa de las Américas, 1981).

"*A mi vagabunda y desmembrada generación,*"

to my vagabond and dismembered generation the world over,

particularly to my generation of Cuban sisters and brothers,

deseándonos ganas de un mundo liberado

y fuerzas para la lucha para lograrlo,

wishing us a deep desire for a liberated world and

the strength to struggle to accomplish it

CONTENTS

PREFACE

I AM A MUJERISTA THEOLOGIAN, an activist theologian committed to the struggle for justice and peace. The poor and oppressed of Lima, Perú, where I had the privilege of living for three years, taught me that without liberation there is no justice and peace and that no one can be liberated at the expense of others or isolated from others. The struggle for liberation is the struggle to be self-determining within the context of community and in view of the common good, and to have the material conditions needed to develop into the fullness of our capacity. This fullness of being to which we are all called cannot become a reality if we cannot do according to what we know. For at the core of our being lies our conscience, our moral consciousness, demanding from us responsible decisions in accord with reasonable judgments. Fullness of being requires a commitment constantly to check, expand, and deepen our understanding of the values according to which we choose, and constantly to strengthen our resolution to decide according to those values at no matter what cost. And for me, to do *mujerista* theology is one of the key ways in which I contribute to and participate in the struggle for fullness of being, for liberation, an indispensable preparation for the coming of the kin-dom of God.[1]

For me to do *mujerista* theology is a vocation: it is the best way I can at present live out who I am and what I believe I am called to do. I do *mujerista* theology not to promote myself, but that fact does not take away from nor contradict the fact that doing *mujerista* theology is fulfilling and life-giving for me. It is a way of responsibly living my Christianity, struggling for survival and liberation as a Latina in the U.S.A.

In doing *mujerista* theology I struggle for liberation because religion is an essential and integral element of Hispanic culture. For a Latina, religion does indeed provide or influence many of the understandings and motivations of daily life. I believe that religious understandings likewise are part of the ideology of the U.S.A., an ideology that grounds and supports societal institutions. I believe that *mujerista* theology, by providing a platform for the voices of grassroot Hispanic Women, can be an effective means of challenging (and, I hope, changing) present ideology and societal structures because they effectively exclude and oppress Latinas.

I come from a hard-working middle-class family with certain privileges that money can buy but with no monetary wealth. As a middle-class woman I am always two or three months away from not having enough money to pay my bills—including my mortgage—but with a certain degree of confidence that such a thing will not happen. As a Latina, I have often experienced ethnic prejudice and sexism: in educational institutions both as a student and as a professor; in women's groups and in organizations where difference is neither understood nor valued; in many diverse situations and places such as stores, conferences, government offices, Latino businesses and organizations. For me, to do *mujerista* theology is an effective way to struggle against the prejudices that oppress me and my Hispanic sisters.

As a *mujerista* theologian, I straddle the academic and the Latino worlds. Hispanic Women are indeed my community of accountability. But I am an academically trained theologian, and part of my praxis has to do with attempting to affect academia, to bring Latinas' religious understandings and practices to bear on the academic world and on academic disciplines, particularly theology. My writings reflect these two worlds, between which I move constantly. Some of the language I use in my writings is certainly alien to the majority of grassroot Hispanic Women, but I am confident it does not betray who they are, their beliefs and expectations. Though I do not speak for them, I speak with them and on behalf of them. *Mujerista* theology is an effective way of doing community advocacy. I also hope that *mujerista* theology's method and insistence on the validity and importance of Latinas' religious understandings and practices will affect not only theology but also the churches and, through them, society.

This self-revelatory statement, as well as the acknowledgments that follow, are meant to make obvious my subjectivity and my social locality. Who I am, where I am coming from, and where I wish to go shapes the method and content of my theological work. Though such self-revelation is always dangerous, I have entered upon it because I believe that the pretense of objectivity by theologians indicates complicity with the status quo, a status that for me and my Hispanic sisters is oppressive.

THERE IS NOT MUCH TO ADD to the self-revelatory Preface of ten years ago. When this book was written I had recently started teaching at Drew University and today I am Professor of Ethics and Theology at that institution. I have published several other books and many articles about *mujerista* theology.

I continue to do *mujerista* theology because I believe it is the best way I can contribute to the struggle for liberation of Latinas in the U.S.A. I also continue to believe it is the best way to live out my own vocation to struggle for justice, a struggle that is today as relevant as it was a decade ago. Hispanic Women continue to be oppressed: we continue to suffer violence and marginalization, we continue to have little or no power, and the majority of us continue to live in poverty. I realize that for many the discourse of oppression and prejudice might sound like a "tired discourse" with nothing new to offer. Others might think that to talk about oppression and prejudice is to fan the flames of hostility between Latinas and Latinos, or between Hispanic Women and other women. That is not my intention nor is it to promote a victim mentality among Latinas. However, as long as prejudice continues to be operative in our lives, as long as Hispanic Women suffer oppression, my theological work has to focus on these realities for they are present in *lo cotidiano*—the everyday lives—of Latinas. It is the reality of Hispanic Women's *cotidiano* that has been and will continue to be the source of *mujerista* theology and, unfortunately, oppression and injustice continue to be at the heart of Latinas' daily experience.

One of the joys and learnings of this past decade that has influenced my theological work has been my being in touch with women—theologians and grass-root women—in different parts of the world. Their reality has given me a new lens through which to look at our reality as Hispanic Women in the U.S.A. Of particular importance has been the ability to go back to my country, Cuba, every year for the last seven years. This has led me to recognize that, in spite of the fact that we are a marginalized community, most Latinas in the U.S.A. enjoy certain privileges. Our task, then, is to use those privileges in ways that can contribute to the struggle for liberation. It is a matter of using privileges to undo dominant structures instead of benefiting from them at the expense of others in this country or in other parts of the world. Ongoing contact with women who live in so-called third world countries also has sharpened for me the issue of representation and of identity. I live in my own flesh as a Cuban in the U.S.A. who is a Latina theologian, struggling to provide a platform in my work for the voices of grassroot Latinas.

PREFACIO

Soy una teóloga mujerista, una teóloga activista comprometida con la lucha por la justicia y la paz. Los pobres y los oprimidos de Lima, Perú, con quienes tuve el privilegio de trabajar por tres años en la década de 1960, me enseñaron que sin liberación no puede haber justicia y paz, y que nadie puede liberarse a costa de otras u otros o sin contar con los demás. La lucha por la liberación es una lucha por la auto-determinación de la persona, la persona siempre como miembro de una comunidad. La liberación de cada persona no puede ser un proceso individualista sino que tiene que darse en vistas al bien de su comunidad. Es también una lucha por crear las condiciones materiales necesarias para el desarrollo pleno de nuestras capacidades humanas. Esta plenitud humana a la que estamos llamadas no puede lograrse sino actuamos de acuerdo a lo que sabemos que tenemos que hacer. Por eso decimos que en el centro de toda persona se encuentra la conciencia, el sentir moral que exige decisiones responsables de acuerdo con juicios razonables. La plenitud humana requiere que constantemente comprobemos, ampliemos y profundicemos los valores que guían nuestras decisiones, y también exige que constantemente reforcemos nuestra decisión de actuar de acuerdo a esos valores, cueste lo que cueste.

Para mí, el hacer teología *mujerista* es una de las formas principales en que contribuyo y participo en la lucha por la plenitud humana, por la liberación de todas y todos, preparación necesaria para poder llegar a ser familia de Dios.[1] Para mí, el hacer teología *mujerista* es una vocación: es la mejor forma de serme fiel a mí misma y la mejor manera de vivir de acuerdo a lo que Dios quiere de mí. Yo hago teología *mujerista* no para vanagloriarme, aunque sí reconozco que ser teóloga *mujerista* me satisface y me da vida. Yo hago teología *mujerista* porque es una forma responsable de vivir mi cristianismo, y es una forma eficaz de contribuir a la lucha por sobrevivir de las latinas en los EE.UU., y, por lo tanto, a la lucha por mi propia liberación.

El hacer teología *mujerista* es luchar por la liberación de las hispanas porque la religión es elemento integral de la cultura hispana. Para las latinas la religión provee o influye en la manera en que entendemos la vida cotidiana y los motivos que nos mueven a vivir como lo hacemos. También creo que la religión es parte de la ideología que apoya y mantiene las instituciones sociales en los EE.UU. Es esta importancia de la religión lo que me lleva a creer que la teología *mujerista*, al proveer una plataforma para las voces de hispanas de la base, puede ser una manera eficaz de retar y de contribuir a cambiar la ideología y las estructuras de este país, tarea necesaria ya que dichas estructuras excluyen y oprimen a las latinas.

Soy de una familia de clase media muy trabajadora. Sin duda, mi familia ha tenido ciertos privilegios usualmente relacionados con tener dinero; aunque por ser una familia numerosa de seis hermanas y dos hermanos el dinero nunca fue mucho. Ser mujer de la clase media quiere decir que, si me quedo sin trabajo, pues sólo tengo dinero para vivir tres meses, aunque vivo con cierto grado de sosiego ya que estoy segura de que siempre podré conseguir trabajo. Como latina que vive en los EE.UU. siempre he sufrido prejuicio étnico y prejuicio por ser mujer. Esa doble carga de prejuicios es una realidad en las instituciones educativas en las que me desenvuelvo como profesora al igual que lo fue cuando fui estudiante, y también impacta mi vida cotidiana cuando voy a las tiendas, a oficinas gubernamentales o de negocios. En las organizaciones y grupos de mujeres sin duda se me margina por ser latina, mientras que en las organizaciones y grupos latinos se me margina por ser mujer. Para mí, el hacer teología *mujerista* es una forma eficaz de luchar en contra de estos prejuicios que me oprimen a mí y a mis hermanas hispanas.

Como teóloga *mujerista* me muevo entre el mundo académico y el de la comunidad latina. Considero que es a las latinas antes que a nadie a quienes tengo que rendir cuentas. Pero soy una teóloga con adiestramiento académico y parte de mi praxis consiste en tratar de impactar a la academia, de hacer que las prácticas religiosas y la manera de entender la fe de las hispanas tengan peso en el mundo académico, en el campo de la teología. Lo que escribo refleja estos dos mundos entre los cuales me muevo. Parte del lenguaje que empleo en las elaboraciones teológicas que publico, sin duda, no le es familiar a la mayoría de las latinas de la base, pero estoy segura de que lo que digo no traiciona quiénes son, sus creencias y lo que esperan de la vida. Aunque no considero que hablo en nombre de ellas, sí hablo como una de ellas y abogo por ellas. La teología *mujerista* es una manera efectiva de abogar por la comunidad latina. También espero que el método que empleamos al hacer teología *mujerista* y nuestra insistencia en la validez e importancia de las creencias y prácticas religiosas de las hispanas impacte no sólo el campo de la teología sino también a las iglesias, y por medio de ellas, a la sociedad.

Este relato personal que aquí hago, al igual que la sección de reconocimientos y agradecimientos que le sigue, tiene como fin el hacer visible mi subjetividad y cómo me sitúo en la sociedad—mi status en la sociedad. Quién soy, de dónde vengo y a dónde quiero ir moldea el método y el contenido de mi trabajo teológico. Aunque creo que este tipo de relato siempre puede ser peligroso, he estado dispuesta a correr ese riesgo porque creo que para la mayoría de los que escriben teología, el presumir objetividad es indicación de complicidad con el *status quo*, es decir, con la realidad de los poderosos que es tan opresiva para mí y mis hermanas hispanas.

No hay mucho que añadir a lo que escribí en este relato personal hace diez años. Cuando se publicó este libro ya enseñaba en la Universidad de Drew donde hoy en día soy catedrática titular de ética y teología. En los años que han pasado he publicado otros libros y muchos artículos sobre teología *mujerista*.

Continúo creyendo que mi trabajo de elaborar una teología *mujerista* es la mejor manera que tengo de contribuir a la lucha por la liberación de las latinas en los EE.UU. También sigo creyendo que es la mejor manera de vivir mi vocación de luchar por la justicia, lucha que sigue siendo tan relevante hoy como lo era hace diez años. Las hispanas continuamos siendo oprimidas: continuamos sufriendo violencia y siendo marginadas; continuamos teniendo muy poco o ningún poder, y la mayoría de nosotras vivimos en la pobreza. Comprendo que para muchas personas—mayormente académicas—el discurso acerca de la opresión y el prejuicio es un "discurso cansado" que no ofrece nada nuevo. Habrá quien piense que hablar de opresión y prejuicio es avivar las llamas de la hostilidad entre latinas y latinos, o entre hispanas y otras mujeres. Éstas no son las razones por las que insisto en hablar de la opresión y el prejuicio. Tampoco lo hago con el afán de crear una mentalidad de víctima entre las latinas. El hecho es que mientras el prejuicio en contra nuestra no cese, mientras que las hispanas sufran opresión, mi labor teológica tiene que centrarse en esas realidades tan presentes en su vivir cotidiano. La vida cotidiana de las hispanas ha sido y continuará siendo la fuente de la teología *mujerista* y, desgraciadamente, la opresión y la injusticia siguen siendo elemento central de las experiencias diarias de las latinas.

En esta última década una de las alegrías y fuentes de aprendizaje que más ha influido mi quehacer teológico ha sido el estar en contacto con mujeres—teólogas y de la base—en diferentes partes del mundo. La realidad que viven me ha dado un lente nuevo a través del cual mirar la realidad de las hispanas en los EE.UU. Particularmente importante para mí ha sido haber regresado a mi patria, Cuba, todos los años durante los últimos siete años. Esta experiencia me ha ayudado a entender mejor que, ya que las latinas en los EE.UU. disfrutamos de ciertos privilegios, a pesar de ser una comunidad marginada, tenemos que ver cómo usamos esos privilegios para lograr cambios estructurales en la sociedad. El disfrutar de ciertos privilegios puede ser una tentación para beneficiarnos de las estructuras presentes sin darnos cuenta de que dichos privilegios son, en su mayoría, a costa de lo que no tienen la mayoría de los seres humanos en otras partes del mundo. El tener contacto repetido con mujeres en países del llamado tercer mundo también me ha ayudado a perfilar cómo entiendo las dificultades que surgen cuando se me ve como representante de otras hispanas. También me ha dado la oportunidad de pensar y re-pensar lo complejo del problema de la identidad de las latinas, problema que siento en mi propia carne como cubana viviendo en los EE.UU. y que, a la vez, es una teóloga hispana—responsable a una comunidad de mujeres de otros países además de Cuba.

ACKNOWLEDGMENTS

"HONRAR, HONRA"—TO HONOR OTHERS HONORS ONE—is a saying of José Martí, one of the literary greats of Latin America, the soul of Cuba's independence at the end of the nineteenth century and of its revolutionary struggles ever since. Although the length may seem extravagant to some, these acknowledgments are my way of honoring those who have blessed me with their friendship and love, and those who have shared with me their experiences and knowledge through the years. It is a way for me to say that I cannot do theology and will not do theology apart from a community of support and accountability. It is also a way of giving the reader a sense of who I am.

My first debt of gratitude is to the Hispanic Women who have in many different ways been my sisters in the struggle. I particularly wish to thank those who have given me so much by sharing with me their religious understandings and practices. I thank Inez, Adela, Marta, Lupe, María, Olivia, Margarita, Esperanza, and Caridad, who speak from the pages of this book. I thank all the other women who participated in the reflection weekends at which Yolanda Tarango and I gathered the material first used in our book *Hispanic Women: Prophetic Voice in the Church,* material which is also reflected throughout this book.

I want to thank my *mujerista* community, particularly Yolanda Tarango, Carmen Villegas, and María Antonietta Berriozábal, whose support has been unswerving. Our friendship was birthed by the struggle, and the struggle is indeed one of our friendship's main sources of nourishment.

For the last ten years I have been a member of the Women's Liturgy Group in New York City. The group has persisted through the years in gathering once a month to celebrate our lives, to explore and deepen our faith. In the process, many of us have become good friends, we are *familia,* and we know we can depend on one another. I thank all of these wonderful women for their support and encouragement. Particularly I am grateful to Mary Ragan, who listens to me and shares with me when I am fit to be tied; to Cindy Derway, whose affirming praise always nourishes me and spurs me on; to Janet Walton, who every single time she sees me affirms my ability to be a theologian; to Eileen King, who first introduced me to her beloved city of New York and who has shared generously with me through the years. Finally, I owe a major debt of gratitude to Ann Patrick Ware. We worked together at Church Women United while I was writing my doctoral dissertation, from which this book draws extensively. Ann Pat helped me at work time and again during those years so I could have time for my studies. She has edited all of my written work during the last six years, always insisting on clarity of thought as well as precise and effective use of the English language. I am most appreciative of her ability to make my English correct without making it sound "non-Cuban."

I want to thank a scattered feminist community that had Union Theological Seminary, from which I graduated in 1990, as its initial point of reference. In particular I want to thank Angela Bauer, Pam Brubaker, Liz Bounds, Hyun Kyung Chung, Marilyn Legge, and Serinity Young. Their friendship has confirmed my belief that the creation of feminist communities is an effective survival strategy.

To all of these sisters I say those wonderful words of Marge Piercy, "Give birth to me, sisters, in the struggle we transform ourselves. . . . This morning we must make each other strong. Change is qualitative: we are each other's miracle."

I am grateful to my doctoral dissertation committee, who guided the work on which this book is based. Beverly Harrison was my adviser at Union Theological Seminary, and her trust enabled me to follow my theological insights and experience as I worked on the initial formulations of *mujerista* theology. Margaret Farley helped me keep in touch with my Roman Catholic roots. Her clear and methodical thinking and her vast knowledge of Roman Catholic theology kept me on a firm footing. Victoria Erickson has been enormously helpful to me regarding the use of social sciences in my theological method. I am particularly grateful to her for teaching me that I am not alone in my convictions regarding the need to have the voices of Latinas in my writings, that there is a whole school of sociologists whose theories back me. Larry Rasmussen became one of my theological dialogue partners through his written work before I met him personally. Larry is a true gentleman, always willing to spare a moment to help me clarify ideas and concepts. I am deeply grateful to all of my committee members for their willingness to work with me and to embrace me as a colleague.

I am grateful to my large family for their loving support and care, which is so intense and has such actuality that although I am the only one of us who lives in New York City I feel that, after all, I do *not* live alone. I especially want to thank the three little ones, Alexandra, Javi, and A.J., who repeatedly give me an opportunity to be concerned about important things like diapers, peanut butter-and jelly-sandwiches, and learning how to swim and to ride bikes. These three little ones, because they concretize for me the future in a very personal way, always offer me hope and refresh me.

I am grateful to Michael West and Lois Torvik, my editors at Fortress Press, and to my copy editor, Sydney Merkel, who also edited the Spanish in this book. Without their support and help this book would not have been possible.

Finally, a word of explanation about the dedication of this work. I finished high school while my country, Cuba, was going through earthshaking events that have radically changed the course of its history and of mine. My generation, whether we came to *el exilio* or stayed in Cuba, was the one that had to struggle to find who we were and how to give meaning to our lives—the task of all teenagers and young adults—in the midst of great turmoil. Those of us who live in the U.S.A. are part of the generation of the 1960s that saw racism challenged by the civil rights movement and the myth of U.S. invincibility challenged by the movement against the war in Vietnam. It was my generation that welcomed the Spirit-filled winds of Vatican II in the Roman Catholic Church and had to learn how to accept and nourish its challenges in our personal lives. This is the generation that has been a key element in and a great beneficiary of the women's movement of the last twenty years. This is the generation that has been so instrumental in the unbelievable unfolding of events the world over—what was the U.S.S.R., Eastern Europe, South Africa, China, Central America, Latin America—during the last few years.

I believe all these experiences, benefits, and challenges have been given to us, whether we have been active participants or not, to prepare us for the task that still lies ahead. They have been given to us to prepare us to move our world to be a life-giving world, one in which liberation is a possibility for all if we are willing to struggle passionately for it instead of believing that justice means only equality for a few at the expense of most others. Our lives up to now have been a preparation so we can work without rest to stop the destruction of our world by ecological devastation even as the threat of nuclear destruction abates.

I dedicate this book especially to my generation of Cuban compatriots called to build bridges between the Cuban community in exile and the community on the island. The future of our country will depend on our ability to understand the depth of Martí's *"la patria es ara, no pedestal,"* the mothercountry is an altar, not a pedestal, and to live accordingly. It will depend on our ability to dream dreams and see visions—to look forward and think of new possibilities instead of trying in vain to bring back what was or to maintain what is. Let us indeed be willing to forge ahead, convinced that to struggle is to live: *la vida es la lucha.*

As LIFE UNFOLDS, ONE'S COMMUNITY of accountability and support tends to grow. At least that has been my experience. So, besides thanking once again Michael West and Ann Delgehausen of Fortress Press and Ann Patrick Ware, SL, my tireless

English editor, for their continuous and generous help, I have to add a few names to the list of people mentioned in this acknowledgment.

I am grateful to Michael Humphreys, a Ph.D. candidate in social ethics at Drew University and my research assistant, for his work in updating the statistics in this book.

In my *mujerista* community, I now count on the friendship and support of many other Latinas. Of particular importance for my work as a theologian has been Milagros Peña.

I am grateful for the never-failing personal support of Nina Torres-Vidal and for her wise advice regarding composition and rhetoric in English as well as in Spanish. I thank her for editing the Spanish sections in this edition of *En la Lucha*.

AGRADECIMIENTOS

"Honrar, honra", es uno de los dichos de José Martí, uno de los grandes literatos de Latino América, y el alma de la lucha por la independencia de la Cuba de finales del siglo diecinueve y de todos sus esfuerzos revolucionarios desde entonces. Aunque lo extenso de esta sección pueda parecer exagerada, el reconocimiento que aquí hago es mi manera de honrar a aquellas personas que me han bendecido con su amistad y cariño y a las que han compartido sus experiencias conmigo a través de los años. Este reconocimiento es una manera de decir que yo no puedo hacer teología y no haré teología sin una comunidad de apoyo a la cual rindo cuentas. Y este reconocimiento es también un modo de compartir con el lector y la lectora una noción de quién soy.

Mi primera deuda de gratitud es con las mujeres hispanas, mis hermanas en la lucha. En particular quiero darles las gracias a quienes han colaborado conmigo en escribir este libro. Mi agradecimiento a Inés, Adela, Marta, Lupe, María, Olivia, Margarita, Esperanza y Caridad, quienes hablan a través de estas páginas.

Gracias a mi comunidad *mujerista,* en particular a Yolanda Tarango, Carmen Villegas y María Antonietta Berriozabal, cuyo apoyo ha sido constante. La lucha dio a luz a nuestra amistad y es también su alimento principal.

Durante los últimos diez años he pertenecido a un grupo de mujeres el que ha perseverado en reunirse una vez al mes para celebrar nuestras vidas, para explorar y profundizar nuestra fe. Hoy día somos amigas, somos familia, y nos da seguridad saber que podemos depender las unas de las otras. Les agradezco a estas mujeres su apoyo y estímulo. En especial le doy las gracias a Mary Ragan, con quien hablo cuando necesito entenderme a mí misma; a Cindy Derway, cuyos elogios me sostienen y estimulan; a Janet Walton, que me anima siempre en mi papel de teóloga; a Eileen King, que me presentó a su amada ciudad de Nueva York y me enseñó a quererla. Finalmente, mi mayor deuda de gratitud es con Ann Patrick Ware. Trabajamos juntas en Church Women United mientras yo escribía mi disertación doctoral. Ann Pat me ayudó repetidamente durante aquellos años para que yo tuviera tiempo para mis estudios. Ella ha corregido el inglés de todos mis escritos durante los últimos seis años, insistiendo siempre en que reflejen tanto la claridad de pensamiento como el uso efectivo de la lengua. Lo que más agradezco es su habilidad de corregir mi inglés sin hacerme dejar de sonar cubana.

Quiero darle las gracias a otro grupo de feministas que aunque disperso geográficamente forma una comunidad de apoyo para mí. Nos conocimos inicialmente en

Union Theological Seminary, de donde me gradué en 1990. Angela Bauer, Pam Brubaker, Liz Bounds, Hyun Kyung Chung, Marilyn Legge y Serinity Young: amigas que confirman mi convicción de que la creación de comunidades feministas es una estrategia efectiva para poder sobrevivir.

A todas estas hermanas digo esas palabras maravillosas de Marge Piercy, "Denme a luz, hermanas, en la lucha nos transformamos nosotras mismas. . . . Hoy tenemos que fortalecernos. El cambio es cualitativo: somos un milagro las unas para las otras".

Gracias a mi comité de disertación doctoral que guió la obra en la que se basa este libro. La confianza en mi capacidad como teóloga de Beverly Harrison, mi consejera en Union Theological Seminary, me permitió seguir mis discernimientos y experiencias y así pude llegar a las formulaciones iniciales de la teología *mujerista*. Margaret Farley me ayudó a mantenerme en contacto con mis raíces católicas. Su pensar claro y metódico y su vasta sabiduría de la teología católica me sostuvieron sobre una base firme. Victoria Erickson me ha ayudado enormemente a incorporar las ciencias sociales a mi método teológico. En particular le agradezco el haberme enseñado que no soy la única que cree en la necesidad de incluir voces específicas en mi trabajo, que hay una escuela entera de sociólogos cuyas teorías apoyan mi pensar. Larry Rasmussen fue uno de mis compañeros de diálogo teológico a través de su obra escrita antes de que lo conociera personalmente. Larry es un verdadero hermano, siempre dispuesto a ayudarme a clarificar ideas y conceptos. Agradezco a todos los miembros de mi comité el estar dispuestos a trabajar conmigo y a aceptarme como colega.

Agradezco a mi familia su apoyo tan cariñoso. Aunque soy la única de la familia que vive en Nueva York, su atención tan intensa y sincera me hace sentir como si no viviera sola. Vaya un agradecimiento especial a Alexandra, Javier y Andrew Joseph, que me dan la oportunidad de interesarme en asuntos importantes como son los pañales, los cuentos infantiles, el aprender a nadar y a montar bicicleta. Alex, Javi y A.J. concretizan el futuro para mí de un modo muy personal y eso me da esperanzas y me anima.

Gracias a Michael West y a Lois Torvik, mis editores en Fortress Press y a la editora del manuscrito, Sydney Merkel, quien también redactó la mayor parte de las secciones en español. Sin su ayuda este libro no hubiera sido posible.

Concluyo con una breve explicación de la dedicatoria de este libro. Terminé mis estudios secundarios mientras en mi patria, Cuba, sucedían acontecimientos de importancia mundial que han cambiado radicalmente el curso de su historia y de la mía. Mi generación, tanto los que vinimos al exilio como los que permanecimos en Cuba, tuvo que luchar para descubrir quiénes éramos y el significado de nuestras vidas—el deber de todo adolescente y joven—en medio de un gran tumulto. Los que vivimos en EE.UU. hemos formado parte de la generación de 1960 que vivió la lucha en contra del prejuicio racial y que vio el mito de la invencibilidad de EE.UU. desafiado por el movimiento contra la guerra en Vietnam. Fue mi generación la que recibió con alegría los vientos llenos del Espíritu Santo que trajo a la Iglesia Católica el Concilio Vaticano Segundo, y la que tuvo que aprender a aceptar y nutrir sus retos en nuestras vidas personales. Ésta es la generación que ha sido elemento central del movimiento feminista y que se ha beneficiado grandemente de él en los últimos veinte años. Ésta es la generación que durante los últimos años ha sido tan instrumental en el desarrollo de increíbles acontecimientos mundiales en lo que fue la Unión Soviética, en Europa Oriental, Sur África, China, América Central y la América del Sur.

Todas estas experiencias, todos los beneficios y desafíos, se nos han dado para prepararnos para la tarea que todavía queda por delante. Tenemos que luchar para que nuestro mundo sea un mundo vivificante. Tenemos que creer que la liberación es posible para todas las personas si estamos dispuestas a luchar apasionadamente por lograrla en vez de contentarnos con creer que "justicia" significa la igualdad para unos pocos a costa de la mayoría de la humanidad. Hasta ahora nuestras experiencias han sido sólo una preparación para poder trabajar sin descanso para detener la destrucción ecológica de nuestro mundo que se acrecienta a la par que la amenaza de la destrucción atómica disminuye.

Dedico este libro especialmente a mi generación de compatriotas cubanas y cubanos, llamada a construir puentes entre la comunidad cubana en el exilio y la comunidad en Cuba. El futuro de nuestra patria depende de que hagamos nuestras las palabras de Martí, "la patria es ara, no pedestal". El futuro de Cuba depende de nuestra capacidad para soñar sueños y ver visiones—para mirar adelante y pensar nuevas posibilidades en vez de esforzarnos inútilmente en hacer que el pasado retorne o en mantener estáticamente el presente. Tenemos que comprometernos a abrir brechas frescas con el convencimiento de que "la vida es la lucha".

CON EL PASAR DE LOS AÑOS LA COMUNIDAD a quien uno le rinde cuentas y de quien se recibe apoyo tiende a crecer. Por lo menos, esa ha sido mi experiencia. Así es que, vuelvo a agradecerles a Michael West y a Ann Delgehausen de Fortress Press, y a Ann Patrick Ware, SL, quien edita mi inglés, su continua y generosa ayuda.

Agradezco a Michael Humphreys, estudiante doctoral en Drew y mi asistente de investigación, su ayuda para poner al día las estadísticas en este libro.

En mi comunidad *mujerista* cuento con la amistad y el apoyo de muchas latinas que no conocía cuando primero publiqué este libro. Muy importante, especialmente para mi labor teológica, ha sido Milagros Peña.

En forma muy especial agradezco a Nina Torres-Vidal su apoyo personal, que nunca falla, al igual que nuestras conversaciones teológicas que siempre afilan mis escritos, y sus sabios consejos en cuanto a redacción y retórica del lenguaje— tanto en inglés como en español. Le doy las gracias por haber editado todas las secciones en español de esta nueva edición de *En la Lucha*.

INTRODUCTION
TO THE TENTH ANNIVERSARY
EDITION

Mujerista Theology at the Beginning of the Twenty-first Century

THE DEVELOPMENT AND GROWTH of Hispanic/Latino theology in the United States since the publication of the first edition of this book, *En la Lucha/In the Struggle: Elaborating a* Mujerista *Theology,* has been significant. During this decade Latina theologians and our male colleagues, using a diversity of methods, have dealt with a considerable variety of theological themes in a sizeable number of theological texts. Without doubt we have created an autochthonous theological school of which *mujerista* theology, a theological praxis that has as its goal the liberation of Latinas, is an integral part. Though there are still not many *mujerista* theologians, those of us who claim this title continue to be committed to offering through our theological work a platform for the religious beliefs and practices of grassroot Latinas. Because religion is a key element in their struggles for survival, we believe these women have a great deal to contribute to the religious thinking and the faith-practice of our churches and society.

Among the books and articles about *mujerista* theology that have been published, *En la Lucha/In the Struggle,* has an important place for it presents the method that we have developed to bring to the attention of the theological world Latinas' voices. The ethnographic method presented in this book is not the only method used in doing *mujerista* theology. Admittedly, we have benefited from exegetical, critical literary and critical historical methods, from methods of correlation and of sociological analysis, and from psychological methods—particularly those of social and pastoral psychology. However, regardless of the method, we always use a hermeneutic of liberation that demands a critical attitude toward any text that does not take into consideration Latinas and our struggles to be able to live fully.

As a theology of liberation, *mujerista* theology is contextual. It deals with a historical context, which in turn we understand to be a social construct. Latinas share many of the elements of our sociohistorical context with others of the "minoritazed,"[1] whether they are ethnic/racial groups, women's groups, or those considered as "other," that is, apart from the dominant group. We have never thought that the sociohistorical status of Latinas is unique. What we have insisted on is our own specificity made up of social characteristics, historical perspectives, and struggles we share with others. In our case, we see these as coming together in a unique way that we call "Latina" or "Hispanic." Our Latina specificity, for example, includes the fact that the majority of us find ways to relate in a concrete way to our countries or communities of origin. We send money on a monthly basis; we often return to visit. Those of us who were born outside the U.S.A. work to be allowed to vote in government elections in the countries from which we come. For these reasons we think of ourselves not only as integral to Hispanic/Latino communities here in the U.S.A. but also in close relation to our native or ancestral communities. Liberation for us, therefore, has to do with more than better participation in the benefits that accrue to us because we live in the U.S.A. It demands much more. It means that we have to struggle to bring about radical sociopolitical change so we will not continue to live at the expense of our sisters and brothers in our countries or communities of origin. Without doubt, the historical project of liberation for us seeks to include the most needy instead of seeking to create certain improvements merely for us and for our communities.

This living between two worlds, the mainstream U.S.A. and our original countries or communities of origin, helps us appreciate the positive aspects of globality that allow rapid access to the countries or communities from which we come, that make it possible to talk by telephone or communicate electronically with families and friends who are far away, that allow us to wire money to distant families and friends in need. Also because of globality there now exists an international working class in which many Latinas work shoulder to shoulder with others from many different countries. Many Latinas thus share our daily lives at an "international level," learning about the reality of many in the third world. In this sense, we can relate much more with people of our own socioeconomic status in other countries than with those of an upper socioeconomic class and different ideology in the same cities where we live. Living between two or more countries helps us understand better the exploitation suffered by so many here and in our countries or communities of origin. We see how the benefits of globality, used to exploit the third world, become the so-called globalization from which only first world countries benefit.

Another specificity of Latinas has to do with *mestizaje-mulatez,* a term that *mujerista* theology uses in a broad way to refer to the coming together of races and cultures—including religion as an element of culture. We Latinas who live in the U.S.A. find ourselves in a place and a historical moment in which people from all over the world come together. In our communities we find people from many different countries of origin. The *mestizaje-mulatez* that has been characteristic of our communities or countries of origin is complex, often bringing together elements of more than two races and many more than two cultures. In *mujerista* theology, this broad racial-cultural richness has made us realize the need to insist on similarities rather than on differences among us. We have also insisted that differences in themselves are amoral. It is prejudice that makes us judge differences as better or worse. *Mujerista* theology insists on the positive elements of differences, in the richness that differences make available to us. This is why we believe that justice demands struggling for a society that values including instead of excluding persons different from the dominant group. In this book, in chapter 1 as well as in chapter 7, I explain more fully the concept of *mestizaje-mulatez*.

In these last ten years we have not stopped seeking for tools that help us analyze and understand better our Latino/Hispanic communities. Different theories and methods of analysis concerning gender, social class, economic status, political organizations, and institutions have helped us understand our reality more fully. From the beginning we insisted that Latinas—most of us poor or working-class women—have been marginalized by the majority of political and economic institutions. This marginalization and the oppression we suffer are not due to one reason separated from another. In other words, we do not experience sexism here, ethnic prejudice/racism there, poverty in still another place. No, we experience marginalization and oppression as one factor, not as an aggregate of conditions. The various reasons for oppressing and marginalizing Latinas operate together. They reinforce and influence each other, becoming "accepted" practices and influencing social institutions in such a way as to maintain and support the status quo that keeps us at the bottom of the social, economic, and political ladder. There are many tools to analyze social constructs, but we find these tools inadequate for explaining the confluence of factors that impact Latinas.

In the U.S.A., from the 1960s on, society has become much more aware of discrimination and the role it plays in oppressing and marginalizing different groups. However, this does not mean that discrimination has ceased to exist, but that it operates in more subtle ways, often making it much more difficult to unmask and understand prejudices. *Mujerista* theologians have insisted on the fact that we need new tools of analysis to be able to understand our communities at the beginning of the 21st century. It is not our task to develop such tools, but often we have had to improvise in order to deal appropriately with the reality we face. For example, when sexism, ethnic prejudice/racism, and classism operate together, what emerges are hegemonic structures and institutions in which power is consolidated in the hands of a few—almost all of them men—with enormous economic privileges. There is a great need for new tools to help us analyze power, both theories of power and practices of power. What constitutes power? What are its various manifestations? How does one acquire power? How does one keep it? Is power always oppressive? Is there a good or positive kind of power? How do we confront oppressive power in an effective way? Do we have to give up all kinds of power and is it possible to do so? In this analysis of or in any discussion about power, we are, as always, not interested in merely theoretical elaborations, though we recognize them as important. What interests us is how discussion and analysis help us to better understand how oppression and marginalization operate in our communities. This information has grave importance because power is a key element of Latinas' context and, without a deep understanding of the reality that Latinas face every day, we cannot elaborate a *mujerista* theology. We cannot understand who is God for us, how is God present and acts in our lives, or what role our religious understandings and practices have in our churches, in organized religion.

Mujerista theology, as a theology of liberation, understands the history of salvation and human history to be one and the same thing. We affirm that the redemptive reality of which our Christian faith speaks is not something apart from our daily reality: it is part of our daily living; it impacts the situations we face day in and day out. This is why every theology of liberation has to maintain a utopian vision of being the family of God, the kin-dom of God, which becomes present in an effective and forceful way in our world. Of course, living as we do in our postmodern world, we are aware that all universal vision is questionable. Hence we do not use "utopia" in an abstract, universal sense, giving it some local flavor—in our case a Latina flavor—to make it palatable. We find it better to speak about a situated universal[2] that we arrive at from our reality and experience, an expectation and vision as to what constitutes liberation-fullness of life.

We have said that in *mujerista* theology liberation is a holistic process: liberation happens at the spiritual, personal, and sociopolitical level. And what is liberation? We have added the phrase "fullness of life" to define in a more concrete way what we mean by liberation. Fullness of life begins with survival, with having what is needed to sustain physical life. Fullness of life requires criteria to be established so that all persons can satisfy their basic needs.[3] However, we have noticed that it is almost impossible to separate what one needs from what one wants. Although they are not the same and in an extremity needs have to prevail, satisfying both is important for Latinas. We have been "indoctrinated" into seeing personal abnegation as something positive without realizing that it can lead us to personal destruction. Since wants and needs are a binomial, satisfying wants as much as satisfying needs has to be a criterion for liberation-fullness of life. In other words, Latinas claim our right to happiness, to "a pleasant daily existence and . . . [the] right to a *joie de vivre*."[4]

The utopian vision becomes concrete in a historical project with many phases that intersect and influence each other repeatedly and in many different ways. When we speak about a historical project, we are referring to concrete processes with material mediations. In such a project, after establishing our goal as liberation-fullness of life, we begin to delineate the means needed to achieve it. And the starting point for considering the means—and this is true also about the starting point for considering the goal—is the reality of Latinas: our daily experiences. Using our daily experiences as a basis, we begin to create spaces, processes, and institutions where we can operate in accord with our goal. At all moments along the processes, we have to keep before our eyes the fact that our lived-experiences are our point of reference. Thus we will be able to continuously evaluate our means and goal so as to shape them according to the reality in which we find ourselves, the needs we have, and what we desire.

It is essential for our historical project that we have the material conditions we need to make the project a reality. We have to take into consideration that, on the one hand, without the needed resources we cannot construct a different reality. On the other hand, having the resources to carry out this or that program or to establish and maintain this or that organization does not ensure that these are good means to our end. In other words, on the road that leads to our carefully elaborated goal we have to keep our criteria always in mind. We have to ask ourselves continually how what we are doing contributes to a true liberation and whether it is helping to bring about the fullness of life that we so desire.

In *mujerista* theology, when we speak about life and fullness of life we are talking, first of all, of the physical-biological aspects of life. But life also has to do with knowledge, feelings, and emotions, which are also dependent on our physical being just as are the evaluative functions of the mind (the basis for ethical-moral thinking). Life takes place at the historical-cultural level, at the ethical-aesthetic level, and at the spiritual-mystical level—all elements of the social aspect of human life. Life as a principle or criterion of the *mujerista* historical project "is not a concept or an idea, an abstract or concrete ontological horizon. Neither is it a 'way of being.' *Human life* is a 'mode of reality'; it is the concrete life of each human being from which reality is faced, constructing it from an ontological horizon...where reality is actualized as true practice."[5] Our historical project has to do with *producing* life (fullness of life in its material aspect), without forgetting that this includes the intellectual functions. It has to do with *reproducing* human life, and with *developing* human life. That is to say, our historical project has to do with values and historical-cultural institutions, the "cultural" here referring to what we humans produce in order to deal with the reality we have to face.[6] All of this happens at the personal level and at the community level, that area of intersubjectivity that is characteristic of human beings. It happens too at the social level and in the social, political, and economic institutions we create.[7]

Our historical project is based on the principle of liberation-fullness of life but in and of itself does not dictate or prescribe universal ethical principles or specific forms of government, economic systems, or social structures. We embrace as a guide in our struggle to reach our goal nonexclusion, being open to all.[8] This is why we insist that liberation-fullness of life cannot become a reality for some but not for others. The *mujerista* historical project does not dictate one given form of social, economic, or political structure.[9] We do not claim to know exclusively what it takes for human beings to enjoy happiness.[10] This is why we accept any kind of social, political, or economic form of institution that does not exclude anyone or any group for any reason whatsoever. All our norms and criteria are subject to one principle: our decisions concerning good and evil, what is obligatory or permissible, have not only to respect but also to promote liberation-fullness of life.

Our historical project brings together our utopian vision with concrete programs: with a liberation praxis. By liberation praxis we understand what we do in a conscious way. The way of life we embrace must lead to radical changes in the oppressive and exclusive practices of society. Our praxis must be, in the first place, firmly planted in the world of possibilities. Second, our liberation praxis is concrete. It refers to what happens in actual places, spaces, situations, and moments. That is to say, our liberation praxis refers to many different claims and ways of acting. For example, to insist on justice in personal relationships, to claim the right of women to participate actively at all levels of the church, to demand opportunities for personal development, to reject being treated as objects, to want to participate actively in making decisions that impact our lives: all of these are different ways of engaging in liberation praxis. "Organic intellectuals" such as *mujerista* theologians do not "invent" liberation praxis. Instead we provide elaborations and understandings that point to liberation praxis as something organic, not artificially created, possessing many different incarnations. We work to create a discourse that points to and organizes in a coherent way the reasons and qualities of our liberation praxis. What we want our theological discourse to show clearly is that radical change happens in small, simultaneous, or consecutive changes in the way we think and act in different areas of our lives.[11] We want our theological discourse to point out and promote the criteria that need to be used to judge liberation praxis, criteria that arise from the everyday lives of Latinas. *Mujerista* theology is part of this liberation praxis. Third, liberation praxis happens in many different places and levels: the person, the intersubjective or communitarian, and the social. Finally, our liberation praxis is part of the process of conscientization that helps us Latinas to become moral agents, subjects of our own history.

From the beginning, *mujerista* theology has denounced sexism in our own Latina/Hispanic culture as well as in the dominant culture in the U.S.A. We created the word *mujerista* to identify the central perspective of our work for three reasons. First, the grassroot Latinas with whom we work, influenced by the press and other patriarchal structures judging feminists to be anti-men and anti-family, did not accept—and continue not to accept—the word "feminist." Though I do not agree with this interpretation, the fact is that this unjust view is powerful and has made it impossible for grassroot Latinas to appropriate the term "feminist." Second, in the field of theology and of women's struggle for liberation in the churches, it has not been easy to make others pay attention to the problems of Latinas, to our perspective, to our vision of the future. We do not deny the good intention of many feminist colleagues, but it is true that Latinas have been kept on the margins, gaining acceptance only when we can be accommodated in the way others think and decide. Third, at the beginning it was almost impossible to make feminist theologians understand how multiple forms of prejudices come together to oppress Latinas. Many insisted, and some still do, that the central oppression for all women is sexism and that is what we should all concentrate on. All of these reasons persuaded us that it was necessary to invent or adopt a name of our own that would identify the perspective of Latinas in the U.S.A. A small group of us started using the word *mujerista*, inviting almost immediately a broad group of Latinas to elaborate the meaning of the word.[12]

As a theology rooted in the religious thought and practice of Latinas, *mujerista* theology has made it possible to give voice to those who so far had not been listened to in any theological elaboration, mainly because they were thought incapable of deep, systematic reflection. The experience of *mujerista* theologians has been exactly the opposite. We have always marveled at the capacity of grassroot Latinas to explain their religious beliefs and how they impact their lives. What has moved us to use the voices of Latina women as the source of *mujerista* theology is the hermeneutical privilege that theologies of liberation—among them feminist theology—claim for their communities. One of the main motives for the work we do is our preferential option for women living in poverty—the majority of Latinas—a concern we extend to all those who are oppressed, no matter for what reason.

Sexism, once it is added to poverty and ethnic prejudice/racism, takes on special characteristics. For example, the physical exploitation of Latinas is not just sexual abuse. The exploitation of their bodies through long working hours under terrible conditions is equally abusive. And that we are exploited at work does not mean that we do not also suffer sexual abuse and exploitation at the hands of Latino men. There is no place where we are totally safe. The ethnic prejudice/racism that Latinas suffer results in lower wages. It is difficult to find a job that pays more than the minimum wage. Add to this the fact that we continue to be responsible for providing and caring for children and the elderly. We often have to use what we need to provide for others. This kind of personal sacrifice, plus the lack of good medical care, puts us at risk and often leads to premature aging.

All of this leads Latinas to understand God and to relate with God in "our own way." For example, the lack of true personal intimacy makes us seek that kind of relationship with God, and for Catholics, with the saints. God for us is very personal. God knows us and is someone on whom we can count at all times, not so much to solve our problems but to walk with us daily. Saints are friends with whom we talk, on whom we can count to help and give us strength, who we know worry about us and want us to honor them by having their statues at our home altars and by lighting candles to them. The lordship of Jesus is not one of domination and control. Jesus is "Our Lord" because he understands us, he walks with us, and, in the worst moments comforts us so we will not give up. The blessings we ask from God, the way in which we hope God will be present in our lives—these are not through miracles. What we expect is that God will give us strength for the struggle and will help us to provide for our children and for all those for whom we are responsible.

Liberation for Latinas is deeply enmeshed in what is personal to us. We have seen repeatedly changes in social structures, but they have not benefited us. What is more, in the U.S.A. we continue to be the first ones impacted negatively when there is a shortfall in governmental programs. We are the first ones laid off when the economy requires cutting jobs. We are the ones who have to be "magicians" to make ends meet when family income decreases. Divine grace for us, then, has to do with having the resources and the strength we need to care for our families, to help those who have less than we do, to struggle to give our children the kind of education we did not have the opportunity to receive. The worst sin for us is precisely not to care for others, to think in an individualistic way, to refuse to cooperate with others. God, Jesus, the Holy Spirit, Mary, the saints, our dead mothers and grandmothers—all of them are for us "faces of the divine" that we try to see despite all the difficulties in life, whose smiles we try to glimpse at the worst moments. In conclusion, we believe in all these manifestations of the divine because God and God's saints believe in us. This gives Latinas courage; this is what comforts us; this is what gives us hope and strength for our everyday struggles.

Our main concern in *mujerista* theology continues to be creating a theological discourse that values the religious beliefs and practices of Latinas. We continue adamantly to do theology in such a way as to contribute to the conscientization of Latinas so we can be moral agents, subjects of our own history. Our goal continues to be to make the academic world and the churches take note of us—who we are, our struggles, our dreams and hopes. And what we want more than anything else is to elaborate a historical project that revolves around the liberation of Latinas—a liberation that will never happen unless it happens for everyone in our communities. On this the tenth anniversary of the original publication of *En la Lucha,* we celebrate having been able to walk with grassroots Latinas. We renew our commitment to elaborate *mujerista* theology as a way of contributing to the liberation of Latinas in the U.S.A.

INTRODUCCIÓN A LA EDICIÓN DÉCIMO ANIVERSARIO

Teología *Mujerista* al Comienzo del Siglo 21

EL CRECIMIENTO Y DESARROLLO de la teología hispano/latina en los EE.UU. desde la publicación de la primera edición de este libro, *En la Lucha/In the Struggle: Elaborating a* Mujerista *Theology,* ha sido significativa. Durante esta década, las teólogas latinas y los teólogos latinos hemos desarrollado un número considerable de temas teológicos utilizando una variedad de métodos. Sin duda hemos creado un pensamiento teológico autóctono del cual la teología *mujerista*—una praxis teológica que tiene como meta la liberación de las hispanas/latinas—es parte integral. Aunque no seamos muchas las teólogas *mujeristas,* las que lo somos continuamos aferradas a nuestro empeño de proveer a través de nuestro quehacer teológico una plataforma para las creencias y prácticas religiosas de las hispanas/latinas de la base. Creemos que ésta es una manera eficaz de las hispanas/latinas contribuir al pensar religioso y la vivencia de la fe de las iglesias y de la sociedad.

Entre los libros y artículos publicados que han ido articulando la teología *mujerista*, este libro, *En la Lucha/In the Struggle,* ocupa un lugar importante ya que presenta el método que hemos elaborado y usado para traer al mundo teológico las voces de las hispanas/latinas para quienes la religión es elemento clave en sus luchas por sobrevivir y por la liberación. El método etnográfico que presentamos en este libro no es el único método de la teología *mujerista.* Sin duda también nos hemos beneficiado de métodos exegéticos, crítico-literarios, crítico-históricos, de correlación, otros métodos de análisis sociológico, y métodos sicológicos, sobre todo de sicología social y sicología pastoral. Sin embargo, no importa el método que usemos, siempre empleamos una hermenéutica de liberación, lo cual nos lleva a una actitud de crítica ante todo trabajo teológico que no tome en consideración a las mujeres hispanas/latinas y a nuestras luchas para lograr plenitud de vida.

Como teología de la liberación, la teología *mujerista* es una teología contextual, contexto que consideramos histórico: una construcción social. Las latinas/hispanas compartimos muchos de los elementos de nuestro contexto histórico-social, con otros grupos "minoritizados",[1] ya sean grupos étnicos/raciales, grupos de mujeres, o grupos de personas consideradas como "otras", es decir, ajenas al grupo dominante en la sociedad. Nunca hemos pensado que el status histórico-social de las hispanas/latinas sea único. En lo que sí hemos insistido es en nuestra especificidad. O sea, que las características sociales, perspectivas históricas y luchas que compartimos con otros grupos se conjugan en nuestro caso en una forma específica, forma que llamamos "lo latino", o "lo hispano". Nuestra especificidad hispana/latina, por ejemplo, incluye el hecho de que la mayoría de nosotras nos relacionamos con nuestros países o comunidades de origen en forma concreta ya sea mandando "remesas" de dinero a familiares y amistades, ya sea regresando a visitar con frecuencia nuestro lugar de origen, o, aún más, insistiendo—las que hemos nacido fuera de EE.UU.—en que se nos dé el derecho a votar por los gobernantes de nuestros países de procedencia. Esto nos lleva a conceptualizarnos en referencia no sólo a las comunidades hispanas/latinas de los EE.UU. sino también tomando en consideración las comunidades en las que nacimos o nacieron nuestros antes pasados. La liberación para nosotras hispanas/latinas, por lo tanto, no sólo tiene que ver con una mayor participación en los beneficios de este país sino que tiene una perspectiva mucho más amplia que nos permite darnos cuenta de que tenemos que luchar por cambios políticos-sociales radicales para no vivir a costa de nuestras hermanas y nuestros hermanos en nuestros países o comunidades de origen. Sin duda, el proyecto histórico de liberación para las hispanas/latinas busca cómo incluir a los más necesitados en vez de crear mejorías sólo para nosotras y nuestras comunidades. Este vivir entre dos mundos, el de los EE.UU. y el de nuestros países o comunidades de origen, nos ayuda a apreciar los aspectos positivos de la globalidad que nos facilita el acceso rápido a los países o comunidades de donde venimos, la comunicación telefónica o electrónica con familiares y amistades que están lejos, las transferencias bancarias casi inmediatas que nos permiten ayudar económicamente a los familiares necesitados que están lejos. Ha surgido también a partir de la globalidad una "clase trabajadora" internacional en la que participamos las hispanas/latinas hombro con hombro con mujeres y hombres de muchos otros países, incluyendo, claro está, los países originarios de las comunidades hispanas/latinas. Muchas hispanas/latinas compartimos nuestras vidas diarias a "nivel internacional", aprendiendo y preocupándonos por la realidad de muchas personas del tercer mundo y relacionándonos, en este sentido, mucho más con personas de nuestra misma esfera social y económica y con las que compartimos perspectivas e intereses en otros países que con las de clases sociales y económicas e ideologías diferentes a las nuestras que viven en las ciudades de EE.UU. donde nosotras residimos. El vivir entre dos o más mundos también nos ayuda a entender con más claridad la explotación que sufren aquí las hispanas/latinas y la que se sufre en nuestros países o comunidades de origen cuando los beneficios de la globalidad, usados para la explotación del tercer mundo, se convierten en la llamada globalización de la cual sólo se benefician los países del primer mundo.

Otra especificidad hispana/latina tiene que ver con el llamado mestizaje-mulatez, término que en la teología *mujerista* usamos en forma amplia para referirnos a la confluencia de razas y culturas—incluyendo en lo cultural las religiones. Las hispanas/latinas que vivimos en EE.UU. nos encontramos en un lugar geográfico y un momento histórico en el cual convergen personas de todas partes del mundo. En las comunidades hispanas/latinas de EE.UU nos reunimos originarias de muchos diferentes países latinos. Pero la confluencia no es sólo entre hispanas/latinas de diferentes países sino también de hispanas/latinas en general con personas de muchos otras nacionalidades que emigran a este país. El mestizaje-mulatez que ha sido característico de nuestras comunidades o países de origen hoy en día es muy complejo, incluyendo elementos de más de dos razas y muchas más que dos culturas. En la teología *mujerista* esta gran riqueza racial-cultural nos ha hecho ver la necesidad de insistir en las similitudes, que son mucho mayores que las diferencias. También hemos insistido en que las diferencias de por sí son a-morales, y que es la discriminación la que nos hace pensar que quiénes son diferentes son o mejores o peores que nosotras. La teología *mujerista* insiste en lo positivo de las diferencias, en las riquezas que aportan. Es por eso que creemos que para que haya justicia tenemos que luchar por una sociedad que vaya incluyendo en vez de excluyendo a personas diferentes a las del grupo dominante. En este libro, tanto en el capítulo 1 como en el 7, explico más ampliamente el concepto de mestizaje-mulatez.

En estos últimos diez años no hemos dejado de buscar herramientas que nos ayuden a analizar y a entender mejor el contexto de nuestras comunidades hispanas/latinas. Diferentes teorías y métodos de análisis sobre género, clase social, status económico, organizaciones e instituciones políticas nos han ayudado a aprehender mejor la realidad que vivimos como hispanas/latinas en los EE.UU. Desde el principio hemos insistido en que en nuestras comunidades y, en general, en la sociedad, las hispanas/latinas—mayormente mujeres de clase pobre o trabajadora—vivimos marginadas por la mayoría de las instituciones políticas y económicas. La marginalidad que se nos impone es una sóla condición y no un agregado de condiciones. O sea, la opresión y marginalidad que sufrimos no es causada por una u otra de estas condiciones—sexismo por un lado, prejuicio étnico/racial por otro, pobreza por otro—sino que estas condiciones se dan a la misma vez, reforzándose unas a otras, constituyendo prácticas e influenciando instituciones sociales que mantienen y apoyan el *status quo* el cual nos sitúa a las hispanas/latinas en los últimos peldaños sociales, económicos y políticos. Sin duda existen muchas herramientas para analizar estas construcciones sociales, las razones por las que existen, y cómo nos impactan. Sin embargo, notamos que no siempre son adecuadas las herramientas que hay para analizar el conjunto de estas discriminaciones, cómo es que operan cuando se unen, cómo nos impactan al formar parte de las estructuras.

También está el hecho de que en los EE.UU. a partir de la década del 1960, se está mucho más consciente de las discriminaciones que marginalizan y oprimen. Sin embargo, esto no quiere decir que se han eliminado las discriminaciones sino que operan en forma más sutil, siendo a menudo, por lo tanto, mucho más difícil entenderlas y desenmascararlas. Las teólogas *mujeristas* hemos insistido en que se necesitan herramientas nuevas para el análisis del contexto de nuestras comunidades. No nos toca elaborarlas pero, sin duda, hemos tenido que improvisar para poder lidiar mejor con nuestra realidad. Por ejemplo, al conjugarse los prejuicios sexistas, étnicos, raciales y clasistas, lo que surgen son situaciones, estructuras e instituciones hegemónicas en donde el poder está consolidado en las manos de unos cuantos, casi todos hombres, casi todos blancos y todos con inmensas ventajas económicas. Creemos que hay una gran necesidad de nuevas herramientas para analizar el poder, herramientas tanto teóricas como prácticas. El poder, ¿en qué consiste? ¿Cómo se hace presente? ¿Cómo se adquiere? ¿Cómo se mantiene? ¿El poder es siempre opresivo? ¿Existe el poder positivo o bueno? ¿Cómo nos enfrentamos al poder en forma efectiva? ¿Hay que renunciar a todo poder? ¿Es eso posible? Como siempre, lo que nos importa en todo este análisis y discusión no son las elaboraciones teóricas, aunque no dejamos de reconocer que son importantes, sino cómo mejor entender la realidad de las hispanas/latinas, cómo mejor apreciar los mecanismos de opresión y marginación que marcan y determinan nuestras comunidades. Sin entender profundamente el contexto de las hispanas/latinas no podemos hacer teología *mujerista,* no podemos entender quién es Dios para nosotras, cómo está presente y actúa Dios en nuestras vidas, y qué papel juegan en nuestra cotidianidad tanto nuestras creencias y prácticas religiosas como las iglesias—la religión organizada.

La teología *mujerista,* como teología de liberación, entiende que la historia de la salvación y la historia humana son una misma cosa. Afirmamos que la realidad salvífica de la que nos habla la fe cristiana no se da sino en medio del diario vivir: es parte de ese diario vivir e impacta las situaciones que vivimos y nuestra cotidianidad. Es por eso que toda teología de liberación tiene que mantener una visión utópica que no es sino una visión de lo que es ser familia de Dios—el llamado "reino de Dios"—que se hace presente en forma efectiva y pujante en nuestro mundo. Claro está que viviendo en el postmodernismo sabemos que toda visión que se considere universal es cuestionable, y no usamos utopía en sentido universal abstracto ni revistiendo lo universal con sabor local, en este caso hispano/latino, para hacerlo pasar por concreto. Nos parece más correcto hablar de un universal situado[2] que se da a partir de nuestras realidades y experiencias y siguiendo nuestras expectativas y visones de lo que es liberación-plenitud de vida.

Hemos hablado antes de que en la teología *mujerista* consideramos liberación en forma holística: la liberación se da en el aspecto espiritual, personal y social-político. Y, ¿qué es la liberación? Pues hemos añadido la frase "plenitud de vida" para poder precisar lo que queremos decir por liberación. Plenitud de vida empieza por poder sobrevivir, por tener lo necesario para sostener la vida física. Al insistir en plenitud de vida necesitamos establecer criterios para que todo ser humano pueda satisfacer sus necesidades.[3] Sin embargo, nos hemos dado cuenta de que es casi imposible separar lo que se necesita de lo que se desea. No podemos considerar que las dos cosas son lo mismo ya que en tiempos de gran necesidad tenemos que aferrarnos al derecho a exigir las condiciones necesarias para poder satisfacer las necesidades. La satisfacción de necesidades y deseos tiene una importancia especial para las hispanas/latinas a las que se les ha inculcado la abnegación como algo positivo y necesario sin tomar en cuenta que a veces lleva a la destrucción personal. Como las necesidades y los deseos en realidad son un binomio, la satisfacción de los deseos tanto como el de las necesidades tiene que ser un criterio para la liberación-plenitud de vida. En otras palabras, las hispanas/latinas reclamamos el derecho a la felicidad, a "una existencia cotidiana agradable y. . . [el] derecho al gusto de vivir".[4]

La visión utópica se concretiza en un proyecto histórico con muchas facetas, facetas que se intersecan e influencian repetidamente y de muchas maneras. Cuando hablamos de un proyecto histórico nos referimos a procesos concretos con mediaciones materiales. En este proyecto histórico, después de establecer que la meta es liberación-plenitud de vida, empezamos a definir los medios necesarios para alcanzar esa meta. Y el punto de partida de los medios, al igual que el de la meta, es la realidad de las hispanas/latinas: nuestras experiencias cotidianas. A partir de ellas vamos creando espacios, procesos e instituciones donde podamos operar en forma acorde con nuestra meta. En todo momento, nuestras experiencias de vida nos sirven como punto de referencia para ir evaluando los medios y el fin, para ir dándoles forma de acuerdo con la realidad que vivimos, las necesidades que tenemos y los deseos que albergamos.

Parte de nuestro proyecto histórico tiene que ver con procurar las condiciones materiales necesarias para realizarlo. Aquí tenemos que tomar en cuenta que, por un lado, sin los recursos necesarios no podemos construir una realidad diferente. Por otro lado, el hecho que tengamos los recursos, que podamos realizar algún proyecto o echar a andar y mantener una organización, no significa que necesariamente sea un medio bueno para llegar a la meta. En otras palabras, en el caminar hacia la meta tanto como en la elaboración y articulación de la meta tenemos que tener siempre presente nuestro criterio y preguntarnos cómo es que lo que hacemos contribuye a la verdadera liberación, a la plenitud de vida a la que aspiramos.

En la teología *mujerista* cuando hablamos de vida y plenitud de vida estamos hablando, en primer lugar, de los aspectos físico-biológicos de la misma. Pero la vida también tiene que ver con lo que captamos a través de los sentidos, los sentimientos, las emociones, las cuales dependen de la vida física o corporal, al igual que depende de ella las funciones evaluativas de la mente (base para el pensar ético-moral). La vida también es y se da en el nivel histórico, cultural, ético-estético y espiritual-místico—todos estos elementos del aspecto social de la vida humana. La vida como principio o criterio del proyecto histórico *mujerista*, "no es un concepto, una idea, un horizonte ontológico abstracto o concreto. No es tampoco un 'modo de ser'. La *vida humana* es un 'modo de realidad'; es la vida concreta de cada ser humano desde donde se encara la realidad constituyéndola desde un horizonte ontológico... donde lo real se actualiza como verdad práctica".[5] Nuestro proyecto histórico tiene que ver con *producir* la vida, la plenitud de vida, en su aspecto material—sin olvidar que esto incluye las funciones intelectuales; tiene que ver con la *reproducción* de la vida humana; y con el *desarrollo* de la vida humana, es decir con los valores y las instituciones históricas-culturales, lo cultural aquí refiriéndose a lo que producimos los seres humanos para poder lidiar con la realidad a la que nos enfrentamos.[6] Todo esto se da en el aspecto personal—aspecto que tiene que ver con cada una de nosotras, en el aspecto comunitario—en la intersubjetividad característica de la persona, y en el aspecto social—en las instituciones sociales, políticas y económicas que creamos.[7]

Nuestro proyecto histórico está basado en el principio de liberación-plenitud de vida pero en sí no dicta ni prescribe principios éticos universales ni formas específicas de gobierno, sistemas económicos o estructuras sociales. Abrazamos como guía para lograr lo que nos proponemos la no-exclusión, el estar abiertas a todas y todos.[8] Es por eso que insistimos en que la liberación-plenitud de vida no se da para algunos si no se da para todos. El proyecto histórico *mujerista* no pretende dictar una forma de organización social, económica o política.[9] No reclamamos ser las que sabemos exclusivamente cómo hacer felices a los seres humanos.[10] Es por eso que consideramos aptas para nuestro proyecto histórico cualquier institución social, política o económica que no sea excluyente, que no deje afuera grupos de personas por la razón que sea. Todas nuestras normas y criterios los juzgamos de acuerdo a este principio: nuestras decisiones acerca del bien y el mal, de lo que es obligatorio o permitido, tienen que no sólo respetar sino también promover la liberación-plenitud de vida.

Nuestro proyecto histórico conjuga la visión utópica con programas concretos: con la praxis liberadora. Por praxis liberadora entendemos lo que concientemente hacemos y maneras de vivir que llevan a un cambio radical en la formas opresivas y exclusivistas que nos oprimen. Nuestra praxis debe tener, en primer lugar, los pies bien plantados en el mundo de las posibilidades. Lo factible, dado el lugar en que estamos y la situación a la que nos enfrentamos, es una de las características de la praxis liberadora. Segundo, nuestra praxis se da en lugares, espacios, situaciones y momentos concretos. O sea, nuestra praxis liberadora tiene muchas formas diferentes como son el insistir en relaciones justas a nivel personal, reclamar el derecho a una participación activa en todos los niveles de las iglesias, exigir oportunidades para el desarrollo personal, rechazar que se nos trate como objetos y querer participar activamente en las decisiones que nos incumben. Los "intelectuales orgánicos", como somos las teólogas *mujeristas*, no inventamos la praxis liberadora sino que proveemos lineamientos para entender nuestra praxis como algo orgánico que se va dando en diferentes formas. Nuestro discurso trata de señalar y organizar las razones y cualidades de una praxis liberadora. Lo que queremos es que nuestro discurso teológico indique claramente que los cambios radicales se dan a partir de pequeños cambios simultáneos o consecutivos en el pensar y forma de actuar en diferentes áreas de la vida.[11] Con nuestro discurso teológico queremos impulsar y hacer resaltar criterios para juzgar la praxis liberadora que surge de la vida cotidiana de las hispanas/latinas. El discurso teológico *mujerista* es en sí parte de esta praxis liberadora. Tercero, la praxis liberadora se da en muchos lugares y momentos, y a diferentes escalas: la personal, la intersubjetiva o comunitaria, la social. Finalmente, nuestra praxis liberadora es parte del proceso de conscientización que hace posible que las hispanas/latinas seamos agentes morales—sujetos de nuestra propia historia.

Desde un principio la teología *mujerista* ha denunciado el sexismo en la cultura hispana/latina y en la cultural dominante en los EE.UU. Creamos el termino *mujerista* para identificar la perspectiva central de nuestro quehacer teológico por tres razones. Primero, las hispanas/latinas de la base no aceptaban—y siguen sin aceptar—el termino "feminista", mayormente influenciada por la prensa y otras estructuras patriarcales que aseguran que las feministas son anti-hombre y anti-familia. Aunque no estoy de acuerdo con esa interpretación, el hecho es que esta visión injusta pero muy poderosa ha hecho muy trabajoso, y hasta imposible, el que las hispanas/latinas se identifiquen con el término "feminista". Segundo, en el campo de la teología y de las luchas por la liberación de las mujeres en las iglesias, de donde surge la teología *mujerista,* no ha sido fácil lograr que se le ponga atención a los problemas de las hispanas/latinas, a nuestras perspectivas, a nuestras esperanzas. No negamos la buena intención de las colegas feministas pero lo cierto es que a las hispanas/latinas se nos ha mantenido al margen, aceptándonos siempre que nos puedan acomodar a lo que ellas piensen y decidan. Tercero, al principio era casi imposible hacerle comprender a las teólogas feministas la multiplicidad de prejuicios que se conjugan para oprimir a las hispanas/latinas. Eso de que el sexismo, el prejuicio étnico-racial y el clasismo se dan en forma inseparable en las vidas de las hispanas/latinas fue algo difícil de hacerles entender. Muchas se empeñaban, y algunas aún se empeñan, en que la opresión central para todas las mujeres es el sexismo y que en eso es que debemos concentrarnos. Todas estas razones nos llevaron a ver la necesidad de inventar y adoptar un nombre propio que identificara la perspectiva de las mujeres hispanas/latinas en los EE.UU. Fue así que un pequeño grupo de nosotras decidimos empezar a usar la palabra *mujerista* invitando casi inmediatamente a un grupo amplio de hispanas/latinas a desarrollar el significado de la palabra.[12]

Como teología centrada en el pensar y la práctica religiosa de hispanas/latinas, la teología *mujerista* ha hecho lo posible por darles voz a mujeres a quienes no se ha tomado en consideración en la elaboración teológica por creérselas incapaces de una reflexión sistemática y profunda. Nosotras las teólogas *mujerista*s hemos experimentado precisamente lo opuesto. Siempre nos hemos maravillado de la capacidad de las hispanas/latinas de la base para explicar sus creencias religiosas y el impacto de las mismas en sus vidas. Lo que nos ha motivado a usar como fuente de nuestro quehacer teológico las voces de las hispanas/latinas es nuestro compromiso con el privilegio hermenéutico que las teologías de la liberación—entre ellas la teología feminista—reclaman para las comunidades de las que surgen. Nos ha motivado la opción preferencial por las mujeres pobres que constituyen la gran mayoría de las hispanas/latinas, opción que extendemos a todas y todos los oprimidos, no importa cuál sea la causa de su opresión.

El sexismo, al conjugarse con la falta de recursos materiales y con el prejuicio étnico-racial, toma un cariz especial. Por ejemplo, la explotación del cuerpo de las hispanas/latinas, no sucede sólo a partir del abuso sexual. La explotación del cuerpo de las hispanas/latinas que se da en las horas interminables de trabajo extenuante en condiciones paupérrimas es tan avasallador y abusivo como lo es la explotación de las hispanas/latinas como objeto sexual. Y la explotación en el trabajo no quita el que también suframos la explotación y el abuso sexual a manos de hombres hispanos/latinos no teniendo, por lo tanto, ningún lugar en el que nos encontremos por completo seguras y a salvo. El prejuicio étnico-racial que sufre la mujer hispana/latina lleva a que se nos pague menos por nuestro trabajo y que tengamos acceso sólo a trabajos de renumeración limitada. Esto, arriba del hecho de que se nos sigue haciendo responsable del cuidado y el sostenimiento de niños

y niñas, ancianas y ancianos, nos hace enfrentarnos con situaciones en las que tenemos que quitarnos lo que personalmente necesitamos para proveérselo a los
demás. Este sacrificio personal llega a poner en riesgo a muchas hispanas/latinas
que no tienen acceso a buen cuidado médico y que sufren de gran desgaste físico
a edad bien temprana.

Todo esto lleva a las mujeres hispanas a concebir a Dios y relacionarse con
Dios en una forma muy nuestra. Por ejemplo, la falta muchas veces de verdadera
intimidad personal nos lleva a buscar esa intimidad en nuestra relación con Dios
y, para las católicas, con los santos. Dios para nosotras es alguien bien personal,
que nos conoce, y es alguien con quien podemos contar, no para solucionar nuestros problemas sino para que nos apoye y dé fuerzas para la lucha cotidiana. Las
santas y los santos son amigas y amigos con los que conversamos, con quienes
negociamos ayuda y favores, quienes sabemos se preocupan por nosotras y
quieren que nosotras las honremos teniendo sus estatuas en nuestros altares hoga-
reños y prendiéndoles velas. El señorío de Jesús no es uno de dominación y control. Jesús es "Nuestro Señor" porque nos entiende, porque camina con nosotros,
y, en los peores momentos, nos conforta para que no nos desesperemos. Las bendiciones que se piden de Dios, la forma en que esperamos que Dios se haga presente en nuestras vidas, no es produciendo milagros que nos libren de las
dificultades. Las bendiciones que esperamos tienen que ver con que Dios nos dé
fuerzas para la lucha y nos ayude a sacar adelante a nuestras hijas, hijos, y a todas
y todos aquellos por los cuales nos ha tocado responsabilizarnos.

La liberación para las hispanas/latinas tiene que estar profundamente
enraizada en la esfera personal. Muchas veces hemos visto cambios en las estructuras sociales pero esos cambios no han repercutido en beneficios para nosotras.
Es más, en los EE.UU. seguimos siendo las primeras a quienes nos impacta los
cortes en la ayuda del gobierno, somos las primeras que dejan cesantes cuando la
economía requiere reajuste en los trabajos, somos las que tenemos que ser magas
cuando hay menos ingresos para la familia ya sea por falta de trabajo o por mer-
mar los recursos para el cuidado de ancianos y enfermos. La gracia divina,
entonces, tiene que ver con tener los recursos y las fuerzas para cuidar a la
familia, para ayudar a los que tienen menos que una, para tratar de darle mejor
educación que la que tuvimos a nuestras hijas e hijos. El pecado mayor es precisamente el no ocuparnos de los demás, el pensar en forma individualista no
tomando en cuenta a los demás, el rehusar cooperar con los demás. Dios, Jesús,
El Espíritu, María, los santos, las santas, las madres y abuelitas que han falle-
cido—todas y todos son para nosotras rostros de lo divino que tratamos de ver a
través de las vicisitudes de la vida, cuyas sonrisas tratamos de vislumbrar aun en
los momentos más difíciles. En resumidas cuentas, creemos en estas manifesta-

ciones de la divinidad porque Dios y sus santas y santos creen en nosotras. Eso es lo que nos da valor, eso es lo que nos conforta, eso es lo que nos alienta y da fuerzas para la vida diaria.

Nuestro empeño en la teología *mujerista* sigue siendo el de crear un discurso teológico que valorice las creencias y prácticas religiosas de las mujeres hispanas/latinas. Seguimos empeñadas en hacer teología en tal forma que podamos contribuir a la conscientización de las hispanas/latinas para que podamos ser agentes morales, sujetos de nuestra propia historia. Nuestros esfuerzos continúan teniendo como meta el que el mundo académico y las iglesias tomen en cuenta quiénes somos, nuestros empeños, nuestras luchas, nuestros sueños y esperanzas. Y nuestra ambición es poder contribuir a construir un proyecto histórico que de verdad haga posible la liberación de las hispanas/latinas—liberación que no se dará sino se da también la liberación de todas y todos en nuestras comunidades. Al cumplirse diez años de la publicación original de *En la Lucha,* celebramos el haber caminado con las hispanas/latinas de la base y renovamos nuestro compromiso de hacer teología, de seguir elaborando la teología *mujerista,* para contribuir a la lucha por la liberación de las mujeres hispanas/latinas en los EE.UU.

INTRODUCTION
TO THE ORIGINAL EDITION

THE APPEARANCE IN 1988 OF THE BOOK *Hispanic Women: Prophetic Voice in the Church* brought to public attention one strand of theological work that Latinas had been doing in the United States. In that book Yolanda Tarango and I began the work of writing *mujerista* theology. Theology at large, it seemed to us, was lacking a key element that has since become the core of our work: providing a platform for the voices of Hispanic Women. For years we had been personally enriched by grassroot Latinas' religious understandings and the way those understandings guide their daily lives. We firmly believe that those religious understandings are part of the ongoing revelation of God, present in the midst of the community of faith and giving strength to Hispanic Women's struggle for liberation. Having been educated in theology, we believe we are responsible for gathering the voices of Latinas because of their value for our own strategies for survival. We believe we also must present the voices of Hispanic Women to the public at large so they can be taken into consideration by all who do theology and thus be reflected in the life and teachings of the church.

This book pushes further and deeper the ideas and methods presented in the earlier book. Like the first one, it is a platform for the voices of Latinas because their lived-experience is the source of *mujerista* theology. To pursue this task I went once again to speak with each of the women whose voices are in the earlier book as well as with two other Hispanic Women.[1] As I spoke with these women, who live in different areas of the U.S.A., who are from different national backgrounds and from different socioeconomic strata, who have different degrees of formal education, different ages, different ways of looking at and practicing their religious beliefs, I became all the more convinced that as Latinas we have a significant contribution to make to the society of the U.S.A. generally and to theology in particular.

I also became convinced that *mujerista* theology, because it is a liberative praxis, must be mainly about the moral agency of Latinas—how we understand ourselves as agents of our own history, how we create meaning in and through our lives, how we exercise our moral agency in spite of the oppression under which we live.[2] Years and years of talking and reflecting with Hispanic Women throughout the U.S.A. had made me aware of my own experience and practice regarding the use of the word *conciencia,* conscience. One of the reasons for this book is the need we have to go deeper into these understandings and examine how they operate in the lives of Latinas in order to strengthen our struggle for liberation. This book examines the links between Hispanic Women's understanding and use of *conciencia,* moral agency, and praxis. This examination demands that we further elaborate *mujerista* theology: how is it a liberative praxis, what is its role in the struggle for survival of Latinas, what are its key understandings?

Naming Ourselves

Two initial challenges confront those of us who understand the importance of a name. To name oneself is one of the most powerful acts any person can do: Should we call ourselves *Latinas* or *Hispanic Women?* And should those of us who struggle for our liberation call ourselves *Hispanic feminists* or *feminist Latinas* or something else? Should we call our theology *feminist Hispanic theology* or *Hispanic Women's liberation theology* (as we did in our earlier work) or something else? Because a name is not just a word by which one is identified but also provides the conceptual framework, the point of reference, the mental constructs that are used in thinking, understanding, and relating to a person, an idea, a movement, we need to address this issue.

In addressing whether we should use *Latinas* or *Hispanic Women* to identify ourselves, the first thing to note is that among ourselves we hardly ever use either of them.[3] Most of us use the national adjective that refers to the countries where we were born or from where our ancestors came: Cuban, Puerto Rican, Colombian. The only exception to this, in general, are Mexican Americans, who refer to themselves in a way that indicates both their ethnic-national roots and the fact that they are citizens by birth of the U.S.A.[4] I believe that unless we are clearly grounded in our own country of origin or that of our ancestry, we will not be able to link arms with those who come from other Latin American and Caribbean countries, and we will not be able to survive in the U.S.A.

Perhaps the difficulty in agreeing on a given word to name the different groups in the U.S.A. has to do not only with how disparate we are but also with our suspicion that by putting us all under one "name" the dominant culture is trying more easily to control and assimilate us. There is also the fact that we cannot be defined racially since all races are part of our peoples. We have no monolithic characteristic except, perhaps, the Spanish language; but we cannot identify ourselves as Spaniards since that is the national adjective used by those born in Spain.

In this book we will take turns and use *Hispanic Women* in chapters 1, 3, 5, 7 and *Latinas* in chapters 2, 4, 6. In other sections of the book we will alternate the two terms. I do this not to avoid choosing but because I think that deciding on one term is premature. I believe that only as our communities gain power will we see the need to decide on one of these terms. The time for this is not yet at hand but might well be upon us sooner than the dominant groups of this society believe.

When it comes to those of us Latinas who feel the need for a name that would indicate the struggle against sexism that is part of our daily bread, a name that would help us identify one another in the trenches as we struggle for our survival within Hispanic communities and U.S.A. at large, what should we call ourselves? Some of us have called ourselves *feministas hispanas,* Hispanic feminists, though it has been an appellation riddled with difficulties because it has meant giving long explanations of what such a phrase does not mean.[5]

Feministas hispanas have been consistently marginalized within the Anglo feminist community because of our critique of its ethnic/racial prejudice and its lack of class analysis. Though Anglo feminists have indeed worked to correct these serious shortcomings in their discourse, in my experience their praxis continues to be flawed in this regard.[6] The phrase *feministas hispanas* has also been rejected by many in the Hispanic community because they consider feminism a concern of Anglo women. Yet Latinas widely agree with an analysis of sexism as an evil within our communities, an evil made into a touchable reality through the different ways in which Hispanic Women are repressed and exploited. In spite of our understanding of sexism and its role in our oppression, however, Latinas have not had a way to name ourselves until recently, when some of us came up with the word *mujerista.*[7]

A *mujerista* is a Hispanic Woman who struggles to liberate herself not as an individual but as a member of a Hispanic community. She is one who builds bridges among Hispanics instead of falling into sectarianism and using divisive tactics. A *mujerista* understands that her task is to gather the hopes and expectations of the people about justice and peace and to work, not for equality within oppressive structures, but for liberation. A *mujerista* is called to gestate new women and new men—Hispanics who are willing to work for the common good, knowing that such work requires us to denounce all destructive sense of self-abnegation. A *mujerista* is a Latina who makes a preferential option for herself and her Hispanic sisters, understanding that our struggle for liberation has to take into consideration how racism/ethnic prejudice, economic oppression, and sexism work together and reinforce each other.

Mujerista Theology and Traditional Classifications in Theology

Mujerista theology has always insisted on the intrinsic unity between what has traditionally been referred to as systematic/dogmatic theology and moral theology/ethics. The exposition of *mujerista* theology as a liberative on praxis in chapter 5 of this book will clarify why *mujerista* theology sees ethics and systematic theology as going together. As we studied the history of "conscience" we came to understand why Catholic moral theology degenerated into a "science of guilt and sin" in the sixteenth, seventeenth, and eighteenth centuries and remained almost exclusively preoccupied with the training of priests as judges until the Vatican II Council in the 1960s: moral theology was "cut off from its speculative roots as well as from dogmatic and spiritual theology."[8]

Another reason why we do not separate moral theology/ethics from systematic/dogmatic theology derives from the fact that the source of *mujerista* theology is the lived-experience of Hispanic Women, and one of its central preoccupations is the enablement of our moral agency. This means that we do not strictly follow standard procedures of ethics but are developing our own. Finally, the common understanding that, in general, moral claims should not be deduced from religious ones or that ethics should not be dependent on theology does not apply here for this reason. In spite of the fact that we live in a secularized society here in the U.S.A., Latinas' culture is not a secularized one. As will be explained later in this work, religion is an integral part of who we are and, therefore, what we do is intimately tied to what we believe.

Another traditional distinction that *mujerista* theology does not embrace is the one between moral theology and ethics. In traditional Roman Catholic theology, moral theology seems to parallel what in Protestant ethics is called *theological ethics*. These terms are used, usually but not exclusively, when referring to the accumulated body of moral teaching or knowledge based on doctrinal teachings, in the case of the Catholic church, and accepted theological teachings, for the Protestant churches. The term *ethics* seems to be used most often when referring to questions of actual behavior and decision making; often it means the application of moral theology or theological ethics to a specific issue, for example, euthanasia or the death penalty. But Christian ethics in most cases does not accept being set apart from moral theology or theological ethics because it often includes theological understandings. Since the distinction is not clear, probably because it is not tenable, in *mujerista* theology we use moral theology, religious ethics, and ethics interchangeably.

In *mujerista* theology ethics is always understood as social ethics. This follows from the centrality of community in our culture and from the fact that *mujeristas* denounce the split between the personal and the political as a false dichotomy used often to oppress Hispanic Women.

The Written English of a Cuban

This book bears the burden of being a work done in translation. I say this not to excuse my writings from the rigor of grammatical correctness but rather to explain the "sound," the "turn of phrases" I use, which, I am told, strikes some dissonance in the Anglo ear. My insistence on my writings' not "sounding" Anglo is because language not only expresses but is an intrinsic element of human understanding. I wish to try to communicate how the world is seen and understood from a Hispanic perspective. Because I am Cuban, my language is full of what others consider exaggerations, hyperboles, repetitions. What seems hyperbolic to the English reader is to me nothing but a needed emphasis; what seems repetitious is a way of connecting ideas and constantly building on what I consider central in the argument. Repetition also has to do with my concern that I may not be understood because English is not my native language and because what I say refers to a world not known by the majority of my readers.

My insistence on sounding in English like myself, and not like someone for whom English is her first language, is a way of preserving my identity, of insisting that to contribute to the theological enterprise Latinas do not need to forget our culture or our language. It is also necessary so that my primary community of accountability can resonate with what I write. It is of utmost importance for me that Latinas who read my work be comfortable with it, find themselves in it.

INTRODUCCIÓN
A LA PRIMERA EDICIÓN

LA PUBLICACIÓN EN 1988 DEL LIBRO *Hispanic Women: Prophetic Voice in the Church,* hizo público una de las vetas del quehacer teológico de las latinas en los EE.UU. Ese libro, del cual somos autoras Yolanda Tarango y yo, fue el primero escrito sobre la teología *mujerista.* Nosotras considerábamos, y así todavía creemos, que, en general, a la teología le faltaba un elemento vital el cual se ha convertido en eje principal de nuestro quehacer teológico: ser un foro abierto para las mujeres hispanas. Por muchos años las creencias religiosas y prácticas de fe de la vida cotidiana de las mujeres latinas han enriquecido nuestras vidas. Creemos que esas creencias y prácticas son parte de la continua revelación de Dios, de un Dios que está presente en nuestras comunidades de fe, dándonos fuerzas para la lucha por la liberación. Por eso estamos convencidas de que las voces de las mujeres hispanas deben ser tomadas en consideración en toda labor teológica y en toda enseñanza y práctica eclesiásticas.

Este libro, *En la Lucha,* continúa desarrollando los conceptos religiosos y métodos teológicos presentados en el primero. Este libro, al igual que el anterior, es un foro para las mujeres latinas porque sus experiencias cotidianas son fuente de la teología *mujerista.* Para continuar desarrollando esta teología fui de nuevo a hablar con cada una de las mujeres cuyas voces se escuchan en este libro y ya habíamos oído en *Hispanic Women.* Al hablar con todas ellas quedé convencida más que nunca de que, como latinas, tenemos una contribución importante que hacer a la sociedad de los EE.UU. y a la labor teológica que aquí se desarrolla.

Estoy convencida también de que la teología *mujerista,* por ser una praxis liberadora, tiene que tener como meta principal el desarrollo y fortalecimiento de las mujeres hispanas como agentes morales; es decir, tiene que ayudarnos a entender que debemos ser sujetos de nuestra propia historia, que tenemos que ser nosotras quienes determinemos lo que significan nuestras vidas, cómo es que creamos significados a través de la manera en que vivimos, cómo es que somos agentes morales a pesar de la opresión que sufrimos. Este libro examina las conexiones entre nuestra manera de entender "conciencia", cómo ésta funciona en nuestro quehacer moral, y el papel que la misma juega en nuestra praxis liberadora. Este análisis además requiere que continuemos elaborando una teología *mujerista:* ¿cómo funciona la teología *mujerista* como praxis liberadora? ¿qué papel juega en la lucha por sobrevivir de las latinas? ¿cuáles son sus propuestas principales?

Nuestro nombre

Nombrarse a sí misma es uno de los actos más poderosos que hay. ¿Nos llamamos latinas o hispanas? Y las que luchamos por la liberación, ¿nos llamamos feministas latinas o feministas hispanas, o usamos otro nombre? ¿Llamamos a nuestra teología "feminista hispana" o la llamamos, como hicimos en el primer libro, teología de la liberación de las mujeres hispanas? Porque un nombre es más que una identificación; un nombre provee el marco conceptual, el punto de referencia, las estructuras mentales que se usan para pensar, entender y relacionarnos con personas, ideas, movimientos. Por eso tenemos que preocuparnos por el nombre que le damos a nuestro quehacer teológico.

En cuanto a los términos "latinas" e "hispanas", hay que hacer notar que entre nosotras casi nunca usamos ni el uno ni el otro. Lo que utilizamos la mayor parte de las veces es el adjetivo que se refiere al país de donde procedemos o de donde vinieron nuestras abuelitas. La única excepción son las méxico-americanas que emplean este apelativo para indicar tanto su origen étnico como el hecho de que son, por nacimiento, ciudadanas de los EE.UU.

A lo mejor encontramos difícil el decidir qué nombre usar no sólo por la variedad de nuestros países de origen sino también porque sospechamos que usar el nombre que nos da la cultura dominante es cooperar, en cierta forma, con los esfuerzos que se hacen constantemente para asimilarnos y controlarnos. También está el hecho de que no se nos puede definir racialmente ya que entre nosotras hay personas de todas las razas. Tenemos una sola característica que todas compartimos: todas hablamos o sabemos usar el español. Pero no nos podemos llamar "españolas" ya que ese es el apelativo que usan los nacidos en España.

En este libro, en los capítulos 1, 3, 5 y 7 usaremos "hispanas"; en los capítulos 2, 4 y 6 usaremos "latinas". No hago esto para evitar el escoger sino porque pienso que el decidirnos por uno de estos términos es prematuro. Yo creo que sólo cuando nuestras comunidades tengan poder, podremos decidir cómo llamarnos. Ese momento no ha llegado pero está más cerca de lo que cree la clase dominante.

Y, ¿qué nombre le damos a la lucha de las latinas que consiste de una lucha en contra del sexismo, del prejuicio étnico, y del clasismo? El llamarnos "feministas hispanas" no ha resultado, ya que muchas mujeres en nuestras comunidades consideran que las feministas de extracción europea no han tomada en cuenta a las hispanas y, por lo tanto, no quieren identificarse con ellas. Sin embargo, las mujeres hispanas sí comprenden y están de acuerdo con que mucha de nuestra opresión se debe al sexismo. Por esta razón un grupo de nosotras ha empezado a usar la palabra *mujerista*.

Una *mujerista* es una mujer latina que lucha para liberarse no sólo ella, individualmente, sino lo hace como miembro de una comunidad hispana. Una *mujerista* establece conexiones entre los miembros de nuestras comunidades hispanas y denuncia todo sectarismo y toda táctica divisiva. Una *mujerista* sabe que su tarea consiste en alimentar las esperanzas y expectativas de justicia y paz en su pueblo, y que tiene que trabajar no para obtener la igualdad con la clase dominante sino para destruir las estructuras de dominación. Las *mujeristas* hacemos una opción preferencial por nosotras mismas y por nuestras hermanas latinas, sabiendo que nuestra lucha por la liberación tiene que comenzar con un análisis profundo de cómo el sexismo, el prejuicio étnico y el clasismo se combinan y refuerzan entre sí para oprimirnos.

La teología *mujerista* y las divisiones de la teología tradicional

La teología *mujerista* siempre ha insistido en que hay una unidad intrínseca entre lo que tradicionalmente se ha llamado teología sistemática o dogmática y la teología moral o la ética. Más adelante, ampliaremos lo que queremos decir con unidad intrínseca, pero por ahora lo importante es precisar lo siguiente. Al estudiar la historia del concepto "conciencia" hemos logrado entender cómo fue que la teología moral católica se degeneró en los siglos XVI, XVII y XVIII hasta llegar a convertirse meramente en una "ciencia de la culpabilidad y del pecado", preocupándose la iglesia, casi exclusivamente, por darles una educación jurídica a los sacerdotes. Hasta el Concilio Vaticano II en el siglo 20, la teología moral católica estuvo separada tanto de sus raíces especulativas como de la teología dogmática y espiritual. Esta separación fue una de las causas principales de su degeneración. La teología *mujerista* no quiere caer en este mismo error. Por eso en nuestro quehacer teológico entrelazamos la teología moral y la teología dogmática.

Otra razón por la cual no separamos la ética de la teología sistemática es porque la experiencia cotidiana de las latinas es la fuente de la teología *mujerista* y su tarea principal en el presente es el desarrollo de las mujeres hispanas como agentes morales. Esto quiere decir que no seguimos los procedimientos tradicionales de hacer teología sino que estamos desarrollando nuestros propios métodos. Finalmente, en la sociedad norteamericana por lo general, se piensa que las exigencias morales no deben depender de la religión ni que la ética debe depender de la teología. En el mundo latino no se piensa así. A pesar de que vivimos en un país secularizado, Estados Unidos, la cultura hispana sigue siendo una cultura religiosa. Como explicaremos más adelante, la religión es parte integral de quiénes somos y por lo tanto, lo que hacemos va mano a mano con nuestras creencias religiosas.

Otra distinción que la teología *mujerista* no acepta es la que usualmente se hace entre teología moral y ética. Nadie parece poder explicar claramente esta distinción, probablemente porque es imposible hacerla. En la teología *mujerista* nosotras usamos teología moral y ética en forma intercambiable.

Por último, para nosotras toda ética es ética social debido a la importancia que tiene la comunidad en nuestra cultura. Es precisamente por la importancia que para las *mujeristas* tiene la comunidad que denunciamos la falsa dicotomía entre lo personal y lo político, dicotomía que a menudo se usa para mantenernos oprimidas.

El inglés de esta cubana

Este libro, aunque fue escrito en inglés, en realidad es una traducción. A pesar de que insisto en que mi inglés sea correcto, no quiero sonar "angla". Quiero que mi inglés me ayude a comunicar cómo se ve y se entiende el mundo desde la perspectiva hispana. El modo en que hablamos los cubanos, no importa qué idioma estemos usando, está lleno de hipérboles y repeticiones que muchos consideran exageraciones. Lo que le parece hiperbólico a los no-hispano hablantes, para mí es un énfasis necesario; lo que parece repetición para quienes no son latinos, para mí es una manera de entrelazar ideas y de incluir en todo momento en mis argumentos elementos que considero importantísimos.

Mi insistencia en "sonar" en el inglés escrito como yo misma y no como alguien para quien el inglés es su lengua materna es una manera de preservar mi identidad, de insistir en que, para contribuir a la tarea teológica, las hispanas no tenemos que olvidar nuestra cultura, nuestro idioma. Para mí es de suma importancia que al leer *En la Lucha: In the Struggle*, en español o en inglés, las mujeres latinas—mi comunidad—sientan que este libro es parte de su mundo, parte de su lucha por la liberación.

CHAPTER 1

Hispanic Ethnicity and Social Locality in *Mujerista* Theology

THE COMMON CONCEPTION OF ETHNICITY is that of a category or classification that includes, among other traits, race, language, country of origin of oneself or one's ancestors, and cultural practices once the person leaves the homeland. But I believe that ethnicity is a social construct and that the construction and maintenance of ethnicity is a vital process of Hispanic Women's struggle to survive. The ethnic identification of any given person is not necessarily a constant but a dynamic self-understanding and self-identification that can vary over time.[1] As a social construct, ethnicity for Hispanic Women is not a collection of "natural" traits such as language, race, country of origin, or gender. It may or may not include some or all of these "natural" traits, but it also includes such other elements as social, economic, and political reasons for being in the U.S.A., the way the dominant culture deals with us, our daily struggle to survive, and our vision of our future.[2]

In our articulation of *mujerista* theology we are using the term *social construct* in reference to ethnicity not as a conceptual framework but as an organizational tool, as a way of gathering the social forces that go into forming Hispanic Women in the U.S.A. We identify our ethnicity as a social construct a posteriori, that is, as a way of describing, of narrating who we are and how we live our daily lives. Ethnicity for *mujerista* theologians starts with givenness, particularity, reality, the specificity of our lives. It is a tool used to speak about the multiple particularities that take into account the personal within the context of community, and of talking about our shared reality as Hispanic Women by bringing together the specific and the particular.

This is the understanding of ethnicity that *mujerista* theology uses. Because the lived-experience of Hispanic Women is the source of *mujerista* theology, our theological articulation must start with an analysis of our ethnicity, of who we are and how we understand ourselves. This first chapter, therefore, presents an exploration of what we consider are three of the main elements of Hispanic Women's ethnicity: *mestizaje,* survival, and our socioeconomic reality. In chapter 2 we will deal with three other elements that are likewise intrinsic elements of our ethnic identity.

Identifying Hispanic Women

Time and again *mujerista* theology talks about the lived-experience of Hispanic Women. Who are these Hispanic Women? To whom does this theology refer and to whom is it important?

Officially, Hispanics are those who describe themselves as "Mexican American, Chicano, Mexican, Mexicano, Puerto Rican, Cuban, Central or South American, or other Spanish origin."[3] In this book, however, we will use *Hispanic* to refer only to the three most populous of these groups: Mexican Americans, Puerto Ricans, and Cubans.

"Hispanics" in this work includes the vast numbers of Mexican Americans whose home for many generations has been the southwestern part of the United States. It is important to remember that this area was not always part of the U.S.A. Because of the Treaty of Guadalupe-Hidalgo in 1848, the border crossed the people who lived there, and not the other way around. Mexican Americans, for the purpose of this work, also include Chicanos—that is, Mexican Americans who are proud of their cultural heritage and the unique way they have adapted to the American society. Chicanos emphasize in their self-understanding the concept of *la raza*,[4] that is, a rejection of materialistic standards of individualistic self-achievement and an adoption of collective goals.[5] Under the rubric "Mexican American" I am also including those born in Mexico, now living and working in the U.S.A., but still maintaining contact with and frequently visiting their native land.

"Hispanics" here also includes the more than two million Puerto Ricans living on the mainland of the U.S.A. Their country of origin was acquired by the U.S.A. from Spain in 1898 without Puerto Ricans having much to say about it. The Jones Act in 1917 gave Puerto Ricans U.S. citizenship and made them eligible for the military draft. The new Puerto Rican constitution, drafted in 1947, which defines Puerto Rico as a free, associated state, has not changed this situation. Puerto Ricans "are still U.S.A. citizens, subject to military draft, but they do not pay income taxes and do not fully participate in federal government social service programs."[6] This means that Puerto Ricans can travel without any restrictions between the mainland and their island. The back-and-forth flow is enormous:

> reaching in one recent year more than 2 million people. . . . The flow of returning people is profoundly important. It means, first, that the Puerto Ricans offer the larger society not only a new and burgeoning minority but also a close relationship to a small and overcrowded Caribbean island with serious economic problems. Second, the nearby island gives Puerto Ricans themselves a sense of intactness, of closeness to an ancient home and reference group.[7]

The third group included in the term "Hispanics" in this work are the Cubans. There are about one million Cubans in the U.S.A., 80 percent of them living in the Miami area, about 20 percent in New York, New Jersey, California, Illinois, and Texas. Though most of these Cubans have been living in the U.S.A. for more than twenty-five years and are not allowed by the Cuban government to return to their country, and although a high percentage of them have become U.S. citizens, this community as a whole continues to maintain close emotional ties with the island.[8] It is not surprising, therefore, that Cubans who have been relocated to other areas of the U.S.A. often return to Miami, the area which has become the center of the Cuban community in the U.S.A. not only because of the high percentage of Cubans living there but also because of its geographical proximity to Cuba. The dense concentration of Cubans in this area and the fact that they have been able to establish a high percentage of the same businesses and services which they owned and operated in Cuba, makes it possible for Cubans in Miami to move almost exclusively within Cuban circles without any need to speak English.[9] In many ways, it is correct to say that the Miami-Dade County area has adapted itself to the Cubans, while they have not had to acculturate themselves to the U.S.A.[10]

Thus, in this work "Hispanics" refers to people who call themselves Mexican Americans or Chicanas, Puerto Ricans, and Cubans, and who are aware and critically conscious of their ethnicity and its role in their lives in this country. What about the rest of the Hispanic Women in this country? I do not wish to be exclusionary, but obviously I have had to set parameters to my research and my work. Though I do not attempt to subsume the rest of Hispanic Women under the three specific groups I deal with in this book, I do believe that much of what I say based on the experiences and understandings of Mexican Americans or Chicanas, Puerto Ricans, and Cubans, is also true about Hispanics from other countries in Latin America and the Caribbean.

When the term *Hispanic Women* is used, it is not to be understood as an attempt to mask differences—some of them important—among us. It is not my intention to represent Hispanic Women at large for that would require a massification that *mujerista* theology specifically rejects. Hispanic Women are too many and too different for any one person or any one group to speak for them. Hispanic Women are not a homogeneous group with no particularities or differences. For us, diversity is not a matter of different expressions of the same truth, but rather points to differences that touch the very core of who we are and what we believe. Our diversity is the source of our richness as a people, and we therefore welcome it and celebrate it. Our diversity is at the core of our *mestizaje.*

Mestizaje—Embracing and Celebrating Diversity

In this book Hispanics or Hispanic Women also refers to the coming together here in the United States of these three groups with their cultural variants. This mingling necessarily brings about cultural modifications and innovations that, over a period of time, will no doubt become distinctive enough to be considered a new culture. The coming together of these three groups and other groups from Latin America and the Spanish-speaking Caribbean adds a new dimension to the concept of *mestizaje,* to *la raza.*[11]

This *mestizaje,* this sense that we are actively contributing to the creation of a new race, *la raza cósmica,* the cosmic race, was originally formulated as a concept by the Mexican philosopher José Vasconcelos in the 1940s. For us Hispanic Women, the creation of a new race is a very real part of our daily lives. *Mestizaje* is grounded in the fact that we live in between, at the intersection of our countries of origin and the U.S.A. In the U.S.A. we are mostly marginalized people relegated to the outskirts of society, not really fully belonging. Regarding our countries of origin, we know that even if or when we do return, it is never really possible to go back.[12] Even for Puerto Rican Women, as well as for a certain segment of Mexican American Women, many of whom live *con un pie in cada lado* (with a foot in each place)—the island and the mainland, or Mexico and the U.S.A.—their travels are never a going back. "In history there is no returning, because all of history is transformation and novelty."[13]

And we also carry with us the mind-set and reality of the *mestizaje* that exists in our countries of origin. It is a fusion of the different lineages and races out of which most of us in Latin America and the Spanish-speaking Caribbean come. Nothing says it better than a popular saying, *un dicho,* from Venezuela: *Aquí todos somos café con leche; unos más café, otros más leche* (Here we all are coffee and milk; some more coffee, others more milk).

It is important for non-Hispanics to understand that for us, *mestizaje* is a reality which we have come to accept and of which many of us are proud. *Mestizaje* for us does not carry the negative connotations associated with miscegenation. It was and is a natural result of the coming together of different races. It is not the attempt of one race to make the other disappear—which seems to be the sense given to miscegenation by both African Americans and whites in this country. *Mujerista* theologians affirm *mestizaje* as the coming together of different races and cultures in a creative way that necessarily precludes the subordination of one to another; we affirm it as the going forward of humankind.[14] *Mestizaje* precludes the exclusion of some groups—Hispanics here in the U.S.A., for example—by other groups that control society. *Mestizaje* for us Hispanics is not only a matter of a mingling of races. As we shall see, this understanding certainly impacts and is defined by our religious beliefs and practices, our use of Spanish in an English-speaking world, and our *proyecto histórico,* our historic project. But before exploring these elements of our ethnicity, it is necessary to understand our socioeconomic reality.

Survival—Hispanic Women's Daily Bread

For Hispanic Women, the questions of ultimate meaning that form the core of *mujerista* theology are basically questions of survival, which here means much more than barely living. Survival has to do with the struggle *to be* fully. To survive, one has to have "the power to decide about one's history and one's vocation or historical mission."[15]

Survival for Hispanic Women means a constant struggle against oppression. Our oppression results in an "anthropological poverty," which both includes and goes beyond material poverty. This anthropological poverty threatens to despoil us of our very being. "Being fully" or "not being" is what survival is all about. As Hispanic Women, we are concerned with whatever can threaten or save us—our very being. For Hispanic Women, "being" designates existence in time and space; it means physical survival, and it means cultural survival, which depends to a large extent on self-determination and self-identity.[16] Survival starts with sustaining physical life, but it does not end there; being or not being also includes the social dimension of life. Hispanic Women need bread, but we also need to celebrate. Today we need a roof over our heads, but we also need to have possibilities for a better future for ourselves and our children—a future with some cultural continuity to our past and our present.

But for us, survival is not something one assures just for oneself. Personal survival for Hispanic Women is integrally linked with the survival of the community and, in a special way, with the survival of the children of the community. The hopes, dreams, visions, and hard work of Hispanic Women are often for the sake of the children. But they are also for our own sake. We need to make our humanity as women and as Hispanics count in this society; we need to participate actively in defining the society in which we live, which is another way of saying that we need to struggle against the classism, ethnic prejudice, and sexism that threaten our very existence.

Our struggle for survival starts with an in-depth analysis of the reality of oppression that we suffer. This oppression has different modes that relate to one another: (1) "domination" due to racist/ethnic and sexist prejudices; (2) "subjugation," which has to do with the creation of oppressed subjects according to these prejudices; (3 & 4) "exploitation" and "repression" that are the result of societal institutions, economical mechanisms, and the state apparatuses.[17] In other words, our oppression has to do with the fact that we are women, that we are Hispanics, and that the majority of us are at the bottom of the economic ladder in the U.S.A. We understand that our gender, our ethnicity, and our economic status have been made into social categories that play a very important role in the domination, subjugation, exploitation, and repression that we suffer.[18]

An integrated analysis of the oppression we suffer is essential for two reasons. First, it is often difficult to determine whether we are being oppressed because of our gender, our ethnicity, or our economic status. For example, the way Hispanic Women who work as maids are treated is at the same time a matter of class, race/ethnic, and gender oppression. Second, we do not experience our oppression differently depending upon which of the modes of oppression is at work; neither do we experience the different modes independently of one another.[19] We do not suffer two or three different kinds of oppression, each stemming from different prejudices, each one at different moments. Rather, the different modes of oppression are compounded into one multilayered burden which touches every aspect of our lives in an ongoing way.[20] None of these modes of oppression, therefore, comes before the other or is more intrinsic to our subordination. None of the prejudices at work in our oppression is paradigmatic, but together they support the structure of oppression at work in our lives. The links among them will be discovered only as we analyze each of them in depth.

The classification of people according to race/ethnicity is based on physical differences—skin color and other physical features—as well as on distinct languages, cultures, and social institutions. Racist thinking developed in Europe in the seventeenth and eighteenth centuries and became part of the Christian worldview.[21] During the nineteenth century, racial/ethnic differences and inequalities were attributed directly to biology: human beings were divided into biologically distinct and unequal races, with whites at the top of the racial hierarchy, "with the right and duty to dominate the others."[22] These racist theories were and are used to justify social, economic, and political practices that have made the nonwhite races *de facto* unequal and have resulted in their subordination.

As Hispanics, it is very obvious to us that racial or ethnic domination is intrinsically linked to economic domination. In our history, our racial/ethnic differences have been used to displace us from land, to use us as cheap labor, to exploit our countries for their prime resources, to insist on the need for us to forgo our culture and values. It is important for us to understand that though a small group of Hispanics are allowed social mobility and rise above whites, all whites have some of us below them. And the oppression we suffer as Hispanic Women has to do not only with racial/ethnic and economic domination but also with sexism.

When we turn to the analysis of gender oppression, we quickly realize that it cannot be understood apart from economic and racial/ethnic considerations. Gender differences across racial/ethnic and economic lines, as well as within Hispanic communities or among people of similar status,

> are based on, but are not the same thing as, biological differences between the sexes. Gender is rooted in societies' beliefs that the sexes are naturally distinct and opposed social beings. These beliefs are turned into self-fulfilling prophecies through sex-role socialization. . . .[23]

The kind of work assigned to men, different from that assigned to women, is an intrinsic element of the social construct called gender and the differences it creates. The differences in kinds of work have contributed greatly to considering the genders as complementary to each other—a complementarity that almost always leads to inequality. Thus, for example, women have been assigned work in the private or domestic sphere while men are assigned work in the public sphere. But women's work in the domestic sphere is unpaid and is considered as having little value. Men in the public world are the ones who have the power, control the wealth, and make decisions that affect the whole world. The work of women in the private, domestic sphere is seen as complementary, as necessary but determined by what the work and the workmen in the public sphere need. When women do venture into the public sphere, their work there is not considered worth the same pay as men's work, nor does it relieve women of responsibilities in the domestic sphere. The situation is similar among Hispanic Women, but not identical to what happens to Anglo women.

An analysis of gender oppression has to take into consideration the fact that sex-role socialization differs according to historical time and culture. This results in different conceptions of what is appropriate gender behavior and, therefore, in different experiences of gender oppression. This is precisely the reason why Hispanic Women resist the conception of sexism as defined by Anglo women. Of course there are similarities, but there are also differences created by different understandings of gender behavior and by the role played by racist/ethnic prejudice.

For example, forced sterilization of Hispanic Women in this country has repeatedly threatened our families and communities.[24] Maintaining our families is an intrinsic part of our struggle. Therefore, we are not willing to accept fully the Anglo feminist understanding of the family as the center of women's oppression.

An important example of the way the dominant group—men and women—mix ethnic prejudice and sexism is seen in the use of the word *machismo* by English-speaking persons nowadays despite the fact that there is a perfectly comparable term, "male chauvinism," in the English language. Use of *machismo* implies that Hispanic men are more sexist than Anglo men. Using *machismo* absolves somewhat the sexism of Anglo men and sets Anglo men and Anglo culture above Hispanic men and Hispanic culture. Hispanic Women do not deny the sexism of our culture or of most Hispanic men. But it is not greater than the sexism of the U.S.A. society in general and of Anglo men in particular.

In the struggle against ethnic and racist prejudice, it has to be recognized that the survival of Hispanic Women is directly related to the fate of Hispanic culture. Our culture is a social reality; it involves Hispanic Women's patterns of thoughts, feelings, and behaviors learned from the human group in which we have grown. Religious understandings and practices that have become part of the patterns of relationships and social structures that we use as a group to organize ourselves are key to what we learn.[25] Hispanic culture has to do with our "symbolic system of meanings, values and norms,"[26] and Christianity plays an essential role in determining and sustaining this system. *Mujerista* theology, therefore, because it is indeed an articulation that has as its source the daily life of Hispanic Women, has to deal with Hispanic culture. But the relationship of *mujerista* theology to culture has another important aspect, and that is to critique Hispanic Women's culture. Using our struggle for survival as its critical lens, *mujerista* theology evaluates culture from within. For example, *mujerista* theology embraces the Chicanas' critique of Hispanic culture and refuses to accept *machismo* simply because it is a cultural trait. Likewise, *mujerista* theology does not accept completely the operative understanding of family in the Hispanic culture, for it limits us by defining us first and foremost as mother, and it refuses to accept families headed by lesbian or gay couples.[27]

How Hispanic Women's future will relate to Hispanic culture depends on whether or not the Hispanic culture here in the U.S.A. develops organically. If an organic development can take place, the distinguishing Hispanic cultural values and traits will not disappear but will be allowed to inform and guide the changes that take place as we come in contact with a different reality from the one we have known. This means that Hispanic values and traits would also play a role in society at large, influencing what is normative for all. But if, in order to survive, we have to deny our cultural roots, to become "Americanized," as the people in our communities say, then the development of the culture will be far from organic, and distortions—often directly related to the negative stereotypes imposed on us—will become increasingly common among Hispanics.

If values and traits are to survive, they have to be enfleshed, to be lived daily by Hispanics. Thus, if we do not know our language or cannot use it, if we are not able to interact with other Hispanics because of the isolation and individualism that often creeps into our way of life in the U.S.A., if we have to deny our own people instead of identifying with them and being loyal to them, if we are encouraged to consider ourselves as just another group of Americans instead of knowing and valuing the specificity of Hispanics, if the demands of society are such that we are not able to stay in generational proximity to our parents and extended family—if in order to survive and move ahead we have to give up all of this, then the Hispanic culture in the U.S.A. will be dead. Only the quaint and exotic aspects of our culture will survive, not having much meaning or value, mainly as a form of entertainment for the dominant culture. Already we are witnessing instrumentalization and commercialization of our culture. Hispanic music, food, typical clothing—that is what is known and accepted by the dominant culture. But what affirmation exists for our deep sense of community, our valuing of the elderly and the children, the religiosity of our culture, the importance of honor as an expression of the worth and value of every single person for us? Will such traits and values survive? Without them, will the Hispanic people in general, and Hispanic Women in particular, survive as Hispanics? Can we consider ourselves to have survived if we lose our culture?

The analysis of economic oppression starts with understanding "the important ways in which economic institutions and practices structure our lives, as well as the important role which the economy plays in creating and sustaining racial-ethnic, gender, and class conflicts."[28] Economic status and class are greatly impacted by gender and racist/ethnic exploitation. For example, access to ownership of the means of production and, concomitantly, to wealth, greatly depends in this country on being male and white. In the early history of the U.S.A., white males established their economic dominance, rationalizing their behavior by using the racist and sexist ideas prevalent in Europe at the time. Once they had done this, they "were able to perpetuate and institutionalize this dominance in the emerging capitalist system, particularly through the monopolization of managerial and other high-level jobs."[29]

Today's capitalist system, however, is quite different from the one that existed in the early history of the U.S.A. The backbone of the economic system has been the working class: those who sell their labor to produce goods that are sold for a profit which belongs to the owners of the wealth who control the means of production. It is to this working class that the majority of Hispanic Women belong. But the economic system has changed dramatically in the last few decades and now depends on highly mechanized and technically sophisticated industries, not on a large workforce. Given the fact that men are still considered by society as the ones who should work outside the home for a family wage, in a shrinking workforce, women and racial/ethnic minorities—and especially racial/ethnic women—are the last ones to be hired. There is no doubt that growing unemployment affects racial/ethnic women the most. This development means that Hispanic Women, if they find work, will do so mainly in the service sector, in which wages are significantly lower than in industry.

Furthermore, because of the diminishing need for industrial workers, Hispanic Women are part of a growing sector of society whose unemployment is not a passing situation, but a permanent one. Hispanic Women are part of a population surplus for which the economic system—and society—has no need, no use, and, therefore, society is not willing to invest money, time, or effort in satisfying our basic needs for food, health, housing, or education. The present system views us as a dangerous sector where prostitution, theft, drugs, and AIDS flourish. This leads to being excluded from, separated from, society at large. Indeed, many of us think that the societal neglect that is part of our daily lives is a strategy of the system to get rid of this population surplus which has no role to play in it.[30]

This multifaceted oppression frames Hispanic Women's everyday lives but does not define us. What is central to our self-understanding is not our suffering oppression, but rather our struggle to overcome that oppression and to survive.[31] Our struggle is made all the more difficult by the dimness of our Hispanic communities' future. It is obvious that the steady inmigration of very poor Hispanics into the U.S.A. will continue. This, coupled with the effects on the poor of cutbacks in federal programs during the Reagan–Bush era (1980–92), is causing havoc in the Hispanic community. Let us take a closer look at some specifics of our economic oppression and how it intersects with sexism and racist/ethnic prejudice.

Socioeconomic Reality of Hispanic Women

A critical socioeconomic analysis of the oppression of Hispanic Women is key to grounding *mujerista* theology in the life of Hispanic Women as it is actually lived. Without such analysis, *mujerista* theology could not investigate the lived-experience of Hispanic Women effectively and hold it up for understanding and, when needed, critique. Ethics as an intrinsic part of *mujerista* theology must not be separated from life as it is actually lived by Hispanic Women or it will be irrelevant to our communities.[32] Also, dealing with our material condition and sociological reality will keep *mujerista* theologians from treating the experience of Hispanic Women abstractly, something we reject completely.[33] Thus, the socioeconomic reality of Hispanic Women is more than a background one has to consider when doing theology; it is a key element of *mujerista* theology's method.[34]

According to information gathered by the U.S. Census Bureau, in 1972 11.9% of all U.S. persons were poor.[35] But the percentage of persons of Hispanic origin who were poor was twice that: 22.8%. In 1989 26.2% of Hispanics were poor compared to 12.8% of all U.S. persons;[36] in 1990 28.1% of all Hispanics were poor while only 12.1% of all non-Hispanics were poor.[37] By 1991 28.7% of all Hispanics were poor. Between 1991 and 1993 the percentage of Hispanics living in poverty peaked at 28.7%. In 2000 the percentage of Hispanics living in poverty was holding at 28%.[38] Those most affected by this unbearable increase in poverty are the young and the elderly, groups usually the responsibility of women in our communities. In 1999, "Hispanics . . . constituted 23.1% of the population living in poverty," one in every four living in poverty, and, like in 1990, nearly half were children—47.2%. Further, more than one in four of children living in poverty were Hispanic—that is, 29% of all children living in poverty.[39]

Poverty increasingly affects Hispanic youth in a special manner. About 38% of all Hispanics under the age of 18 in 1990 belonged to families living in poverty. In 1999 30.3% of Hispanics under the age of 18 lived in poverty.[40] The high unemployment rate among Hispanic teenagers does not help their situation. In February 1992 30.3% of Hispanic youth between the ages of 16 and 19 were unemployed compared to 38.4% of African Americans, and 17.4% of whites.[41] In 2001 unemployment has decreased, with 17.7% of Hispanic youth unemployed.[42]

Elderly Hispanics have not fared better than the youth. The relative number of Hispanics 65 and older who live in poverty decreased from 23% to 22.5% between 1978 and 1990, while during the same period the white elderly poor population decreased from 12% to 10%.[43] By 1999, the percentage of Hispanics 65 and older was 20.4, while the percentage for whites had decreased to 7.6%.[44]

For Hispanic families, the median income in 1990 was about 7.1% that of white households. This means a Hispanic family earning the median income received about $8,900 less than a white family of median income.[45] In 1999 the median income of Hispanic families was 60.2% that of white families. This means that a Hispanic earning the median income for Hispanic families earned $21,829 less per year than the income earned by a white family.[46] This represents the largest disparity between Hispanic and whites represented in the data gathered from the 2000 Census. The percentage of Hispanic families living under the poverty line in 2000 was 20.1%. This is basically the same that it was in 1978 when it was 20.9%. This compares to 5.5% of white families living in poverty in 2000 and 6.3% in 1978.[47] The breakdown of Hispanic families living in poverty by countries of origin indicates a shift in the previous ten years. In 1990, 13.8% of Cuban families lived below the poverty line and in 1999 the percentage had grown to 15%. In 1990, 37% of Puerto Rican families lived in poverty and that has decreased to 23%. In 1990, 25% of Mexican American families were poor and that percentage has also decreased to 21.2%.[48]

Whether seen as a result or as a cause, the increasing poverty of Hispanics is connected to the increase in the proportion of households headed by women. In 1970, 16.9% of all Hispanic families with children were headed by women, as opposed to only 10.8% of all American families. In 1981 the Hispanic figure had grown considerably to 21.8%, compared with 18.8% of all American families with children under 18.[49] By 1981 23.8% of Hispanic families were headed by women with no husband present. By 1999 there seemed to be no difference with 23.4% of Hispanic families headed by women compared to 17.6% for all families and 9.3% for white families.[50] Of the families headed by Hispanic Women in 1999, 57% are of Mexican origin, 15.5% are Puerto Rican, and 3.9% are Cuban.[51]

Looked at from the perspective of children, these statistics mean that in 1980 only 72% of Hispanic children lived with both parents, compared with 84% of whites.[52] By 1988 the percentage had dropped to 66% of Hispanic children living with both parents.[53] In 1996 the situation had barely changed, with 68.2% of Hispanic children living with both parents.[54] Moreover, the number of Hispanic children continues to increase at a rate faster than that of African American families and white families. In 1990 70.2% of Hispanic families had children under 18, compared to 67.8% of African American families and 49.5% of white families.[55] In 2000, 63.5% of Hispanic families had children under 18%, compared to 55.5% of African American families and 44.8% of white families.[56]

Another result of the severe economic limitations of Hispanic Women and the children who depend on them is the abysmal educational picture presented by Hispanic youth. For example, the overall high school completion rate for the general 18 to 24 population grew slightly to 84.1% in 2000 from 81.2% in 1988. But the Hispanic high school completion rate continued to drop. It was 51% in 2000, 55.2% in 1988, 59.9% in 1986 and 61.2% in 1987. Hispanic Women continue to complete school at a somewhat higher rate than Hispanic men.[57] The picture is somewhat more encouraging concerning Hispanics who go on to college. In 1998, the number of Hispanics who enrolled in college was 8.8% of the total number of persons so enrolled compared to 5.5% in 1990. "All four major ethnic minority groups experienced enrollment increases at two- and four-year institutions from 1997 to 1998. Among these groups, Hispanics recorded the largest increase, 4.3%, for four-year colleges and universities.[58]

What are the job possibilities for Hispanics being less than 10% of those going on to college? The picture is pretty grim given that the job market in the twenty-first century will continue to decline in low-skill jobs. Occupations now and in the future will require more education than just high school for there will be fewer jobs described as "helpers and laborers, hand workers, machine setters, transport workers, farmers, precision production, administrative, construction, and marketing and sales."[59] Jobs which will exist in greater numbers are described as "technicians, teachers, management, engineers, lawyers, natural scientists."[60]

The participation of Hispanic Women in the job market is less likely than that of Anglo women or African American women. This is apparently due to cultural prescriptions and imperatives, although these are often stretched to the limit by the need for survival.[61] Only a third of Puerto Rican Women are gainfully employed or even looking for work, though on the mainland there are more Puerto Rican Women working outside the home than on the island. Mexican American Women since the 1970s are tending to work more and more frequently outside the home, but they still do so less than Anglo women. Cuban Women, however, tend to work outside the home more frequently than do Anglo women.[62] Comparisons among Hispanic Women of different national roots seem to indicate that other factors, such as education and the number of children, coupled with cultural expectations, play a significant role in determining whether Hispanic Women work outside the home or not. Cuban Women, for example, are more educated and have fewer children than other Hispanic Women.

Most of the Hispanic Women who do work outside the home do so in marginal jobs, that is, jobs that have a combination of low wages, poor working conditions, high turnover, and few or no fringe benefits, precisely the kind of jobs of which there will be fewer and fewer in the future. Again, the combination of better education and fewer children seems to help Cuban Women obtain better jobs and higher income than most other Hispanic Women.

Cuban Women who work year round in 1999 had a median income of $23,888, while Puerto Rican Women's median income was $22,298, and Mexican Americans' was $18,089. Of the jobs held by Cuban Women, 25.8% are at the managerial and professional level, and 45.2% are at the technical, sales, and administrative-support level. This results in 47.9% of the Cuban Women who work year round earning more than $25,000—with 11.41% of them earning over $50,000. This compares to 44% of the Puerto Rican Women earning more than $25,000 a year—with only 7.6% of them earning over $50,000. The picture for Mexican American Women is dismal, with only 30.5% of them earning more than $25,000 a year—with only 4.1% of them earning over $50,000.[63]

The economic stratum of Hispanics is not the only factor, and in some circumstances not the most important factor, that determines class status among Hispanics. For example, the longer a family has been a member of a given community, the higher is its class status. If a family has been among the founders of a town, parish, or organization, the class status of its members has little to do with their economic standing. Contributing factors to the class status of a person may also be the social position of his or her *comadres* and *compadres* (nonblood relatives who enter the family by being sponsors of the children at baptism) or *madrinas* and *padrinos* (sponsors of all sort of different family enterprises). *Comadres, compadres, madrinas, padrinos*—they are all advocates for and protectors of the family, so their economic status within the community reflects on the family to which they become related. These factors, however, are mainly operative only within the Hispanic community and are not relevant in our dealings with society at large.

"Middle-class" Hispanic Women, like women in general in U.S. society, own hardly any property or investments. Most of us have only our labor power to sell, which, strictly speaking, makes us members of the working class. But, though the actual money that middle-class Hispanic Women have may be limited, they do profit from the privileges of the relatives and friends—both male and female— who belong to the dominant group and control their lives to a greater extent than is the case for Hispanic Women in lower economic strata.[64] In other words, survival for middle-class Hispanic Women is a strong possibility. However, even for middle-class Hispanic Women, the possibility of survival is often threatened by the ethnic prejudice we suffer. We are keenly aware that maintenance of membership in the middle class often depends on our ability and willingness to conform to Anglo culture. We also realize that, like all other women, we are often "a man away from welfare"—that our economic status and privileges are, in great part, determined by whose daughters, sisters, and wives we are.

Though the struggle for physical survival is not a daily factor in the lives of middle-class Hispanic Women, survival is still our main preoccupation for, as we have already seen, survival for us is not only a matter of economics but is also cultural: "the cultural struggle is a struggle for life."[65] It has to do with questions of self-definition and self-determination. Survival for middle-class Hispanic Women is related to the difficult task of living in a culture that is not our own; it comes down repeatedly to choosing between faithfulness to self or, at the risk of losing cultural values and identity, adopting the values and behavior of the dominant culture in order to maintain our status, to survive.

FIRST OF ALL I WANT TO CALL ATTENTION to what I said in the Introduction: the statistics in this chapter have been updated. There are two issues I deal with in this chapter that need clarification.

Ten years ago I claimed that the oppression Hispanic Women suffer results in an "anthropological poverty" that threatens our material and cultural survival and also threatens to despoil us of our very being. Poverty, I claimed then and continue to claim now, affects us at the ontological level. This affirmation, of course, does not mean that the human nature of the poor is different from the human nature of those who are not poor. Poverty does not "alter" the essence of human nature. But the fact is that human nature does not exist in a pure form anywhere. Human nature, in a way, is always being altered by the context in which it lives. Poverty, precisely because it limits possibilities and options, alters what human nature is capable of becoming. It is at this level that I consider that poverty is "anthropological"—a menace not only to what we can have, but to what we can become as a Hispanic community and as human beings.

The second clarification has to do with the concept of *mestizaje*. I have continued to develop this concept during the last ten years. (See my article "A New *Mestizaje/Mulatez:* Reconceptualizing Difference," in *A Dream Unfinished: Theological Reflections on America from the Margins,* ed. Eleazar S. Fernandez and Fernando F. Segovia [Maryknoll: Orbis, 2001].) I have found it absolutely necessary to add *mulatez* to *mestizaje* using it as a binomial: *mestizaje-mulatez.* I have added *mulatez* to make it absolutely clear that there is no Hispanic culture in the U.S.A. (and no culture in our countries of origin) that is without elements of African culture and race. In this chapter I lay out the "material base" of *mestizaje-mulatez* and in the last chapter I develop this concept and make clear its importance for *mujerista* theology. What I mention here now has to do with the present-day discussion of the use of these two words, *mestizaje* and *mulatez*.

There are Hispanic scholars in this country who do not want to use these words because, they insist, they "whiten" our Hispanic culture. They say that instead of highlighting the Amerindian and African elements of our cultures, these words tend to hide them, whether consciously or not. This is indeed not an uncommon way of thinking in the U.S.A., particularly among African Americans.

However, these reasons or attitudes are not the ones behind the use of *mestiza* and *mulata* in our cultures of origin, much less in Hispanic/Latino theology in general and *mujerista* theology in particular. *Mestiza* and *mulata* in our cultures of origin continue to be, for the most part, a way of identifying features of the Amerindian and African races and cultures. A sign of this is that these words are often used in a pejorative sense. It is precisely for this reason that here in the United States, in *mujerista* theology, we use *mestizaje-mulatez* as an indication of essential elements of our Hispanic identity and not to whiten our culture. On the contrary, what we are trying to do in using *mestizaje-mulatez* is to make very clear that the Amerindian and African races and cultures are an integral part of Hispanic culture.

I recognize we need to understand and welcome the perspectives of African American women in the U.S.A. But I also believe that we have to hold on to our Hispanic perspective in this matter just as we do with Euro-American feminist perspectives. Of course our understandings have to remain open, but we need to insist on claiming that our way of dealing with issues of race and ethnicity has something to contribute to our social context in this country.

Síntesis del Capítulo 1
Etnicidad hispana y medio social local en la teología *mujerista*

Para la teología *mujerista* la etnicidad no es una simple colección de características dadas, tales como el idioma, la raza, el país de origen, sino que es un concepto que ha sido construido socialmente—lo cual señala un proceso de auto-identificación que es dinámico. Este capítulo analiza tres de los elementos de la etnicidad hispana: el mestizaje, la sobrevivencia y la realidad socioeconómica.

Mestizaje en la comunidad hispana

En este libro nos hemos concentrado en los tres grupos de hispanas más numerosos en EE.UU.: las méxico-americanas, las puertorriqueñas y las cubanas. "Mujeres hispanas" aquí se refiere a las mujeres de estos tres grupos que están conscientes del papel que juega el ser hispana en el modo en que se desenvuelven sus vidas en este país. El uso de "mujeres hispanas" en este libro no pretende esconder las muchas diferencias que existen entre nosotras. Al contrario, vemos la diversidad como un elemento positivo que subraya la riqueza que existe en nuestra cultura. En esta diversidad encontramos la semilla del mestizaje.

Cuando hablamos de "mestizaje" nos referimos a la confluencia en este país de tres variantes de la cultura hispana propias de méxico-americanas, puertorriqueñas y cubanas. Este sentido de mestizaje lo añadimos al concepto de "la raza cósmica" presentado inicialmente por el filósofo mexicano José Vasconcelos en la década de 1940. Este nuevo mestizaje que se está desarrollando en EE.UU. se nutre de la experiencia única de vivir entre el-aquí-y-el-allá: vivimos con un pie en nuestros países o culturas de origen y con el otro en la sociedad de EE.UU.

Mestizaje tiene que ver con la mezcla de razas, y aunque existe prejuicio racial entre nosotras las hispanas, sabemos que la mayoría somos, como indica un dicho venezolano, "café con leche: unas más café, otras más leche". La clase de mestizaje que la teología *mujerista* abraza es un mestizaje que no resulta en la opresión de una raza por otra. El mestizaje que abrazamos tiene que ver no sólo con mezcla de razas sino también con la mezcla de culturas africanas, amerindias, y la cultura española.

Sobrevivir: el pan de cada día para las mujeres hispanas

Cuando hablamos de "sobrevivir" no nos referimos a vivir en el nivel más bajo posible. En la teología *mujerista* sobrevivir tiene que ver con la lucha por ser plenamente, por poder decidir cuál ha de ser nuestra historia, nuestra misión, nuestra vocación. Sobrevivimos porque luchamos en contra de la opresión que, en nuestro caso, tiene cuatro modalidades: dominación—basada en el racismo y los prejuicios étnicos del grupo dominante; subyugación—que nos convierte en seres oprimidos por dichos prejuicios; y explotación y represión—llevadas a cabo a través de las instituciones y los mecanismos del estado, la economía y las instituciones sociales. La opresión que sufrimos nos lleva a una "pobreza antropológica" que amenaza nuestro ser, no sólo en el aspecto material, sino también en el cultural y hasta en el ontológico. Sabemos que para que la lucha en contra de la opresión sea efectiva, tenemos que hacerla como comunidad, teniendo en cuenta que nadie se puede salvar a costa de nadie, y que nadie se puede salvar en forma individual—dejando atrás a las demás.

Para que nuestra lucha sea efectiva empezamos por analizar a fondo la situación que vivimos, tomando en consideración los prejuicios étnicos y sexistas y la explotación económica. No sufrimos diferentes formas de opresión por separado sino que experimentamos los diferentes prejuicios y la explotación económica simultáneamente—como una opresión compleja de muchas capas, que afecta todos los aspectos de nuestras vidas. Nos resulta obvio, por lo tanto, que el prejuicio racial o étnico está ligado a la dominación económica que sufrimos aquí tanto como a la explotación económica en nuestros países de origen. Y sabemos que nuestra opresión como mujeres no se puede separar de las opresiones étnicas y económicas.

La opresión que sufrimos las mujeres hispanas a causa del sexismo tiene mucho que ver con la división que existe en las sociedades entre el ámbito público y el privado. La socialización que nos ha formado asigna a los hombres el ámbito público en donde sus trabajos reciben mejor renumeración y mayor reconocimiento. A las mujeres se nos asigna el ámbito privado donde el trabajo no es remunerado o recibe una remuneración muy baja. Cuando por diferentes razones trabajamos en el sector público, los trabajos que conseguimos son casi siempre una extensión de los que hacemos en la casa: costureras, enfermeras, maestras. Estos trabajos, aunque realizados en el sector público, reciben una paga inferior que los trabajos equivalentes realizados por los hombres.

Aunque hay similitudes, la manera en que somos socializadas varía de acuerdo a las diferentes culturas, de lo cual resulta que el comportamiento que se espera de las mujeres y de los hombres en la cultura hispana sea diferente al que se espera en EE.UU. Esta variación es una de las razones por lo que las mujeres hispanas tenemos una orientación distinta a la de las mujeres anglas en nuestra lucha contra el sexismo.

La lucha de la mujer hispana en contra del racismo y el prejuicio étnico es una lucha por sobrevivir que está intrínsecamente ligada a la lucha por salvar la cultura hispana. La teología *mujerista* reconoce que la cultura tiene que ver con el modo de estructurar relaciones, la manera de pensar, los sentimientos y comportamientos del grupo humano en el cual nacemos y crecemos. Estando ligada a nuestras vidas diarias, la religión cristiana tiene un papel muy importante en nuestra cultura. Por tal razón, la fuente de la teología *mujerista* es la experiencia diaria de las mujeres hispanas, lo que hace posible el que la teología *mujerista* también tenga como una de sus funciones la crítica de la cultura hispana usando como lente la perspectiva de género. Hay aspectos de nuestra cultura, como es el machismo, que la teología *mujerista* denuncia.

En el futuro, las mujeres hispanas nos relacionaremos con nuestra cultura, en parte dependiendo de cómo ésta se desenvuelva y sobreviva en la sociedad de EE.UU. Desgraciadamente ya estamos experimentando la instrumentalización y comercialización de nuestra cultura: lo que se acepta y usa es aquello que ayuda a mantenernos como grupo "minoritario" en este país y lo que trae ganancia económica—como es la comercialización de nuestras comidas típicas, nuestra música y bailes. Al no existir por parte de la cultura dominante una afirmación de nuestros valores, este uso de la cultura hispana se convierte en explotación y va resultando en una distorsión de nuestra cultura.

El análisis económico de nuestra realidad tiene que tomar en cuenta las diferentes maneras en que la economía estructura nuestras vidas y sostiene el prejuicio étnico/racial y el sexismo. Tenemos que comprender que hoy en día el sistema capitalista de EE.UU. es muy diferente a como era cuando otros grupos étnicos vinieron a este país antes e inmediatamente después de la Segunda Guerra Mundial. En aquel entonces las industrias necesitaban trabajadores y les era posible a familias que se sacrificaban y trabajaban mucho, mejorar económicamente. Pero hoy en día el capitalismo usa tecnología y maquinarias que requieren cada vez menos trabajadores. Por eso existe tanto desempleo, que afecta en primer lugar a los grupos minoritarios—los hispanos entre ellos. Y entre los hispanos, las que primero quedan desempleadas son las mujeres ya que se nos considera siempre como una fuerza laboral secundaria.

El resultado de toda esta situación es una opresión multifacética presente en la vida de las mujeres hispanas. Ante esta realidad las mujeres hispanas no nos damos por vencidas sino, al contrario, luchamos en contra de la opresión, nos negamos a doblegarnos ante los prejuicios que existen en la sociedad de los EE.UU. y en nuestra propia cultura, y luchamos por sobrevivir en todo momento.

Realidad socioeconómica de la mujer hispana

La teología *mujerista* insiste en un análisis crítico de la realidad socioeconómica de la mujer hispana ya que sin ello no puede entenderse nuestra experiencia diaria, fuente de nuestra teología. A continuación ofrecemos algunas estadísticas sobre nuestra realidad socioeconómica en los EE.UU.

• En 1972 el 22.8% de hispanos vivía bajo el nivel de pobreza, comparado con el 11.9% de la población de los EE.UU. en general. En 1989, 12.8% de la población total y 26.2% de los hispanos era pobre. Entre 1991 y 1993 el porcentaje de hispanos viviendo bajo el nivel de pobreza llegó al máximo: 28.7%. En el año 2000 28% de los hispanos eran pobres.

• La mayoría de los pobres son niños-niñas y ancianos-ancianas y por lo general son las mujeres hispanas las encargadas de estas personas.

• La pobreza afecta especialmente a la juventud hispana. En 1990, el 38% de los hispanos de 18 años o menos vivía en familias pobres. En 1999, 30.3% de los hispanos menores de 18 años vivían bajo el nivel de pobreza.

• En febrero de 1992, el 30% de la juventud hispana entre 16 y 19 años no tenía empleo, comparado con un 38.4% entre los afro-americanos y un 17.4% entre los anglos. En 2001 la situación había mejorado con 17.7% de la juventud hispana desempleada.

• En 1990, el 22.5% de la población anciana hispana vivía en pobreza; en 1999 la población hispana anciana viviendo bajo el nivel de pobreza era de 20.4% comparada con 7.6% para la población anciana blanca.

• En 1990 una familia recibiendo el average de las entradas que reciben las familias hispanas recibía $8,900 menos que el average de las entradas de las familias blanca. En 1999 la diferencia había aumentado enormemente a $21,829 de diferencia entre el average de las entradas de las familias hispanas y el average de las entradas de las familias blancas.

• En 1990 13.8% de las familias cubanas vivían bajo el nivel pobreza. En 1999 sólo entre los cubanos ha crecido el número de familias pobres al 15%. El porcentaje de familias puertorriqueñas pobres ha disminuido del 37% en 1990 al

23% en 1999. En 1990, 25% de las familias méxico-americanas eran pobres y en 1999 el porcentaje era de 21.2%.

• Otro elemento que contribuye a la pobreza es la educación. En 1988, sólo 55.2% de la juventud hispana, entre 18 y 24 años, completaron secundaria (high school), comparado con 81.2% de la juventud angla. En 2000 la situación había empeorado con sólo 51% de los hispanos terminando high school comparado con 84.1% de la población en general terminando sus estudios de secundaria.

• En 1998 de las personas matriculadas en "college", 8.8% eran hispanos comparado con 5.5% en 1990. Siendo menos del 10% de las personas que van a "college", la posibilidad de trabajos ventajosos para los hispanos y las hispanas es mínimo dado que en el siglo 21 habrá menos trabajos que no requieran "college".

• Son menos las mujeres hispanas que las mujeres anglas o las africanas-americanas que trabajan fuera del hogar. Esto se debe en parte a factores culturales, en parte al número de hijos y en parte al nivel de educación académica.

• Entre las mujeres hispanas, las diferencias económicas son las mismas que entre las familias de diferentes grupos hispanos. En 1999 las entradas medio para las cubanas que trabajan fue de $23,888; para las puertorriqueñas fue de $22,298; y para las méxico-americanas fue de $18,089.

Entre los hispanos, otros factores, aparte de los económicos, juegan un papel en la determinación de clase social. Entre estos factores se encuentra el tiempo que la familia ha vivido en una localidad, si alguien en la familia es líder en alguna de las asociaciones o instituciones importantes para la comunidad y los parientes carnales o políticos de cada cual.

Las mujeres hispanas de clase media, al igual que las mujeres anglas, raramente tienen capital o riquezas propias. Ser clase media en gran parte depende del capital de sus padres o esposos y por eso siempre corren el riesgo de volverse pobres. Por ejemplo, el divorcio frecuentemente mueve a las mujeres a una clase económica más baja pero no al punto de que tengan que preocuparse de sobrevivir materialmente como sí les ocurre a las mujeres pobres. Sin embargo, al igual que las mujeres hispanas de clase pobre, las de clase media también son oprimidas por el prejuicio sexista y el étnico/racial, y todas nos tenemos que preocupar por nuestra supervivencia cultural.

***

Lo primero es reiterar lo que se indicó en la introducción del libro: las estadísticas en este capítulo han sido actualizadas. Hay dos puntos que se mencionan en este capítulo sobre los cuales quisiera hacer algunos señalamientos.

Primero, una aclaración que tiene que ver con la afirmación que hice hace diez años, y que continúo haciendo hoy día, de que la opresión que sufrimos las hispanas nos lleva a una "pobreza antropológica" que amenaza nuestro propio ser no sólo en el aspecto material, sino también en el cultural y hasta en el ontológico. Claro está que esto no significa que la naturaleza humana de las mujeres y los hombres pobres sea diferente a la naturaleza humana de los que no son pobres. La pobreza "altera" la naturaleza humana. El hecho es que la naturaleza humana nunca se da en forma "pura". La naturaleza humana siempre es "alterada" por el contexto en el que se da. La pobreza, al ir limitando posibilidades y opciones, va alterando lo que es la naturaleza humana para cada ser. Es en ese nivel y de esa forma que considero que la pobreza es una condición "antropológica", una condición que amenaza lo que pudiéramos ser, no sólo en cuanto a lo que tenemos, sino en cuanto a lo que somos como comunidad hispana y como seres humanos.

Lo segundo tiene que ver con "mestizaje". Mucho he trabajado en los últimos diez años con este concepto del mestizaje. (Ver mi artículo "A New Mestizaje/Mulatez: Reconceptualizing Difference," in A Dream Unfinished: Theological Reflections on America from the Margins [Maryknoll: Orbis, 2001].) Con el pasar del tiempo he encontrado necesario añadirle a "mestizaje" la palabra "mulatez", usándolas como un binomio: mestizaje-mulatez. He añadido "mulatez" para dejar por sentado que no existe cultura hispana en los EE.UU. (y no existe cultura en nuestros países de origen) que no tenga elementos de las culturas africanas y de la raza negra. En este capítulo he dado las bases "materiales" del mestizaje-mulatez y más tarde en el último capítulo elaboro este concepto y su importancia en la teología *mujerista*. Lo que añado aquí tiene que ver con la discusión que existe hoy día en cuanto al uso de las palabras mestizaje-mulatez.

Hay estudiosas hispanas y estudiosos hispanos en este país que critican el uso de mestizaje-mulatez ya que entienden que el uso de este concepto conlleva una intención velada—más o menos consciente—de "blanquear" la cultura hispana en los EE.UU. Insisten en que, en vez de hacer resaltar lo que de amerindio y africano tienen nuestras culturas, lo que hacen estas palabras es ocultarlo. Este es un enfoque bastante generalizado en los EE.UU. mayormente entre los africanos-americanos.

Sin embargo, estas razones o actitudes no son las operantes en el uso de mestiza y mulata en nuestras culturas de origen, y mucho menos en la teología hispana/latina en general y, en particular, en la teología *mujerista*. Mestiza y mulata siguen siendo mayormente en nuestras culturas de origen una manera de identificar rasgos de las razas y culturas amerindias y africanas. Indicación de esto, debido al racismo que existe en las culturas hispanas/latinas, es que muchas veces

se usan estos apelativos en forma peyorativa. Basándonos, entonces, en el significado que tienen estas dos palabras en nuestras culturas de origen, y debido al prejuicio étnico/racial que existe en contra de las hispanas en los EE.UU., en la
teología *mujerista,* hemos adoptado el uso de mestizaje-mulatez como parte esencial de nuestra identidad hispana no para "blanquear" nuestra cultura sino, al contrario, para dejar claro que las razas y culturas amerindias y africanas son
elementos centrales de nuestra cultura.

No dejo de reconocer la necesidad que tenemos de comprender y compene-
trarnos con las perspectivas de las mujeres africanas-americanas en EE.UU. Pero
al igual que con las perspectivas feministas euro-americanas, nosotras las hispanas
tenemos que mantener nuestro punto de vista a la vez que insistimos en una perspectiva abierta a otros puntos de vistas y otras experiencias.

CHAPTER 2

Popular Religiosity, Spanish, and *Proyecto Histórico:* Elements of Latinas' Ethnicity

WHEN THE PRESENT IS LIMITING—oppressive—one looks to the future to find a reason for living. Historically, religion has been used to encourage the poor and the oppressed to postpone hopes and expectations to "the next world." But liberation theologies turn the focus of the hopes and expectations of the poor and the oppressed from "the next world" to this world. For this reason liberation theologies are feared and opposed by those interested in maintaining the status quo.

In this chapter we will explore the hopes and expectations of Latinas grounded in our reality and aimed at historical fruition. It is the contention of *mujerista* theology that the *proyecto histórico*, historical project, of Latinas is one of the key elements in constructing our reality. We will then analyze popular religiosity and the role it plays in Latinas' struggle for survival, and how the Spanish language functions as part of Latinas' self-understanding and ethnic identification.

Latinas' Preferred Future: Our *Proyecto Histórico*

Mujerista theology uses the term *proyecto histórico* to refer to our liberation and the historical specifics needed to attain it. Though the plan is not a blueprint, it is "a historical project defined enough to force options."[1] It is a plan that deals with the structures of our churches, as well as with social, political, and economic institutions of society. The articulation of Latinas' *proyecto histórico* presented here is not only an explanation but also a strategy: it aims to help shape Latinas' understandings in our day-to-day struggle to survive, and our identity as a community. This articulation springs from our lived-experience and is a prediction of "our hopes and dreams toward survival,"[2] of our *lucha*—struggle.

Latinas' *proyecto histórico* is based on an understanding of salvation and liberation as two aspects of one process. This is grounded in the belief that there is but one human history that has at its very heart the history of salvation. By "history of salvation" we refer to what we believe are divine actions—creation, incarnation, redemption—as well as our human responses to them, whether positive or negative. For us Latinas, salvation refers to having a relationship with God, a relationship that does not exist if we do not love our neighbor. Our relationship with God affects all aspects of our lives, all human reality. As Latinas become increasingly aware of the injustices we suffer, we reject any concept of salvation that does not affect our present and future reality. For us, salvation occurs in history and is intrinsically connected to our liberation.[3]

For Latinas, liberation has to do with becoming agents of our own history, with having what one needs to live and to be able to strive toward human fulfillment. Liberation is the realization of our *proyecto histórico,* which we are always seeking to make a reality, while accepting that its fullness will never be accomplished in history. Liberation is realized in concrete events which at the same time point to a more comprehensive and concrete realization.[4] For Latinas, salvation, liberation, and the coming of the kin-dom of God are one and the same thing. Historical events are never clearly nor completely the fulfillment of the kin-dom of God, but they affect such fulfillment; they are "eschatological glimpses," part of the unfolding of the kin-dom which we do not make happen but which requires us to take responsibility for making justice a reality in our world.

The realization of the kin-dom of God—liberation—is related to our present reality. Our *proyecto histórico* is not divorced from the present but rather is rooted in it, giving meaning and value to our daily struggle for survival. The present reality of Latinas makes it clear that in order to accomplish what we are struggling for, we need to understand fully which structures are oppressive, denounce them, and announce what it is that we are struggling for.[5] Our struggle for liberation has to start with an analysis of the root causes of our oppression. Such an analysis shows our oppression to be multifaceted—an intersection of ethnic prejudice or racism, sexism, and economic oppression—all of which are intrinsic elements of patriarchal and hierarchical structures. Analysis of oppression must then lead to effective denunciation.

Denunciation as part of Latinas' *proyecto histórico* is a challenge to understand and deal with present reality in the name of the future. Such a challenge does not consist only in criticizing, reproaching, and attacking those who maintain the structures that oppress us. Denunciation also has to do with repudiating such structures—not aspiring to participate in them—and refusing to benefit from them.[6] Therefore, *mujerista* theology is not to be only a resource for social criticism from the perspective of Latinas but is also sociocritical at its point of departure.[7] This means that we insist on our preferred future from the very beginning and insist that our *proyecto histórico* grounds our theological task, which we understand to be a liberative praxis.

To denounce oppressive structures without having a sense of what we believe our future should be is irresponsible. For Latinas' denunciation of oppression to be effective, we must also announce, that is, proclaim, what is not yet but what we are committed to bringing about. In this context, annunciation, like analysis and denunciation, is indeed a liberative praxis, an exercise that is intended to yield tangible results. Denunciation and annunciation have to contribute effectively to the creation of new structures that make possible the liberation of Latinas and of all humanity. To announce is an intrinsic part of our insistence on fullness of life against all odds and in spite of all obstacles. Such insistence is incarnated in the concrete daily struggle of Latinas, a struggle which makes tomorrow a possibility. Whether that tomorrow is for ourselves or for our children makes no difference to us. Our annunciation becomes reality in our struggle to find or create spaces for self-determination, a key factor in the struggle for liberation. The challenge to be agents of our own history is what pushes us on to do the analysis, denounce those who oppress us, and engage in building a future society with alternative values, no matter how foolish our efforts appear to those with power.[8]

Liberation is a single process that has three different aspects or levels[9] which must not be confused or identified in any simplistic way. Each one maintains its specificity; each is distinct but affects the other; none is ever present without the others. None of those aspects exists in isolation from the others.[10] These three aspects of liberation also serve as points of entry for Latinas into the struggle for liberation because they are concrete aspects of our *proyecto histórico*. We refer to these different aspects of liberation as *libertad, comunidad de fe,* and *justicia:* freedom, faith community, and justice.

Libertad has to do with acting as agents of our own history. This aspect of liberation involves the process of conscientization, with how we understand ourselves personally in view of our preferred future. *Libertad* has to do with a self-fulfillment that renounces any and all self-promotion while recognizing that commitment to the struggle and involvement in it are indeed self-realizing. *Comunidad de fe* is the aspect of liberation that makes us face sin, both personal and social sin. *Comunidad de fe* is both our goal (rejecting sin) and the community that makes rejecting sin possible. *Justicia* here refers to the political, economic, and social structures we struggle to build that will make oppression of anyone impossible. *Justicia* has to do with the understandings that guide us, challenge us, and enable us to survive daily.

Since these three aspects of liberation are interconnected and happen simultaneously, it is difficult to speak about them separately. We do so to distinguish each from the other, to explain and understand how they interrelate without confusing them. The specifics we discuss as part of each of these three elements are not to be understood as relating only to a single element. Each of the specifics has implications for and relates to all three elements.[11]

The first element we will consider is *libertad*. In Latinas' struggle for survival we must take great care not to oppose structural change to personal liberation. What is "personal" for us Latinas is neither individual nor necessarily private. For us the term "individual" carries a pejorative meaning, a sense of egocentrism and selfishness that we believe to be inherently bad since it works against what is of great value to us, our communities. Our sense of community keeps us from arrogating a sense of privacy to all aspects of the personal. Therefore, for us, *libertad* involves being aware of the role we play in our own oppression and in the struggle for liberation. It includes being conscious of the role we must play as agents of our own history. *Libertad* has to do with being self-determining, rejecting any and all forms of determinism, whether materialistic, economic, or psychological.[12] It has to do with recognizing that the internal aspiration for personal freedom is truly powerful, as both a motive and a goal of liberation.[13]

Libertad as an element of liberation for us Latinas happens, then, at the psychological and the social level. The two main obstacles to *libertad* among Latinas are apathy and fear.[14] As an oppressed group within the richest country in the world, Latinas view our liberation as such an immense task that a common response is apathy. We often think of our task as beyond accomplishment, and apathy appears as a protection against frustration. For those of us for whom the *proyecto histórico* becomes a motivational actor strong enough to enable us to shake off our apathy, our next struggle is with fear. Our fear is not mainly the fear of failing—fear of trying and not accomplishing what we set out to do—but rather the fear of being co-opted by the status quo.[15]

A central and powerful myth in the U.S.A. tells all those who come here, as well as everyone in the world, that, because this is the best of all societies, whether one accomplishes what one wants or not depends on the individual. It depends on whether one is ambitious enough, gets a good education (which the myth maintains is available to everyone), and is willing to work hard and sacrifice oneself.[16] This myth is promulgated constantly in the most pervasive way possible. It contributes significantly to the negative self-image of Latinas who cannot get ahead, not because we do not try hard, but because of socioeconomic realities that militate against us in all areas of life. If a negative self-image is oppressive, the fact that this myth fills us with fear, often robbing us of even envisioning our *proyecto histórico*, is insidious.

In order to counteract apathy and fear, we have to continue to elaborate our vision of the future at the same time that we work to articulate the details of our *proyecto histórico*. Making our preferred future a reality needs much more than vague generalities. Latinas' *proyecto histórico* has to be specific enough for each of us to know how we are to participate in the struggle to make it a reality, and what our task will be when it becomes a reality. All Latinas must know what it is we are being asked to contribute. Our *proyecto histórico* must have concreteness and specificity. Only when we know the concrete details can we face our shortcomings and the tremendous obstacles that we find along the way. Knowing concrete details can also help us face and conquer the fear that an unknown future brings. We can mitigate our fear by insisting on particulars, by being precise, by concretizing our vision of the future. The more tangible our *proyecto histórico* becomes, the more realizable it will be, since once it moves from vision to implementable plan, we will be able to transfer to this task of building our preferred future all the skills we do have—those skills we use effectively to survive every day.

Our explanation of *comunidad de fe* as an element of liberation starts by recognizing that Latinas' relationship with the divine is a very intimate one. It is not only a matter of believing that God is with us in our daily struggle, but that we can and do relate to God the same way we relate to all our loved ones.[17] We argue with God, barter with God, get upset with God, are grateful and recompense God, use endearing terms for God. This intimate relationship with the divine is what is at the heart of our *comunidad de fe*. For Latinas, it makes no sense to say one believes in God if one does not relate to the divine on a daily basis.[18]

Because Latinas relate intimately to the divine, we know that sin hurts such a relationship. We know that sin, while personal, is not private, for it is something that affects our communities negatively. The reflections of grassroot Latinas about evil give a clear sense of their understanding of sin:

> Sin is not a matter of disobedience but of not being for others. Not going to church is not a sin. But not to care for the children of the community—that is a sin, a crime! And the women take direct responsibility for what they do or do not do. Though they have a certain sense of predestination, they do not blame anyone but themselves for what goes wrong. On the other hand, God is given credit for the good that they do, the good that occurs in their lives.[19]

The analysis that our *proyecto histórico* demands can help us deepen our understanding of how sin affects those around us by helping us to understand "structural sin" and the role it plays in our oppression. We need to recognize that there are structures that have been set up to maintain the privilege of a few at the expense of the many and that those structures are sinful. Our analysis of oppressive structures will help us understand that sin is "according to the Bible the ultimate cause of poverty, injustice, and the oppression in which [we] . . . live."[20]

To understand the structural implications of sin, Latinas need to actualize our sense of *comunidades de fe* by setting up communities which are praxis-oriented, which bring together personal support and community action, and which have as a central organizing principle our religious understandings and practices as well as our needs.[21]

We have to accept, however, that most of the time we will not be able to depend on church structures and personnel to help us develop our communities. Once again we are going to have to depend on ourselves and, perhaps, we will be able to find help in the few national Latina organizations that claim to be committed to the struggle for liberation. Our *comunidades de fe* must also find ways of relating to community organizations. Where there are no Latina community organizations, the *comunidades de fe* becomes "support groups" that separate our lives into realms: the personal from the communal, the spiritual from the struggle for justice.

Our *comunidades de fe* must also be ecumenical. We must embrace the grass-root ecumenism practiced by many Latinas who relate to more than one denomination because of their need to avail themselves of help no matter what its source. For others of us, our ecumenicism has to do with our belief that the struggle for liberation—and not the fact that we belong to the same church—must be the common ground of our *comunidades de fe*. Our ecumenism must take into consideration and capitalize on our *religiosidad popular,* popular religiosity.

Finally, the *comunidades de fe* have to develop their own models of leadership, communal leadership that recognizes and uses effectively the gifts of Latinas. Characteristics emerging from our historical reality will make it possible for the *comunidades de fe* to contribute effectively to the building of our *proyecto histórico*.

The third element of liberation is *justicia.* Justice as a virtue does not refer only or mainly to attitudes but to a tangible way of acting and being; it involves not only personal conduct but also the way social institutions—the building blocks of societal structures—are organized, the way they operate, prioritize issues, and use resources. Justice is not only a matter of taking care of the basic needs of the members of society, nor is it a utilitarianism that insists on the greatest happiness for the majority of people.[22] Justice is not a matter of "to each according to one's needs," as Marxist principles proclaim.[23] For *mujerista* theologians, justice is all of this and much more. Justice is a Christian requirement: one cannot call oneself a Christian and not struggle for justice.

Our understanding of justice is based on the lived-experience of Latinas, an experience that has as its core multifaceted oppression. In *mujerista* theology *justicia* is a matter of permitting and requiring each person to participate in the production of the goods needed to sustain and promote human life. It has to do with rights and with the participation of all Latinas in all areas of life. Justice is indeed understood as the "common good." But striving for the "common good" can never be done at the expense of anyone. The "common good" is to be judged by the rights and participation of the poorest in society; it never places the rights of individuals against or over the rights and participation in society of others, particularly of the poor. It understands "welfare" in a holistic way and not just as limited to the physical necessities of life. In *mujerista* theology *justicia* is concretely expressed by being in effective solidarity with and having a preferential option for Latinas.[24]

Effective solidarity with Latinas is not a matter of agreeing with, being supportive of, or being inspired by our cause. Solidarity starts with recognizing the commonality of responsibilities and interests that all of us have despite differences of race or ethnicity, class, sex, sexual preference, age. Solidarity has to do with recognizing and affirming, valuing and defending a community of interests, feelings, purposes and actions with the poor and the oppressed. The two main, interdependent elements of solidarity are mutuality and praxis. Mutuality keeps solidarity from being a merely altruistic praxis by making clear that, if it is true that solidarity benefits the poor and the oppressed, it is also true that the salvation and liberation of the rich and the oppressors depend on it. Solidarity is truly praxis, because in order for a genuine community of interests, feelings, and purposes to exist between the oppressed and the oppressor, there must be a radical action on the part of the oppressors that leads to the undoing of oppression. Thus, for solidarity to be a praxis of mutuality, it has to struggle to be politically effective; it has to have as its objective radical structural change.[25]

Effective solidarity with Latinas demands a preferential option for the oppressed. This preferential option is not based on our moral superiority. It is based on the fact that Latinas' point of view,

> pierced by suffering and attracted by hope, allows them, in their struggles, to conceive another reality. Because the poor suffer the weight of alienation, they can conceive a different project of hope and provide dynamism to a new way of organizing human life for all.[26]

Solidarity with Latinas as oppressed people is a call to a fundamental moral option, an option that makes it possible and requires one to struggle for radical change of oppressive structures even when the specifics of what one is opting for are not known. As a matter of fact, only opting for a radical change of oppressive structures will allow the specifics of new societal structures to begin to appear.

The ability of Latinas to conceive "another reality," a different kind of social, political, and economic structure, is greatly hampered, as explained above, by the powerful U.S. myth regarding the possibility of success in this country for every-one. Poor and oppressed women in the shantytowns that surround Lima, Peru, for example, know very well that they will never be able to live—except as maids—in San Isidro, one of the rich neighborhoods in that city. Knowing that they cannot benefit from the present societal structures helps them to understand the need for radical change and to work for it. But it is not unusual to find Latinas living in the most oppressed conditions in the inner cities of the U.S.A. who think that if they work hard and sacrifice themselves, their children will benefit from the present order, and that they will eventually have the material goods and priv-ileges this society claims to offer to all. I believe that this possibility, which becomes a reality for only the tiniest minority of Latinas and their children, hin-ders our ability to understand structural oppression. It keeps us from under-standing that if we succeed in the present system, it will be because someone else takes our place at the bottom of the socioeconomic-political ladder.

In order to overcome the temptation to leave behind oppression individually and at the expense of others, Latinas need to continue to set up strong commu-nity organizations. Such organizations are most important in constructing our own identity and strengthening our moral agency. Community organizations are fertile settings for supporting our liberative praxis. They provide spaces for us to gather our political will and power to help us question the present structures. Community organizations provide or help us to move into spaces that can bring together different political projects. These projects enable us to participate in the creation of a different kind of society—a participation that must be present if socioeconomic transformation is to happen. Without community organizations that make it possible for us to analyze our reality and to explore alternatives, we will not be able to participate politically, socially, or economically at all levels of society; we will not be able to be agents of our own history, to make our *proyecto histórico* a reality.[27]

Our community organizing will be helped if those with privileges in this society are willing to stand in solidarity with us. To be in solidarity with Latinas is to use one's privileges to bring about radical change instead of spending time denying that one has privileges. For our part, Latinas must embrace the mutuality of solidarity; we have to be open to the positive role that those who become our friends by being in solidarity with us can play in our struggle for liberation. By culture and socialization Latinas are not separatists; we do not exclude others from our lives and from *la lucha,* nor do we struggle exclusively for ourselves. We extend this same sense of community to those who are in solidarity with us. They can enable us in our process of conscientization; they can help us see the decep-tion behind the U.S. myth. They can assist us in getting rid of the oppressor within who at times makes us seek vengeance and disfigures our *proyecto histórico* when we seek to exchange places with present-day oppressors.[28]

At present the unfolding of our *proyecto histórico* requires that Latinas organize to bring about an economic democracy in the U.S.A. that would transform an economy controlled by a few to the economy of a participatory community. Concretely, we must insist on a national commitment to full employment, an adequate minimum wage, redistribution of wealth through redistributive inheritance and wealth taxes, and comparable remuneration for comparable work regardless of sex, sexual preference, race, ethnicity, or age. Radical changes in the economics of the family that will encourage more "symmetrical marriages, allow a better balance between family and work for both men and women, and make parenting a less difficult and impoverishing act for single parents," the majority of whom are women, are a must.[29] We need a national health-care plan with particular emphasis on preventive health care. Latinas call for a restructuring of the educational system so that our children and all those interested can study Latino culture and Spanish. We also call for a restructuring of the financing of public education so that its quality does not depend on the economics of those who live in the neighborhood served by a given school but is the responsibility of the whole community of that area, region, or state. Latinas must have access to political office to ensure adequate representation of our community. Access to public means of communication including entertainment TV and movies is necessary so that the values of Latinas can begin to impact the culture of the nation at large.

Working for these change in the U.S. system might not be considered radical enough. But we believe that these kinds of changes within the present system do strike at the

> essential arrangements in the class-power-ideology structure. To respond to these . . . [demands] would necessitate such a fundamental change in the ownership and use of domestic and international wealth as to undercut the ruling class's position in American society and in the world, a development of revolutionary rather than reformist dimensions.[30]

These reforms demanded by Latinas significantly modify economic structures, gender, cultural relationships, and social and political institutions. Working for such changes also enhances our ability to build coalitions with other oppressed groups struggling for liberation. Thus we can have the numbers we need to be politically effective. Working for these changes strengthens our communities of struggle and makes our survival possible by enabling us to be self-defining and to strengthen our moral agency.[31]

Latinas' *proyecto histórico* is based on our lived-experience, which is mainly one of struggle against oppression. It has been argued that the subjectivity of lived-experience makes it impossible to consider it an adequate normative base. But the fact is that so-called adequate normative bases, such as different theories of justice, spring from the understandings of men, understandings that are based on and are influenced by *their* experiences. The liberative praxis of Latinas, having as its source our lived-experience, is an adequate base for moral norms and values because it enables our moral agency and empowers us to understand and define ourselves—to comprehend what our human existence is all about and what its goal is.[32]

Popular Religiosity as an Element of *Mujerista* Theology[33]

The starting point for a study of the popular religiosity of Latinas is our struggle to survive.[34] Popular religiosity for us is a means of self-identification and our insistence on it is part of the struggle to exist with our own characteristics and peculiarities. Popular religiosity allows religion to remain central to our culture in spite of the neglect we suffer as a people from most organized religions in this country.[35]

It should not be surprising that Latinas, as persons who are "vitally engaged in historical realities with specific times and places,"[36] and as persons who have to struggle for survival, are involved with and reflect on matters of ultimate concern. This reflection includes religious consideration that form "a system of symbols which acts to establish powerful, pervasive, and long-lasting moods and motivations . . . by formulating conceptions of a general order of existence and clothing these conceptions with such an aura of factuality that the moods and motivations seem uniquely realistic."[37]

Many of these powerful symbols arise from a certain kind of "official" Christian tradition. "Official" here refers to "those prescribed beliefs and norms of an institution promulgated and monitored by a group of religious specialists,"[38] the clergy and, in particular, the hierarchy of the church. Without question Christianity is the religion of Latinas—Catholicism being the specific form of Christianity which about 80 percent claim and pass on to our children. But the Christianity to which we relate, our way of relating with the divine and expressing such connection, is not "official" Christianity, nor does it necessarily have the church—either Catholic or Protestant—as its main point of reference. The Christianity of Latinas is of a very specific variety because of its history in the countries of our ethnic roots.

Christianity came to Latin America at the time of the *conquista,* the Conquest. It came not only, or even primarily, in the form of organized religion, but as an intrinsic part of the conquering culture. Theology was indeed "the main discourse in the ideological production of the sixteenth century."[39] This is why the *conquistadores,* the conquerors, planted crosses to symbolize their taking possession of the land, and named the territories and the natives in the same way as species and persons are named or renamed in the Bible—to indicate their having authority over them.[40] The *conquista* was not just a political conquest, but a conquest in which even the religious world of the conquered suffered total devastation. Christianity not only was imposed on the natives but also played a very important role as moral justifier in the whole process of the *conquista.*

When the Spanish world and the world of the indigenous people of what was to become the Americas met, a process of acculturation was set in motion during which the culture of the conqueror was imposed unilaterally on the conquered people. Real enculturation—"the process of making personal the traditional culture of the society," that is, the society of the *conquistadores*—did not take place because education was not made available to the vast majority of the population. Instead, what resulted was a "culturization" of Christianity; Christianity became culture. It has become a cultural expression in a continent in which the Spanish and the indigenous cultures have come together to give birth to a new culture.[41]

The Christianity that became and is an intrinsic part of Latino culture is one that uses the Bible in a very limited way, emphasizing instead the traditions and customs of the Spanish church.[42] Therefore, the Bible, biblical truth, and revelation are not repudiated by Latinas but, for the majority of Latinas, they are not central, they are not considered very important, they do not play a prominent role in our lives. Most of us seldom read the Bible and know instead popularized versions of biblical stories—versions Latinas create to make a point. One can consider these versions to be distortions, but for us they are "valid" interpretations, albeit imaginative ones, insofar as they contribute to the liberation of Latinas.[43]

The Christianity of Latinas also includes religious traditions brought to Latin America and the Caribbean by African slaves, and the Amerindian traditions bequeathed by the great Aztec, Maya, and Inca civilizations, as well as other Amerindian cultures, such as Taino, Siboney, Caribe, Araucanian. The mingling of sixteenth-century Spanish Catholicism with religious understandings and beliefs of the African and Amerindian religions in these regions is what has given birth to Latino popular religiosity.[44]

Popular religiosity refers to the religious understandings and practices of the masses, in contrast to "official" Christianity or the Christianity of certain minorities that eschew popular religiosity. Popular religiosity is

> the set of experiences, beliefs and rituals which more-or-less peripherical [sic] human groups create, assume and develop (within concrete socio-cultural and historical contexts, and as an answer to these contexts) and which to a greater or lesser degree distance themselves from what is recognized by the Church and the society within which they are situated, striving through rituals, experiences and beliefs to find an access to God and salvation which they feel they cannot find in what Church and society have regulated as normative.[45]

Concretely, we can say that the popular religiosity of Latinas has five general characteristics. First, it is a real religious subculture in the sense that it is a way of thinking and acting in their religious sphere not as individuals but as a group of persons. As a religious subculture, popular religiosity includes beliefs, attitudes, values, rituals, and so forth, that express the religiosity of Latinos. Second, insofar as rituals are concerned, a central position is given to certain aspects of the Catholic tradition considered marginal, for example, "sacramentals."[46] Third, popular religiosity, as I have already begun to suggest, is syncretic for it invests Catholic religious practices with meaning from other religious traditions. Fourth, "official" religious practices are reinterpreted and given a different meaning. For example, Baptism and First Communion become rituals of passage; the Mass becomes a public ceremony used to solemnize the most important moments in the life of a person or a group of people. Fifth, all these behaviors are transmitted as part of the Latino culture in contrast to being personal options.[47]

In *mujerista* theology we see popular religiosity as an essential part of popular culture and, therefore, as a part of the identity of and central to the lived-experience of the people. It is an essential part of our deepest constitutive element.[48] In many ways, popular religiosity is one of the most creative and original parts of our heritage and our culture, being a significant element in providing *fuerzas para la lucha,* strength for the struggle. In this sense, popular religiosity is valuable not only culturally but also "in relation to its capacity for strengthening the political consciousness and mobilization of the people."[49]

Mujeristas take popular religiosity very seriously, then, finding it to be an essential source of our theology because it is operative in the lives of Latinas as a "system of values and ideas, and a complex of symbolic practices, discursive and non-discursive, enacted in ritual drama and materialized in visual images," relating us to the sacred, originated and maintained in a large measure by Latinas as poor and oppressed people.[50] But this does not exempt popular religiosity from being examined through the critical lens of the liberation of Latinas. As *mujerista* theologians, we recognize that the popular religiosity of Latinas has its failings and ambiguities, as do other cultural forms of Catholicism and Christianity.[51] Using a liberative lens, *mujerista* theology recognizes that popular religiosity has elements that legitimize the oppression of Latinas. However, this does not lead us to minimize or dismiss it.

The evangelizing role that popular religiosity has had and continues to have among Latinas and within the Latino community is instrumental in the struggle for liberation because it is a major force in preserving the Latino community. "The historical neglect to which Latinos have been submitted in this country, by Church and society, added to the constant pressure to become 'anglicized,' would have long ago done away with Catholicism among Latinos and with Latino culture in general."[52] Instead, Latino Christianity and culture are alive today thanks to the evangelizing role of popular religiosity through which Latinas transmit the religious, cultural, and social values of our people. Moreover, it has provided common ground for the great variety of Latinos who live in the U.S.A., thus binding the different Latino communities together.[53]

For Latinas, popular religiosity also has another important role: it allows us to experience the sacred in our everyday lives. In many ways it makes it possible for us to live our religiosity as an intrinsic element of who we are and all that we do; it makes it possible to integrate the sacred and the secular. It is through the practices of popular religiosity that Latinas are aware of the sacred in the private as well as the public, in the personal as well as the social.[54]

"Official" churches, instead of seeing popular religiosity as a positive element,[55] either denounce it and work actively against it or look for ways of purifying it, of "baptizing" it into Christianity—accepting only those elements that can be Christianized.[56] In *mujerista* theology we will not dismiss "the normative, graced, and even universal dimension of the 'salvific' manifestations of non-Christian religions."[57] As *mujerista* theologians, we are suspicious of an imperialistic approach that refuses to recognize and accept as true, good, and life-giving any and all religious understandings and practices that do not directly relate to a magisterial understanding and interpretation of the gospel, that do not have Christ as center, model, and norm.[58] We take exception to such refusal because it does violence to a valid understanding of Jesus as portrayed in Scripture: Jesus clearly indicated that his mission was not to point to himself, but rather to point the way to God.

This imperialistic attitude on the part of "official" churches, particularly vis-à-vis the Amerindian and African strands in popular religiosity, is anticultural, and in this case, anti-Latino. To insist on imposing the divinity of Jesus as the only true and relevant expression of the divine on people who because of cultural factors either believe differently or for whom such claim is irrelevant shows a lack of respect for a people whose religion includes other claims, and whose religion is central to their culture.[59] Is this imperialistic attitude not one of the main reasons for the lack of pastoral care and inclusion of Latinos in the life of the church in the U.S.A.?

Latinas' Christianity is indeed a mixture, a fusion of different religious strands. In this regard it follows in the footsteps of "official" Christianity. For example, Christmas is celebrated at the time of the year when the Feast of the Unconquered Sun took place at Rome in the late third and early fourth centuries;[60] pagan buildings such as the Pantheon were turned into churches; civil offices and the garbs of different periods and cultures have become religious offices and liturgical garb; Greek philosophical concepts of substance are used by Catholics to talk about the Eucharist. Once this syncretism became official, however, it has been used as an orthodox norm which has excluded and continues to exclude other syncretisms.

But such an exclusion does not obliterate syncretism from the Latinas' *religiosidad popular,* popular religiosity. Is Our Lady of Guadalupe the Mother of Jesus, or is she Tonantzin, the Aztec goddess, Mother of the Gods on whose pilgrimage site, the hill of Tepeyac, Our Lady of Guadalupe appeared?[61] In their hearts, and often quite openly, Latinas with Caribbean roots who pray to St. Barbara are identifying her, directly or indirectly, with Chango, the Yoruban God of Thunder. The hierarchy's decision to declare the story of St. Barbara a legend and the improbability that such a person ever existed is irrelevant to them.

The history of Christianity shows that orthodox objections to syncretism have less to do with the purity of faith and more with who has the right to determine what is to be considered normative and official. For the articulation of religious understandings, beliefs, and practices to be an act of liberation, it has to be an act of self-determination, not an attempt to comply with what the "official" church says, with what it considers to be orthodox. This is why *mujerista* theology does not shrink from claiming that the fusion of Christian, Amerindian, and African religious strands operative in the lives of Latinas may be good and life-giving.

Popular religiosity as a subculture pervades the lives of Latinas. Perhaps because of the precariousness of our lives, perhaps because our variety of Christianity is an intrinsic part of our culture, and because we are keenly aware of our culture since it is different from the dominant one, religion, religious thinking and practices, provide for us the moods and motivations operative in our day-to-day life. Questions of ultimate meaning, understandings of the divine and of ourselves and of our relationship to the divine, are not matters for religion experts only. No, they are matters which preoccupy, touch, and affect everyone. "*Si Dios quiere,*" God willing, is not an empty phrase for us. The belief that the divine cares about us and participates in our lives is something very real for us, something constantly taken into consideration. There is no doubt for us that what we are able to accomplish is due to much hard work; but it is also a fact that God has had something to do with it, and due credit is given to the divine by fulfilling promises at any physical or monetary cost.[62]

The day-to-day acknowledgment of the role the divine plays in our lives, as well as a firm belief in the ongoing revelation of God in the midst of and through the community of faith, is what leads us to claim the lived-experience of Latinas as the source of *mujerista* theology. This belief continues the long tradition very much present in the Hebrew Scriptures that God's revelation happens in and through the history of Israel's people. Salvation history is not something different from what actually happened to the Jewish people. Salvation history *is* precisely what happened to them; it has to do with how they interpreted what happened to them, with the role that God played in their struggles and accomplishments. Our claiming Latinas' lived-experience as the source of our theology is firmly rooted in this biblical understanding of the revelation of God. Knowing that as Latinas we have indeed been created in the image and likeness of God, trusting that our struggle to be faithful to our understandings of the divine makes us worthy member of the Christian community of faith, we believe that God's revelation happens in the day-to-day living of Latinas.

Spanish: "The Language of the Angels"

The Spanish language functions for Latinas not only as a means of communication but as a means of identification.[63] Spanish has become "the incarnation and symbol" of our whole culture, making us feel that here in the U.S.A. we are one people, no matter what our country of origin is. The Spanish language identifies us by distinguishing us from the rest of society. It gives us a specificity that we need to be a certain kind of people within a culture not our own.[64]

White Americans are willing to accept Latinos who are "white enough" as one of them when we become sufficiently middle-class and sufficiently "Anglicized." Many African Americans are also ready to claim black Latinos. But Latinas in general consider ourselves neither white nor black:[65]

> . . . for Hispanics the prime identifier is not color, but language, and so the Hispanic, whether black or white, tends to think that those who speak Spanish are "his [sic] people" no matter what their color, while those who speak English (whether black or white) are "the others." For Hispanics the "Anglo" is not the Anglo-Saxon, but the Anglophone.[66]

The Spanish language for us Latinos here in the U.S.A. has become "the bearer of identity and values."[67] Our attachment to it is such that even those Latinos born and raised in the U.S.A. who understand a little Spanish and can speak only a few words insist on saying that they do know Spanish. Since the importance of Spanish for Latinas is not so much to be able to communicate but to be able to identify each other, grammatical and pronunciation correctness is totally secondary. For us, Spanish is indeed a social construct and, therefore, we do not use Spanish to exclude from our communities those who know little Spanish or use it improperly.[68]

Our insistence on Spanish has to do, perhaps mostly at an unconscious but not all the less real level, with the fact that we resist the empire building of the U.S.A. at the expense of many of our countries of origin, which were either conquered, acquired, or dominated by the U.S.A. Many of us Latinas and Latinos are in the U.S.A. or are part of the U.S.A. by force, unlike European immigrants who came here seeking citizenship, cutting ties with their native lands and accepting "a subsidiary status, if any, for their native tongues."[69] Latinas' insistence on using Spanish and seeing it as a marker of our identity is a constant reminder to the dominant culture and to us that neither conquering a people nor the passing of generations means that a culture will disappear. As a matter of fact, our marginalization in a way assures us the continuation of our culture for, "if conquered people feel themselves systematically mistreated by their conquerors, they inevitably turn their language and culture into weapons or resistance, into tools with which precisely they demand full equality within the conquering society."[70] But with language, as with many other cultural elements, our insistence on our particularities is not a matter of wanting to Balkanize the U.S.A. Our insistence has to do with our desire to be included, to contribute to what is normative in this society. We will not give our Spanish up; on the contrary, Spanish seems to grow stronger in our communities and we are clearer in our demands for using our language widely within the U.S.A.

In an in-depth market study released in October 2000 that looks at the values, attitudes and behavioral patterns among the Hispanic market, Hispanics' preference for the Spanish language is on the rise: from 44% in 1997 to 53.1%; 22.4% preferred English and 24.3% had no preference.[71] 69.2% of Hispanics indicated that the Spanish language is more important to them now than it was five years earlier. When asked what language they spoke at home, 63.4% said Spanish was the dominant language and 15.5% said English. 47.2% indicated that they spoke Spanish all the time at home, while only 6.1% said they spoke English all the time at home. English and Spanish are used equally by 21%. Finally, in looking into the future and the role that the Spanish language plays in the maintenance of our culture, it is important to notice that only 38.9% of those polled strongly agreed with the statement "I feel that 50 years from now Hispanics in this country will lose their language and culture and become like everybody else in the United States," with 61.1% disagreeing, and 21.8% strongly disagreeing.

Yet maintaining fluency in Spanish is no easy task for Latinas. In the U.S.A., the governing principle in this regard continues to be "one population—one language . . . [and it] has assumed overtones of moral, social, and psychological normalcy."[72] The recent successful attempts in several parts of the U.S.A. where Latinos are numerous to pass a law declaring English *the* official language make this obvious. At the same time, this insistence on having an English-as-official-language law indicates that Spanish is used widely in certain states in the U.S.A. Laws will not stop Latinas from using Spanish, because it is a social construct that has enormous importance in maintaining our identity, and we will do everything in our power to continue to speak it and teach it to our children. We are aware that as an oppressed group we are not able to preserve the use of Spanish because we are "limited in being able to establish and control institutions of language monitoring, language ideologization [*sic*] and, most particularly, language use via the establishment and control of significant political and economic bases of . . . [our] own."[73] It is our hope, however, that the constant flow of new Spanish-speaking people into the U.S.A., plus the frequent return to their country of origin, will help Latinos us preserve Spanish.

Latino Ethnicity: Social Construct

In these two first chapters I have analyzed the main elements of Latino ethnicity: *mestizaje,* our multilayered oppression and struggle for survival, our socioeconomic reality, popular religiosity, the insistence on speaking Spanish, and our *proyecto histórico*—all of these are pieces that together constitute and shape Latinas' ethnicity. It is the intersection and interplay of all of these elements that give us our peculiarities and distinctiveness as Latina Women. In other words, the shared cultural norms, values, identities, and behaviors that form the core of our ethnicity are linked to these six elements we have explored.

At the same time, we know that these cultural norms, values, identities, and behaviors are irreversibly impacted by the prejudice and discrimination to which we are subjected in this society.[74] This means that the oppression we suffer as Latinas has become an integral part of our ethnicity—of Latino ethnicity—and, therefore, it impacts every aspect of our lives, as does our daily struggle to survive.

I CONTINUE TO CONSIDER the six elements that I examine in these two first chapters key characteristics of our identity as Latinas in the U.S.A. These are the characteristics that define our position in relation to other groups in society. It is also in and through these elements that we relate among ourselves within the Latina community. These six elements—*mestizaje-mulatez,* survival, socioeconomic status, popular religiosity, Spanish, and our historical project—are also the elements that influence and mold our surroundings and how we develop within it. Daily life—*la vida cotidiana*—of Latinas, the reality in which we live and which we are creating, is important because *mujerista* theology is a reflection on those beliefs and practices of Latinas which are part of our daily lives. In other words, we have to know the reality in which religious faith happens in order to understand it and explain it.

In the last ten years, much has been written about popular religiosity. We have come to understand the religious value it has for Latinas and that is why now we refer to it as "popular religion" instead of "popular religiosity," a term that seems to indicate a lower level of importance than that given to "official" religion. Religious practices outside the church are as religious as those in the church, that is to say, they express what we believe about the divine and how they affect our lives as much as do official religious practices. What is more, many of us believe that popular religion has been and continues to be one of the main avenues we Latinas have to express our faith since the churches do not always understand or pay attention to our religious perspectives and practices. Popular religion, then, is often one of the main vehicles for Latinas to keep our faith alive.

The majority of Hispanic Protestant theologians do not see popular religion as a central element in their denominations, nor do they claim it to be a means of divine revelation. Yet they do accept the fact that there exist popular religious devotions—popular, of course, in the sense that they belong to the people, not that they have wide acceptance—and that there is a popular spirituality that often is not valued by the churches. These popular religious devotions do inform Hispanic Protestant theology and center on the Bible, sermons, witnessing to the Lord's presence in life, prayer vigils and religious songs—particularly the *coritos* and *estribillos.*

The syncretism of Christian-Catholic practice with *santería, curanderismo,* and spiritualism continues to be an integral part of the lives of many Latinas. Many priests and ministers consider that such syncretism points to religious confusion. However, when one speaks with Latinas and Latinos, one does not perceive any confusion. Therefore, if we take these beliefs seriously, what we learn is that for them different religious systems or different systems of beliefs do not exclude one another. Latinas and Latinos embrace at the same time more than one system, moving between them with great ease, guided by the many needs that they face daily.

In reference to the use of Spanish, I am more and more convinced of how important this is for Latino identity in the U.S.A., as a sign of our hybridity, and as an element we use in positioning ourselves in relation to the dominant group. The "Spanglish" that mixes English and Spanish in one same word—*rainenado* meaning "raining," *rufa* meaning "roof"—continues to function as a sort of mid-point that allows us, or so we imagine, to be understood in both languages. Our Spanish as well as our English is full of "linguistic transferences," in which we use cognates that do not necessarily mean the same in both languages and grammatical constructions of one of the languages in the other one. This, without doubt, exasperates language scholars but, on the other hand, it indicates the need we have to keep, no matter how minimally, elements of our own language. The fact is that even those of us who work as professors need our Spanish to be edited as well as our English. Yet, we are willing to risk not being able to express ourselves perfectly in either language, rather than give up Spanish.

Regardless of the blemishes we inflict on the Spanish language and all the difficulties speaking Spanish gives us, we insist on the use of Spanish not only because it is an element of our identity but also because of its epistemological value. The language we speak not only allows us to express what we think but also provides us with the categories we use to think, to argue, and to explain what we understand to ourselves as well as to others. When we think "in Spanish," even if it is in a faulty Spanish, we are able to think in a way closer to the one we learned in our countries or communities of origin. I believe, therefore, that Spanish is a key element in the preservation of our Latina culture in the U.S.A.—in the preservation of our values and customs.

Síntesis del Capítulo 2
Religiosidad Popular, Idioma Español y Proyecto Histórico:
Elementos de la Etnicidad de las Latinas

En este capítulo examinamos las esperanzas y expectativas arraigadas en la realidad cotidiana de las latinas, y mantenidas por la esperanza de que en algún momento darán frutos en este mundo. Lo que llamamos nuestro proyecto histórico es la realidad que nos esforzamos por construir y, por lo tanto, es uno de los elementos centrales de nuestra identidad latina. Otros dos elementos importantes de nuestra identidad y realidad latina que también analizamos en este capítulo son la religiosidad popular y el uso del idioma español.

El proyecto histórico

El proyecto histórico de las mujeres latinas es nuestra liberación y los pasos específicos que necesitamos dar para lograrlo. Aunque este proyecto histórico no es un plan detallado, sí es un proyecto lo suficientemente concreto como para forzar a las personas a escoger valores y formas de vivir. Este capítulo recoge no sólo un esbozo de nuestro proyecto histórico sino también las estrategias que nos ayudan a moldear nuestra lucha cotidiana por sobrevivir al igual que nuestra identidad como comunidad. Lo que aquí decimos del proyecto histórico de las mujeres latinas está basado en las experiencias que hemos vivido y es, a la vez, la meta que nos esforzamos por alcanzar.

Nuestro proyecto histórico se basa en un entendimiento de en qué consiste la salvación cristiana y la liberación—realidades que entendemos como dos aspectos de un mismo proceso histórico. La historia de la salvación se refiere al actuar de Dios—creación, encarnación, redención—tanto como a la respuesta humana a este actuar de Dios. Para nosotras las latinas la salvación tiene que ver con nuestra relación con Dios, relación que no existe si no amamos a nuestro prójimo. Nuestra relación con Dios afecta todos los aspectos de nuestras vidas. Para nosotras el proceso salvífico se da en la historia y está íntimamente relacionado con nuestra liberación.

Liberación para las latinas tiene que ver con ser sujetos de nuestra historia y tener lo que necesitamos para vivir y poder realizarnos plenamente como seres humanos. Para las latinas, la plenitud del reino de Dios—el ser plenamente la familia de Dios—significa a la vez salvación y liberación. Nosotras creemos que nuestra labor en favor de la justicia y la paz en este mundo es indispensable para la realización plena del reino de Dios, el ser familia de Dios.

El ser plenamente familia de Dios está relacionado con nuestra realidad diaria, la cual requiere que denunciemos la injusticia a la vez que anunciamos el futuro por el que luchamos. La denuncia como parte de nuestro proyecto histórico requiere que analicemos profundamente las estructuras que nos oprimen a la vez que criticamos y censuramos a quienes las mantienen y se benefician de ellas. La denuncia también tiene que llevarnos a repudiar estas estructuras opresivas, no a que aspiremos a participar en ellas o a beneficiarnos de ellas. Esta insistencia en la denuncia hace que uno de los puntos de partida de la teología *mujerista* sea la crítica social.

Denunciar sin anunciar el futuro que queremos y necesitamos es irresponsable. Es más, para que la denuncia sea efectiva tiene que ir acompañada del anuncio de la meta por la que luchamos. El anunciar en medio de la opresión ya es en sí una manera efectiva de luchar por nuestra liberación.

El proceso de liberación tiene tres aspectos, los cuales no se deben confundir. Cada uno es específico y distinto pero todos se afectan entre sí, y ninguno está presente sin que lo estén los otros. Estos tres aspectos del proceso de liberación son elementos del proyecto histórico. Las latinas nos referimos a estos tres niveles o aspectos del proceso de liberación como "libertad", "comunidad de fe", y "justicia".

"Libertad" aquí se refiere a nuestra lucha por ser sujetos históricos. En esta lucha por la libertad, las latinas tenemos que tener cuidado de no creer que pueden darse cambios estructurales sin que haya liberación personal o viceversa. Lo "personal" para nosotras no excluye a las demás personas ni se da en el ámbito privado. Esta manera de entender la "libertad" también nos ayuda a las latinas a comprender el papel que nosotras mismas jugamos en nuestra opresión a la vez que nos llama a luchar para poder ser nosotras las que determinemos quiénes somos y qué hacemos.

La "libertad" como aspecto del proceso de liberación se refiere al aspecto sicológico tanto como el social. Los dos obstáculos principales para que las latinas logremos "libertad" son la apatía y el miedo. Al sabernos un grupo oprimido dentro del país más rico del mundo, las latinas sentimos que la lucha es tan ardua y dura que nos descorazonamos y nos volvemos apáticas. Nuestra meta—nuestra liberación—nos parece tan lejana que la apatía surge como forma de protección en contra de la frustración. Aquéllas de nosotras que logramos evitar la frustración y la apatía tenemos que luchar contra el miedo: el miedo a fracasar, a no lograr lo que queremos, y aún más, el miedo a que vayamos a aceptar el *status quo* y a que, a fin de cuentas, acabemos por acomodarnos para poder beneficiarnos de las estructuras opresivas de la sociedad.

Para poder contrarrestar la apatía y el miedo, las mujeres latinas tenemos que continuar elaborando nuestra visión del futuro a la vez que vamos articulando los detalles de cómo lograr lo que queremos. Uno de los aspectos más importantes es empeñarnos en que cada una puede participar en el proceso de convertir nuestra visión en realidad.

"Comunidad de fe" como aspecto del proceso liberador de las latinas tiene como eje central nuestra íntima relación con lo divino. Esta relación se basa no sólo en nuestra creencia en que Dios está con nosotras en nuestro caminar cotidiano sino también en que nosotras nos relacionamos con Dios de la forma familiar y constante en que nos relacionamos con nuestros seres queridos. Discutimos con Dios, peleamos con Dios, nos contrariamos con Dios, les estamos agradecidas a Dios, halagamos a Dios, ¡hasta recompensamos a Dios!

Esta forma de pensar y vivir nos hace ver que el pecado daña nuestra relación con Dios a la vez que afecta negativamente nuestras comunidades. Para las latinas el pecado no es tanto un desobedecer los mandamientos de Dios y de la iglesia como es un no ocuparnos de los demás, un no ser responsables por los demás, por quiénes somos y por lo que hacemos. El análisis de la realidad opresiva que sufrimos nos puede ayudar a entender mejor que el pecado tiene siempre un elemento social porque afecta a la comunidad. Entendemos que el pecado social es el pecado encarnado en estructuras que explotan y oprimen, y que por eso es que tenemos que luchar para cambiar esas estructuras.

Las latinas tenemos que actualizar nuestro sentido comunitario trabajando en grupos y organizaciones que tengan una orientación práctica y que nos apoyen tanto personalmente como en nuestros proyectos comunitarios. Es importante que no perdamos el tiempo en organizaciones y grupos cuyo enfoque sea lo espiritual—entendido como algo ajeno a la lucha por la justicia; o que se dediquen al apoyo personal pero no al comunitario. Tenemos que aceptar el hecho de que aunque nuestras creencias religiosas son, la mayor parte de las veces, la motivación principal para nuestro trabajo comunitario, desgraciadamente no podemos contar mucho con la ayuda de las iglesias. Por el contrario, una vez más, vamos a tener que depender de nosotras mismas y, a lo mejor, de las pocas organizaciones nacionales de latinas que dicen estar comprometidas con la lucha por nuestra liberación.

Nuestras "comunidades de fe" tienen que ser ecuménicas. Es imperativo abrazar el sentido ecuménico que existe, casi siempre sin ser nombrado, entre las latinas de la base que se relacionan con diferentes iglesias sin experimentar contradicción alguna al hacerlo. La base del ecumenismo tendría que ser, no la uniformidad de creencia, sino la lucha por la liberación. Nuestro esfuerzo ecuménico tiene que tomar en consideración la religiosidad popular que muchas compartimos a pesar de pertenecer a diferentes iglesias. Por último, nuestras "comunidades de fe" tienen que desarrollar su propio estilo de liderazgo. Necesitamos líderes comunitarios que reconozcan y utilicen los dones de las latinas, líderes que posibiliten y capaciten a las demás en vez de convertirse, con una rapidez vertiginosa, en caciques.

El tercer aspecto de la lucha por la liberación es la "justicia." La justicia es una virtud que tiene que ver principalmente con la manera en que actuamos, la manera como las instituciones sociales están organizadas, las prioridades que tienen y la forma en que usan sus recursos. La justicia como aspecto central de la lucha por la liberación tiene que ver con mucho más que el proveer las necesidades básicas de todos los miembros de la sociedad. Más allá de ser una virtud utilitaria, la verdadera justicia tiene que ver con lograr la plenitud humana: la felicidad de cada persona. La verdadera justicia no es sólo cuestión de "a cada uno de acuerdo con sus necesidades", como dice el dictamen marxista. Para nosotras en la teología *mujerista* la justicia es un requisito del cristianismo que le permite a cada persona y requiere de cada una el participar en decisiones acerca de lo que necesita la comunidad—tanto los bienes morales como los materiales—para mantener y promover la plenitud de vida. Y, como ya hemos dicho, la justicia tiene que ver con el derecho de las latinas a participar plenamente en todas las instituciones sociales, incluyendo las iglesias. La justicia es la lucha por el bien común que no se puede lograr a costa de nadie ni puede poner los derechos individuales de las personas por encima de la participación de todos—en especial de los pobres—en la sociedad. El éxito del bien común se determina a partir de los derechos y las necesidades de las más pobres y oprimidas. El bien común tiene que ver no sólo con las necesidades físicas sino también con lo que les permite a las personas expandir sus horizontes: la educación, el arte, la música.

La justicia, desde la perspectiva *mujerista,* requiere una opción preferencial por las latinas, opción que encuentra expresión en una solidaridad efectiva entre nosotras y con nosotras. Dicha solidaridad requiere que quienes se benefician de las estructuras presentes, pongan sus privilegios al servicio de cambios sociales necesarios para que florezca la justicia. Aquéllas que se hacen solidarias con la causa de las latinas nos pueden ayudar a no caer en la tentación de creer que se puede lograr la justicia dentro de las presentes estructuras; quienes se hacen solidarios con nuestra causa nos pueden ayudar a deshacernos del "opresor internalizado" que a veces nos hace ser vengativas, desfigurando así nuestro proyecto histórico.

La religiosidad popular como elemento de la teología *mujerista*

El punto de partida para el estudio de la religiosidad popular de las latinas es nuestra lucha cotidiana por sobrevivir. Para nosotras la religiosidad popular es parte de nuestra auto-identificación; nuestra insistencia en valorar la religiosidad popular es parte de la lucha por mantener las características y peculiaridades propias que nos definen como latinas. Es gracias a la religiosidad popular que la religión continúa siendo elemento central de la cultura latina a pesar del descuido de las iglesias por nuestras comunidades en este país.

El cristianismo que es, sin duda, la religión de la vasta mayoría de las latinas, no es el cristianismo "oficial", y no tiene necesariamente a las instituciones eclesiásticas como punto central de referencia. Nuestro cristianismo tiene su base en la religión que trajeron los conquistadores españoles a América Latina, un cristianismo que fue parte del violento proceso de la conquista y que ayudó a aniquilar el mundo y la cosmología de los nativos. Este cristianismo que se convirtió en parte integral de la cultura latina, usaba la Biblia en forma muy limitada haciendo en vez énfasis en las tradiciones y costumbres de la iglesia española. El cristianismo de las latinas hoy día incluye también las tradiciones religiosas de los esclavos africanos al igual que las de las culturas amerindias. Es precisamente de la mezcla del cristianismo español del siglo XVI, las religiones africanas de los esclavos y las creencias y prácticas religiosas de las culturas amerindias que surge la religiosidad popular latina.

Por religiosidad popular entendemos las experiencias, creencias y ritos que, como grupos marginados, hemos creado, asumido y desarrollado como respuesta a situaciones socioculturales específicas. Estas experiencias, creencias y ritos se distancian de las instituciones eclesiásticas y los grupos dominantes de la sociedad tratando de encontrar acceso a Dios y a la salvación, cosa que las latinas no creemos poder lograr a través de las iglesias "oficiales" y de las instituciones de la sociedad dominante.

La religiosidad popular de las latinas tiene cinco características. 1) Es una subcultura religiosa ya que es una manera de pensar y actuar no de algunos individuos sino de todo un grupo de personas. 2) Los ritos que se usan se basan mayormente en tradiciones católicas, tales como los sacramentales, que la iglesia "oficial" considera secundarias. 3) La religiosidad popular es sincrética ya que le da a prácticas religiosas católicas significados que vienen de otras religiones. 4) Hay prácticas "oficiales" que al ser reinterpretadas adquieren otros significados. 5) Todas estas características se transmiten como parte de la cultura latina.

La teología *mujerista* considera que la religiosidad popular es uno de los elementos más creativos y originales de nuestra cultura y de nuestra herencia, y que es uno de los elementos que más nos anima en la lucha por la liberación. La religiosidad popular es una fuente importante de la teología *mujerista* porque es un sistema de valores, ideas y prácticas simbólicas representadas por medio de ritos y materializados en imágenes visuales que relacionan a las latinas con lo divino y que surgen de nuestra situación de grupo marginal. Pero el que no sea oficial no la excluye de ser examinada bajo el lente de la liberación. Como teólogas *mujeristas* reconocemos que la religiosidad popular tiene sus fallas y ambigüedades al igual que las tienen otras formas culturales del catolicismo y el cristianismo. Reconocemos que algunos de los elementos de la religiosidad popular son opresivos para las latinas. Por otro lado reconocemos el papel evangelizador que ha jugado la religiosidad popular y el rol tan importante que tiene en preservar nuestra cultura.

Otro papel importante de la religiosidad popular para las latinas es que nos ayuda a encontrar lo sagrado en lo cotidiano, en lo ordinario y corriente de nuestras vidas. Es precisamente la religiosidad popular lo que hace posible que no sea desacralizada nuestra cultura. Son las prácticas de la religiosidad popular las que nos permiten a las latinas estar conscientes de lo sagrado en todos los aspectos de nuestras vidas: tanto en lo público como en lo privado, tanto en el orden personal como en el social. Sin embargo, las iglesias "oficiales" en vez de considerar la religiosidad popular como algo positivo, o la denuncian y trabajan activamente en contra de ella, o buscan maneras de purificarla, de "bautizarla", aceptando sólo aquellos elementos que puedan reconciliarse con el cristianismo "oficial". Pero no importa cuánto hayan tratado, las iglesias "oficiales" no han podido hacer que el pueblo latino en general y en particular las mujeres latinas dejemos de recurrir a Santa Bárbara—identificada con Changó, orisha de la religión yoruba—para que nos ayude en la lucha diaria; o que sea en Guadalupe—identificada con la divinidad azteca Tonantzín—en quien pensamos cuando sentimos que necesitamos ayuda divina.

El español: "el idioma de los ángeles"

El español funciona para las latinas no sólo como medio de comunicación sino también como medio de identificación. El idioma español se ha convertido en este país en símbolo de nuestra cultura, haciendo posible que sintamos que somos un solo pueblo aquí en los EE.UU. El español nos identifica y nos distingue del resto de la sociedad, dándonos la especificidad que necesitamos para sobrevivir como grupo dentro de una cultura que no es la nuestra. Las que hablan o entienden el español son de las nuestras; las que no lo hacen, esas pertenecen a "las otras". El idioma español para nosotras aquí en EE.UU., es vehículo fácilmente reconocible de nuestra identidad y de nuestros valores. Sin embargo, lo importante, no es tanto que nos podamos comunicar efectivamente en español, como que lo reclamemos como nuestro, como lo que nos identifica como latinas.

Es precisamente porque el idioma español es elemento de cohesión para las latinas y los latinos que hay tanta oposición al uso del español en esta sociedad. La clase dominante entiende que el uso del español sigue siendo elemento importantísimo en la construcción social de nuestra identidad latina. Sabemos que debido a que no podemos influenciar las decisiones sobre el uso del español—parte de la ideología lingüística de este país—se nos hace muy difícil mantener el uso del español. Tampoco tenemos los medios económicos y políticos para insistir en el uso de nuestro idioma en el ámbito público. Pero confiamos en que la constante llegada a los EE.UU. de nuevos inmigrantes hispanohablantes y las frecuentes visitas a nuestros países de origen nos ayuden en la lucha por preservar el español.

Presentamos estadísticas del 2000 que indican lo importante que sigue siendo el uso del español para las latinas.

• 53.1% de los latinos y las latinas en el 2000 prefieren hablar español comparado con 44% en 1997.

- 69.2% indica que el uso del español es ahora más importante que hace cinco años.
- Para 63.4% de los latinos y las latinas el español es el idioma dominante en sus hogares. Sólo el 15.5% dijo que el idioma dominante era el inglés.
- Sólo el 6.1% dijo que hablaba inglés en el hogar todo el tiempo.
- A la propuesta, "siento que de aquí a 50 años los hispanos en este país perderán su idioma y su cultura y serán como todos los demás en los EE.UU.", sólo 38.9% está muy de acuerdo, mientras que 61.1% está en desacuerdo y 21.8% está muy en desacuerdo.

La etnicidad latina como construcción social

En estos dos primeros capítulos hemos analizado seis elementos principales de nuestra etnicidad latina: el mestizaje, nuestra opresión y la lucha por sobrevivir, nuestra realidad socioeconómica, la religiosidad popular, el español y nuestro proyecto histórico. La interacción entre estos elementos es lo que constituye y le da forma a la identidad latina aquí en los EE.UU. En otras palabras, estos elementos están relacionados con las normas culturales, los valores, las formas de comportamiento, y la forma como nos identificamos, que son el corazón de nuestra etnicidad. Pero el afirmar nuestra identidad cultural latina no es cosa fácil debido al impacto negativo que tienen el prejuicio y la discriminación a que estamos sometidas en esta sociedad. Esta discriminación—esta opresión que sufrimos por ser latinas—es parte integral de lo que quiere decir ser latina, por lo tanto, es una realidad que impacta en forma negativa todos los aspectos de nuestras vidas. Nuestra esperanza está en que la opresión también nos impacte en forma positiva. Es decir que nos haga valorar lo mejor de lo que tenemos y nos haga insistir en nuestra lucha cotidiana por la liberación.

Sigo considerando los seis elementos que examino en estos dos primeros capítulos características centrales de nuestra identidad como latinas en los EE.UU. Es a partir de estos elementos que las latinas nos posicionamos en relación con los otros grupos en la sociedad. Es también en relación a estos elementos que nos relacionamos entre nosotras, en la comunidad latina. Estos seis elementos—mestizaje-mulatez, sobrevivencia, estado socioeconómico, religiosidad popular, el idioma español y el proyecto histórico—también son elementos que influyen y moldean nuestro medio ambiente y cómo nos desarrollamos en él. La vida cotidiana de las latinas—la realidad en la que vivimos y que vamos creando—es importante porque la teología *mujerista* es una reflexión acerca de las creencias y prácticas religiosas de las latinas, creencias y prácticas que se dan en el vivir diario. En otras palabras, tenemos que conocer el medio ambiente en el que se da la fe religiosa para poderla conocer y explicar.

En los últimos diez años mucho se ha escrito acerca de la religiosidad popular. Hemos comprendido el significado teológico y el valor religioso que tiene para las latinas y es por eso que hablamos hoy día de "religión popular" en vez de "religiosidad popular", apelativo que parece poner estas prácticas de fe a un nivel inferior que las que se dan en torno a las iglesias "oficiales". Las prácticas religiosas fuera de las iglesias son tan religiosas como las prácticas que se dan en las iglesias; es decir, las prácticas que se dan fuera de las iglesias expresan lo que creemos acerca de lo divino y el papel que estas creencias tienen en nuestras vidas tanto como las prácticas oficiales ecclesiales. Es más, muchas y muchos mantenemos que la religión popular ha sido y continúa siendo una de las formas principales que tenemos las latinas de expresar nuestra fe y, dado que toda fe en realidad es una vivencia—una forma de entender y vivir la vida—la religión popular a menudo es la única manera que tenemos de mantener viva la fe ya que las iglesias no siempre entienden o atienden nuestras perpectivas y pácticas religiosas.

Las teólogas y los teólogos protestantes hispanos no ven la religión popular como elemento central de sus denominaciones y no la reclaman como vehículo de la revelación divina y, por lo tanto, del quehacer teológico hispano protestante. Sin embargo, dejan por sentado que existen devociones religiosas populares—popular, claro está, en el sentido de que pertenecen al pueblo y no en el sentido de algo que tiene gran aceptación—y que existe una espiritualidad popular que muchas veces no es valorada por las iglesias, y que esta religiosidad popular sin duda informa el quehacer teológico hispano protestante. Estas prácticas se centran en la Biblia, sermones, testimonios, devocionales, vigilias de oración y canciones religiosas—en especial los coritos y estribillos.

El sincretismo de lo cristiano-católico con expresiones y creencias religiosas como la santería, el curanderismo y el espiritismo continúa siendo parte integral de la vida de muchas latinas. El que las iglesias cristianas—tanto protestantes como católicas—denuncien este sincretismo no quiere decir que no exista. Muchos sacerdotes, ministras y ministros consideran que el sincretismo lo que indica es la confusión religiosa que existe en las comunidades latinas. Sin embargo, cuando se habla con las latinas y los latinos se percibe que no se sienten confundidos. Por lo tanto, si se toman en serio sus creencias lo que aprendemos es que para ellas y ellos los diferentes sistemas religiosos o sistemas de creencias no se excluyen el uno al otro. Las latinas y los latinos abrazan más de un sistema de creencias a la vez, moviéndose entre ellos con gran fluidez, guiados por las necesidades de la vida cotidiana.

En referencia al uso del español, estoy más y más convencida de la importancia que tiene para mantener la identidad latina en los EE.UU., para señalar nuestra hibridez, y para posicionarnos en relación a la clase dominante. El "espanglés" en el cual se mezcla el inglés y el español en una misma palabra—"raineando" para decir lloviendo, la "rufa" de *roof* para referirse al techo—continua siendo como el punto medio que nos permite, o así nos lo parece, que se nos entienda en los dos idiomas. Nuestro español y nuestro inglés están llenos de las llamadas "transferencias lingüísticas" en las que usamos construcciones gramaticales propias de un idioma en el otro. Esto sin duda exaspera a los eruditos del idioma pero, por otro lado, indica la necesidad que tenemos de mantener, sea como sea, algo de nuestro idioma. La realidad es que incluso las que pertenecemos al mundo académico necesitamos que se nos edite tanto en inglés como en español, pero estamos dispuestas a no poder expresarnos perfectamente en ninguno de los idiomas antes que dejar de usar el español aunque sea en forma limitada.

Con todas las desfiguraciones que le hacemos sufrir a la lengua y todas las dificultades que nos causa, insistimos en el uso del español no sólo como elemento de nuestra identidad sino también por el valor epistemológico que tiene el lenguaje. El idioma que hablamos nos permite no sólo expresar lo que pensamos sino que provee los esquemas que usamos para pensar, para armar los argumentos y las explicaciones que nos damos a nosotras mismas y a otras. Cuando pensamos "en español", aunque sea un español con faltas, nos es posible pensar en forma más cercana a la que aprendimos en nuestros países de origen. Creo, entonces, que el uso del español es uno de los vehículos principales para conservar nuestra cultura latina en los EE.UU.: nuestros valores y costumbres.

CHAPTER 3

Mujerista Theology's Methods:
Understandings and Procedure

BEGINNING AN ARTICULATION OF MUJERISTA THEOLOGY and ethics with an explanation of Hispanic Women's ethnicity indicates the significance of our everyday world, how we understand and describe our bodily and material existence as Hispanic Women for this enterprise. That social locality is central to *mujerista* theology is consistent with our insistence on the lived-experience of Hispanic Women as the source of our theology, which calls for a theological method that not only explicitly identifies such experience but also presents it as unmediated as possible. Likewise important is the commitment of *mujerista* theology to provide—to be—a platform for the voices of Hispanic Women. Such requirement and commitment have led to an exploration of the social sciences to find understandings and methods that will not objectify us and our experience, that will not ultimately discard it, but rather will enable us to gather our lived-experience, to explore it and present it to others with integrity.

This chapter presents a mosaic of *mujerista* theology's methods, a mosaic that will be seen in its totality only if one first notices and studies the pieces. First, we present an overview of the main sociological considerations that ground our method. A brief exposition of ethnomethodology—a critique of professional social sciences that focuses on the particularities of the persons being investigated—follows. Then comes an analysis of the role of *mujerista* theologians as researchers. Two qualitative research methods (ethnography and meta-ethnography) used to gather the voices and lived-experiences of Hispanic Women are then explained.

The chapter ends by arguing that *mujerista* theologians must present in our writings particular voices from the communities in which our theology is rooted. Otherwise we will either run the risk of objectifying grassroot Hispanic Women by talking about "them" and for "them," or we will speak exclusively for and by ourselves instead of providing a forum for the theological voice of our communities. Only if *mujerista* theology is a theological discourse that serves as a platform for oppressed Hispanic Women's voices can it claim to be a liberative praxis.

Sociological Methods and Theories

Precisely because of the absence of Hispanic Women's voices from theological discourses, our lives, our understandings, and meanings are what *mujerista* theology seeks to bring to light. But as important as bringing them to light is the way in which this is done. Often we have seen the experiences of other marginalized groups, including Hispanics, molded to fit into the accepted formats of theological discourse. We believe this has led to distortions that have resulted in new ways of silencing these groups, such as using their experiences as examples to illumine answers to questions determined by those who control the systems, while never allowing the marginalized groups to pose the questions. To avoid this, when considering what method to use in elaborating *mujerista* theology, we have kept in mind two things. First, the moral agency of Hispanic Women has to be the determining factor in our methodological considerations. Therefore, second, though we understand the elaboration itself of *mujerista* theology to be a liberative praxis, *mujerista* theology as a discourse cannot be considered more important than Hispanic Women's development as agents of our own lives and of our own history.

In struggling to maintain Hispanic Women as agents and subjects, instead of making them into objects, *mujerista* theologians discovered that we needed the voices of Hispanic Women themselves to be present in the theological discourse. These voices do not claim to be representative. Neither are they to be understood as examples of a worldview or perspective. We believe that the voices of particular Hispanic Women have validity in themselves and that without claiming to be representative they point to the reality of all Hispanic Women because they make our reality more understandable. Instead of attempting to present a universal voice, our attempt has been to point to the universal by being as specific as possible. Just as radical immanence is a different way of understanding what up to now has been called transcendence, so, too, the more specific and particular the voices we present in *mujerista* theology, the more they encompass the reality of all Hispanic Women.

But we realized this was not enough when we saw that no matter how faithfully we present specific Hispanic Women's voices, there are always numerous mediations that tend to muffle them. We also had, first of all, to investigate and understand—an ongoing process that we do not think will ever end—who we are, how we understand ourselves and elaborate meaning for ourselves. Understanding our Hispanicness, our ethnicity, as a social construct and identifying the key elements in it has helped us to grasp better our world and the situation of oppression in which Hispanic Women live. The second element has to do with the dialogic relationship those of us conducting the research and doing the writing of *mujerista* theology have established with the Hispanic Women whose voices we include in our discourse. Furthermore, a very important role here also is the role our religious understandings and practices play in *mujerista* theology.

Third, we have worked with the women whose voices we include so that the process of gathering the voices helps them to understand better their daily struggle to survive. Our attempt has been not to turn them into "types" but to see them as they see themselves, as persons who seek to know the meaning of their lives, of their daily struggles.[1] One of our goals has been to enable the development of their moral agency, not by analyzing their religious understandings and practices but rather by seeing how they construct those understandings and practices.

Our methods have had as their objective to help these women come to know themselves, to know what they think about questions of ultimate meaning, and how these questions are used in Hispanic Women's everyday struggle to survive in the midst of great oppression. One of our objectives has been to hold up our everyday religious practices and to value them. Grounding our methods has been the firm conviction that our task is not to present already fixed representations, "pretheorized reality."[2] On the contrary, our insistence on presenting the voices of Hispanic Women has been to destabilize the balance of power and knowledge that exists between Hispanics and the dominant groups in the U.S.A., and between Hispanic Women and women of the dominant groups in the U.S.A. Such destabilizing will make possible—at the same time that it is partially caused by—the critical consciousness and practice of Hispanic Women.[3]

Gathering and presenting their voices allows Hispanic Women to be subjects of their own history, to see and present themselves as moral agents with a critical consciousness. It also makes it possible for them to understand and to present to others "powerful and insightful commentaries on the social order" that are embedded in their self-disclosing discourse. What they have shared in their narratives they understand as relating not just to themselves. They understand who they are and what they go through as something that goes beyond them, as something that has to do with the Hispanic community at large and with the whole of society.

As we gather and present the voices of grassroot Hispanic Women, *mujerista* theologians have come to understand more clearly that the conceptual frameworks and epistemological presuppositions of the world of theology cannot hold the meaning of our daily lives and our concerns, knowledge, and understandings of the divine without distorting them. The old wineskins cannot hold new wine, but if by chance they do, the new wine will turn into vinegar!

Ethnomethodology

Ethnomethodology is a critique of professional social sciences initially proposed by Harvard social psychologist Harold Garfinkel. His primary criticism is that in professional sociology there is no "actor," but rather an ideal type, a dummy. Ethnomethodologists argue that it is difficult to find in sociological studies a real person with a biography and a history. The person to whom the studies keep referring is the creation of the social scientists, and therefore the self-understanding and everyday life of that person are absent from consideration. Ethnomethodology, on the other hand, is a theory of everyday life.

The basic presuppositions of ethnomethodology provide a pointed explanation of this "new" method that wants to be available for everyone to use in any discipline. The first presupposition is that people have and use "practical rationality," that is, people accomplish everyday life. Second, everyday life is reflexive, that is, it is contextual and self-descriptive, not explanatory. Reflexivity in this context refers to people's everyday creation of life and their holding each other accountable for appropriate participation in it. Reflexivity here has to do with the definition of the situation at hand, with its integrity in itself. The third presupposition is that social interaction can be indexed, it can be documented. These last two presuppositions are undergirded by an understanding of language—gestures, expressions, symbols, deportment—which create the social world.

Because of the centrality of description to ethnomethodology, the test of whether or not what one has observed corresponds to the self-understanding of the person being described is critical. In the case of the written accounts of *mujerista* theology, the test will be whether or not Hispanic Women can say, "Yes, this is my life, this is what I understand, this is what I mean."[4]

Ethnography

Mujerista theology recognizes and makes explicit the culture of the community out of which it arises, the Hispanic culture. It is appropriate, therefore, for those of us doing *mujerista* theology to avail ourselves of the techniques and principles of qualitative research which is concerned with coming to know by "watching people in heir own territory and interacting with them in their own language, on their own terms."[5] Furthermore, because qualitative research "involves sustained interaction with the people being studied,"[6] it is a highly appropriate technique for *mujerista* theologians, who should be an integral part of the community out of which the theology they are formulating arises. Qualitative research is " 'grounded' in the everyday lives of people,"[7] and looks for explanations of "social or cultural events based upon the perspectives and experiences of the people."[8]

Of the different methods used in qualitative research, ethnography is one particularly well suited to doing *mujerista* theology. It is used by social sciences to describe and classify cultures by dealing with the distinctive characteristics and customs of those cultures. Ethnography is a way of conducting research that has as its foundation "the complex relationship between the researcher and his [*sic*] informants."[9] Ethnographical principles call for participation of the informants, of those who are being studied, in developing the method used. Ethnography calls for as little mediation as possible in describing and making known the culture in question.

Using ethnographic principles, *mujerista* theology presents the understandings and opinions of Hispanic Women, as much as possible, in their own words. To do this we conduct ethnographic interviews. These interviews are much more a conversation, a dialogue, than the standard survey form of questions and answers. In contrast to other kinds of interviews, ethnographical interviews have as their goal "to learn from people, to be taught by them,"[10] instead of just gathering information about them. This learning from the people occurs in the dialogic process that takes place between the researcher and the informants. Ethnographic interviews also make it possible to hear many voices instead of only the voices of the leaders of the community. They provide an opportunity for different members of the community to reflect on their experiences, to grasp better what they believe and how those beliefs impact their everyday lives. The interviews, therefore, are part of a liberative praxis; they are a consciousness-raising experience for Hispanic Women not only because it gives them an opportunity for reflection but also because they are often a vehicle for Hispanic Women to develop their own voices. Without this voice of one's own, Hispanic Women are not able to be agents of our own history.[11]

In doing *mujerista* theology I have conducted ethnographic interviews in two different settings. One is what the women who participated called "retreats," that is, reflection done in community during a weekend. The information gathered during these weekends has proved to be extremely rich. The women sparked and challenged each other to become more and more reflective and explicit about their experiences and understandings. These weekends have included celebrations as well as the development of strategies for dealing with problematic circumstances at home, in the workplace, or in the community at large.[12] I prefer this way of conducting ethnographic studies.

When this process has not been possible because of lack of money or time, the interviews have been conducted individually in the homes of the Hispanic Women or wherever they have chosen. In these one-on-one interviews, as in group interviews, I have freely mixed techniques used for focused interviews, free-story interviews, case studies, and life histories. Because I have an ongoing relationship with most of the Hispanic Women whose voices are heard in the studies I have done, they themselves have provided me with extensive information about their life histories and their process of socialization. The fact that I have worked with them, that we have engaged in praxis together, has helped me to comprehend better their religious understandings, and to see how those understandings motivate them and are rooted in their actions.

Given the great variety among Hispanic Women, I had to make sure that the group of Hispanic Women chosen for this study were generally representative of the total population.[13] Therefore, I have included in the sampling not only Hispanic Women I know and have worked with, but also Hispanic Women from communities in areas of the United States where I have been only marginally involved. I have interviewed Hispanic Women with Mexican American, Puerto Rican, and Cuban roots. Those I have worked with in articulating a *mujerista* theology come from different socioeconomic strata and different degrees of formal schooling. They vary in age from the early thirties to the late sixties. Some are deeply involved in the church at the local, regional, and even national level. For others, the church is something, at best, marginal to their lives.

In order to ensure diversity in the sampling, I asked Hispanics working in different parts of the country, Hispanic Women with whom I do not have much in common or whose praxis is very different from mine, to choose persons from their communities for interviews. I have also gathered information from Hispanic Women whose point of view differs from mine and, indeed, I have incorporated that information if it is not an isolated opinion or experience and if it contributes to the struggle for liberation.

Beyond the gathering of information through interviews, ethnographers need to include in their cultural research social, economic, and political elements. Knowing about these different elements of culture helps the researcher understand what she is seeing and hearing;[14] they help her develop a critical awareness of the everyday reality of those whose culture is being studied.

Meta-Ethnography

Mujerista theology is shaped by the experience of a great variety of Hispanic Women with historical roots in different countries and in different socioeconomic contexts. In order to bring together multiple ethnographic accounts, I use the basic understandings and techniques of meta-ethnography.[15] The meta-ethnography I use does not attempt to aggregate the information gathered in interviews but rather to interpret it. First I present the different accounts as they were actually voiced by Hispanic Women. I then attempt to bring together the single accounts by pointing out some of their commonalities and differences. This results in what meta-ethnography calls "knowledge synthesis," a synthesis which is both inductive and interpretive.[16]

This knowledge synthesis (or interpretive synthesis) uses an *emic* approach that is holistic and considers alternatives.[17] As used in *mujerista* theology, an emic approach is one that does not judge the religious understandings and practices of Hispanic Women, nor does it try to make them fit into traditional theological frameworks or those articulated by others. *Mujerista* theology, then, not only is concerned with theological answers but, more importantly, asks theological questions from the perspective of Hispanic Women. This emic approach is holistic because it takes into consideration the cultural context of Hispanic Women. In other words, it does not present their religious understandings as something apart from their day-to-day living. In fact, in many ways, *mujerista* theology is an accomplishment of everyday life.

Finally, *mujerista* theology takes into consideration alternative interpretations of the understandings and experiences of Hispanic Women. There is no desire on the part of *mujerista* theology to present a single voice. On the contrary, we recognize that differences are part of the specific identity of each person. We consider differences to be a reality which enriches our theology, helping to keep it vital and viable.

What is the process used in meta-ethnography to arrive at knowledge synthesis? After the information is gathered from different persons over a certain period of time, the accounts of that information are read repeatedly, and commonalities and differences noted. Key ideas and understandings begin to emerge. The next step in the process is that of "translating the accounts into one another":

> Translations are especially unique syntheses, because they protect the particular, respect holism, and enable comparison. An adequate translation maintains the central metaphors and/or concepts of each account in their relation to the other key metaphors or concepts in that account. It also compares both the metaphors or concepts and their interactions in one account with the metaphors or concepts and their interactions in the other accounts.[18]

In an attempt to avoid reductionism as much as possible, meta-ethnography, instead of combining accounts, uses analogies. For example, meta-ethnography does not posit that "Olivia and Lupe say the same thing or mean the same thing when they say . . ." Instead, meta-ethnography brings together what the two women say by indicating that "Olivia's experience seems to be similar to Lupe's except that . . ." Olivia's experience is not incorporated into Lupe's or vice versa, but one is understood in comparison to the other. The differences between their experiences are not erased but read together; the similarities they suggest create the themes which *mujerista* theology must take into consideration.

The purpose in doing "translations" for *mujerista* theology is to discover the themes that are important to the women, the ones about which they feel the strongest, which move them, which motivate them. In *mujerista* theology we refer to these themes as generative words.[19] They emerge from the world of Hispanic Women and express the situations they have to grapple with as well as their understanding of themselves in those situations. These generative words or themes are not only those "with existential meaning, and therefore, with greatest emotional content, but they also are typical of the people."[20]

Because of the goal of *mujerista* theology and the value it places on community, the process of "translating" differs somewhat from the process used in other meta-ethnographies. The latter place both the similarities and the differences found in the various individual accounts into an interpretative order which results in what is called a "lines-of-argument synthesis," which has as its goal to interpret what each one of the persons involved is saying.[21] In *mujerista* theology, however, the main interest and ultimate goal is a liberative praxis of Hispanic Women that uses interpretation but does not stop there. Another difference is that the interpretation used in arriving at generative themes in *mujerista* theology is not drawn from what one person says but rather from the lived-experience which makes up the daily life of Hispanic Women as a community.

From the very beginning, the mental constructs and experience of the person conducting the ethnographic investigation and the meta-ethnographic analysis play a significant role in the process. But at the point when the writer explains, from her own perspective, of course, similarities and differences, she becomes, in a very special way, a key element in the process. At this point the materials gathered are "translated" into the experiences and understandings of the writer and, one hopes, a reverse process also takes place. This is another reason why writers of Hispanic theologies should be immersed in their communities.

Mujerista Professional Theologians as Insiders

Mujerista professional theologians do theology from within our own communities.[22] Therefore, the understanding of researcher as insider is most appropriate for us. There are three important points to consider in this regard. First, the role of insider corresponds with the understanding that the doing of *mujerista* theology is a liberative praxis—a praxis that contributes to the liberation of *mujerista* professional theologians as well as of their community. In other words, as insiders, *mujerista* professional theologians also profit from their doing of theology.

Second, one of the characteristics of ethnographic methodology is the dialogic relationship between the researcher and those being researched. Dialogue is a horizontal relationship between equals which involves communication and intercommunication. Dialogue refers to a "relation of 'empathy' between two 'poles' who are engaged in a joint search,"[23] a joint effort to understand and articulate meaning. The professional theologian-researcher is one pole; the community being researched is the other. The joint search is a valuable strategy in our struggle for liberation as Hispanic Women. When the professional theologian is not herself part of the community—that is, when she has no vested interest in the liberation of those involved because her liberation is not connected to the liberation of others in the group—the dialogue becomes dishonest, the group being researched is objectified, and theology itself becomes a tool of oppression.[24]

Also, as insiders *mujerista* professional theologians are able to establish this dialogic relationship much more readily than an outsider could. Very often the research is made possible or enhanced by long-term relationships between the *mujerista* professional theologian and the community, or the research itself becomes the beginning of an ongoing relationship.[25] This has made it possible for me not only to listen intensely but also to share my own insights openly while conducting interviews.

But I have had to accept the fact that I am both an insider and an outsider in the community of Hispanic Women. I have struggled to distinguish what I hold in common with the respondents (because I am a woman and Hispanic) from what is different, that is, class, age, role, degree of formal education, and so forth.[26] It is important to recognize that identities are always complex and multifaceted, and, therefore, no researcher is ever totally an insider.

The third consideration has to do with factoring in the experience and understanding of a professional theologian-researcher who is more an insider than an outsider. Initially I tried to listen to everyone but myself. I soon realized that it would be impossible to stay away from my own experience. I realized that whether I wanted to or not, my voice would play a role and that I needed to listen to it instead of allowing it to operate surreptitiously. I came to understand that I had to pay attention to my own voice, to observe carefully and reflect methodically on my own experience as a Hispanic Woman working for many years with my own people. The challenge for me has been and will always be not to allow my experience and my understandings to become a sifter for the experiences and understandings of others. Two things have helped me avoid this. First of all, as an insider and because of the dynamics of liberative praxis, I accept seriously my responsibility to take back to the community, in a way that is meaningful to it and in a way that can be used as a tool for liberation, the understandings gained from the community.[27] If the community fails to recognize itself in the *mujerista* theology that I present, then it is obvious that I have manipulated and changed the voices of Hispanic Women instead of providing a platform for them. Second, I am eager to have the informants assess my work. I take their critique very seriously and I am committed to changing whatever they identify as not coming from them or as misrepresenting them.[28]

What can be done when the professional theologian is less an insider than an outsider? The less the professional theologian is an insider, the more she must be immersed in and stand in solidarity with the community. In other words, she must allow herself to be deeply engaged by the community so that she can, as much as possible, come to understand the community from within. The difference between her context and that of the community will not disappear, but at least she may be better able to grasp the perspectives, understandings, and experiences of the community. This will lessen the likelihood of equivocation and will steer the writer away from erroneous understandings and explanations of the commonalities and differences among Hispanic Women.[29]

Why We Use Ethnography and Meta-Ethnography in *Mujerista* Theology

Ethnography and meta-ethnography provide understandings and techniques that make it possible to discover, organize, present, and interpret the source of *mujerista* theology: the lived-experience of Hispanic Women. The reasons for using ethnography and meta-ethnography, then, are to be found in the reasons we have for placing this lived-experience at the center of our theological task.

Though the expression "lived-experience" might seem tautological to some, in the context of *mujerista* theology it refers not only to what has happened— what a person has endured or made happen—but to that experience upon which she reflects in order to understand its significance and to value it accordingly.[30] Because of the centrality of religion in the day-to-day life of Hispanic Women, our understandings about the divine and about questions of ultimate meaning play a very important role in the process of giving significance to and valuing our experience. It is imperative for us, therefore, to comprehend better how religious understandings and practices impact our lives. In order to do this, we need to start from what we know—ourselves, our everyday surroundings and experiences.

In society, the dominant understandings and practices that are considered as having important religious significance, the ones that carry weight and impact societal norms, arise from the experience of the dominant culture, class, race, and gender. Whether or not those people actually invest themselves in these understandings and practices, they abide by the understandings, consciously or unconsciously. These are elements of the structures that keep them in power. By using our lived-experience as the source of theology, Hispanic Women start from a place outside those structures, outside the traditional theology which is controlled by the dominant group. This gives us an opportunity to be self-defining, to give fresh answers, and, what is most important, to ask new questions.

For us who do *mujerista* theology it is essential to look at the questions being asked in theology.[31] Our task, in general, is not that of answering centuries-old questions from a different perspective without looking at the questions themselves. Our task is not to use grassroot Hispanic Women's answers to old questions. This results in "new" answers, which are most often nothing but reinterpretations of old answers, old answers with different words and different emphases, but basically within the parameters of the old answers. We consciously seek to avoid manipulating what grassroot Hispanic Women say to fit the parameters established by traditional questions and "old" answers.

For example, some Hispanic theologians give great importance to Scripture. Their goal is to present Jesus in such a way that the common folk can relate to him. Undoubtedly, the experience of Hispanics also plays a part in the hermeneutical work of these theologians. But in their work, the fact that the great majority of Hispanics relate very little to Jesus is never confronted. Instead, it is glossed over. This results, therefore, in a "new" emphasis on Jesus but never in new questions about Jesus or about how Jesus has been used by theologians and those with power in the churches to oppress and marginalize Hispanic Women.[32]

Mujerista theology, on the other hand, using the lived-experience of Hispanic Women as its main source, pushes out the old parameters and insists on new questions. In the case of Jesus, for example, we ask, Why is it that the majority of Hispanic Women do not relate to Jesus? What does this mean about their understanding of the divine and the presence of the divine in their lives? *Mujerista* theology, then, often becomes a subversive act by enabling Hispanic Women to be suspicious of what we have not participated in defining.

A third reason for insisting on the lived-experience of Hispanic Women as a source for *mujerista* theology concerns our struggle for liberation and our sanity. As people who live submerged within a culture which is not ours, we often question our ability to comprehend "reality." In a very real way, as Hispanic Women, we have to "go out of our minds" in order to survive physically.[33] You can often hear Hispanic Women, especially older women, respond to "that's the way things are done here" with the phrase, *en qué cabeza cabe eso?*, in what kind of head does that fit? The reality that impacts our daily lives is often incomprehensible to us. What we say does not count; our cultural customs—dance, food, dress—are divorced from us and are commercialized; our values hardly count in society; our language is considered a threat, and millions have voted to have Spanish declared "not an official language"; our social reality is ignored. As a people we continue to slip into poverty and to suffer from the social ills prevalent in the culture of poverty.

By using our lived-experience as the source of *mujerista* theology, we are trying to validate our world, our reality, our values. We are trying to reverse the schizophrenia that attacks our lives by insisting that who we are and what we do is revelatory of the divine. The lived-experience of Hispanic Women constitutes our common and shared reality. The "common sense" of Hispanic Women is not wrong. We can trust it to inform and guide our day-to-day life. *Mujerista* theology wants to affirm the worldview of Hispanic Women, shaped as it is by our lived-experience. For it is precisely in our worldview, in our paradigm of social reality, that we find "the categories and concepts through and by which we construct and understand the world,"[34] and understanding and constructing our world is a liberative praxis.

Finally, what much of the above implies is that the centrality of the lived-experience of Hispanic Women in *mujerista* theology is based on what liberation theologies call the epistemological privilege of the poor and the oppressed. This privilege is not based on the moral or intellectual superiority of the oppressed; it does not mean that Hispanic Women personally are better or more innocent or more intelligent or purer in our motivations. No, this epistemological privilege is based on the possibility the oppressed have

> to see and to understand what the rich and the powerful cannot see nor understand. It is not that their sight is perfect, it is the place where they are which makes the difference. Power and richness have a distortionary effect—they freeze our view of reality. The point of view of the poor, on the other hand, pierced by suffering and attracted by hope, allows them, in their struggles, to conceive another reality. Because the poor suffer the weight of alienation, they can conceive a different project of hope and provide dynamism to a new way of organizing human life for all.[35]

The lived-experience of Hispanic Women, therefore, brings a new dynamism to theology. It is our lived-experience which allows us to conceive another theological reality, a new theological reality, a liberative praxis, which we call *mujerista* theology.

The Ethnographic Interview

Because we understand *mujerista* theology to be an integral part of the process of the liberation of Hispanic Women, the first consideration in designing interviews conducted specifically for this study was to use the kind of questions that allow people to reflect on their experience and to articulate it in their own words.[36] The main purpose of the interviews was to provide Hispanic Women with an opportunity to reflect on themselves as decision makers, to enable them to enhance their moral agency. The questions were designed to illumine their process of decision making, to investigate how they exercise their moral agency, thus creating meaning in and through their lives. The same core, grand tour questions around the issue of moral decision making were asked of each of the interviewees. When at times one of the questions that had been planned did not elicit a response, I put that question aside and formulated another one or relied on one of the other prepared questions to elicit the information I hoped to gather. Supplementary structural and attributional questions helped in the interaction and clarified the meaning of the core questions or explored different topics brought up in the Hispanic Women's answers.

The first few questions sought to elicit general information about the self-understanding of the person being interviewed.[37] The important thing initially was to elicit enough information to indicate the areas which would need to be explored as the interview continued. I asked no questions about the general background of the person except in two instances (when those being interviewed had not participated in the previous research project I had conducted). With women whom I knew earlier, I did ask questions to update the information I had and I did call back some of the interviewees to ask for further details.

The next set of questions was conceived as "warm-up" questions and consisted of third-person or hypothetical questions. These allowed the person being interviewed to voice her values, disvalues, criteria for decision making, and so forth. It also gave her an example of the kind of situation in her own life that the third set of questions would ask her to identify. Close to the time of the interview, several of the Hispanic Women interviewed, however, had been faced with very important decisions in their lives, so the "warm-up" questions were not necessary at the beginning. They were used later in the interview to clarify issues brought up in the conversations.

The third set of questions formed the core of the research. These questions were designed to elicit values operative within the lives of Hispanic Women and in their decision-making process. I asked them to describe two very important decisions they have had to make in their lives. Asking for more than one important decision-making situation made it possible for me to begin to discern patterns instead of criteria and processes used only in an unusually serious situation.

In most cases, it was only toward the end of each interview that I used words such as *moral* and *immoral*. By then I felt I could risk using words that are not part of the women's daily vocabulary but are the regular ones used by "church people." The confidence we had established, as well as what I had already learned about the person I was interviewing, helped me ascertain whether she was giving me "catechism" answers or whether she was answering out of reflection on her own experience.[38]

The interviews were intense, lasting one to two hours (not a lengthy interview considering the concept of time in the Hispanic culture). The relative brevity of the interview was possible because, as I have indicated before, most of those interviewed had participated in a previous weekend-long research project. Of course, the success of this kind of in-depth interview depends to a large extent on the "rapport, mutuality of trust, and sense of reciprocity"[39] that is established between interviewer and interviewee. Since I have known the majority of the interviewees for a long time and all of them had previously shared at length with me, trust already existed between us.

In order for interviews to yield valuable information, four elements must be taken into consideration: commitment, meaning, fluidity, and assimilation.[40] Commitment to the interaction determines the quality of what the interviewee shares. All along, the interviewee determines, consciously or unconsciously, how much to share, how candid to be in view of what impression she wants to make. For example, one of the interviewees asked me to send her the questions ahead of time so she could prepare "good answers." She was indeed committed to the interview but was too preoccupied with the impression she would make. When I came over to her house for the interview, she criticized her input in the previous process and told me she hoped she could do better this time. Her critique of herself, her willingness to see me for the interview during a holiday, her desire to "have the answers ready," and the fact that she considered it a privilege that I wanted her to participate in this second project all show her commitment to the interaction. Her concern also shows that participation in this project enhances her self-esteem. This is consistent with how she had felt when she participated in the last project. She insisted I use her real name when publishing the materials to which she had contributed.

The second element to be taken into consideration is meaning: "the ability of each party to understand the true intent of the other's actions and statements."[41] In intense interviewing—the kind of interviewing done for this study—it is always possible to obtain clarification of what the interviewee is saying. Different ways of phrasing the questions, customizing them according to the clarification one needs from each of the interviewees, cannot, however, interfere with "equivalence of meaning." The questions asked should "have the same meaning to each interviewee, even though [they] may have to be phrased differently from interview to interview to achieve the goal."[42] The second set of questions in the interview was important in establishing equivalence of meaning. These questions helped the interviewees understand the meaning of the central set of questions in the interview, that is, the third set.

During the interview the conversation must be fluid. To achieve this, the interviewer has to adapt content and course of the conversation to meet both her need and the needs of the interviewee. The more the interview is in the mode of normal discourse, the more at ease the interviewee will be and the more she will be able to open up and respond according to her experience without being concerned about what the interviewer wants to hear.

The fourth element that has to be taken into consideration is assimilation. Since I personally interviewed the Hispanic Women whose voices are presented here, I had the opportunity "to assimilate or digest the results of one interview before undertaking another."[43] This made it possible for me to modify and mold my expectations of the interviews according to the information I was gathering from the different women. The interviewees themselves, one by one, helped me find the best possible way of describing and bringing together what I heard from them.

Intensive interviewing is an appropriate technique to use in doing *mujerista* theology because it provides an opportunity for the interviewees to articulate their lived-experience, to tell their own story in a way that makes them understand what being agents of their own history is all about. Whereas structured questionnaires tend to mold answers, intensive interviews allow for free-flowing answers which are not unduly directed or shaped by the questions. Given that meta-ethnography is not a quantitative analytical tool, the limitations of intensive interviewing are not detrimental to the results needed for doing *mujerista* theology.

———

THE INSISTENCE THAT HISPANIC WOMEN are admirably capable of reflecting on their beliefs and religious practices and articulating what we think is a key element in the method that we have used always in *mujerista* theology. I have repeated often that the lived experience of Hispanic women is the source of our theology because our religious beliefs play an important part in our every day life. In no way have I wanted to homogenize or universalize the experience of Hispanic women. That is why we continue to use meta-ethnography as an interpretative method since it allows us to respect what is specific in the experience of different Hispanic women. When it is not possible to use a variety of Hispanic voices, we insist on talking about "lived-experience," precisely to insist on the specificity of different Hispanic women's understandings, and to distance ourselves from any elaboration that might be interpreted as "universalizing."

The use of ethnography has allowed us, during these last ten years, to continue to be grounded in the Hispanic communities in the U.S.A. and, therefore, it has allowed us to elaborate *mujerista* theology from an ecclesiological perspective with pastoral goals in mind. During all this time we have struggled to honor our decision not to elaborate theological themes that we have not first discussed with Hispanic women in our communities. Ethnography has allowed us to contextualize *mujerista* theology, to enmesh it in the daily lives of Hispanic women. The fact that we always take as our starting point the way Hispanic women explain their religious faith has helped us to continue "doing" theology and to keep in mind that the goal of our work is the liberation of Hispanic women. *Mujerista* theology is a liberation praxis, among other things, because it continues to be a platform for the voices of Hispanic women: it continues to offer them an opportunity to be subjects of their own history.

Finally, ethnography has made it possible, precisely because it enmeshes us in the specificity of the lives of Hispanic women, not to enclose ourselves in the particular. It is through the specific that we enter into a "renewed universal," a "situated universal" that does not think about what is specific as a universal "applied" to the particular. In a "situated universal" what is concrete in the voices of Hispanic women is not lost or synthesized. On the contrary, the "situated universal" makes it possible for differences to emerge, differences without which humanity cannot exist or be imagined. The voices of Hispanic women remind us that what is universal is not given a priori but rises from the specific and the concrete. The lived-experience of Hispanic women—the source of our theological work—reminds us at all times that *mujerista* theology must insist on being effective in promoting justice and peace.

The method that we use in *mujerista* theology has made us reflect on the issue of representation. First of all, the use of grassroot Hispanic women's voices was born out of deep respect. Because we see *mujerista* theology as a liberation praxis, it has been a strategy to include the voices of grassroot Hispanic women to break the hegemony of the women of the dominant race in the area of theology. We are aware of the responsibility we have with grassroot women who contribute to *mujerista* theology to work for their liberation. As an activist-theologian, I believe I have to be accountable to the community that embraces me and is so life-giving. I have always thought that the main question about everything I write and say as a *mujerista* theologian has to do with what it contributes to the liberation of Hispanic women. I have never thought that I speak for Hispanic women or that I represent them. I speak merely as a Hispanic woman. As a *mujerista* theologian, I speak deeply aware of the responsibility I have with Hispanic women in the U.S.A.

Síntesis del Capítulo 3
Métodos de la teología *mujerista*: propuestas y procesos básicos

En los dos primeros capítulos de este libro hemos explicado el contexto social de las mujeres hispanas en los EE.UU., y los elementos claves de su identificación étnica-cultural. Este enfoque refuerza nuestra insistencia en que la teología *mujerista* tiene sus raíces en la experiencia vivida por las hispanas y de que nuestra teología tiene que ser un foro para sus voces. Esta manera de pensar nos ha llevado a explorar las ciencias sociales con el fin de encontrar métodos de investigación que no nos conviertan a las hispanas, a nuestras experiencias y realidad, en meros objetos de estudio e investigación. Este capítulo presenta los métodos que usamos en la teología *mujerista* y las teorías que los sostienen.

Métodos y teorías sociológicas

Los métodos que hemos escogido para investigar y presentar las prácticas y creencias religiosas de las hispanas son aquéllos que hemos juzgados que no distorsionan lo que dicen las mujeres tratando de encasillarlas en esquemas ya establecidos. Lo más importante para nosotras ha sido escoger métodos que, a la vez que hacen posible la investigación, sirvan para que las hispanas amplíen su agencia moral—el proceso de auto-determinarse y auto-definirse—lo que nos permite reclamar que la teología *mujerista* es en sí una praxis liberadora.

Precisamente porque queremos que la teología *mujerista* contribuya al desarrollo de la agencia moral de las hispanas, decidimos que en nuestras elaboraciones teológicas teníamos que incluir las voces de las mujeres hispanas. Estas voces no se presentan como representativas ni como ejemplos de un punto de vista general de todas las hispanas. Creemos que las voces de estas hispanas tienen validez en sí y no necesitan ser representativas para señalar la realidad de las mujeres hispanas. Por lo tanto, el punto de partida ha sido la particularidad de las hispanas que desde su perspectiva específica apunta hacia lo universal.

El segundo punto que consideramos al escoger los métodos fue el papel de las investigadoras y escritoras de la teología *mujerista*. Vimos la importancia de establecer un verdadero diálogo entre ellas y las mujeres hispanas cuyas voces incluimos en nuestro quehacer teológico. Tercero, al recopilar las voces de estas hispanas hemos tratado de hacerlo en tal forma que les sea una manera efectiva de conscientizarse acerca de su lucha cotidiana por sobrevivir. Para ayudarlas a comprenderse y a determinar mejor lo que quieren para sí mismas, lo que hemos hecho es tratar de entender cómo ellas entienden y construyen el significado de sus propias prácticas religiosas en vez de simplemente analizar esas prácticas desde afuera. Hemos tratado de no convertirlas en "tipos" sino de verlas como ellas se ven a sí mismas: como personas que reflexionan sobre sus luchas diarias para poder entender el significado de sus vidas. En esta tarea nos ha ayudado el que nuestro fin no haya sido descubrir lo relevante de la teología tradicional para las hispanas. Al contrario: en la teología *mujerista* presentamos el entendimiento de estas hispanas para desestabilizar el balance que existe entre el poder y el conocimiento de los "encargados" de la teología y las iglesias, entre la comunidad hispana y el grupo dominante en esta sociedad, entre las mujeres hispanas y las mujeres del grupo dominante. Por eso las voces que presentamos no sólo nos permiten escuchar una revelación personal y comunitaria sino que también proveen un comentario intuitivo y poderoso del orden social.

El proceso de recolectar y presentar las voces de las mujeres hispanas ha llevado a las teólogas *mujeristas* a comprender que las categorías conceptuales y las presuposiciones epistemológicas del mundo teológico tradicional, ni abarcan el significado de las vidas de las mujeres hispanas, ni sirven para explicar sin distorsionar nuestras preocupaciones cotidianas y lo que sabemos y entendemos de lo divino. Las viejas botas de vino—los conceptos y la etimología teológica tradicional—no pueden usarse para guardar vino nuevo, y si se usan ¡lo más probable es que estropeen el vino!

Etnometodología

La etnometodología es una teoría sociológica que critica a las ciencias sociales por usualmente presentar a las personas no como "actores" sino como idealizaciones tipológicas—como "muñecos". Esta teoría insiste en lo difícil que se hace encontrar en estudios sociológicos a personas reales con sus propias historias y biografías. Las personas a quienes los estudios usualmente se refieren son la "creación" de los científicos sociales. En las consideraciones de estos científicos no está presente la realidad cotidiana de dichas personas ni la forma en que ellas se entienden a sí mismas. La etnometodología, al contrario, es precisamente una teoría sobre la vida cotidiana.

Las presuposiciones básicas de la etnometodología son las siguientes. Primero, las personas tenemos y usamos una "racionalidad práctica", que nos ayuda a vivir cada día. Segundo, la vida diaria es reflexiva, es contextual y descriptiva, no explicativa. Lo reflexivo aquí se refiere al hecho de que la gente, día a día, crea su vida, su mundo y hace que los demás participen en él en forma responsable. Reflexivo también se refiere a cómo se define la situación presente y la integridad interna de esa situación. Tercero, la interacción social se puede documentar.

Etnografía

En la teología *mujerista* usamos métodos cualitativos de investigación los cuales nos hacen posible el observar a la gente en su propio ambiente, y el relacionarnos con ellas usando su propio idioma y de acuerdo a sus costumbres. Los métodos cualitativos son técnicas que las teólogas *mujeristas* consideramos apropiadas ya que permiten y "requieren una relación prolongada con las personas que están siendo investigadas", personas que pertenecen a la misma comunidad de la cual nosotras, teólogas-investigadoras, somos parte integral. La investigación cualitativa, al igual que la teología *mujerista,* se centra en la vida cotidiana de la gente y busca saber cuáles son las explicaciones que la misma gente tiene de eventos culturales y sociales.

Entre los diferentes métodos de investigación cualitativa el que más usa la teología *mujerista* es la etnografía. Las ciencias sociales usan la etnografía para describir y clasificar culturas, sus características peculiares y sus costumbres. La etnografía depende en gran parte de la relación que se establece entre las investigadoras y las informantes. Se supone que las personas que son investigadas participen en el desarrollo de los métodos que se usan para el estudio de su cultura. La etnografía requiere la menor mediación posible entre lo que es y lo que se presenta en el estudio. Por eso la teología *mujerista* cita directa y extensamente las palabras de las mujeres hispanas.

Las entrevistas etnográficas que tenemos con las mujeres consisten en algo más que preguntas y repuestas; son más bien una conversación, un diálogo. Nuestro fin no es aprender acerca de las mujeres hispanas sólo lo que nos interesa sino ir dejando que ellas guíen el proceso de aprendizaje y nos lleven a lo que ellas consideran importante. Nuestro fin no es aprender sólo de las líderes de la comunidad sino aprender de la mayor variedad posible de mujeres hispanas.

Para que las entrevistas que hacemos provean información valiosa tienen que incluir cuatro elementos. Primero, todas las que participan tienen que comprometerse a hacer posible, facilitar y alimentar la interacción en el grupo, estando dispuestas a compartir abiertamente y no tratando de decir lo que creen que las demás quieren que digan. Segundo, hay que saber entender lo que se dice y lo que se oye. Es decir, hay que ir más allá del significado de las palabras para abarcar también el contexto en que se desarrolla lo que las participantes están explicando. Es importante tratar de que todas las que participan entiendan las preguntas por igual aunque para eso haya que repetirlas de diferentes maneras. Tercero, la entrevista tiene que ser una conversación fluida para que todas se sientan a gusto y puedan participar plenamente. Mantener estrictamente el formato de pregunta-respuesta puede resultar en que las informantes se sientan interrogadas y no estén a gusto durante el proceso. Cuarto, la investigadora debe asimilar bien lo que está diciendo una persona antes de pasar a escuchar a la próxima. Por lo tanto, en el proceso del diálogo hay que puntualizar lo que se va entendiendo. Este ejercicio lleva a que al final de las entrevistas pueda hacerse, sin mucha dificultad, una síntesis del conocimiento—de lo que se ha aprendido.

Las mujeres hispanas con las que hemos dialogado han sido escogidas de la mayor variedad posible de trasfondos socioeconómicos, de diferentes edades y con maneras muy diferentes de relacionarse con las iglesias. A propósito he invitado a hispanas que sabía que pensaban distinto a como pienso yo, siendo el requisito imprescindible que las participantes tengan un sentido de la lucha por la liberación.

Meta-etnografía

En la teología *mujerista* usamos la meta-etnografía para entrelazar la información que se recoge de las diferentes mujeres hispanas. La meta-etnografía es un método interpretativo. Primero es imprescindible presentar las voces de cada hispana; después se entrelazan señalando lo que tienen en común al igual que las diferencias. Esto es lo que la meta-etnografía llama "síntesis de conocimiento", una síntesis que es integral, inductiva e interpretativa, considera alternativas, y es holística, porque relaciona diferentes elementos entre sí en vez de referirlos a una clasificación general impuesta desde afuera. Usamos una metodología holística porque no queremos encasillar el pensamiento religioso de las mujeres hispanas en los esquemas tradicionales de la teología y porque nos permite darle importancia a las preguntas que surgen de lo que dicen las hispanas que participan en el proceso. Finalmente, la síntesis del conocimiento, al entrelazar las diferentes voces, no las reduce a una sola voz sino que permite que se distinga la identidad de cada voz, la particularidad y especificidad de cada hispana.

La síntesis del conocimiento se logra leyendo repetidamente lo que han dicho las hispanas hasta que se empieza a ver y entender cuáles son los temas centrales. Entonces se ve lo que cada cuál dice sobre esos temas sin reducirlo a una sola voz.

Es por eso que en vez de combinar las voces se comparan unas con otras en forma analógica. Por ejemplo, no decimos "Olivia y Lupe dicen tal cosa". En vez decimos, "Lo que dice Olivia es similar a lo que dice Lupe excepto en tal cosa". Las diferencias entre ellas no se borran sino que se leen juntas; y las similitudes nos llevan a los temas centrales. Durante esta parte del proceso las investigadoras-teólogas tenemos que tener mucho cuidado de no influenciar indebidamente el material recopilado. En esta fase se aprecia mejor la importancia de que la investigadora sea parte de la comunidad que se está investigando.

Las teólogas mujeristas como participantes-observadoras

Las teólogas *mujeristas* hacemos teología desde adentro. Como miembros de la comunidad de mujeres hispanas somos participantes en todos los diferentes momentos del quehacer teológico *mujerista*. Este quehacer teológico es liberador para las investigadoras y escritoras tanto como para las mujeres hispanas que hablan a través de este texto. Nuestra liberación está íntimamente relacionada con la liberación de todas las mujeres hispanas. El dialogar, que es parte del método etnográfico de la teología *mujerista,* se facilita grandemente porque las teólogas *mujeristas* somos parte de la comunidad que investigamos.

Pero además de participante también soy observadora: la cercanía que me aportan mis lazos con las mujeres que entrevisto se suavizan por el hecho de también ser observadora. He tratado constantemente de notar y entender las diferencias que hay entre mi realidad y la de las mujeres que entrevisto. Compartimos mucho pero también hay diferencias considerables entre nosotras, y el hecho de que yo sea la investigadora crea una diferencia importante que no puedo dejar de lado. Inicialmente esta diferencia me llevó a tratar de no escucharme a mí misma. Pero pronto me di cuenta de que era imposible dejar de ser parte del proceso. Fue entonces que decidí que era importante prestarme atención a mí misma, escucharme, reflexionar metódicamente sobre lo que pienso, y ver cómo influenciaba lo que pasaba en el proceso de las entrevistas. Para tener controles externos que me ayudasen a no excluir aquellas voces que no están de acuerdo conmigo, me he comprometido a discutir lo que escribo con mujeres hispanas para ver si ellas se encuentran reflejadas en lo que he escrito. También he tratado de darle a leer a las informantes el texto escrito y estoy dispuesta a cambiar lo que crean que no representa adecuadamente lo que ellas han dicho o han querido decir.

¿Y si la teóloga es más observadora que participante por no ser miembro de la comunidad sobre la que escribe? En ese caso sólo una verdadera solidaridad le hará posible a la teóloga comprender adecuadamente a la comunidad de mujeres hispanas. La solidaridad tiene que ser tal, que a pesar de no ser una mujer hispana, la liberación de la teóloga esté entrelazada con la de las mujeres hispanas.

Razones para el uso de la etnografía y la meta-etnografía

La etnografía y la meta-etnografía se usan en la teología *mujerista* porque son las técnicas que hemos encontrado que más nos ayudan a descubrir, organizar, presentar e interpretar la experiencia cotidiana de las mujeres hispanas—fuente de este quehacer teológico. La experiencia cotidiana de las hispanas es fuente de nuestra teología, entre otras razones por la importancia que tiene la religión para nosotras las hispanas. Para nosotras es imprescindible entender mejor cómo la religión impacta nuestras vidas. En segundo lugar, la experiencia cotidiana de las hispanas no se valora en los EE.UU., no impacta lo que es normativo en esta sociedad. Al usarla como fuente de nuestra teología lo que hacemos es evitar que la experiencia del grupo dominante sea lo que controle la teología *mujerista*. La utilización de la experiencia de las hispanas como fuente nos lleva a de proveer nuestras respuestas a preguntas tradicionales—respuestas que son mayormente reinterpretaciones de las respuestas tradicionales con algo de "sabor" hispano añadido. Nuestro propósito es ampliar los horizontes conceptuales y los de la praxis insistiendo en nuestras propias preguntas. Por eso la teología *mujerista* es subversiva, animando a las mujeres hispanas a sospechar lo que no hemos participado en definir.

Una tercera razón para insistir en la experiencia cotidiana de las mujeres hispanas como fuente de la teología *mujerista* tiene que ver con nuestra liberación y nuestra salud mental. Como vivimos dentro de una cultura ajena, a veces nos preguntamos si entendemos lo que está pasando, lo que estamos viviendo. En una forma muy concreta, como hispanas tenemos que dejar a un lado lo que es nuestra realidad y tenemos que volvernos "locas"—ir constantemente más allá de nuestros esquemas mentales—para sobrevivir en circunstancias tan opresivas. A menudo escuchamos a hispanas, especialmente a mujeres mayores, responder a la frase, "así es como se hace eso aquí," con la expresión, "¿en qué cabeza cabe eso?" La realidad que impacta nuestra vida diaria a menudo nos es incomprensible. El uso de nuestra experiencia cotidiana como fuente de la teología *mujerista* es un tratar de valorizarnos a nosotras mismas; es insistir en que la revelación de Dios continúa a través de nuestra experiencia cotidiana; es un antídoto contra la esquizofrenia que nos ataca de todas partes. La experiencia cotidiana de las mujeres hispanas es fuente de la teología *mujerista* porque es nuestra realidad común. Lo que pensamos, nuestro sentido común, no está equivocado; podemos confiar en que nuestro sentido común nos puede informar y guiar día a día. La teología *mujerista* quiere afirmar la perspectiva e ideología de las mujeres hispanas ya que ahí se encuentran las categorías y los conceptos que usamos para construir y entender nuestro mundo—praxis liberadora por excelencia.

Mucho de esto que acabamos de decir se basa en lo que otros teólogos de la liberación han llamado el privilegio hermenéutico de los oprimidos. El privilegio hermenéutico de las mujeres hispanas no se basa en una superioridad intelectual o moral; no creemos que seamos mejores o más inocentes o más inteligentes o que nuestros motivos sean más puros. Nuestro privilegio hermenéutico se basa en el hecho de que porque el orden social presente no nos beneficia, podemos concebir una realidad diferente—cosa que los que tienen privilegios en la sociedad no son capaces de imaginarse. Debido a la alienación que sufrimos en la sociedad de los EE.UU. el proyecto histórico de las mujeres hispanas puede proveer el dinamismo que se necesita para organizar esta sociedad en tal forma que no haya ni opresores ni oprimidos.

La insistencia en que las mujeres hispanas somos admirablemente capaces de reflexionar acerca de nuestras creencias y prácticas religiosas y de articular lo que pensamos es el elemento principal del método que hemos usado siempre en la teología *mujerista*. He repetido constantemente que la experiencia vivida de las hispanas es la fuente de nuestro quehacer teológico ya que la fe juega un papel muy importante en nuestra cotidianidad. De ninguna manera he querido ni homogenizar ni universalizar la experiencia de las hispanas. Por eso seguimos usando la meta-etnografía como método interpretativo ya que respeta lo específico de las experiencias de distantes hispanas. Y cuando no es posible usar una variedad de voces hispanas, insistimos en hablar de "experiencia vivida"—lo cual se nos ha criticado como tautológico—precisamente para insistir en la especificidad a la que nos referimos y alejarnos de enunciados que se puedan interpretar como "universalizantes".

El uso de la etnografía nos ha permitido, durante estos últimos diez años, continuar ancladas en las comunidades hispanas en EE.UU. y, por lo tanto, nos ha permitido elaborar la teología *mujerista* desde una perspectiva ecclesiológica y con fines netamente pastorales. Durante todo este tiempo hemos luchado por honrar nuestro compromiso de no elaborar temas teológicos que no hayamos discutido con las hispanas de la base. El uso de la etnografía también nos ha facilitado la contextualización de la teología *mujerista* a partir de la cotidianidad de las hispanas. El tomar siempre como punto de partida la manera en que las hispanas entienden y explican su fe religiosa nos ha ayudado a seguir haciendo teología—es decir, a elaborar la teología *mujerista* teniendo en cuenta que la meta es la liberación de las hispanas. La teología *mujerista* es una praxis liberadora entre otras cosas porque sigue siendo una plataforma para las voces de las hispanas: les sigue brindando una oportunidad para contribuir a ser agentes de sus propias historias.

Por último, el uso de la etnografía nos ha hecho posible, precisamente porque nos enraíza en lo específico de las hispanas, el no encerrarnos en lo particular. Es precisamente en lo específico y a través de ello que entramos en una "universalidad renovada", una "universalidad situada" que no piensa en lo concreto como un universal particularizado. En la "universalidad situada" lo concreto, lo específico de las voces de las hispanas, nunca se pierde ni se sintetiza sino que hace posible que surjan las diferencias sin las cuales no puede existir ni la humanidad ni un concepto de ella. Las voces de las hispanas nos recuerdan que lo universal no está dado sino que surge de lo específico y lo concreto. Las experiencias vividas de las hispanas que constituyen la fuente de nuestro quehacer teológico nos recuerdan en forma pujante que la teología *mujerista* debe de insistir en ser efectiva y en promover la justicia y la paz.

El método que usamos en la teología *mujerista* nos ha llevado a reflexionar en un tema que, al igual que el de la "identidad", es muy discutido: la representatividad. Ante todo, el uso de las voces de las hispanas de la base en la teología *mujerista* nació del profundo respeto que las que iniciamos esta labor teológica les tenemos. Sin duda, porque vemos la teología *mujerista* como una praxis liberadora, el incluir las voces de las hispanas de la base ha sido una estrategia para romper la hegemonía de las voces de las mujeres de la raza dominante en el campo de la teología. Estamos conscientes de la responsabilidad que tenemos con las mujeres de la base que cooperan con nosotras, la responsabilidad que tenemos de contribuir con nuestra tarea teológica a su liberación. Como activista-teóloga siempre he considerado, y sigo considerando, que debo rendir cuentas a la comunidad que me abriga y da vida, y que la pregunta principal sobre lo que escribo y digo como teóloga *mujerista* tiene que ver con cuánto contribuye este esfuerzo a la liberación de las hispanas. Nunca he pensado que hablaba por las demás hispanas ni que las representaba. Siempre he hablado como hispana consciente de la responsabilidad que como teóloga *mujerista* tengo con las hispanas en los EE.UU.

CHAPTER 4

In Their Own Words:
Latinas as Moral Agents

THE FIRST AND MAIN REASON FOR INTERVIEWING LATINAS for this study was to enhance the moral agency of Latinas by helping those I spoke with to reflect on how they deal with their everyday world and by helping them to grasp how they are self-defining as they struggle to survive and to be liberated. Given the influence of Catholicism in Latino culture, it is not surprising that one of the key elements Latinas use to talk about their ability and efforts to be self-defining is that of "conscience." Also, I had long ago noticed how the institutional churches often use "conscience," knowingly or unknowingly, as an instrument of control and domination. And then there is the fact, which I will discuss in the next chapter, that helping Latinas become conscious of their oppression is a necessary beginning in the process of liberation. These are the reasons I structured my conversation with Latinas for this project around "conscience."

Presenting the voices of nine Latinas in this chapter makes their lived-experience available for other Latinas as we struggle to be agents of our own history. To be self-determining one has to speak for oneself—a second reason why *mujerista* theology provides a platform for the voices of Latinas instead of telling about their lived-experience.

There are four other reasons why the voices of Latinas are presented in *mujerista* theology as unmediated as possible. First, there is the richness of the understandings and experiences Latinas have shared and been willing to entrust to me. It is impossible for any author to say better, more eloquently, more simply, or with greater pathos what they say. Second, the materials presented here and in other texts of *mujerista* theology fill a vacuum. One reason why the theological world at large has paid little attention to Latinas' religious experiences and practices is that they have not been available. We have had little opportunity to speak and much less to be heard. Third, there is a need to listen to Latinas to understand how and why religion is a central vivifying element of Latino culture. The voices we present here help one to see how the religious dimension in their lives constitutes a "revolutionary urge," the desire to continue to struggle for survival, for liberation, and the strength to do it.[1]

Finally, *mujerista* theology wishes to respect variations among Latinas' religious moods, motivations, and practices, and such variations can best be appreciated by listening to what the women themselves have to say. Although their own words are used, I do not claim that the material presented in this chapter is raw data. Even with a concern not to shape what the women say according to my own thought patterns and words, I realize that there is always some filtering in the process of selection and in the ordering of its presentation. Besides, some adaptation of what the interviewees have said occurs when it is transposed from oral to written form, and, in several cases, when it is translated from Spanish, "Spanglish,"[2] or *mexicano*[3] into English. The only corrective to the bias of the interviewer that can be introduced here is to recall once again the presuppositions and goals that undergird and help to form *mujerista* theology.

The second part of this chapter begins to formulate what meta-ethnography calls "knowledge synthesis." Knowledge synthesis points out commonalities and differences; it provides generative themes, central elements in the enablement of the moral agency of Latinas;[4] it protects *mujerista* theology from schemas imposed from the outside on the reality—that is, practical, everyday living (survival)—of Latinas. In short, knowledge synthesis is part of the method that *mujerista* theologians use to gather the lived-experience of Latinas as the source of our theology.

The purpose of this knowledge synthesis is not to establish norms and values—though they may be deduced quite easily—but to elucidate the self-understanding of Latinas in order to contribute to the enhancement of their moral agency. The purpose of this knowledge synthesis is not to create categories, illumine issues, or answer classical theological questions, but to enable Latinas to grasp better their daily lives so they can more effectively struggle for survival and liberation. The purpose of knowledge synthesis is not to examine what the women say to the point where the analysis and not the lived-experience of Latinas becomes central to the theological enterprise, but to allow the voices of Latinas to be heard because they have the right to be heard. The purpose of knowledge synthesis is not to instrumentalize—objectify—the lived-experience of Latinas, but to recognize the right Latinas have to express how they view and understand their reality. The purpose of knowledge synthesis is not to translate Latinas' reality into a theological discourse that claims to be scientific, but to present the voices of Latinas as a central element in a hermeneutics of suspicion about the role of religion and theology in our lives.

Who Are These Latinas?

INEZ is a Puerto Rican born in the U.S.A. and taken to Puerto Rico when she was a little girl.[5] Raised there in a rural setting by her grandparents, Inez finished high school in the early 1970s, entered the convent, and was sent to Venezuela to do her novitiate. There she spent three difficult and painful years and, in the end, was not allowed to take religious vows by the superiors of the congregation she had entered. After that she moved to the U.S.A., which she calls "the cold country."

Inez is an extremely articulate person, deeply committed to working with grassroot women—a classification she ascribes to herself. Most of her involvement is related to Puerto Rican Women's participation in the Roman Catholic Church. Inez worked for many years in a job that combines both advocacy and service. When her responsibilities there became more managerial and she was less involved with the people, she left. At present she is working for a large hospital in the public relations office. Her ambition is to find a job in the field of public communication and this is why she recently completed a Master's in Communication. Inez lives by herself in an apartment in the South Bronx, an area of New York City heavily populated by Latinos. Her father, with whom she had lived since her mother died over twelve years ago, died this last year.

Inez likes herself and has a very healthy self-understanding. A happy and gregarious person, she prefers to talk in Spanish whenever possible. This preference reflects not only the fact that her Spanish is very good while her English is somewhat limited, but also that she sees speaking Spanish as a means of preserving her Puerto Rican roots, a means of self-identification for Puerto Ricans. For her, to speak Spanish is a political action. She rarely speaks English or Spanglish. Inez is an *independentista*—never giving up hope that one day Puerto Rico will be independent.

ADELA Is a single mother of two, a boy and a girl about to become teenagers. She was married in Mexico when she was very young, but the marriage did not last. Until very recently she lived in one of the border cities of Texas. Listening to her story, one has to marvel at her resiliency. On different occasions she attempted to find a job in the U.S.A., and each time she suffered great injustices. Once when she worked as a maid, the woman she worked for drove her back across the border, and as Adela got out of the car, paid her only one-third of what she owed her. At that time, Adela found that all her belongings, which she had stored in someone's house during her U.S.A. stay, had disappeared.

One of the times she crossed the border into the U.S., Adela found some stability, mostly because she lived with a man who fathered her two children. But that relationship did not last long and Adela was again on her own. She has raised her two children by herself—a task made all the more difficult since her son has a learning disability as a result of childhood encephalitis.[6] For several years Adela also "mothered" a girl who was no relation to her. Adela's own mother, who lives in Mexico, had taken the girl in, and one of the times Adela went to visit, the girl came back with her. This young woman is now married to one of Adela's brothers and is living in Mexico.

When I first met Adela about five years ago, she had no legal documents, but now she has her U.S. residency papers. At the time, she was the cook in a parish rectory, a steady job which she did not mind except for the fact that one of the priests dealt with her always as if she were a "nonentity," to quote Adela.

When I tried to contact Adela to interview her for this project, I could not find her. I spoke with key people in the Latino community of the city where she lived, all to no avail. She seemed to have disappeared, and people thought she might either have moved to the West Coast or gone back to Mexico. One day I received a note from her, giving me her new address. Someone who knew I was looking for her had seen her and given her my address. We were able to talk on the phone and I flew out to interview her.

She seemed to be doing well and felt in control of her life. She had a job as a day caretaker for older folks and was going to school at night to learn English. She had her son in a school for children with learning disabilities and her daughter was doing well in school. She told me about her plans to move to another state in a couple of years and start a small business, a bakery perhaps. Four months after I interviewed her she called me. She had fallen, and though now she had recuperated fully, the agency for which she was working was giving her only part-time work. She called to ask me if I could arrange for her to move in with some people I knew because her landlord was evicting her for back rent. She was concerned, but not desperate. Adela is the kind of person who never seems to get in a panic. She is a hard worker and trusts herself to be able to move ahead. My friends have visited her and are in the process of helping her obtain some government aid for her rent.

MARTA was born and raised in Cuba. Married in Cuba, she has a married son and is a grandmother. She also has a daughter in her twenties who has recently married. In the early 1960s Marta came to the United States as part of the large exodus of Cubans who left the island because of the Castro regime. She has been a single woman for the last eight years. Her sister, also a single woman, has lived with her for the last fifteen years. They both brought up the children and share equally now in maintaining the household.

After managing a highly profitable import-export business for several years, Marta has established her own business. She is a hardworking woman, highly motivated. She belongs to the so-called upper middle class: she lives in an elegant condominium, owns a boat, and vacations away from the city where she lives.

Marta speaks a mixture of English and Spanish—a sentence might begin in English and finish in Spanish or vice versa. Marta is extremely articulate and likes to express what she thinks, to grapple with it, and to be sure that she is communicating adequately what she believes. Marta went to an American school in Cuba, but has not pursued her studies further.

LUPE is a Mexican American who has lived all her life in the Southwest. The oldest of a large family, she helped her parents raise her younger brothers and sisters and helped the family out financially. She finished her college education when she was older, is now married, and has no children. Lupe is a business woman in a large corporation and in her job she can relate directly to grassroot people—something she chooses to do as much as possible. Her job has brought her high visibility, and, being very civic-minded, she has become involved in many community activities and is also very active in the church.

Lupe made it very clear when I started the interview that she has grown much since participating in the weekend retreat that provided data for *Hispanic Women: Prophetic Voice in the Church*. She often refers to that weekend as a very important event in her life. Lupe gives much thought to what she does, to what she should do, and the reasons for both. So it was not hard for her to respond to the questions I posed. Lupe speaks mostly in English, using Spanish only for emphasis.

MARÍA was born in Puerto Rico but was brought to the U.S.A. when she was very small. She was the youngest of eleven children, and her mother gave her to an aunt to bring up. María married and had twelve children; three died when they were young.

María has been involved in church affairs and in politics in her neighborhood for many years. She has been a district leader and also has been elected to the school board. Though she now lives by herself—her husband died of cancer—she is very close to her children and travels to different cities in the U.S.A. where they now live. A few months before our conversation, she was mugged in the elevator of her building and no longer felt safe. Some of her children urged her to move to a different city from the one María had insisted on living in since coming from Puerto Rico. María finally agreed to move but only with the proviso that she would have her own place to live. The situation in the new city did not work out for María and she is now back to the place she has lived most of her life.

María speaks both English and Spanish and used both languages for this interview. She is very precise and expresses herself with great ease.

OLIVIA is a Texas-born Mexican American who moved with her young family to the Midwest almost thirty years ago. They drove for three days in an old station wagon with only eighty dollars in their pockets, and three very small children—two sons and a daughter. Olivia has been married for more than thirty years and now has several grandchildren. At present she works in a bakery just a few blocks from her house and is working on getting her G.E.D. in order to become a teacher's aide.

Olivia was very enthusiastic about participating in this study. She said repeatedly she was honored to be chosen. She has a boundless enthusiasm when speaking about religion and is single-minded about her relationship with God. As the interview progressed it became obvious that her religious convictions run very deep.

Our interview took place in her kitchen on Mother's Day. Later I had lunch with her family, a bountiful meal which I was honored to share. Though Olivia can understand Spanish, she asked me to put the questions to her in English. Though she said she would answer in "Mexicano," the fact is that she spoke almost exclusively in English.

MARGARITA is a Cuban who has lived in New York City for many years. She came here forty years ago, invited by her aunt. She married a man born of Cuban parents in Tampa, but they did not stay together for long. She had twins; her son is now a father of six children; her daughter is single and lives with Margarita.

Margarita is a deeply religious person. When she was growing up she wanted to be a nun, but she says that she never found a way of following that calling because she was poor and black. After she moved to the U.S.A., she followed her second preference and became a licensed practical nurse. She has worked the night shift in one of the city hospitals for the last nineteen years. She has recently retired but is going to do volunteer work at the hospital so as not to get bored. Her plans are to work with senior citizens as much as possible.

Margarita speaks both Spanish and English with great ease. The interview was conducted in Spanish.

JULIETA is the poorest of the women interviewed for this study.[7] She is a Mexican who lives in Los Angeles. As a matter of fact, I got in touch with her through a shelter for women with which I have had some contact for several years. She is thirty-four years old and has been in the U.S.A. for twelve years. Julieta's mother had twenty-one children, of whom only half survived. Julieta has six, the oldest one eighteen years old and the youngest five. One of her children died of bronchial pneumonia. Julieta goes back to Mexico once in a while to see her mother. The first time she came over she paid the "coyote," the man who guided them across the border, four hundred dollars. After that she learned the way and now crosses on her own.

Julieta's mother is a religious person who took time to teach her children about God. Julieta says that for her, God is the greatest thing that exists. In her problem-ridden life Julieta has always gone to church to "ask God" whenever she has a problem. "And I feel that it helps me. Maybe it is the faith that I have, because

I believe much in God, and if I have great pressures, I go into a church, and I come out more at peace." Her mother taught her the little bit she knew and Julieta learned the regular prayers and made her First Holy Communion. Julieta's faith may be considered simple but it is not unreflective.

The day I interviewed Julieta at the women's shelter, she told me that to get enough money to eat the previous day she and her husband had sold some merchandise on the sidewalk. Her husband has an old, dilapidated truck, which is of great value to them. One of the ways they get money is by driving around and picking up discarded mattresses from the sidewalks. They can sell each for about five or six dollars. She tries to find work as a maid, but having a little one to take care of does not make that easy. She does not have her immigration papers and, therefore, cannot work in a factory without running the risk of being picked up by the *migra* (the Immigration and Naturalization Service).[8]

When I interviewed her, her husband was also out of work so they were surviving on welfare. She feels bad that she had to lie about her husband not living with her in order to get welfare, but if not, "we would starve to death." At the end of the interview I gave her, "as a sign of gratefulness for helping me," twenty dollars. But she did not want to accept it. She told me that she was not going to accept money for talking about religion. I explained to her that I was hoping eventually to publish this study and that I would make a profit then, that this little bit of money was my way of sharing something of that profit with those who helped me. It took a while but she finally accepted the money.[9]

CARIDAD was born and raised in Cuba.[10] She lived in the countryside and her family was very poor. They lived about ten kilometers from the nearest small town and they did not go to church. She does remember her mother invoking Our Lady of Charity—the title under which Mary is venerated in Cuba—and she remembers that there was a picture of the Guardian Angel on the wall above their bed. She was baptized in the Catholic church when she was born but that was the extent of her religious upbringing, though she did marry in the church *"en este país,"* in this country.[11] Caridad and her husband go to church but do not receive communion. So her boy started to ask them why. Since this is a second marriage for both of them, they decided to look into having their previous marriages annulled so they could get married in the church.

Caridad has found religious instruction to be very good for her. "I begin to feel full of something that I know was not in me before." She goes to church now, but not because she has strong beliefs; "those beliefs are strong when they are inculcated in you in your home," she says. She goes because "something has to exist, I have to have some beliefs, because I cannot just drift. And after my son was born, I do not want things to be for him the way they were for me. I do not blame my mother, but I want my son to receive the sacraments, to have some faith inculcated in him. My husband is different. I do not know if there is a connection between religiousness and class. He comes from a family that had means, so he went to Catholic school, and so forth."

Caridad is extremely honest with herself. She realizes that she goes through certain religious mechanics like making the sign of the cross, but that she does not really believe. She wants to, she wants God to be revealed to her, but she says she really does not have faith: "I am cold inside."

Caridad came to the U.S.A. in 1969 and is now forty years old. Everything about her is energetic and said or done with great determination. She understands very little English and speaks Spanish at great speed!

Initial Explorations of Latinas' Decision-Making Process

The material that follows is but a small part of what these Latinas shared during the interviews. The order in which the material is presented does not necessarily follow the order of conversation. I have included only the back-and-forth dialogue when I sense that my response or further questions on a specific point may have influenced the course of the conversation.

QUESTION: *What should a mother do who has no money to feed her child?*

INEZ: "Well, she has to look for a way to provide for the child. I think that to want to do it means to be able to do it, and if she really wants to feed her child, she is going to find a way to buy food. Maybe she has to be a maid or beg in the streets. As they said in the Middle Ages, the end justifies the means, so if I have a son and I love that son, I am going to do what seems impossible, to look for food for that son. To beg, to do what seems impossible. If she is really interested she could do something not so—well, I would not call it low; something so desperate as to beg. I think that if she looks she will find something [a job]."

How can she go to work with a child?

"She can take the child with her."

As a maid they are not going to let her take her child.

"I think that if she looks . . . What else can I suggest? If she looks she can find something."

And if she finds no other way, should she steal?

"I think that if she uses all other means and cannot find anything, well, if you have to steal for your son, steal. But it has to be a drastic measure. I think that what is essential is not to allow the child to die of hunger. I do not know. For some people it is an option to give him up for adoption, give him to someone else."

Who is going to want the children of the poor?

"No one. So I think that the mother of the child should always stay with him. I think she must do even the impossible until she finds something."

MARTA: "I think that the survival of a son justifies everything except killing another person. Everything, stealing, everything to save his life. In very difficult times, in the worst of times—well, imagine, very few people find themselves in this kind of situation in the Western world. But in a place where there is famine, one has to make all kinds of decisions. But you can understand that if a person has a son who is starving to death, to steal some apples from an orchard, for me that is *pecatta minuta* (a small sin)."[12]

LUPE: "For me—very quickly I say—you need something, you go get it. The most important thing is to keep that baby. Give him food. We can get into a long discussion of the places where the people can get . . ."

What about the poor guy who owns the store from which the woman takes what she needs for her child. What about him? He is going to be out of money?

"I can only think of a mother and a child. It is not the normal thing that a mother has to see her children starve. A mother will do anything for her child, things she would not have done before. Like the cannibals that have eaten each other . . . You can do a lot of things. And I think that when there is a great imme-diate necessity that has to do with a life . . . To me it is just not any big moral prob-lem. If that is the only way out . . . You can always say, there is always a place where she can go to get food so she does not have to steal. I am considering the question thinking that there is no other way for her to get food. No matter what value any-thing else has, it is overshadowed by the necessity of the mother to see that the child is fed. She'll have to take the consequences if she is caught. It is hard."

MARÍA: "I think I would even steal, if I had to do it. You have to feed that *criatura,* infant, at all costs.[13] I would beg, I would supplicate, and if it comes to the point where I cannot get food any other way, I would steal. I lived with my chil-dren *una época bien fuerte,* very difficult times, *bien fuerte, bien fuerte.*[14] When I was raising them and the situation was really bad . . . I remember my husband and I selling newspapers at night. We would wait for the newspaper truck and buy the newspapers at two cents and sell them at five cents, and that helped us a lot. And I remember going to bed hungry so my children could have enough to eat because in the house there was not enough for everyone to eat. So I think that a mother goes to any extreme when she sees that her child is hungry. God has given us that thing so beautiful, to have the right to be mothers. But at the same time God has given us a really hard job not only of carrying the child for nine months, and bringing it into the world, but also the responsibility goes on because the work contract of a mother never finishes. It is for all eternity. And I am surprised at times when I see how mothers, with great ease, wash their hands of their children and, if the children have problems, let them have them! But I believe that the one that has real maternal instinct, the job of being a mother goes on, that job never ends. On the contrary, I believe that it multiplies because when they get married, the question is whether you get to love the daughter's husband or not; because, be it as it may, he is already part of your family, so then he also becomes your concern. Then the grandchildren arrive, and your responsibility keeps stretching."

OLIVIA: "First of all I would tell her to get to the Lord in prayer."

After she prays she still has to feed her baby.

"Does she have any relatives?"

No.

"I would go for help to a neighbor, with a friend."

Do you think she should steal or let the baby die?

"No, she should not let the baby die. She has to do whatever she has to do and pay the consequences afterwards. If there is absolutely no other, I mean no other way, she has to do what she has to do to feed the baby. A life is much more important than the consequences she is going to have to pay if she has to go to jail or something . . . I would do it, sure, I would not let the child die."

MARGARITA: "I do not think stealing would be good. The children would not die of hunger because there is always a neighbor who gives one a helping hand. I do not think it is possible for there to be no other way, because I struggled, I struggled with my children and I never had to steal. Because there is always a good soul who gives you something. I do not think that stealing is good because one does it once and then one becomes used to doing it and, without realizing it, one commits other crimes. And besides, it is bad example for the children. One becomes used to doing it, it was easy to take something, so I do it the next time around, I continue to do it and give my children bad example."

QUESTION: *Faced with having to choose which of your two baby children you have to surrender to be killed when only one is allowed to live, what would you do?*[15]

INEZ: "I think I would tell him, 'There is no way that I can decide.' Look, I remember something very similar, that really happened. In the early 1970s many of my cousins were in the Vietnam War—I remember especially all the work we had to do around Christmas time to cook *pasteles* for them.[16] There was this lady whom I heard talking to my aunt. The lady had two sons, and both were drafted. And her friends kept saying to her, 'That is wrong, they are not supposed to take both of your sons. You have to write a letter to the Red Cross, or whoever, and tell them that you want one of your sons home, because you do not want both of them to be in danger of being killed.' But the lady insisted she did not have the heart to do anything like that. 'If I, for example, ask them to send Rafael back, the one son, Daniel, is going to feel inferior and is going to say I love Rafael more. And if I ask for Daniel, Rafael is going to think I love Daniel more. So I place all of this in God's hands and let God decide. I cannot decide.' The same with this example you give me, I cannot decide."

Then they are going to kill both of them.

"But what am I going to decide? It would be a very difficult decision. I do not have children but I would like to have a daughter. I could say, 'Well, I'll keep the girl.' But I will always have it on my conscience that I gave up my son. Another person might say, 'I am going to keep the son so the name of the family can be carried on.' But I think that in moments like that you do not think about anything like that. I think that under such intense pain one cannot decide. That is what I would tell the man, 'I cannot decide.' I would beg the man not to kill them, that they are all I have, that they are my children, and I *los adoro,* adore them, with all my heart. That if they have to kill someone in the family, well, I believe I would give my life for my children. I think it is very difficult for me or for any other woman."

He is not going to settle for anything but for you to decide between one of your children.

"I really could not decide. I have never been in a situation like that. I would beg the man not to kill them. Neither one or the other; and they are not even one year old. I would decide that if they are going to kill one, let them kill all three of us and that is that."

Do you think that human beings are capable of making such a decision?

"I do think that human beings can make such a decision. My conscience would tell me, I cannot give you to kill either of them. It would be difficult, very difficult to decide."

Do you think God would punish if you decided one way or the other?

"I do not think of God, I do not think of being punished . . . none of that. I think that I in particular, for me it would be something that would always stay in my conscience. No, God . . . I don't bring God into this."

ADELA: "I tell you the truth, if I had a pill or something [to commit suicide], I would share it with my children. Having to keep only one child or dying, I would prefer to die with my two children. I would do that. It would be impossible to decide. How can one live without a child? No, no. This is like the story in the Bible when the women were arguing and saying, 'No, no, I am the real mother.' And the real one said, 'Do not divide the child.' My children know this story because I show them the Bible I have in my house. And they say, 'She was right, mami, to let her child go with the other women so nothing happens to the baby.' Oh no, if they asked me to decide . . ."

MARTA: "Between one child and the other, *concho* [expletive], twins! Well I can imagine what must go through a mother's mind to be able to make such a decision. Only God knows that would go through my mind if I was in that situation. Imagine I have two children. What would I decide? I don't have the foggiest idea. I think that one has to be really in that situation, all kinds of things would go through one's mind. If one of the two has children, right now maybe I would decide for my son who has a child than for my daughter who is single. When they were small, I simply cannot imagine. I imagine that if one is sickly and the other one has a better chance of survival . . . Imagine, in a concentration camp when people have to make this kind of decision, only God knows how they would evaluate the situation. I imagine that it must be devastating for a parent to make such a decision. Thanks be to God, many people are not placed in that situation. I think that at that moment the person would evaluate a whole bunch of things: who is more needed, who has a better chance to survive, who . . . I don't know, I don't know what type of evaluations would be needed."

MARÍA: "What a thing for a mother to face! If I had to choose . . . Was there no other alternative? I would have to choose? [Long pause] Well, I would consider two points. If the son lives, he can carry on the family line, the family name will be preserved. If the girl lives, she would have a greater opportunity of expanding the family, of having more children, of carrying on. But it is too difficult a decision, too difficult."

OLIVIA: "That is a very bad decision to make because you do not love one child more than another. See, I have two *hijos,* children, and there is no way I could decide. I get more frustrated with one than with the other but I do not love him any less. You are asking me what I would do?"

Let's say you have to advise someone else.

"About how old are the kids?"

They were twins, a girl and a boy, one or two years old.

"Actually I do not do anything without praying. I would pray over it and whatever the guidance would be . . ."

But what do you think the guidance would be?

"Let him decide."

If she said, "You decide," he would kill them both.

[Silence]

Do you think one choice would be better than another?

"No, it's hard, it's the hardest thing a mother has to do. When it's life, it's so precious that you cannot make a decision like that. When it comes to life you just can't. See, my belief is so strong, my faith is so strong that . . . If you were not going to be able to live with it, let him do whatever he has to do."

If you do not decide, you decide by default. Both are going to die.

"This is it, you love them both so much . . . If you have ten you love them so much. I could not tell her what decision to make."

O.K., if you were in this situation, what would you do?

"My faith is so strong that I figure that if that is God's will, that is what it's going to be, if God wanted to take them both, he was going to take them both. If not, God was going to find a way, a way . . . I do not know how God does it."

But God finds a way to act through you; God is going to give you entendimiento, *enlightenment . . .*

"Right, that is what I was telling Sr. Lupe. What blows my mind is that I do my part and he [God] does the rest. The rest . . ."

My abuelita, *grandmother, used to repeat the saying,* "A Dios rogando, y con el mazo dando," *Pray to God at the same time that you strike with the hammer;* "God helps those who help themselves."

"You see, I would not make a decision."

But in not choosing you are choosing.

"Thank God, I hope we never have to be in that situation. Let met put it that way, because as a mother, I could not choose. If they would ask me, which one are you more frustrated about, I could say this one. But that is the one that I put first in my prayer list, he's got more . . . But as far as making a decision . . ."

MARGARITA: "What a dilemma. I would say, 'Take my life and let them live.' I would decide for them, because they are children that still have a life to live and one, well, one already has lived one's life . . ."

The soldier insists that you and only one of them are going to live.

"No, I would tell him he could have to kill me also. 'If you are going to kill my son, kill me also.' How can you destroy the life of a *criatura,* creature, who is without any guilt whatsoever? But I would not let my son die. Look at the Virgin Mary, she struggled and struggled for her son. What anguish, what pain to have one's daughter killed! Let them also kill me because, why would I want to continue to live? Because the decision to terminate life does not belong to man but to God. God gives life and when he calls, then we go. It is a very hard decision."

CARIDAD: [Long silence] "I think I would choose, at least I would have one child left. If not, I would have none. It would be very difficult because, if they tell me they are going to take my son away, I would die. So imagine, it would be very difficult, very difficult. I would never want to be in those shoes, ever." [Long silence][17]

QUESTION: *What is the most important decision you ever have had to make and how did you go about making it?*

INEZ: "I can think of three: canceling my wedding a week before it was to happen, leaving the convent, and most recently, leaving my job that I have had for over ten years."

Tell me about the last one first. Why did you leave?

"Number one, the racist policy of the office.[18] Number two, when I was a client advocate, I really felt I helped the people. I remember that when the people had to go to a hearing to get their Social Security benefits I would tell them, 'You have to say this and this.' And I felt that I was really helping them. But then they promoted me to coordinator and that meant that I had to support the policies and points of view of the government. Three particular events helped me make the decision. First, we had an advisory board and its members for that agency were considered very radical. They were called "Disabled in Action." They were the ones who fought to have public transportation accessible to the handicapped. They were the ones who fought to have voting places accessible, and they were the ones who wanted to take the mayor and all his administration to court because a bunch of shelters were not accessible—there are a lot of the homeless who are handicapped and cannot get into the shelters. And I was in total agreement with these folks and in disagreement with the racist policies. For example, the city pays $8,000 for a family who is living in a welfare hotel but it will not pay $600 monthly rent for them for an apartment. So, when we were at meetings I would speak out and I would start by saying, 'Look, I am not talking here as an employee of this government related office, I am speaking as Inez.' But my boss found that out and told me I could not speak out, that I was not an advocate any longer, that I represented the official position. Well, things started moving inside my head and I said to myself, 'I am selling out to these people.'

The second thing was when they were going to pass a bill forcing people who have buildings that have commercial use on the bottom floor and the rest is supposed to be for housing but they have them empty—the bill was to force them to fix the housing part and put it to use. The bill did not pass, but I was in favor of it and they did not want me to speak out. I said to myself, 'I have to get out of here.' The third thing was a specific case. There were two old women who were roommates and paid $800 rent. One of them died and the other one kept paying the $400 she always did. She only got $500 from social security so that left her only $100 for food and to get by until the next check arrived. The old woman started receiving notices that she was behind in her rent, and finally she got the seventy-two hours: she had seventy-two hours to pay or she would be evicted! The person who was working as house specialist gave me all the information and I took over the case. So I started by calling the marshal's office and letting him know that this was a handicapped person. That gives an immediate reprieve of twenty days. But no matter how much I argued that they could not evict the woman—you have to remember that the lawyer of the landlord was arguing that she had to be evicted because his client was losing so much money. I got the office to give the woman a lawyer. I personally went to the landlord's lawyer and argued with him. I was supposed as a coordinator just to write memos and oversee the whole thing. But not me, I was right there doing it all myself. I tried to see if I could get for her a special service, that if you are behind in your rent, the government will pay for five or six months if it is a one-shot deal, which means that you have to show that from then on you will be able to continue to pay. Well, this would not have worked in this case but I tried anyway. Well, they finally evicted her. I did not go the day the marshal put her out. I could not stand it. But the old woman called me to let me know that they had thrown her out and she said, 'You see, nothing mattered, they still put me out and the first thing they took out and put on the sidewalk was my Christmas tree.'

"Then to top it all off they started marking us late if we came in after 9:06 in the morning. When you depend on public transportation, it is not always possible to be there at the exact minute. That was when I said, 'Forget it, I am leaving. I will not put up with this any longer!' And when I talked to my boss, she did not care. She had a job to protect. I also wanted to protect my job. It was a good salary. When I started to talk about leaving, my family and friends argued against it, 'How are you going to leave after so many years? And that is a prestigious job, and your pension . . .' There was one thing of which I was very conscious: I could not leave until I had another job because I am the mainstay of my home. In other words, I was conscious of my responsibility because I have to pay the bills. Therefore I could not leave until I found something else. . . . I was disgusted with the whole thing to the point that I knew if I did not leave, I would have a nervous breakdown, because I could not even get up in the mornings to go work. When you reach such extremes, you have to leave. And I was lucky that I found something else."

Did you consult with anyone, talk to anyone else about this decision?

"Oh yes, I talked with my women friends, with someone from that office who had left before I did and who always said to me, 'What are you doing here? You have so much talent.' And that was also another thing. I did not feel I was using my talents because there came the moment when they were really pressuring me because my boss began saying that I was acting like an advocate instead of an administrator. She told me that every time I went to a meeting she wanted a memo, a report, of what I was going to say. So the time came when anyone would say, 'Who wants to continue under such circumstances?'"

Why did you cancel the wedding?[19]

"He lied. He had no intention of coming to marry me and when his brother assured me he would see to it that he came, I said, 'Forget it.' You cannot live with a person you do not trust. You are never going to be happy. You are never going to be at peace. Some members of my family, my aunts, said, 'Get married and then you divorce.' You know how people are. They were concerned about the embarrassment of canceling the wedding a week before. But no, people can laugh all they want but I have my values. In other words, for me it is a value that you marry someone because you love him, because you want to live with that person, and you want to share your life with that person. You do not get married knowing that you are going to divorce. In that situation, no wedding!"

What about leaving the convent?

"It became obvious to me, even though I was young, that in order to stay I had to stop being myself. The novices were treated like maids while the professed, but especially the superiors, lived the good life."

But did you not think that you could endure such a rough life for a while and then you could have the privileges the professed had?

"No, look, I realized that I was never going to get to be superior, because it was an Italian congregation and I was not Italian. But besides, I saw too much hypocrisy. And then, I was too young. I was not diplomatic at all. I did not think about how I could say things in a less confrontational way. But there was this class system—no, forget it! Besides, I started to get scared because for a year and a half I did not menstruate because of the pressure of the situation. I did not seek much advice. I simply decided by myself."

ADELA: [Adela had recently picked up and moved to another part of the country with her three children. Nobody knew why or how. So during the interview we explored why and how she came to decide to move.]

"I came here because I have a friend with whom I was in the shelter where I first stayed when I came to this country. But I have not gotten in touch with her because if I do she will tell the administrator of the shelter."

So what? He will be happy to see that you are . . .

"Safe and sound? No, I don't know, I simply said to myself, I am going to go. I had been thinking about it. When I arrived I stood there in the bus depot and I said to myself, 'My mother, and now what?' I do not know anyone and if I go to a hotel, I will run out of money. So we called a shelter. I do not speak English so I put my daughter on the phone. She is eleven and my son is twelve. The shelter said they would take us but they had no way of coming to get me. The bus had arrived at 6 P.M. and we were still in the depot at 11:30 P.M. Finally the shelter called the police and we arrived at the shelter in a police car. There we stayed.

They gave me a month to get established. They sent for my welfare check. There I became friends with a woman, and we started making all the arrangements to get a place to live together. We found a place to share. I got a job in a nursing home. The children would be alone; they would take care of everything at the house. It was a very hard job, an ugly job to have to deal only with really old people. Then the woman I was living with got back with her husband so she left me. She left me with everything, bills, rent, everything. In a month I moved from that place and went to live with another friend. She lives in government-subsidized housing and she is waiting for her husband to come live with her, so she needed someone to help her pay rent. So I agreed to that. But she did not want the children to go out, to shout, nothing, nothing, nothing. She wanted to have them as prisoners in the room all day long. For me that was not right. Then she wanted to raise my rent. I simply couldn't. So I made many sacrifices, and I moved to a little apartment by myself with my children. Right now I am working with a company that provides health services for disabled people. I help them prepare their meals, clean their apartments. I give them their medicine. I am very happy doing this. They pay me $3.35 an hour. I feel good about my job.

Did you talk to anyone about this move?

"No, only I know . . . My mother does know. She is in Mexico but after two months here I could not stand it any more and I called her. . . .

"I did not tell anyone I was coming here, I did not consult with anyone. I had problems with the landlord where I was. They broke into my house several times so I sued him because I am convinced he was involved. So then he sued me, so I left. We brought two or three things and a big box. I did not consult with anyone because I knew they were going to try to dissuade me from leaving. And I knew inside me that I had to go, I and my children. When I have something to decide, I decide by myself for me and my children. God puts one on the right road. As the saying goes, 'God is never away from his son.' And he puts in our thoughts which way one is to move to solve a problem."

How come you have so much courage, such an adventurous spirit? Is your mother like that?[20]

"No, my mother is not like that. My father was also very calm, and a first-rate father. No, I do not know where this sense of adventure of mine comes from. I think that it comes from all the suffering that I have lived through, all the silence I have had to keep, all that I have seen in my life. In the fifteen years I have been in the U.S.A. I have seen so much, and so much has happened to me, and I have suffered so much. I think this is what has made me be this way. Life made me this way. But I still have my heart, my same sentiments. But I feel strong, I feel that when I say, 'I am going to do this,' I do it. And I do not rest, I do not rest until I do it. I always go; I am going to do it because it is good for me, something moves me to do this. What is going to happen? I will see when it happens. What I hope for will happen, don't ask me how."

MARTA: "When I got divorced, I had to come to the point of forcing my husband to leave. For me at that moment, for him to stay and torture us emotionally did more damage than having him leave the family nucleus. So, it came to the point that the damage was so big that there was no way of justifying postponing the decision. Of course you also then have to weigh the decision. You think, 'If I do this, maybe he will react and act differently.' In my case my decision, my reasoning was 'It is not worthwhile for him to stay, given the Chinese torture he is putting us through,' because he was torturing all of us, and at least in my case, he was torturing me in a way that could have been harmful to my own children. If I had lost all personal control, I would go crazy, and the children were not going to be in much better condition than I. The children, even if they did not know what was happening, were being affected by all that was going on around them. And he was going to do whatever was necessary to force me to be the one to make the decision. I have seen this often, that women are forced . . . In very few marriages nowadays are women not the ones who forced the divorce or the separation. Very few men are the ones who take the decision and say, 'I am going to leave.' They almost always force the women to throw them out. Of course, the throwing them out is because of the deterioration of the relationship, of the Chinese torture, as I say, to the point that forces the break. But you begin to think, and that one thought comes back time and again, 'Maybe forcing him out is my last chance of reconciliation, because it might force him to react and change his behavior.'

"For myself it came to the point that I was going crazy. I thought, 'If I continue this way I am not going to be able to carry on, and the children will be affected very much.' Did I think more of myself than of the children? No, I do not think so. For me I was doing it for the children. Was I in reality using them to justify to myself what I was doing, saying that it was for the sake of the kids but in reality was it for my own sake that I did not want to continue in that situation? I don't know."

Was it an either-or question, either for your good or for the good of the children?

"I would not have minded going crazy if the children had not been involved. That is, 'What is going to happen to the children if I lose my mind?' If the father is letting go of family responsibility and I go crazy, then we will really be in bad shape. It was responsibility for the children that always made me take a whole bunch of decisions, and looking back upon them, one can always say, 'Maybe I should not have done this.' You know you can always say, 'I should have done it a little bit different.' But there are many women who withstood more aggravation, more humiliation, and they were able to save their marriage. I do not think that I would have been able ever to save mine, and, anyway, maybe it was not worth it. But the doubt always remains, would it not have been better for the children if I had done differently?

"I think things worked out very well for me. But later on when there are problems with the children, the thought comes back, what if I had done it differently? It is a question mark. In one's life everything is a question mark.

"Yes, I sought the advice of my sister. My parents were living abroad and they had nothing to say about it. Besides, I was convinced, well, maybe not one hundred percent, but I was quite certain that they were going to side with him because for them he always was the perfect one. Everything he did was perfect. So imagine, I was too weak emotionally to understand that as soon as they knew the facts . . . Now I realize that it was stupid for me to think that way, and if I told my mother and father they would be insulted that I could have had *la más mínima duda,* the most minimal doubt, that, knowing all the factors . . . Besides, I did not want to cause them pain. I kept saying, 'Maybe this can get fixed! Maybe he will react and change. And then they will never forget, especially my father.' So they did not advise me at all. Later, yes, after the separation. But then, not really because they were as lost as I was. My sister, yes, my sister, for example, was the one that helped me to get psychological help. She would say, 'You cannot continue this way. You cannot go into total depression because you will not be able to do anything. If this is what you were avoiding, the fact is that now we are worse each time.' She was the one that always pushed me to do certain things, and also, to get control of myself, to get ahold of myself."

Do you now feel good about the decision you took?

"Of course, every time you evaluate something you measure the pros and the cons. Yes, I feel good because my ex-husband is a person who still has not gotten rid of the problems he has that cause him to behave in a way that does so much damage to those around him. Then, to live with a person like that, to be in a relationship with someone that brings suffering. I can see it and I know that I have gotten rid of that source of suffering."

You recently decided not to apply for the position of CEO of your company. Take me through that process of decision making.[21]

LUPE: "I was thinking of applying for the position, and my decision not to do it has overshadowed the event in my life that I used to consider the saddest and most difficult decision I had had to make . . . My husband wanted so badly for me to apply, and to see it in his face that he wanted it so bad and to have to say no . . . I decided not to apply for the position because I did not think I would be chosen. But what made it worse was that the people who traditionally had been helping me, fizzled. My closest advisers fizzled. 'If you want it, we will be there of course,' they would say. But when people start saying that, then all the *ánimo,* fortitude, hardiness, has to come out of me, everything has to come out of me. It was going to be real hard and we all know it. Those who know the board well told me, 'Wait for the next opportunity.[22] Meanwhile, let's get ready.' But I was saying, 'No, it's got to be now, I have to do it now or never.' My friends were saying, 'If you want to apply I would support you but . . .' The pain I had was to be left alone, because at the end, at the very end, it was me and my secretary; she was the only one whose thinking was, 'Whatever you do, I'll be there.'

"Everybody thought I was going to apply for the position. Some chicanos on the board had already indicated that they were going to vote for someone else. I would have had to mount a huge campaign among the members of the community so they could pressure the board. But even the people of the community with whom I have worked for so long were not clearly behind me. Even the *viejitos,* the old folk, would not support me. 'Lupe has done so much, but she is too young.' They were favoring another person who had applied for the position, one who is much older and in their eyes, because he was older, would know better how to run the organization. Faced with all of this, I did not have it in me. I did not think I would be able to do it by myself. And it would have been something I would have had to do by myself, at least when it came to making the decision and, at the beginning at least, start lobbying the board members. And that hurt a lot. What I learned, and it is not a bad lesson to learn, is that people outgrow each other. Not as friends, but if I am going to be in that kind of position, the people who are going to be with me have to be there because they want to help me. Somebody has to help me openly. They have to be out there in the front lines, and I learned that they will be people that are not themselves so high up. Your frontline workers are the ones that do not have anything at stake themselves in what I do.

"I feel that they failed me. Maybe that is harsh. I wanted to apply because I think one owes something to people and not just because I think I could do the job. I could not please my husband, and that hurts a lot because he never asks for anything. I have to say, here take some, take more . . .

"In order to apply, you need to think that you can get the job. Unless you think it would be worthwhile to give the other people applying a good fight . . . For two weeks I decided, 'What the heck, let's do it. We are going to get publicity galore and I am going to make a name for myself. I am going to make of myself a Hispanic leader in this country.' But then I started to listen to the *viejitos.* One man came in and said, '*Oye, Lupe,* what is this that you are going to apply for the CEO position? What are we going to do without you?' I said to him, "Ay, Mr. García, do not worry. You are all very shrewd and you will get someone to replace me in my job who will help you all.' But the person who applied for my job is someone I do not trust. So then I thought, 'Forget it, I might not get the CEO job and I will also lose my present job.'[23] I asked myself, 'What do you want to do, stay in your present job so you can continue to be a thorn in their side by not shutting up, or what?' The fact that I did not have people really behind me, ready to help me lobby the board . . . You can go and hire professionals to do that but I did not have that kind of money. I did not have enough inside me to make up for all those negatives. That is what hurts. It makes me feel very very bad. So what if I am a great Hispanic leader? Who is going to take care of the *viejitos?* And if I do not get to be CEO, I will have lost my present job, and people listen to me now because of the job I have. I hurt a lot and I am trying to learn from it. The other thing is this. What I do, the job I have, is for a purpose. It gives me the opportunity to do with my life what I have to do. Things will work out because I am doing what I have to do. I think the people need leaders who belong to them, not leaders who sell out. The people need leaders. And how are we going to have more leaders who remain true to the people if we beat them so much? How do I go and talk to other people to do the kind of job that I do? It is such a difficult job. Does it work to do it my way?

"I consider myself the property of the people. Other people point out that I am being used. And I say, '*¡Pues qué bueno! ¡Que me usen los viejitos, que me usen!,* it's all right! Let the old folk use me!' They want this or that, sure I will fight for them. They are little things, they are good things. I am very proud to say I am the property of the people, and I want other people to think the same. It is not just me; we need to find leaders from among the people. And if we find this guy who says he is going to do it, well, what am I going to do but help him, because he is like a community asset? I have to think that way or *me volviera loca,* I would go crazy. It is very good and very important for me to feel anchored to my community. It is very good and it is very important. I mean, that is what it is all about."

So one of the elements in choosing is to consider how the choice is going to be implemented?

"Yes. In the end it was my choice. I was saying, 'I know I can get the job,' but I was saying it without it being inside of me. And I have a very difficult time acting when it is not inside of me. I pretended, but it was only possible to carry on like that for a little while and then I had to decide against it.

"In my present job I like it when I am out there giving a speech. I identify for the people what it is that they need and explain to them what I can do for them. I like it because I like to be out there with the people."

Now as you look back, was it a good decision?

"Yes, other situations have come and I have taken a position different from that of the majority of the board and we have divided the community. I do not say that in the future I will not apply for the position, but I need to be more ready.

"I think it was a good decision because I know now that I would not have gotten the job. If I had seen that it would have been of great value to people, to people I care about, then doing it, even if I had not gotten it, would have been O.K. But it would not have been a fair fight. I was outgunned, it would not have been a fair fight.

"I feel sorry I did not apply for the job, but I do not regret it, I do not regret it. When I was making the decision, God was with me and I think, I hope, I was with him. . . .

"In two years I will have to make that decision again. I have started to do different things. First of all, I have started grooming a different group of people. I am not going to depend on the same ones ever, for that. I'll have them do big things . . . but not help me at the level of lobbying and pressuring the board because we outgrew each other at that level. Their support is at another level, and I have to understand that.

"I am good at grooming other people. I am good at that. Because the reason why some of these people are where they are is because I helped them along and I put them in places. I did not give them anything. I have a job that gave me a chance to appoint them, and they have taken advantage of it. So during the next two years I have to open my circle more, bring more people in and actually ask for help. That is something I had never done. I have never asked the people in the community to help me move up in my job. I will now and we'll be more ready. I feel it was the right decision for this time but I am not happy about it.

"I feel bad about the friends who pushed me not to run, even if it was the right decision, because they did it to advance their own agenda. . . . Their advice was not out of their concern for me but because they had their own agenda. I feel bad also because it is no fun to feel all alone."

But when push comes to shove, we stand alone.

"And I have come to understand that in my head. But I care about people. They are my friends and I care for them. I have cared for years and years and years. . . .

"One thing I have done is I have kept the board straight. I sit there and watch. To me it is very important when there is something that is not helpful for poor people, even if they have the majority of the votes, not to let them have a unanimous vote. I have often been the only "nay" vote and it feels so good. The reason I talk so much is because I want it to be on record that when such and such was approved, there was one person who talked a lot and opposed it. Let history show that it was not a unanimous action. No matter what the issue is, always to bring out a certain point of view is very important. I am very process oriented and I want to see that the process is fair, and that it takes into account the little people. That is my philosophy and it is injected into everything that is happening, and this is very important for me. Public accountability is very important. One has to be account-able to the people . . . Like the church is not accountable to the people. . . .

"I have a great need to know that what I do counts. Maybe it is because I do not have children. I want to leave something behind."

MARÍA: "When my husband got sick, he began to feel ill here, and especially he was very depressed. He had just retired. . . . So I took him to several doctors and none of them found anything wrong with him. All of them told me the same thing, that it was depression, that this happened to many men, that after they stopped working, they felt they were not useful any longer, that they were not needed, and so on, and so forth. . . . Then I called the children in Texas and told them what was happening. And I asked them what they thought about my sending their father down there, because he liked the countryside very much. He liked to plant. And they thought it was a good idea. 'Maybe here he will stop being depressed.' So my oldest son came to get him and take him down there, but he continued with the same depression. One day my daughter called me and said they were going to take him to emergency because all the household remedies for constipation had failed and he was not doing well. I reminded them that this was a problem he had had before. See, he left in May, and my plans were that as soon as the school year was over in June, I would go down to join them.

"My daughter called me from the hospital and told me that they had removed the blockage and that he was feeling well and they would call me from the house. Time went by and they did not call and I was all worried so I called them. But my son-in-law said they were not back yet. Finally my daughter called me and said that they had left him in the hospital. They had asked if he had back problems because they said that back problems and constipation at times go together. He had had problems with a disc before, so they took an X-ray and they found a mass. I immediately said, 'Ay, don't talk to me about a mass, that is cancer.' She told me not to be so fast with a diagnosis, to allow the doctors to do their jobs. I told her I was catching the next plane and I did just that.

"When I got there they said it was cancer but it did not appear to have spread beyond the lung and that he was healthy. They thought that if they operated, his life could certainly be prolonged. That same night he had a heart attack. So that was the end of that, you know. The efforts from then on were to keep him alive. He was like that for three months, each day worse. It was September and the school year had started. I had to make a decision: should I stay with my husband who needed me or come back here to my job that I needed?

"His sister had come to see him and she said, '*Vete en paz*, go in peace, you need your job and they need you there particularly at the beginning of the semester. Leave him here. His children will take care of him and you can come see him every other weekend.' I really had to struggle with this decision. I would tell my daughters, 'You are not helping me to decide.' I even got a bit hysterical. My daughters said to me, 'Mom, the decision has to be yours. We will support you in whatever you decide, but you are the one that has to decide.'

"One night I came up with the solution, obviously because I was thinking with my heart and not with my head. I said to myself, 'I am going to take him up north with me. I can find there someone to look after him. I can rent a hospital bed, and I'll do this and I'll do that, and I will take him with me.' So he was just this size; he weighed seventy pounds. I talked to the doctor, and he said I could bring him if the airline allowed it. But he had to travel with an IV, and I also had to get an oxygen tank in case he needed it on the plane. Nothing frightened me, nothing made me change my mind. When I called the airline, they placed many obstacles in my way. So my youngest son said he would accompany me. Finally the airline gave in. I went and I bought my husband a pair of trousers in the children's department and fixed them for him, and everything was ready. We were set to go the next day. I was about to leave for the hospital to pick him up on the way to the airport when they called to say he had taken a turn for the worse and I was to go right away. The truth is, he was already dead.

"That decision I had to make with my heart instead of my head. Afterwards I thought, 'How foolish I was! How could I imagine I was going to be able to manage all of that by myself up north, when he was so sick?'"

When you say you were thinking with your heart instead of with your head, what do you mean?

"I felt sorry about leaving him, even if his own sister was telling me to do it, that he would be all right with his children."

Were you thinking that he was going to think you were abandoning him?

"No. It surprised the doctors that he was not very lucid. Even if the cancer did not affect his mind, he had such a loss of potassium that he was confused, out of it, you understand? So he would not have noticed that I was not there, but I would have known that I was not carrying out my obligations as a wife, that when he needed me I was going to abandon him and keep going on with my life. Yes, because here I would have not only gone to my job, but I would have continued to participate in the many things I have always been involved in. I say with the heart instead of with the head because I had other options that I never thought of at the time. First of all, I could have called my job and asked for a leave. But above all, I thought that the logical thing to do was to have my husband with me and that he was my responsibility and not that of the children. I made all the arrangements to bring him here. Maybe he would have even died in the airplane, and how difficult it would all have been for my son who was coming with me."

You came back and you have lived here for ten years by yourself, but now you have decided to move to Texas.

"Yes. I remember ten years ago the night that we buried him the children said to me, 'Mom, what are you going to do? You have to decide, and you cannot stay in the north alone. Are you going to come live here or are you going to go live in Miami?' where I have one of my children. And I answered them, 'Right now I am not going to do anything. I am fine in the north, I love to be there.' They started to argue with me. You know I had just buried my husband and I was traumatized. My oldest daughter was the one who said, 'Leave mother alone, let Mom decide whatever she wants. She can live wherever she feels the happiest.' So ten years ago they were pressuring me, almost obliging me. And now ten years later I am deciding on my own. They were surprised when I called to tell them I was moving down there but I did not want to live with any of them. I want my own place. Near them, yes, but not with them. . . .

"Many different things are making me decide to leave. Maybe, in a special a way this last incident [being mugged in the elevator of her own apartment building] that happened to me pushed me to this decision."

OLIVIA: "The latest big decision I have had to make was when my husband got laid off. He was offered another job, but it was going to be three hundred miles away from here. We had to make a decision because the job was his if he wanted it. So I said, 'Well, we have to make the decision but it has to be God's will, not what we want but what he wants for us,' because he guides the way daily. For us that was very hard because first we had come two thousand miles, from Texas to Michigan. So I go, 'Lord, I know that three hundred miles to you is nothing but for me and my children and my grandchildren it would be a very hard decision. But if that is what you want us to do we will do it.' After praying for two weeks . . ."

Did you ask advice from someone?

"No, the advice I get is from the Psalms, from the Scriptures. He talks daily to each one of us, you know. And no matter what the circumstances he gives you the answer. Sometimes you go through something, and you realize, Wow! Here is the answer!"

And how did you come to decide to stay?

"After two weeks of praying, I told my husband, 'Let us not talk about the job at all. There is going to be no conversation about the job at all. There is going to be prayer and listening, listening to what he is going to tell each one of us.' At the beginning of the two weeks I said, 'Lord, if it is thy will that we stay, let my husband's opinion and mine . . . let us both be thinking the same. And that would be a sign that you want us to stay here because he would be getting his job back. But if he has a different opinion, if he wants to go and I want to stay or the other way around, it means that we have to go, because we are not in agreement.' I told my children also, 'I am going to need the votes of all five of us to see what your decision is. Each one has to decide what is best, because God will be talking to each one of us. There are five, if there are three with the same answer, we are staying.'[24] So for two weeks we did not talk about anything. On a Sunday morning, I asked my husband what he wanted to do. And he said that he wanted to stay, that God would provide. On Friday night I had written my answer, so when I asked him, my answer had been written down because I had been guided to an answer. My husband said, 'I want to stay and I will get my job back.' So we went to church and I told Father we were going to stay. He was happy about it and asked if my husband had gotten his job back, and I said, 'No, but he will!' A month after that he got called back to work. The younger one of my kids had decided that whatever we decided he would go with us, but he preferred to stay."

Did you read a specific part of Scripture . . . ?

"Let me show you what I read." [Olivia showed me several books and magazines. One was by Billy Graham, one was the story of Mother Teresa, also "The Official Magazine of Life," by the Study Fellowship of Northern Connecticut, and the New International Version of the Holy Bible.]

Do you work mostly with the Psalms?

"I have different prayers that I work with. I read them over and over."

Do you remember specific Scripture passages that helped you during the two weeks you were praying?

"What I do is I stop and think of the people he has helped in Scripture and then I try to look them up and—look what Job went through, Daniel and the lions, Noah and the ark—and I read the stories of how they trusted in him and he guided them to the right way, the right decisions. I read the Psalms, I mean I just love to praise him and glorify him. I got music . . . every day before I get to the Scriptures I play three songs. I do not know why he has chosen me, but I say, 'Whatever you will, I will it too. I praise you, I thank you.'"

When you say "he," are you talking about God?

"Yes."

You are not talking about Jesus?

"Well, I have to believe in Jesus in order to know God. I know that God sent his son. Jesus said, 'If you know me you know my father.' If God had not sent his son we would not be saved, there would be no hope for us."

I ask because the examples you have given me are about the time before Jesus.

"Yes. How about the miracles? They are Jesus'. Look at the blind man, all that Jesus did to him, he put mud on him, you know. Look at the lady that had been bleeding for seven years. She just touched his garment and right away she was healed. And I went through a lot myself. I imagine I have a better chance than people from the Old Testament because he came down, he has proven that it can be done, but he has to do it. We do what we have to do, and he does the rest."

MARGARITA: "For me it was not difficult to leave Cuba. I was really young, it was not difficult. And the situation was not as precarious as it is now. I came out—not bad, my aunt sent for me, and I came over here fine. I have not had any difficulty since I arrived in this country. I worked, then I decided to go to school at night, which was quite easy to do. It was a bit more difficult once my children were born because I had to bring them up. When they were a certain age I was able to start evening classes because I wanted to become proficient in English. I took that decision. It was not difficult after that. I decided to pursue being a nurse, which I had liked ever since I was small and since I could not be a nun."

Why could you not be a nun?

"Well, you know the difficulties the poor had in Cuba. Frankly, you know that in our Cuba—since we are both Cubans I will tell you—there was also some racism. That we know for sure. I continued to go to church, I paid no attention to not being able to be a nun. Then I thought I would like to follow a medical career. And that is what I have done and what I enjoy. I like my career. It is true that at times I have difficulties on the floor. But I continue to do it because it is something I like very much. I am responsible for my floor at night."[25]

JULIETA: "The most difficult thing for me was to decide to leave my first husband. Because when I came from Mexico he made me work in a place where I had to dance, I was not a prostitute but a dancer. And I left him because I felt so bad that he was making me work in things that I did not want. It was difficult to leave him because I thought that my children would suffer as a consequence of leaving him, because they loved their father very much. And up to now at times I think that it was a decision I took for my sake, but not for the good of my children. Still now they miss him and they ask me why I left him. And I cannot tell them. The oldest one does know and he does not think that I am a bad mother; he understands me. Maybe it is because he now is suffering with his wife and his daughter going from one place to another."

When you made that decision did you think about it for a long time? Did you discuss it with other people?

"I did not need to talk to others, because I knew they would not understand me. They did not know how I felt. I felt really ugly. I thought, 'If I leave my husband, my children are going to suffer.' But I like . . . Whenever I feel something like that I go to God, I go to church and I pray and I feel relief. Maybe I asked God to help me, to give me strength to be able to do it and then to resign myself to it. Because I loved my husband very much, but I also love my children and a life like that one was not going to be good for me.

"I left him because of my children. Because I think that if it had been only he and I, I would have stayed. The only thing he liked was for me to work. He also worked. For me it was difficult to do it, but I did it and God has given me resignation."

And the decision to have to work in prostitution when you went back to Mexico?

"Oh, that was the hardest decision of my life. Because I thought and would tell myself, 'If someday my children find out about this, they will never forgive me.' But every time I arrived home—I lived with my mother and father—I saw one of my brothers—by the way, he is the one living with me now—hiding the tortillas from my children. I think maybe he was just kidding around because I could not think he was doing it because he is bad. But I would always arrive and my children would have their little bellies empty, without shoes, sick, and I had nothing. I looked for work in a factory and I got a job that paid 80 pesos a week, and that did not cover hardly anything. I had three children, food for me, food for them, and I would give the money to my mother but it was not enough for her. I understood that it was not enough. 'What should I do? What should I do? For me it is very difficult. I work all week long to give my mother 80 pesos and it is not enough. What am I going to do?' And a friend told me about this place, 'Look, you can make . . .' 'I don't want to,' I told her. 'I have my children and if I get involved in that, they are never going to forgive me. If I want to marry again, the man is not going to want me because he is going to know what I was.' It was a decision about which I thought and I thought much, but I decided to do it for my children. Because I say it is like this: if I am not going to make headway for them, who is going to do it? And they would ask me for shoes to go to school, for books, and I could not buy them anything. And I had always suffered from that. I had suffered hunger; I had to do it.

"I was not there very long, three or four months. I met my present husband in the street, not there; but I have never wanted to hide anything from him and I told him. Maybe that was a mistake, to have told him. But then I felt more at peace, but now I am paying the consequences. He makes my life impossible. He tells me very ugly things. Yes, he is the one who has told me that God will not forgive me, 'You think God is going to forgive you those things?' But I tell him, 'But God even pardons whose who kill, those who steal. How can he not forgive me what I did when I did it for my children? You think he is not going to forgive me?'

'Who knows?' he says. 'You are always sick and sick and that is God's punishment.'"

And you think God punishes you?

"No, I don't think so. God has given me many good things. If I think that he was punishing me, he would not give me all that he gives me. At least I am not missing a hand, a foot. I am not missing anything. I have the main thing, my health, the health of my children, my children that are mine. If God had not pardoned me he would not send me children. I would not be here, I would be suffering. . . . I don't think so, I am sure God pardons me. Even if my husband does not forgive me, with God forgiving me, I am at peace and satisfied. God knows that I did it for my children, I did not do it for no good reason. If it was for no good reason I would be doing it now, I would still be doing it if I had done it for no good reason. I did it because I had great needs."

CARIDAD: "One of the decisions was marrying my present husband.[26] I met him at a part-time job I had on Saturday as a manicurist at a barber shop. I had gone out with only one other client about my age. My present husband invited me out and I said no, I was very tired. He insisted on asking me to go with him to eat, and I agreed to that. At the time he did not have the final papers of his divorce. When he had them, he told me that I was the woman with whom he wanted to re-do his life. I told him I was not getting married with papers and everything one more time so fast. I was the one who made the proposition—this is usually done by the man—'If you want, we can live together. We can live together for a year and then we can see, and during that year we will have no children.' Because I am a daughter of divorced parents, and I have gone through a lot and I do not want to have a child and have that child go through what I have gone through. He said, 'That's fine if that is what you want. Those were not my intentions but . . .' I called my mother because I was living alone at the time. That was another big decision I had made. . . ."

What process did you follow, how did you decide to live alone?

"The decision to move out and be on my own? I put it in front of me, and I decided. I told my mother, 'I want four walls for me alone, where I am the one who decides, a place I can call my own, my own house, my own closet, my own kitchen.' My mother told me that I was crazy, that the money I made would not cover my expenses. 'Mom, you are right, it is not enough money but I have two arms, and I am strong, and work does not frighten me.' And I worked in a factory and at another job and part-time in the barber shop, and that still was not enough. I had no insurance, no telephone, nothing, but I did it."

Do you ever think of the consequences your actions can have?

"Never, never in my life have I thought about the consequences of my actions.

When the consequences come, I deal with them, but I never think about conse-quences when I decide to do something."

Have you ever made a bad decision, a wrong decision?

"Yes, I made a decision and the outcome was not good. I think, 'I took this decision and things turned out bad.' I analyze it as an experience, and I keep it in mind so I do not do it again. I cannot live thinking of consequences."

Latinas' Understanding of Themselves

The material presented above shows unequivocally that Latinas produce practical reality as they struggle to survive. It also shows that their lives are self-descriptive, that is, Latinas are aware that their lives happen within a certain context, a given social reality constituted by a historical-political situation, economics, religious-cultural background, and personal decisions. Their telling of their stories shows how their struggle to survive includes praxis, reflective action.

In this section we will look into how Latinas understand what they have shared in their stories. Our attempt here is to go further by translating into one another some of their accounts and other explanations about the process they shared. This is a process that steers clear of reductionism and generalities while attempting to elucidate the relationship between the different texts. The goal here is not to create an explanation of "what they mean." The goal is to throw light on Latinas' exercise of their moral agency in order to advance it further.

The purpose of the interviews was to look at Latinas' moral agency by elicit-ing the process they use in making decisions. Since I could not perceive, nor did they identify, any process per se, initially I concluded that they had not reflected much on their ability to be self-determining and still less on their right to be so. But after the third interview I began to see the responses differently. These women found it difficult to deal with the "process" because they see and under-stand it within the much broader scope of what constitutes the fiber of their moral being. They quite appropriately resisted dissecting their experiences in order to identify the process of decision making. However, they were eager to share their experiences and give their opinion about how to proceed in hypothetical situa-tions. Their common sense, formed within the Latino cultural ethos and sharp-ened by their struggle for survival, provides them the moral wisdom they need in their everyday lives.[27]

Margarita seems to go through life calmly, thinking that, in general, she has not had to take many decisions, thinking that things have fallen into place nicely for her. Her sense that she has had to make no momentous decisions seems to indicate a strong inner core which she intuitively trusts. Her life story reveals that in her own quiet way she has been able to find alternatives when things have not gone the way she wanted. She could not be a nun, so she became a nurse. As a poor person in Cuba her possibilities were extremely limited so she decided to accept the invitation of her aunt and come to the U.S.A. Margarita believes in doing for herself. "The first decisions are learned at home and at times what one hears preached in the church helps. But I am going to tell you the truth; one helps oneself."

People have been there for Margarita, even her in-laws after she and her husband went separate ways. So it is inconceivable to her that anyone would need to steal to feed her child: "There is always a good soul who gives you something." However, in the face of having to decide which of two innocent children should live, she will die rather than decide for one or the other. She talks about how God helps us to make decisions. "God gives us strength to go on, to know what it is that one has to do. Right now I have a friend who is having a thousand and one difficulties with her daughter. I advise her, 'Do not get desperate. Pray to the Virgin,' and she does and then when her daughter arrives they sit down and talk."

In her interview she talked about being in charge of her floor during the night shift in a hospital. Part of her responsibility is to take care of people hooked up to respirators. No, she would not disconnect them in spite of the cost and all the talk about the lack of quality of life for these persons. "No," she jumps in to say, "money is nothing; what is important is life." Twice she reminded me of the oath to defend life that she took when she became a nurse. It is not surprising, therefore, that Margarita thinks the best thing that has happened to her is to have survived being run over by a car. And the worst thing going on in the world today is the drug problem, because to use drugs is to toy with death.

But Margarita is no pushover. She angrily told me about the times when drugs addicts tried to attack her in the hospital. "They insult me and at times they try to hit me. Last night I said to one of them: 'Let me make it perfectly clear; you hit me and I'll hit you back.' I'll lose my job but I am not going to be looking at patients' right. Like I said to my supervisor, 'Sure, patients' right, but where are the rights of the nurses?'"

Neither is Julieta a pushover in spite of her trying life and most difficult present circumstances. Her decisions are basic ones: she left her first husband because the kind of life he was insisting she lead was not, in her opinion, something she considered good for herself. She wanted her children to look up to her and for that to happen, she needed to do what she thought was right even if she worries that it might not have been good for the children. "And I left him because I felt so bad that he was making me work in things that I did not want. It was difficult to leave him because I thought my children would suffer as a consequence of my leaving him. . . . And up to now at times I think it was a decision I took for my sake, but not for the good of the children." But when the situation became desperate and it was a matter of the survival of her children, she went ahead and worked as a prostitute. Her decision made after long deliberation convinced her at the end that she had to take this course if her children were not to suffer what she had suffered: hunger. She thought about it for a long time, she says. It was not the easy way out because if it were, she insists she would be doing it now.

Julieta does not complain. When her present husband puts her down by telling her God may not have forgiven her for what she did, Julieta rests assured that God has forgiven her because she did it for the sake of her children. She insists that God has given her many good things, her health, her children, and for her these are signs that God has forgiven her. "I am grateful to God for having my children. I always thank God for being the way I am. As I say to my husband, I am a good mother and I feel, I feel that I am somebody even if they say that I do not do anything. I think I am somebody of value, because I am valued by God even if I am not valued by anyone else. I am also valued by my children, who love me very much."

Unlike Margarita, Julieta has had to depend mostly on herself for her survival and that of her children, despite some small help from her parents. The men in Julieta's life, like the man in Margarita's life, have not been very helpful. "If I leave this one, I do not think I am going to take up with anyone else." And also like Margarita, who stands up for her rights against abusive patients because she has rights too, Julieta is adamant about her self-worth: "This is what I tell my husband, God knows that I have always had enough to eat and for my children to eat. . . . God says, 'Help yourself and I will help you.' I cannot expect God to give me everything. God says, I will help you, but you have to do for yourself."

Like Margarita, Inez is not willing to admit too quickly that in order to feed her child a woman can steal. Margarita was adamant about saying that there is always another way of coping. Inez did finally give in and say that "if there is no other means, then if she has to steal, she has to seal. But it is a very drastic measure . . . maybe she can give the child up for adoption." Like Margarita and Julieta, Inez is determined to do what is good for her. In order to be faithful to her own self she left the convent because, as she says, in order to stay, "you had to stop being yourself." And she preferred to be embarrassed, to lose face and cancel her wedding a week before it was to happen, rather than live a lie.[28] Finally, when her job of many years kept her from being directly involved with her people, an intrinsic part of what she considers to be her calling in this life, she knew she had to leave. "I feel most fulfilled when I am about constructing community; that happens when you are with the people, when you share what you know with the people. . . . What satisfies me most is to see that I have done something with the people and they have responded. . . . It satisfied me when I went to preach in that Catholic church because I was able to communicate well the message I wanted. . . . It satisfies me to see what the people can accomplish, because if you are supportive, the people can grow and better themselves."

Though Inez is deeply involved in church activities, her relationship with God seems to be different from that of Margarita and Julieta. The latter pray to God and advise others to pray to God. Not Inez. Her relationship with God is identified with her relationship with her people. For her, God is present in her struggle to keep the old lady in her apartment. Inez called me recently to share with me what happened in her parish church on Holy Thursday, 1990. After the traditional Eucharist, Inez had prepared an *agape* in the church hall. She could not contain her excitement as she told me that over two hundred people came to the *agape* after the church services ended. "The people really shared what Eucharist means for them. I could have stood up and given a speech, but no, we went around and people said what it meant for them. And then, since not everyone had talked, I said, 'Now we will go around and let us hear in just one word what the Eucharist means for you.' And the people started to shout, 'Joy, hope, resurrection, love. . .' I was crying and if you had been there you also would have been crying."

This sense of her people, of the possibilities in her people, of the role that the church could play in the lives of her people, is the core of Inez's life. To finish the interview I asked her what she would ask for if she were "Queen for a Day." "I would ask that the Puerto Rican people stop having such an identity crisis. And I would ask that conscientious Catholics, men and women who understand their Catholicism as building community, be allowed to take over the church just for one day, just for one day, because they would spend it on human things and not on so much nonsense."

Like Inez, Lupe's commitment to her people is intrinsically linked to her understanding of herself and of God. "There is the journey to the inside . . . But I have to reconcile more my two lives, my two worlds, as I call them. The world of action as a Christian, what you do, which always has been there, but there is more meaning to that now. . . . And then there is the journey inside, a very personal journey, but that has everything to do with what I do outwardly. . . . God is in me, God is in me. That is why I like myself. . . . I am beginning to understand what I have heard for many years, for many years. God speaks more through the poor and in the poor and with the poor than in anybody else because they do not have anything." Vehemently Lupe insists that if the *viejitos* use her, that is good.

Unlike Inez and Margarita, Lupe very quickly says that if a child is starving, the mother has to find food wherever she can. "Whatever value is in anything else is overshadowed by the necessity of the mother to see that the child is fed. She'll have to accept the consequences if she is caught."

In this Lupe resembles Caridad, who insists that she never thinks about consequences when she is deciding what to do. She does it and that is that, she insists. Caridad's "electrical style," as she describes herself, is very different from Margarita's, but the underpinnings of their moral character seem to be the same: a self-affirming, self-valuing that significantly limits the weight they give to what others say or think about them.

Lupe is in a stage of her life in which she finds that in herself the inward and the outward are interconnected. Although on the surface she may seem to resemble Olivia, closer examination shows that there are significant differences. Olivia prays to find guidance and waits for that guidance from God to be very specific. She tried to find ways to be perfectly sure of what God wants her to do. Lupe, on the other hand, has come to realize that God is in the poor, and that she will know what God wants from her by advocating and working for the poor. But like Olivia, Lupe is convinced that through all of this she is following what God wants from her, "though I am still not there." Olivia finds great joy in getting down on her knees and praising and thanking God daily. Julieta thanks God for all that she has, her health, her children, even in the midst of a life so insecure that she does not actually know how she is going to get something to eat each day. She lives, nevertheless, convinced that "God does not leave us. . . . God is here already. I do not think that God is going to come, but that God is here with us. We are the ones that do not see him because of our sins."

Like Olivia and Julieta, María's trust in God is unflinching. Asked what elements play a role in her decision making, she answered, "Maybe my trust in God. I always think that what one does in life is because they are part of a larger scheme. And I always think that when I make a decision, it is because God is taking me towards that decision." But this does not take away her sense of responsibility. "My sense of responsibility is very great, not only for my children, but in all matters. . . . My sense of responsibility, maybe it is because of all that I did not have, but also because I am a bit demanding. . . . I have a sense of keeping my word. For example, some musicians in my parish did not do what they said they were going to do. And I say, 'How can they call themselves men? They have no money but at least they could have the honor of their word.' Because I think one's word is of great value and we should be responsible. . . . I do not consult with anyone. Maybe that is why I am so strong in my decisions, maybe because I think, when I was small I did not have a mother to whom I could go and ask, "What do you think?"[29]

Like Inez, when asked what she would wish for if she were "Queen for a Day," her requests have to do with the good of the community. First, she would ask for love in the community. "By that I mean that we would share, that we would take each other into consideration, that we would be more sensitive. . . . Then I would like to see this world free of drugs because I believe that if we got rid of drugs we would get rid of many other things. . . . One can be happy being poor but people feel inadequate, they do not value themselves. . . . These kids need role models. . . . The drug situation is totally out of control. In the beginning, when all of this started, Puerto Ricans and blacks were the ones who were taking drugs, the ones who were dying and killing, and the government did not pay much attention. But when the people from the suburbs and the whites began to come to Harlem for drugs, the government tried to do something, but it was too late to try to control the situation. When one building is burning, the firefighters can get control of the flames, but when it is a whole block of buildings, it is impossible for anyone to control it. . . . And the last thing I would ask is that my children be happy." María's last words to me were these: "The other day I read somewhere a phrase that I like very much, 'I love my God and I love my people and I hope to serve them both.' I'm going to use that in one of my speeches someday because it is exactly what I think."

Like María and especially like Julieta, Adela's children are central. She had lost a baby in Mexico before she ever came to this country. At that time the doctors told her she would never have another child. But she never doubted that she would. When she got pregnant with her son she was overjoyed. And then she said to God, "You have given me a son, if you could please give me another child. And when I found out that I was pregnant a second time, I was the happiest person in the world." No wonder that putting herself in the shoes of the mother who is asked to decide which of her two children she would hand over to be killed, Adela immediately thinks of death for all three of them. For Adela, her children are a cause of personal satisfaction. "Oh, yes! It is such a great satisfaction for me to have these two children. I want nothing, nothing, nothing, nothing, in this world but to live. I do not want wealth, I do not want luxury, I do not want anything. I only want what is sufficient for me and my children to live. I tell them: 'When I am gone I want to have left you with a little base so you can build upon it, and above all I want to leave you with the greatest thing, an education.' I tell them: 'What pleases me most is to see you going to school. I do not want you saying to me one day you do not want to go to school.' I see how they get up in the morning eager to get going, they clean up, get dressed . . ."

Though Marta's circumstances are very different from Adela's and Julieta's, she also made her most difficult decision in life, to ask her husband to leave the house, because of the children. For her, her own mental health and the safety of the children were all linked together. "It came to the point that I was going crazy. I thought, 'If I continue this way I am not going to be able to carry on and the children will be affected very much.' I would not have minded going crazy if the children had not been involved. That is, 'What is going to happen to the children if I lose my mind?'" Unlike Julieta, who in spite of her husband's harassment believes that she is of value, Marta has doubts about herself. "I am very insecure and I am near the edge of not being very healthy. People do not notice because I fight tooth and nail for the sake of those I love. But I have a very low self-esteem. People do not see it because I put up a front. It has nothing to do with good. Capable, I am not capable. It has nothing to do with good or bad. I am not bad, I am very good. I am not capable. I cannot do things in a way that obtains for me what I want. I'm talking about what I want emotionally because in my business I am an ace. I have accomplished so much in my business but I do not get the highs that I see my son and my father getting when they do a good business deal. I can't. We as women— well, one has accomplishments outside—so what? But it comes down to the fact that I am not married and outside accomplishments are worthless."

Marta stopped going to church once she could not agree with its position on birth control. "But I have all my convictions, and my religion is a matter between my God and me. I have my religion and my God, very, very, very much in mind. . . . I do not go to church because the church is against remarrying. So, since I have always said that if I find the right man I will marry him, I do not go to church." Inez feels free nowadays not to go to church every Sunday. The priests and the way they treat the people make her angry. But like Marta, not going to church does not take away from her relationship with God. Julieta goes to church to be near God; for her the church is a place of refuge when she needs to think, to get rid of her frustration. But she does not go to Mass on any regular basis and does not partake of the sacraments. Margarita finds, when she has to make a decision, that she can use some of the things she hears in sermons. Lupe, on the other hand, feels that her relationship with God is growing as she goes deeper into herself and connects that with what she considers her vocation: to serve her people. She says, "The more I travel into me and come to know who my God is, the more separated I become from my church. It's now to the point that just seeing certain people offends me, just seeing representatives of the institution offends me because they are with power and they are with money, and they are now with the people. And they leave us alone, those of us who stick our necks out, they leave us alone. They do not want to touch us with a ten-foot pole. I think the church is going to fall apart. I do not know how long it is going to take. . . ."

Generative Themes Central to Latinas

Mujerista social ethics seeks to discover the themes that are important to Latinas, the ones they feel strongest about, the ones that motivate them. In the process of identifying some generative themes from the "translations" just made, more comes into play than the information gathered through the ethnographic interviews. The information produced by the socioeconomic and the cultural-religious analysis is also a very important part of this process. Likewise, the understandings and perspectives of the meta-ethnographer are of great significance at this point, and this is why I have argued that this person should be an insider.[30] Also of importance here is a factor that cannot be translated into either oral or written language—the modulation of the voices of the women during the interviews, their gestures, the knowledge the researcher has of them, all of which goes well beyond the actual recording of the interviews.[31] Aware of all the different factors that play a role in this next step of the process, here are two of the key themes that have emerged from this study.

Above all else, there is a sense in these Latinas that they have to act, that whatever is going to happen is going to happen because they see to it that it happens. But their doing is not a thoughtless process, a routine kind of action, empty of reflection. On the contrary, the more critical the action becomes, the more reflection it requires. Even behind Caridad's assertion that she decides "just like that" is a vast amount of reflection on past experience which leads her to know almost intuitively what she must do for her own sake.[32] And Julieta insists that she never stops thinking, trying to find ways to feed her family. In her shines forth that extraordinary creativity of the people that finds thousands of ways of surviving. For Lupe, her way of coming to know herself and her God is to *"dale y dale y dale"* (an expression which combines the sense of being engaged in doing something, doing it repeatedly, and doing it over the long haul). All of them insist in their own way that only if they depend on themselves can they depend on God.

Second, there is in these women a strong awareness, almost a passion, for claiming and asserting their value and their self-worth. Even Marta, who claims to have low self-esteem, struggles valiantly to separate that negative image from her belief, her knowing, that she is good, very good. Julieta's husband tries to control her by insisting that God might not have forgiven her working as a prostitute, and at times he seems to succeed in planting in her a seed of uncertainty. But then, almost out of nowhere, comes Julieta's assertion that she knows she is of value to God, that she is a good mother, that her children love her. Adela is more than pleased with her adventurous self and the way she has succeeded in providing for her children. She makes plans to have a small business in the near future because she believes in herself. Margarita defends herself against abusive drug addicts even if it means risking the loss of her job just before retirement. Caridad emphasizes that she is indeed a good mother for her young son. She ended the interview by saying she wished she could convince her husband to have another child so she could prove herself once again as a mother. Lupe is sad about not having applied for the CEO position in her company, but she is immensely consoled by her reason for not doing it, namely, that it was not worth the risk of her present job in which she can do much for the welfare of her people.

Even the circumstances surrounding the interviews show how they value themselves, how self-determining they are, and how they do want their voices to be heard. Most of them had participated in the weekend gatherings we conducted around the country a few years ago to gather the materials found in the book *Hispanic Women: Prophetic Voice in the Church*. At that time they had all felt that the process was very valuable for them personally. Therefore, in choosing to participate this time, they were doing so not only to help me, but, as most of them verbalized, to help themselves, in spite of the fact that the time set for the interviews was not very convenient for most of them. Olivia gave this project the best part of Mother's Day. In order to be interviewed when I was in the city where she lives, Marta had had to work late the previous evening and then shuffle her schedule to make time for our meeting. Lupe canceled appointments and took the whole day to participate as fully as she could. Julieta materialized out of nowhere at the women's shelter where she had agreed to meet me, and when her husband dropped by during the interview and tried to get her to leave, she firmly told him he would have to wait until we were finished! Adela got in touch with me after meeting by chance with someone who knew I was looking for her. That meant that she had to write to me, and writing is definitely not one of her strengths. Margarita was willing to be interviewed in one of her few precious weekends when she is not working at the hospital. Caridad went without lunch the day of the interview since that was the only time we could find. María had to arrange for us to meet at her church since there was some kind of construction going on at her house. Inez insisted on finding time one Saturday morning before going to an important meeting. By the time I interviewed the last of them, I was more convinced than ever that these women want their voices heard, that they believe they have a contribution to make to the doing of *mujerista* theology.

In the language used by liberation theologies, two of the main generative themes that emerged from our interviews with the women are praxis and moral agency. These are the themes that we will elaborate in the next two chapters.

THE INSISTENCE ON PRESENTING THE VOICES of Latinas in *mujerista* theology means today that I reject all universal and essentialist claims that insist on saying that the nature of women has inherent female characteristics the same for all women, no matter where they live, their age, or their culture. I also reject universal or essentialist women experiences: I do not believe that all Latinas, because we are Latinas, have the same experiences and, much less, that we interpret them the same way. The sources that I use are the understandings and practices of *particular* Latinas. They are specific voices but they are not unique. They are specific but they resonate with other Latinas' voices. Usually when grassroot Latinas get together to reflect one notices how each woman weaves what she is saying with what already has been said, thus creating a tapestry in which one can see the similarity of experiences much more than dissimilar experiences. This is how, starting with the particular, we can arrive at "Latinas say." Of course this does not mean that all Latinas agree with us. However, the voices of Latinas we hear in this chapter find resonance in the lives of other Latinas. What they say is similar to what many other Latinas in their same situation would say because Latinas share a similar world-view—similar ways of ways of looking at life and dealing with reality.

The voices of the women we hear in this chapter create a narrative that makes clear how issues of gender affect their lives and how their gender influences the way they see life. If we know how to listen to them we will understand how sexism and ethnic/racial prejudice impact their lives and how they have adapted themselves in order to deal with them: in some circumstances they pretend motives and ways of being with which they really are not in agreement; at other times, they simply refuse to pretend. The narrative allows one to see how, despite immense odds, Latinas create small spaces where they can be self-defining and self-determining. The narrative is subversive in the sense that it uncovers the way the academy, the churches, and society have ignored us and refuse to take us into consideration. The voices of Latinas point out the way they intuit, think, and act—breaking the hegemony established by those who control the ecclesial and social structures. Perhaps, at this time, we Latinas will not be able to accomplish much, that is to say, we will continue to be invisible to the dominant groups and structures. But the space that *mujerista* theology offers Latinas to speak and listen to themselves and others is a step forward in the struggle to be subjects of our own history. To provide a platform for the voices of Latinas is a way of beginning to make known who we are and the valuable contribution to society we want to make. We know, however, that there is a long road ahead of us before what we say will be taken into consideration by the churches and by society. However, the narrative that arises from the voices of Latinas allows us to continue to conceive—and to start living—a life "beyond" present oppressions. This we can do precisely because the narrative allows us to read ourselves differently from the common interpretation of others, an interpretation that oppresses and marginalizes Latinas.

Síntesis del Capítulo 4
En sus propias palabras: latinas como agentes morales

Son cuatro las razones principales que me llevaron a estructurar el proyecto de investigación que presento en este libro en la forma en que lo hice. Primero, sabía que al entrevistar a las mujeres cuyas voces se escuchan en este capítulo, al ayudarlas a reflexionar sobre su mundo cotidiano y sobre el modo cómo van tomando decisiones en la lucha diaria, ellas entenderían cómo es que se van auto-definiendo y este entender les ayudaría a fortalecer y ampliar su rol como agentes morales. Segundo, sabía por experiencia propia que, dada la influencia del catolicismo en la cultura latina, el tema de la "conciencia" es bien conocido por las mujeres latinas, y que usamos "conciencia" para referirnos a nuestra habilidad y esfuerzos por decidir qué hacer en nuestras vidas y con nosotras mismas. Tercero, había notado que las iglesias institucionales a menudo usan "la conciencia" como instrumento de dominación y control, y quería saber cuánto de ese control hemos internalizado las hispanas. Cuarto, la reflexión que propició este proceso nos ayudaría a las hispanas a entender cómo funciona la opresión en nuestras vidas, lo que es importante porque, como explicaré en el próximo capítulo, cuanto más conscientes estemos de esta opresión, mejor podremos luchar por nuestra liberación.

Presentamos en este capítulo las voces de nueve latinas, convencidas de que sus voces son un recurso importante en la lucha que libramos todas las mujeres por ser sujetos de nuestra propia historia. Para ser sujetos tenemos que apropiarnos de nuestra voz—otra de las razones por las cuales la teología *mujerista* trata de ser un foro para las mujeres latinas en vez de sólo referirse a ellas.

Hay otras cuatro razones para incluir aquí las voces de las mujeres latinas. Primero, es imposible decir en forma más elocuente o más sencilla, ni de mejor manera que en sus propias palabras, lo que las mujeres han compartido conmigo. Segundo, en el mundo de la teología, las mujeres latinas no hemos tenido oportunidad de hablar y de ser escuchadas. Esperamos que las voces que aquí se presentan ayuden a cambiar esta situación. Tercero, necesitamos escuchar a las latinas para entender cómo la religión es elemento vivificante de la cultura latina, y cómo funciona como "empuje revolucionario" en nuestra lucha por sobrevivir, en nuestra liberación. Cuarto, la teología *mujerista* respeta la diversidad existente en maneras de entender y practicar la religión entre los grupos de las mujeres latinas. Escuchar estas diferentes voces permite presentar una muestra de esta diversidad.

Al presentar aquí las voces de las mujeres no indico ni sugiero que el material de este capítulo es objetivo, libre de interpretación. Aunque he tratado de no imponer mis esquemas interpretativos, sé que el proceso de seleccionar y organizar lo que han dicho las latinas constituye en sí mismo una especie de filtro. Incluso el transcribir lo que dijeron y el traducir del español, "espanglish," "mexicano," "cubano" o "puertorriqueño" al inglés, constituye ya una adaptación por mi parte como autora de lo que estas mujeres han dicho. La mejor forma en que puedo corregir el papel de mi voz de autora es identificando mi subjetividad para que quienes lean conozcan el lente que uso en mis interpretaciones; para que sepan cuál es mi punto de vista tanto teológico como de la vida en general.

En este capítulo, después de las voces de las latinas, voces que por falta de espacio no podemos incluir también en español, presentamos la parte del proceso que la meta-etnografía llama "síntesis del conocimiento". La síntesis del conocimiento tiene un fin triple: apunta diferencias y similitudes, facilita el descubrimiento de temas generadores—los cuales explicaremos en detalle más adelante—e impide que se impongan esquemas analíticos ajenos a la realidad de las latinas. El propósito de la síntesis del conocimiento no es establecer normas y valores, sino elucidar para las latinas nuestra manera de pensar para que podamos fortalecer nuestro rol como agentes morales. El propósito de este proceso no es analizar lo que dicen las mujeres latinas, sino ayudar a que oigan mejor sus voces simplemente porque las latinas tenemos el derecho a ser escuchadas. El propósito no es instrumentalizar, convertir en objeto, las experiencias de las latinas, sino reconocer el derecho que tenemos de expresar nuestro punto de vista y nuestra manera de entender la realidad. El propósito de la síntesis del conocimiento no es construir un discurso teológico acerca de la realidad de las latinas, sino presentar sus voces como elemento clave de una hermenéutica de la sospecha que usamos para analizar el papel que la religión y la teología tienen en nuestras vidas.

¿Quiénes son las latinas que nos hablan?

Inés, de clase trabajadora, nació en los EE.UU. pero creció en la casa de sus abuelos en la campiña puertorriqueña. A principios de la década de 1970 entró en un convento pero después de un año muy difícil, salió de la congregación y se vino a vivir a los EE.UU. Su lucha y su trabajo tienen como foco principal los derechos de las mujeres, sobre todo en la iglesia católica en la cual participa en el ámbito local, regional y nacional. Inés trabaja en la administración de un hospital. Tiene una maestría en comunicaciones y su ambición es trabajar en radio o TV. Inés se siente muy a gusto consigo misma y es una persona muy amigable. Prefiere hablar en español no sólo porque le es más fácil sino también porque ve la necesidad de hacerlo para preservar su cultura. Inés no pierde las esperanzas de que algún día Puerto Rico sea soberano.

Adela es madre soltera de una hija y un hijo. Nació y vivió en México los primeros 15 años de su vida. Después, hasta hace poco, vivió en Texas. Al hablar con ella enseguida se nota que está acostumbrada a lidiar con situaciones muy difíciles y tiene gran habilidad para salir adelante. Las injusticias que ha sufrido en los diferentes trabajos en los que se ha ganado la vida la han llevado a soñar con tener su propio negocio: una panadería. Su hija y su hijo son lo más importante para ella y los empuja constantemente a que estudien diciéndoles que la educación es la única herencia que les puede dejar.

Marta nació y se crió en Cuba. Es madre de una hija y un hijo, los dos casados, y ya es abuela por segunda vez. Lleva como 8 años divorciada—aunque preferiría estar casada—y vive con su hermana soltera. Marta es sumamente trabajadora y es la dueña de un negocio muy lucrativo. De clase media alta, es dueña de su casa, tiene un bote, viaja durante sus vacaciones y disfruta de muchas otras amenidades. Marta se expresa muy bien en una mezcla de inglés y español y disfruta al poder compartir lo que siente, lo que cree, las razones por las cuales es como es.

Lupe es méxico-americana y toda su vida ha vivido en la ciudad donde nació en el suroeste de los EE.UU. Es la mayor de una familia muy pobre, y ayudó a criar a sus hermanas y hermanos. Terminó sus estudios universitarios ya algo mayor; está casada y no tiene hijos. Cuando la entrevisté, Lupe trabajaba en una corporación y en su trabajo lidiaba directamente con gente de la base. Su trabajo le ha dado gran visibilidad en la comunidad. Lupe labora como voluntaria en muchas organizaciones cívicas y en grupos relacionados con su iglesia. Lupe piensa bien las cosas y pone mucho empeño en tratar de decidir qué hacer con su vida.

María nació en Puerto Rico pero vino a los EE.UU. cuando era niña. Es la menor de once hijos y su mamá la dio a una tía para que la criara. María es viuda y tuvo doce hijos—tres de los cuales murieron cuando eran jóvenes. María ha estado involucrada con la iglesia y en la política en la comunidad por muchos años, habiendo sido electa miembro de la junta escolar. Aunque vive sola, María está muy apegada a sus hijos los cuales le siguen causando preocupaciones y sufrimientos al igual que consuelo y alegría. Hace poco se mudó a otra ciudad a vivir cerca de una hija pero no resultó el arreglo y ahora se ha vuelto a donde había vivido casi toda su vida.

Olivia es méxico-americana nacida en Texas y ha vivido la mayor parte de su vida en la parte central de los EE.UU. Está casada hace más de 30 años y tiene varios nietos. Cuando la entrevisté, estaba trabajando en una panadería y estudiando para graduarse de secundaria ya que quiere ser ayudante de maestra. Olivia disfrutó participando en este proyecto e insistió en que usara su nombre verdadero. Olivia habla con gran entusiasmo acerca de la religión y de la presencia de Dios en su vida.

Margarita es cubana y ha vivido en la ciudad de Nueva York por muchos años. Vino de Cuba hace más de cuarenta años invitada por su tía. Se casó con un hombre nacido en Tampa de padres cubanos pero el matrimonio no duró mucho. Su hijo está casado y tiene mellizos varones; su hija es soltera y vive con ella.

Margarita es estricta en asuntos religiosos. De joven le hubiera gustado ser monja, pero dice que nunca encontró cómo seguir ese llamado ya que era pobre y negra. Después de mudarse a los EE.UU., estudió enfermería y durante los últimos 19 años ha trabajado el turno de noche en uno de los hospitales de Nueva York. Cuando la entrevisté, Margarita estaba a punto de retirarse.

Julieta es, de las latinas que entrevisté, la más pobre. Es mexicana y ha vivido en los EE.UU. por 12 años. Su mamá tuvo 21 hijos de los cuales sólo la mitad sobrevivió. Julieta tiene 6, el mayor tiene 18 años y el más pequeño, que estaba con ella durante la entrevista, tiene 5. Uno de sus hijos murió de bronquitis. Ella va de vez en cuando a México a ver a su mamá. El día que entrevisté a Julieta me dijo que ni ella ni su marido tenían trabajo y que el día anterior habían recogido por las calles unos colchones viejos y los habían vendido para tener dinero para la comida. Ella es indocumentada y no puede arriesgarse a trabajar en una fábrica ya que la "migra" (el Servicio de Inmigración y Naturalización) puede encontrarla y deportarla a México.

Caridad nació y se crió en el campo en Cuba, en condiciones de gran pobreza. La bautizaron al nacer pero no ha participado mucho en nada que tenga que ver con la religión. Ahora se ocupa más de ir a la iglesia ya que tiene un hijo y quiere que él sí vaya. Cuando va a la iglesia no es porque crea lo que allí se dice sino porque, según ella, alguien más allá de este mundo tiene que existir y "tengo que dejar de andar sin rumbo en esta vida y creer en algo." Caridad es muy honesta consigo misma y ha salido adelante teniendo a veces hasta tres trabajos. Hablando con una rapidez increíble y sin reservarse opinión alguna, ella misma dice que es "eléctrica".

Cómo las latinas entienden su propia realidad

Las entrevistas con estas mujeres muestran cómo las latinas construyen su propia realidad a través de la lucha diaria. Estas latinas se dan cuenta del contexto dentro del cual se desarrollan sus vidas; están conscientes del papel que juegan en su realidad social su situación histórica, política y económica, del trasfondo religioso-cultural de sus vidas, y de las decisiones personales que van tomando día a día. Es obvio cuando se habla con ellas que la lucha cotidiana de estas mujeres es una verdadera praxis: actúan después de analizar bien la situación y después siguen reflexionando sobre lo que han hecho.

Estudiamos detenidamente lo que compartieron estas latinas en las entrevistas, comparando lo que dijeron unas y otras, para identificar cómo es que se van auto-determinando en el quehacer cotidiano. Nos fijamos principalmente en el proceso que emplean para tomar decisiones, en cómo es que deciden. Vimos que sus decisiones no surgen de un proceso predeterminado o específico. Estas latinas toman decisiones dentro del ámbito general de sus vidas, y así se van desarrollando como seres morales al enfrentarse a la realidad cotidiana—realidad que no consiste de decisiones muy transcendentales sino de muchas decisiones pequeñas. El sentido común que han ido desarrollando, usando elementos de la cultura latina perfilados por la lucha por la vida—eso es lo que les da la sabiduría moral que necesitan en su vivir cotidiano.

Temas generadores

La teología *mujerista* trata de descubrir los temas que son importantes para las latinas. ¿Cuáles ideas, problemas y situaciones las motivan y conllevan gran carga emocional? En la teología *mujerista* vamos descubriendo estos temas al analizar lo que dicen las latinas pero también estudiando la información que arrojan los análisis socioeconómicos y culturales-religiosos de sus vidas. En este proceso también juega un papel fundamental la información que se recoge al estar con estas mujeres, la información que nos dan sus sonrisas y lágrimas, el tono de sus voces, la postura de sus cuerpos, la manera en que reaccionan a lo que dicen las demás. Significativo en este proceso es la sensibilidad y perspectiva de la persona que está haciendo el estudio.

Teniendo estos aspectos en cuenta presentamos dos de los temas generadores que han surgido en este estudio. Primero, más que nada hay un sentido en estas latinas de que tienen que actuar, de que lo que va a suceder, va a pasar porque ellas actúan. Y el actuar de ellas no es algo que hacen sin pensar, sin reflexionar, en forma rutinaria. Al contrario, cuanto más crítica es la situación, más y más piensan y reflexionan. Aun Caridad quien nos dijo que ella decide "en un abrir y cerrar de ojos", reflexiona muchísimo sobre sus experiencias pasadas y ha aprendido tanto de ellas que por eso le parece instantáneo o intuitivo cómo decide y actúa. Y Julieta insiste en que ella nunca para de pensar, por ejemplo, tratando de ver qué hacer para poder alimentar a sus hijos. Julieta ejemplifica esa extraordinaria creatividad del pueblo que se manifiesta en la ingeniosa manera en que inventan miles de formas de sobrevivir. Para Lupe la manera en que ella ha llegado a conocerse a sí misma y a su Dios es a través del "dale y dale y dale". Todas ellas insisten que sólo pueden depender de Dios si dependen de sí mismas.

Segundo, estas mujeres están muy conscientes de que tienen que afirmar apasionadamente su valor como personas. Aun Marta, quien insiste en que no tiene mucha estima personal, lucha por separar la imagen negativa que tiene de sí misma de lo que sabe intelectualmente: "que yo soy buena, muy buena". El marido de Julieta trata de controlarla, insistiendo en que Dios no le perdona que haya trabajado como prostituta para darle de comer a sus hijos. Ella confiesa que a veces él le hace dudar; pero en el fondo ella siempre sabe que ante los ojos de

Dios ella tiene valor, ella es una buena madre. Adela está más que satisfecha consigo misma, con su espíritu aventurero y la manera en que ha logrado proveer para sus hijos. Ella no duda que en el futuro podrá tener su propia panadería porque confía en sí misma. Margarita se defiende contra los drogadictos que vienen al hospital y vituperan a las enfermeras aunque sabe que al hacerlo corre el riesgo de que la boten de su trabajo. Caridad afirmó muchas veces que ella es una buena madre y lo quisiera probar teniendo más hijos, cosa que su marido no quiere. Y Lupe, está triste por no haber solicitado el puesto de directora de la compañía donde trabaja, pero le consuela el que no lo hizo porque no merecía la pena correr el riesgo de perder su posición presente en la cual puede ayudar a la comunidad hispana.

Cuando terminé de entrevistar a estas mujeres latinas, estaba más convencida que nunca de que ellas se valoran, que quieren ser escuchadas, que creen que tienen algo importante que contribuir al mundo en el que se desarrollan, a la vida de sus hijas e hijos y a la de otras personas con las que se relacionan. Participar en este proceso las llevó a convencerse de que lo que ellas dicen sobre Dios es importante, y que nos ayuda en la elaboración de la teología *mujerista*. Usando el lenguaje de las teologías de la liberación podemos decir que dos de los temas generadores que surgen de las entrevistas con estas mujeres latinas son la importancia de la "praxis" y la "agencia moral". Estos son los temas de los próximos dos capítulos.

La insistencia en presentar las voces de las latinas en los textos *mujeristas* hoy en día sirve para dejar por sentado que rechazo reclamos universales y esencialistas que insisten en que la mujer tiene su naturaleza propia de hembra con características inherentes, y que dichas características son iguales para toda mujer no importa donde viva, la edad que tenga o su cultura. Este rechazo lo extiendo al campo de las experiencias: no creo que todas las latinas por ser latinas tengamos las mismas experiencias y mucho menos que las interpretemos igual. Es mi intención que las voces de las latinas presentadas en este capítulo den por sentado que elaboro la teología *mujerista* a partir de voces específicas y, por lo tanto, voces particulares. Mi reclamo y propuesta es que *no* por ser específicas, son "únicas", *no* por ser particulares, se refieren—representan/identifican—sólo a la persona que habla. Lo más común cuando nos reunimos con las latinas a reflexionar sobre cualquier tema es que cada una vaya ensartando lo que dice con lo que ya han dicho las otras creando así un tapiz en el cual lo que prevalece son las similitudes en vez de experiencias e interpretaciones opuestas. En esta forma es que, a partir de lo específico y particular, llegamos a poder decir, "las latinas dicen". Claro está que al hablar así no estamos diciendo que no hay latinas que no dirían lo opuesto. Lo que estamos sugiriendo es que lo que dicen las latinas que escuchamos en este capítulo es válido más allá de los límites de las vidas de estas mujeres. Es válido en el sentido de que lo que dicen estas latinas es similar a lo que dirían muchas otras. Es válido en el sentido de que lo que dicen se basa en experiencias vividas y ha afectado—ha tenido y tiene efecto—en sus vidas sirviendo como motivo y afirmación de que merece la pena la forma en que entienden lo que les pasa y las decisiones que toman. Que merece la pena quiere decir que les permite vivir de una manera que las satisface personalmente, que les hace vivir con un sentido de que son responsables de sus vidas y pueden afectar lo que les pasa.

Las voces de las mujeres que aquí presentamos van creando una narrativa que va dejando en claro cómo el género influye en lo que viven, y el papel que juega el género en cómo entienden lo que viven. Si sabemos escucharlas entenderemos cómo el sexismo y los prejuicios étnicos/raciales afectan sus vidas, y cómo ellas han ido conscientemente adaptándose: en ciertas circunstancias aparentando motivos y formas de ser con las que no están de acuerdo, en otras rehusando fingir—tretas que le sirven para poder sobrevivir. Lo que la narrativa que se va hilando de las voces de las latinas nos muestra es cómo responden a determinadas situaciones en sus vidas para por lo menos crear pequeños espacios donde autodefinirse y auto-determinarse. La narrativa de las latinas que aquí presentamos es una narrativa subversiva en el sentido de que pone al descubierto lo que la sociedad, las iglesias y la academia han ignorado o rehusado tomar en consideración. Las voces de las latinas indican que la forma en que ellas intuyen, piensan y actúan, rompe con la hegemonía que establecen los que controlan las estructuras sociales y eclesiales. A lo mejor, de inmediato, las latinas no logremos mucho, es decir, seguiremos siendo invisibles para los grupos y estructuras dominantes. Pero el hecho de que el quehacer teológico *mujerista* les brinda un espacio para hablar y escucharse a sí mismas y a las demás, es un paso en la lucha de las latinas por ser sujetos de nuestra propia historia. El proveer una plataforma para las voces de las latinas es una manera de empezar a dar a conocer quiénes somos y lo que contribuimos a la sociedad. Sabemos, sin embargo, que nos queda mucho camino por recorrer para lograr que lo que decimos impacte a la sociedad en general y a nuestras iglesias en particular. Pero la narrativa que surge a partir de las voces de las latinas nos permite seguir concibiendo—y empezar a vivir—una vida "más allá" de la opresión precisamente porque nos permite leernos a nosotras mismas de una manera diferente a como nos leen los que nos oprimen y marginan.

CHAPTER 5

Conscience, Conscientization, and Moral Agency in *Mujerista* Theology

ONE OF THE MAIN GOALS OF MUJERISTA THEOLOGY is to enhance the development of the moral agency of Hispanic Women—a theme usually studied under what is called moral theology or ethics. In order further to enable the moral agency of Hispanic Women, it is important to understand the significance and role that conscience plays in the lives of Hispanic Women. Our starting place is Hispanic Women's fundamental assumptions in this regard—assumptions evident in our language and experiences. It is necessary also to show how these assumptions, because of the symbiotic relationship between Hispanic culture and Roman Catholicism, are grounded in the appreciation of conscience in this tradition. An understanding of conscience in Roman Catholicism will help clarify and reinforce its significance for Hispanic Women, and point out the part it plays in *mujerista* social ethics. Our brief analysis will be especially useful in helping us guard against the corrosion of the primacy of conscience being attempted by some of the Catholic hierarchy as well as in combating certain forms of fundamentalist biblical perspectives and influences to which Hispanic Women are exposed.

"*Mi conciencia me dice*," my conscience tells me, is a phrase often heard among Hispanic Women. Appealing to one's conscience in regular conversations, in discussions, and even arguments of small consequence, is not unusual for us. In the Hispanic culture conscience is not something that comes into play only when considering matters of grave importance or when making critical decisions. Conscience is invoked frequently but not lightly. Advising others, appealing to them to act according to their conscience, "*haz lo que tu conciencia to indique*," do what your conscience tells you, shaming others for what they have done or have decided to do, "*parece mentira que no re remuerda la conciencia*," it is a shame you have no remorse of conscience, indicating disagreement or condemnation of what another person has done by referring to conscience, or "*la conciencia no le va a dejar tranquilo*," her conscience is not going to let her have any peace—this kind of usage of "conscience" in our conversations is a daily occurrence. To make known that in small as well as in important issues conscience plays a role lets others know that you have considered the matter, that you are not talking off the top of your head, that you are investing yourself in what you say. It is also a way of giving yourself some importance, of making it known that you can think, have an opinion, decide.

The fact that we readily recognize the importance of conscience and the role it plays in our lives makes it all the more difficult to act *"a pesar de lo que mi conciencia me dice,"* in spite of what my conscience tells me, because of circumstances beyond our control. An awareness that we are repeatedly obliged, for whatever reasons, to act against something as central as our conscience contributes greatly to the sense of being oppressed. It is obvious to us that the violation of our conscience impinges on our honor, and such a violation is all the more painful since honor—a term we use to connote our personal worth as human beings—is another basic understanding and value in our culture. To act against one's conscience is to destroy one's integrity: How can you be a person of honor if you do not act according to what you know in the core of your being, in your conscience, is right?

In the context of Hispanic Women's religious experience in the U.S.A., the increased influence of the official Roman Catholic Church on Hispanic Women— or even its possibility—worries *mujerista* theologians because of recent blatant attempts by the Roman Curia to stifle opinions and understandings in the church to the point of threatening primacy of conscience (that is, threatening to subordinate conscience to obedience to Rome in ethical matters as well as in matters of church discipline).[1] This, we believe, disempowers Hispanic Women in our attempt to strengthen our moral agency, an essential component in our struggle for liberation.[2]

If Hispanic Women related very loosely to the official church structures in the U.S.A. as we do in our countries of origin, the task of *mujerista* social ethics in this matter would be only to enhance our sensitivity to conscience and to show how prominently it figures in the development of moral agency. But in the U.S.A., the Roman Catholic Church tends to have much more influence and control over our lives for two reasons. First, the Roman Catholic Church is operative at the neighborhood level through well-organized parishes that provide a strong presence of the official church among the people. This is quite different from the situation in our countries of origin, where, because of lack of priests and because the concept of belonging to a parish is not operative in most cases, the church lacks tight organization and is not able to exert significant control. Second, here in the U.S.A., because of the availability of means of communication, the church reaches people much more frequently than in Latin America and the Caribbean. Thus, the church has more opportunity to influence what people think and believe. Therefore, our task as *mujerista* theologians is much more extensive in regard to encouraging the growth of moral agency. Not only do we have to support and enhance its development but we also have to argue for it and help Hispanic Women to defend their right and duty to develop their own moral agency. This task is made obvious by the present practices of the Catholic hierarchy, which we now examine briefly.

Catholic Bishops' Understanding of Conscience Today

Although the teaching of the primacy of conscience has a long tradition in the church and is firmly entrenched in Roman Catholic theological understandings and teachings, in general it has been kept a secret from the faithful and does not enjoy much respect today among a significant number of members of the hierarchy. Their understanding of conscience, of its nature and function, is closely related to their understanding of the role they have in determining what is truth and their authority in imposing that truth. More and more, those who belong to the hierarchy of the church insist on making the authoritative hierarchical magisterium[3] the decisive factor in the teaching function of the church. Their claims do not stop there, however, but go much further. Addressing moral theologians in 1988, John Paul II stated that "conscience is the 'place' where man [sic] is illuminated by a light . . . [coming] from the Wisdom of the Word. . . ."[4] He then goes on to claim that since "the magisterium of the Church was created by Christ the Lord to enlighten conscience, then to appeal to that conscience precisely to contest the truth of what is taught by the magisterium implies rejection of the Catholic concept of the magisterium and moral conscience."[5] Here John Paul II is claiming that the magisterium of the church enlightens the Wisdom of the Word or at least he is equating that magisterium with the Wisdom of the Word.[6] This is in keeping with what one of his delegates had claimed a few years earlier when he said that there is "no substantial difference between the word of God and the word of the pope."[7]

This mode of reasoning by the hierarchy results in an amplification of the dogma of papal infallibility.[8] If what the magisterium says, even when not speaking in its official capacity of teacher of the faith—*ex cathedra*—has the same authority as the word of God, then what is to be the response of Catholics but total assent in all circumstances? Until now the hierarchy has not claimed that infallibility can be applied to moral issues for, though there are universal moral principles, the application of those principles always involves a particular situation and, therefore, there cannot be a universal application.[9] Furthermore, in moral matters the church's role is limited by the possibility of inadequacy. This has to do with the fact that as temporal beings persons are subject to evolution and change:

It is distinctly possible that what once was good, truly helpful to persons, truly serving this humanization and spiritualization, may someday become the opposite. Thus, while a Church teaching may well have been both adequate and accurate at one time, it does not follow that it will always be so. On the contrary, there may well be need for revision and rearticulation. What was once adequate teaching has become inadequate. And we ought not to be surprised.[10]

The hierarchy, like everyone else, can certainly have opinions about moral issues and no one disputes their right to make them public. However, what is of concern to moral theologians and Catholics in general is the hierarchy's vesting their opinions with the same authority as the word of God. This amplification of infallibility leaves no room for dissent regarding noninfallible matters, including moral issues one has to decide about, issues for which one is responsible. This position by the hierarchy violates the moral obligation to follow one's conscience.

Curtailment of Freedom of Conscience

To deny the possibility of dissent from noninfallible church teaching results in curtailment of freedom of conscience. When church authorities are pressed on this matter, they defend themselves by indicating that the issue is not the right to dissent from noninfallible teaching, but the right to dissent publicly.[11] But their insistence on obedience and their threats of punitive measures against those who do not abide by what they say, their emphasis on knowing and keeping the laws, all results ordinarily in an "authoritarian" conscience (the internalization of an external authority). The "authoritarian" conscience follows the law because it is where authority resides, not because it reflects or embodies one's own value judgment.[12] The main sin of an "authoritarian" conscience is disobedience. It has no right to question or to criticize. "If there seem to be reasons for criticizing the authority, it is the individual subject to the authority who must be at fault; and the mere fact that such an individual dares to criticize is *ipso facto* proof that he [sic] is guilty."[13]

There are two important corollaries to this discussion of "authoritarian" conscience that help to explain the present self-understanding of the Roman Curia and their insistence on not allowing public dissent. First, if obedience is the main virtue of an authoritarian conscience, then it is "blind" obedience that the hierarchy of the church believes it has the right and duty to demand from Catholics today.[14] Second, one of the main tenets of the authoritarian conscience is the fundamental inequality between the one in a position of authority and the rest of us. The one in authority has "the privilege of being the only one who does not follow another's will, but who himself [sic] wills; who is not a means but an end in himself [*sic*]; who created and is not created."[15] This tenet may explain the unwillingness of the hierarchy to accept the role of theologians in the magisterial function of the church; the hierarchy will not see themselves following, nor even being influenced by, anyone else.

This insight into authoritarian conscience also helps to explain the hierarchy's attempt to ignore the centuries-old Catholic belief in the *sensus fidelium*— "the body of the faithful as a whole, anointed as they are by the Holy One (cf. Jn. 2:20, 27), cannot err in matters of belief."[16] The *sensus fidelium* certainly does not assert the inerrancy of the faithful apart from the hierarchy. Nor does it provide, I believe, for the inerrancy of the hierarchy apart from the faithful unless the hierarchy considers itself as separate from the People of God: "Thanks to a supernatural sense of the faith which characterizes the People as a whole, it manifests this unerring quality when 'from the bishops down to the last member of the laity,' it shows universal agreement in matters of faith and morals."[17]

The "authoritarian conscience" that the church hierarchy is promoting feels good to one who is obedient, feeling dependent, powerless, and sinful. On the other hand, the "authoritarian conscience" feels guilt whenever a person has a feeling of strength, independence, productiveness, and pride. Paradoxically, then, the "guilty conscience" becomes the basis for a "good conscience."[18] The "good conscience" helps one to move away from understanding conscience apart from the rest of the person by making it possible for one to see conscience, not in relation to an external norm, but as a revelation of who the person is. One then begins to understand that

> not only are actions expressive and revelatory of the person, but by one's actions the individual shapes and constitutes the self as agent. . . . Truly the individual human person has the opportunity and the destiny to create one's own moral self.[19]

This is the understanding which is common, though mostly not consciously cultivated, among Hispanic Women, as witnessed by the examples given at the beginning of this chapter. The understanding of the "good conscience" is also an understanding we claim is faithful to the more traditional view of conscience in the Catholic tradition.

Historical Developments in the Catholic Tradition

Unfortunately, from the sixteenth century to the second half of the twentieth century moral theology in the Roman Catholic tradition became a very practical discipline concerned with training confessors for the Sacrament of Penance especially in their role as judges about the existence and gravity of sin. Moral theology was cut off from its speculative roots as well as from dogmatic and spiritual theology.[20]

This shift had to do in great part with the Reformation and the Counter-Reformation.[21] It is beyond the scope of this work to analyze at length the intricacies of self-understanding of the Catholic church during this period and the repercussions for moral theology in general. Suffice it to say that to the threat presented by the Protestant Reformation the Catholic church responded by convening the Council of Trent in 1545. Trent sought to homogenize church teaching and to centralize church practice in attempt to protect the Catholic church. Its disciplinary decrees were given predominance and the post-Tridentine popes vigorously carried them out. That a siege mentality was indeed developed by the post-Tridentine church is clear, for example, in the establishment of the Holy Office. Though at times difficult to understand and accept, the fact seems to be that "the motivation behind such defensive measures was often a genuine pastoral fear that the faith of the mass of the people would be endangered by 'heresy' and therefore needed to be protected from it."[22] But this positive motivation does not change the fact that the training priests received and the way the main purpose of the Sacrament of Penance was understood, in view of this need to "protect the faithful," resulted in a most legalistic understanding of the nature and role of conscience.

Catholic moral theology entered the twentieth century totally preoccupied with conscience. Its basic approach to conscience had been minimalist and legalistic, resulting in "an extrinsic understanding of morality and the moral life."[23] Conscience had been considered apart from the person. Therefore, usually no consideration has been given to the person as a whole as the doer of the action. This has meant that the understanding of conscience has been almost exclusively rationalistic, with no consideration given to affectivity. It is important to note that, even though at times Catholic moral teachings about conscience have curtailed and diminished primacy of conscience, primacy of conscience per se—the obligation to follow conscience above anything else—has never been denied.

Beginning with the Second Vatican Council, the understanding of conscience has moved away from the minimalist and juridical approach of ages past and has attempted to be more holistic and expansive. Most moral theologians today stay away from a concise definition of conscience and instead attempt to understand conscience by dealing with it from different perspectives. Though one can still find some theologians who define conscience as a faculty, for example, Bernard Häring,[24] even in those cases the attempt is made to broaden the concept of conscience by relating it to both "the practical intellect seeking truth and the natural yearning of the will and heart of man [sic] for the true good."[25] Nowadays when the subject is conscience, emphasis is placed on the need to include consideration of the emotions, of affectivity.[26] As a matter of fact, conscience is seen as "the spiritual instinct for self-preservation arising from the urge for complete unity and harmony . . . which is possible only through unity with the world of the true and the good."[27] This unity with the true and the world is not to be seen as an abstraction or an ideal but rather refers to the concrete, "the order of experience in which the self is existentially implicated."[28]

Looked at from the perspective of Christianity, conscience is said to have "a voice of itself, but not a word of its own; it is the word of Christ (spoken in creation, in the Incarnation of the Word, through the influence of grace) which speaks through this voice."[29] Furthermore, the natural function of conscience is

to make us partakers of the eternal law of God through the created nature around us and through our rational nature. Our bond with the natural moral law is an exalted participation in the eternal law of God manifested in our conscience whose natural function is to reveal our likeness to God.[30]

This results not in direct revelation by God to a particular person but rather a conferring by the Holy Spirit on conscience of "a delicacy of perception and tenderness of tact so that in the light of divine revelation projected on all the circumstances in which one is involved in particular instances one readily discerns the divine will."[31]

But this does not mean that the person has nothing to contribute of her own in making a decision. On the contrary, the rational insights of the person are her responsibility; conscience as the voice of God simply impels one to act according to those rational insights. Therefore, conscience cannot "draw truth from its own obscure depth or even create it."[32] But for many centuries the church has insisted that conscience does have to conform to what the person has come to believe is true, correct, and valid. For example, Thomas Aquinas (c. 1225–74), a key figure in all theologies, dealt with the obligatory aspect of conscience, asserting that conscience binds whether it is correct or erroneous.[33] However, it must be noted that Aquinas insisted on the fact that it is sinful to follow an erroneous conscience if it is wrong because of ignorance that is voluntary or vincible, which Aquinas calls "consequent ignorance." He indicated that there are two kinds of consequent ignorance. "First, and positively, the ignorance may be willed, as when somebody chooses not to be informed, in order to find some excuse for sin or for not avoiding it . . . this is called affected ignorance. Second, and negatively, ignorance may be voluntary . . . :

it is an ignorance of what we can and should know."[34] However, if it is invincibly erroneous, conscience does excuse from guilt. One can readily see, therefore, that when there is no agreement as to what is true, correct, and valid, even if the person one is disagreeing with is in a position of authority and power, one may not obey that person in opposition to the judgment of one's conscience.

One's right to freedom of conscience is based on the absolute duty one has never to act against conscience. In this context the term *right* involves both the person claiming to have the right and the claim that such a right makes on the institutional church, on the Roman Curia. One question, then, is whether one can make such a claim on the institutional church. Rights are based on the ultimate end of the person, and "end" for *mujerista* theology is understood as the liberation of the person. The question, then, is whether the institutional church exists to help the person attain her end, or whether the end of the person is secondary to the end of the church. The institutional church is a human construct, a sociological and historical reality—just as the law of the Sabbath—created for the person and not the person for the institutional church. Therefore, the faithful have this claim on the institutional church: it must recognize the right of the person to follow one's conscience. This means that the faithful must have essential, inner freedom, as well as effective, external freedom. The institutional church must not coerce anyone to act against conscience, and this means that each person must have "immunity from external force compelling one to act against one's conscience, and the 'full possession of privilege,' the faculty and freedom to perform these actions which conscience enjoins, without let or hindrance."[35]

The attempt by the hierarchy to restrict dissent contradicts the documents issues by the Second Vatican Council as well as the new Code of Canon Law, both official church documents.[36] For example, in the Vatican II Dogmatic Constitution on the Church, #25 indicates that the appropriate response to noninfallible teaching is *obsequium religiosum*.[37] This phrase has been translated as "religious assent," "submission," "due respect." With very few exceptions, regardless of how it is translated, theologians understand this phrase as not precluding dissent. This was the understanding, too, of those who wrote the document. When it was being formulated, a revision was requested that would make specific the possibility of dissent. The official response to the request was that such a revision was not necessary because the phrasing of *obsequium religiosum* meant that dissent was possible.[38]

Two issues raised here of particular interest to *mujerista* theology are the role of theologians in the magisterium of the church, and the way the hierarchy treats the laity. The magisterial function, the teaching function of the church as such, is not limited to the teaching function of the hierarchy, though that is the prevailing operating understanding of the Roman Curia. The fact is that the term *the authoritative hierarchical magisterium,* much used today, only came into existence in the nineteenth century. But more important than the "recent" date of this understanding is the fact that "history shows instances of errors in hierarchical teaching which were later corrected, at least partially due to theological dissent."[39]

All Catholics participate to a certain extent in the teaching function of the church.[40] Through Baptism all Christians receive the gifs of the Spirit and share in the prophetic and teaching office of Jesus. This does not mean that there is no hierarchical teaching function but it does mean that "there can be no absolute division between the hierarchy as the teaching church and the rest of the faithful as the learning church."[41] The role of the hierarchical teaching office of the church is to proclaim and safeguard Christian faith. The role of theology is "to understand and interpret the reality of the Christian mystery in the world in which we live."[42] Obviously these roles, though different, are not contradictory. On the contrary, they are interrelated, but distinct.

> The role of theology is not totally absorbed into or entirely subordinated to the hierarchical magisterium, but theology must give due weight to the authoritative hierarchical teachings. Yes, error and heresy are possible in theology. Yes, the hierarchical teaching office has a God-given role to protect the church from heresy. But in making such judgments the hierarchical teaching office is somewhat dependent on theology and, in all but its solemn statements, is subject to the possibility of error.[43]

What about the possibility that public dissent from noninfallible teaching causes scandal? Scandal has to do with an action or omission that might cause others to sin. Scandal also has to do with the wonderment and confusion caused by an action or omission. This great concern of the hierarchy about scandal is rooted in the paternalistic and authoritarian manner in which they view the people of God. For them, the faithful are poor and ignorant, in need of protection and guidance. But the faithful are not ignorant. Since Vatican II, an increasing number of the laity have become well educated in matters of theology. The faithful are far from being poor sheep who can be easily manipulated or who cannot judge for themselves.[44]

> Too often we worry about protecting the weak and the scandal that might be given to them. What about the scandal of the strong? Many intelligent lay Catholics would be scandalized if Catholic theologians were not searching for better understandings and proposing new theories. Look at the number who have left the church because the Christian message seems to be no longer meaningful for them in their world. At the very least there are both weak and strong in the church.[45]

Instead of being so concerned about scandal, the hierarchy of the church should carry out vigorously its theological task of increasing religious education, of assisting in the formation of conscience, including imparting knowledge about what many call the best kept secret in the church: primacy of conscience. Formation of conscience must also include education about the rights of all the members of the church in all areas, including religion, and including the right to dissent from noninfallible church teaching.

Conscience in Historical Protestant, Fundamentalist, and Pentecostal Churches

Another reason why it is important for *mujerista* social ethics to argue for and defend the development of Hispanic Women's moral agency has to do with the fact that 20 percent of the Hispanics in the U.S.A. belong or relate to Protestant denominations. In the Protestant tradition, because of the emphasis on faith over works, there is a tendency to understand conscience as playing a theological rather than an ethical role. The function of conscience here has been to make people aware of their transgressions and the consequences. The emphasis has been upon guilt and damnation, reminding people that in their life of faith they must face an angry God. This tendency in much of Protestant theology results, in general, in understanding conscience as having no directive role before the action takes place.[46]

This is because in Protestantism sin is peripheral to the relation of the person to God. Salvation comes through "God's imputation of righteousness to persons."[47] Therefore, to discuss the proper role of conscience or its nature is not important because an emphasis on morality could lead to legalism. Luther's and Calvin's reaction against the Catholic morality of their epoch, intent as it was on detailing sin and appropriate penance and restitution, led them to insist that persons cannot earn salvation on the basis of moral merit. Although this is not what the Catholic doctrine was or is, "the practical preoccupation with sins as deterrents to union with God" does give some basis to this Protestant understanding.[48] Such reaction led Protestantism to think of the moral life as not having the same "religious seriousness" as before. "It is serious, but it is set in a different religious and theological context. Ethics and moral theology no longer have the same theological significance,"[49] and conscience is not important since it is understood mainly in reference to sin.

In fundamentalist, Pentecostal, and storefront churches, this general Protestant theological understanding of conscience, coupled with an emphasis on discipline and obedience, greatly threatens the role of conscience as one of the main aids of self-determination for Hispanic Women. Much of what we have already said regarding an authoritarian conscience is applicable in these churches. Whether based on a fundamentalist understanding of the Bible, or on the authority of the ministers who claim to have been "baptized in the Spirit," members of these churches follow what is understood as the law because it is where authority resides and not because it reflects or embodies their own value judgment.[50]

It is important to examine the fact that the great majority of these churches have male ministers and that their so-called rules of discipline have to do much more with directing and controlling the behavior of women than that of men. Many of the rules of discipline, for example, involve dress codes for women, and forbid women to wear makeup and jewelry—something Hispanic Women find greatly restrictive. Since the main sin of an "authoritarian conscience" is disobedience, Hispanic Women in these churches often find themselves in internal turmoil at the same time that they are ostracized for such things as wearing pants or painting their lips.[51]

The fundamentalist or pietistic way in which the Bible is used in these churches also leads to an "authoritarian conscience." The fact is that fundamentalist use of the Bible denies any mediation between the Bible as the word of God and the way the Bible is understood. Even if the way the Bible is used by Pentecostals were understood along the sacramental lines proposed by some, the fact remains that what the Bible says is equated to the way it is understood, and the Bible is considered authoritative in all areas of life.[52] Furthermore, the way the Bible is preached, what the ministers say the Bible says, is understood to be *indeed* what the word of God is by the majority of Hispanic Pentecostals and fundamentalists. In addition, what the ministers say the Bible says is directly applied to concrete situations, resulting not in responsible Christian living but in oppressive situations in which "blind" obedience is demanded. Such use of the Bible in these churches promotes an exclusively deontological type of ethics which tends to diminish the moral agency of Hispanic Women.[53]

From Conscience to Moral Consciousness and Conscientization

Understanding conscience in a holistic way, as an integral part of the person and not as a faculty that can be ascertained and examine separately, focuses on the person as agent of her own life, able to determine, and responsible for, who she is and what she does.[54] This allows seeing the moral life as other than obedience to extrinsic laws, and formation of conscience as more than a matter of learning laws. One of the important consequences of focusing on the person as agent instead of on conscience as an isolated part of the individual is that ethical considerations are not confined just to decision making but rather focus on "the self who continues from decision through decision and who actually affirms and creates one's moral self in and through those decisions."[55] Conscience, then, should not be understood as a faculty or power but instead should be identified with the "moral consciousness" of the person.[56] Consciousness here refers to awareness of oneself as agent, awareness of oneself in one's own experiencing, understanding, judging, and deciding.[57]

Consciousness starts at the level of sensitivity at which one perceives and senses. Human beings share this level of consciousness with animals, but can transcend it. The second level transcends the first level, "presupposes, complements and incorporates it (sublation),"[58] a process that continues through all the levels. At this level human beings understand what they have sensed. The third level is the one at which we judge. The key operation of the fourth level is to choose or decide. It is at this level, therefore, that consciousness becomes moral. At the level of moral consciousness one asks questions about value; then these questions are answered in judgment of values; and finally one decides in accordance with the judgment of values. This decision is always made according to the person's—the moral agent's—"exigence for self-consistency, for making one's decision, one's choices in accord with one's best judgment about what he or she should do."[59] And, for a Hispanic Woman, what she should do has to do with survival, and liberation.

Formation of moral consciousness has to be understood quite differently from the way formation of conscience has previously been understood, as instruction in the law. In *mujerista* moral theology conscience is understood as the agent herself as morally conscious, and since consciousness is constitutive of the human person as agent, the formation of moral consciousness has to do with enabling the process of conscientization of the person. Conscientization is an integral part of the understanding of an the struggle for liberation and involves:

(1) recognizing the distinction between nature in its inevitability and culture in its changeability; (2) unmasking the myths that allow oppressors to dominate society by blurring this distinction; and (3) exploring the alternatives available under the fundamental "generative theme" of our epoch, namely, liberation.[60]

For *mujerista* moral theology there are two especially significant points about the process of conscientization: the importance of praxis in its relationship to liberation, and the meaning and purpose of generative themes. Insofar as praxis is concerned, conscientization is an ongoing process of critical reflection on action, which leads to critical awareness, and this in turn becomes an essential building block in deciding the next action. This reflection on action is one of the moments of praxis and it cannot be separated from action:

One cannot change consciousness outside of praxis. But it must be emphasized that the praxis by which consciousness is changed is not only action but action and reflection. Thus there is a unity between practice and theory in which both are constructed, shaped and reshaped in constant movement from practice to theory, then back to a new practice. . . . [Conscientization] must . . . be a critical attempt to reveal reality. . . . It must . . . be related to political involvement. There is no conscientization if the result is not the conscious action of the oppressed as an exploited social class, struggling for liberation. What is more, no one conscienticizes anyone else. The educator and the people together conscienticize themselves, thanks to the dialectical movement which relates critical reflection on past action to the continuous struggle.[61]

Another element of conscientization that needs further explanation is that of the generative themes. Generative themes are the issues that are important to the person, those issues about which she feels the strongest. The deep feelings, the emotions around an issue incite the person to action; they motivate her to take the initiative and move out of her apathy.[62] The overarching generative theme for Hispanic Women is the binomial survival-liberation. In the process of conscientization, in the formation of moral consciousness, this generative theme unfolds, gaining specificity and thus becoming the basis for praxis.

At the end of the previous chapter we presented some of these specifics by elucidating how the Hispanic Women whose voices are presented in this work value themselves, and know that they must act for themselves. These two themes will always play a key role in their process of conscientization, in further enabling their own self-determination and their participation in the liberative praxis of the Hispanic community. Other themes emerging from the "translations" also have an important role to play in the process of conscientization. One very directly connected to survival-liberation is the value of life for Hispanic Women.

It was difficult for most of the women interviewed to imagine that anyone would be so cruel as to make a mother choose which one of her children would be killed. Most of them refused to choose and insisted on trying to find a way out of the situation. Women who often deal with their own survival and that of their children or their people with such determination that it seems almost effortless could not decide in this case because they refused to think it could really happen. Likewise, for most of the women, it presented no moral dilemma to have to steal to feed a baby. But the example for them was farfetched because they take for granted that life is so important that there will always be someone to help the mother of a hungry child. In their own lives they have been so creative about survival, they have managed with the help of others to survive, why would it be different for this mother I was telling them about?

Life is life if it is linked to others, whether to their people or their children. It is not a matter of Hispanic Women denying themselves, sacrificing themselves for their children or their people. It is their sense of responsibility to their families and communities that becomes their standard for judging and doing. They do for their children and their people because that is what fulfills them, what *"me hace sentir satisfecha,"* makes me feel satisfied, as Inez says. María has found such joy and satisfaction in bringing up her children that it is difficult for her to understand mothers who take no responsibility for their children or have no time for them. She tries to be understanding and not to criticize, but she could not resist sharing how, when her daughters complain about their children, she refuses to listen to them. One of her proudest moments was when the children were small and she went to a parent-teacher conference. When she introduced herself, the teacher said for all to hear, "You do not know how much I have been wanting to meet a mother who has twelve children and has time to help them with their homework and to play with them." For Julieta, her real concern is not that God might not have forgiven her for having had to work as a prostitute, but that her husband will tell her children. All she has done is for her children; how they think of her is most important. It is impossible to describe her tenderness with her five-year-old son who hovered around us during our long conversation.

In the midst of all the comings and goings of life, there is always the presence of a God who understands, who forgives, who is on their side; there is no doubt about it. Marta knows that the church is not on her side, but that has nothing to do with her relationship with God. "I am no agnostic," she says with determination. For Inez, Eucharist happens in the people's celebration she organized in the basement of her church on Holy Thursday. That is when God is really present, not in the ceremonies of the church where the people "did not have a chance to say anything." God gives guidance to Olivia in everything, and for Adela there is no doubt that God puts her on the road she must travel. María prays to every saint anyone mentions. She says that with so many children she has many different kinds of needs and the saints are like friends who help her—a dimension of the divine in her life. Her closing words in the interview were to express her desire to serve her God and her people. Lupe has come to realize in her heart what she knew in her head, that her work with the poor people of the community, with her *viejitos,* is not separate from knowing God for it is through them that God is known.

Generative themes provide the starting place for the process of conscientization. These themes can and should be used to enable Hispanic Women to understand how they make decisions, the values those decisions reflect, how the socioeconomic situation in which they live affects their decision making. Listening to Lupe, Inez, Marta, and the other women, it is clear what it is that awakens and sustains them in the development of their moral consciousness. This is why these generative words are the jumping off point into the process of conscientization.

The process of conscientization involves the totality of the person. It operates at the empirical level in which one perceives and senses, at the intellectual level of understanding, and at the rational level of judgment in which women, by defining themselves in the context of struggling to survive and judging by a standard of responsibility and community building, affirm themselves.[63] It is at this level that one becomes moral because values enter the picture, in this case the values of responsibility and care. The Hispanic Women heard in this study repeatedly emphasize the centrality in their lives of responsibility and community building expressed through care. María asserts that she is very responsible perhaps because she grew up without her mother and had to start making decisions for herself at such a young age. And she readily admits to loving her children to excess—the starting point for her involvement with her community *"que me encanta,"* which enchants me, which I love, because it is so satisfying. Marta's central reason for divorce was her responsibility and care for her children. But she knows that intimately linked with her concern for her children is caring and being responsible for herself. For Lupe, care for and responsibility to the community are part of her own inward journey to know and value herself.

Therefore, for *mujerista* moral theology it is essential to understand these values of responsibility and care as the response of a moral consciousness which has at its very heart loving and caring for oneself. Authentic love of self becomes the basis for a relationship with the divine, with God transformed from one who is radically beyond the person as agent, to one radically immanent to the agent, the God who is the *"algo me lo decía dentro de mí,"* knew inside me that I had to go, of Adela, or the daily guidance from God of which Olivia speaks so readily.

The research done for this work illumines only in passing the second aspect of generative themes within the process of conscientization, the problematization of the themes themselves. The themes become issues when the Hispanic Women realize that their self-determination is thwarted by factors which they cannot control and which are unjust. The problematization of what is important to Hispanic Women is precisely one of the goals of the process of conscientization; that is the spark of suspicion that will move them to liberative praxis.[64] What this process entails and how it happens is beyond the scope of this work but needs to be indicated here in order to complete the explanation of conscientization.

The process of conscientization calls for us to accept our freedom and responsibility without which we cannot truly participate in liberative praxis. An intrinsic part of this process is the realization of the dangers involved in judging and deciding, the two basic ones being human finitude and sinfulness.

Finitude is different from sinfulness. As a result of our finitude we are limited; we see only a partial aspect of reality; we cannot achieve all possible goods or values. Human sinfulness, on the other hand, stems not from creation itself but from the actions of ourselves or others and can be seen in the sinfulness both of the individual and of the society in which we live.[65]

But the process of conscientization pushes us beyond realization to the overcoming of those dangers. This requires a strong spirit of openness which presses us always to search deeper and more ardently for what is true and what is good; it impels us to a liberative praxis that has as its goal the creation of nonoppressive structures. This kind of openness is what humility is all about. Humility is not a matter of self-effacement and self-negation but of being open always to new ways of being responsible and of caring.

The process of conscientization is a personal process. For us Hispanic Women what is personal is related to the Hispanic community. Besides our own communities there are different communities that we Hispanic Women must relate to in our process of conscientization. There is the community of the "popular church," the community which lives a Christianity that brings together the tenets of Catholicism with those of Amerindian and African religions, as well as with the day-to-day struggle for survival of Hispanic Women.[66] Then there are the other communities of struggle: the feminist community, the African American community—especially the Womanist community, the gay and lesbian community, the Native American community, the Asian American community, and so forth. Our dialogue with these communities results in a deep praxis of solidarity which resists any attempts to engage in horizontal violence.[67]

For *mujerista* moral theology to insist on the understanding of moral consciousness presented here is imperative. Our task as *mujerista* theologians is to continue to develop such understanding and to facilitate the development of moral consciousness of Hispanic Women in all circumstances. Given the centrality of the struggle for liberation in the lives of Hispanic Women, this is perhaps the best way in which *mujerista* theology can carry on both its creative role and its critical role, central roles that each and every true theology is called upon to play.

IN THE DECADE THAT HAS GONE BY SINCE I WROTE THIS BOOK, ecclesial authorities continue to insist on obedience as the essential virtue. I think mainly of Roman Catholic authorities, but I think this also happens with officials of the Protestant churches. Those in charge continue to think that what we in the pew must do is to obey while they—mostly men—understand their pastoral activity in a way that promotes an "authoritarian conscience." Such a conscience limits and hampers instead of helping one be a responsible person, responsible for oneself and one's actions. An "authoritarian conscience" is an effective way of controlling, dominating, and oppressing. This is why today more than ever, from our *mujerista* perspective, we insist on the need for educating a liberating conscience, for a process of conscientization that helps us to be responsible for ourselves and to become true subjects of our own personal and communitarian history.

The process of conscientization continues to be, from the *mujerista* perspective, a practical and effective way of struggling for the liberation of Hispanic women. It is important to note three elements in this process. First, conscientization helps us Hispanic women confront ourselves: to deal with how we have internalized the "myths" of the oppressor, how we have internalized the oppressor to such a point that we become strangers even to our own selves. The process of conscientization happens in community and for the sake of community. True, it is a process that one can facilitate for another, but still each one has to engage in it personally. Conscientization has as its goal to explore alternatives. What does the future that we are struggling for look like? What is the future that we want, that we prefer? What do we have to do to make that future a reality? It is in this sense that conscientization, a process that never ends, becomes an effective way of knowing ourselves, and of understanding that we know reality only when we become responsible for it, and embrace it by accepting it or struggling to change it.

Second, because it is personal but not individualistic, conscientization is not something that happens in isolation. For Hispanic women, family functions as community and is not limited only to those with whom we have blood ties. Family is so central that we understand subjectivity as an intrinsic element of our personality but one that happens in view of others. Conscience, one modality of our subjectivity, is present and works in our daily lives. Conscience helps us establish who we are and how we are, and this happens in the middle of relating to others. The process of conscientization makes clear, therefore, that subjectivity and moral agency evolve in the midst of community and in-so-far as we participate in community. Moral agency is nothing else than the way we take responsibility for who we are and what we do individually and communally.

Finally, the process of conscientization helps us understand that the moral agency of a person is ongoing and is not at work only in the moment when we have to take a decision. We become subjects of our own history in the midst of the innumerable decisions, more or less important and weighty, that we take every day. The process of conscientization allows us to see how what we decide becomes part of who we are, helping or hindering us to struggle for our liberation, for fullness of life. The process of conscientization makes it possible for a person to see the connections between the different spheres of her life. It makes it possible to see the relevancy of what she learns in one area for other areas of life, to understand that the way she faces personal relationships may have to do with the way she is not valued at work or to see that the way she confronts an abusive boss helps her to do the same with an abusive companion. In other words, the process of conscientization facilitates the development of a person in a holistic way.

Síntesis del Capítulo 5
Conciencia, conscientización y agencia moral en la teología *mujerista*

Hemos investigado, como parte del compromiso de la teología *mujerista* de ser una praxis liberadora, el significado que tiene y el papel que juega para nosotras las mujeres hispanas la conciencia. El fin ha sido contribuir al desarrollo de la agencia moral de las hispanas.

"Mi conciencia me dice" es una frase usada a menudo por mujeres hispanas. Es común para nosotras recurrir a "la conciencia" aun en discusiones de poca importancia, aunque eso no quiere decir que tomemos la conciencia a la ligera. Cuando aconsejamos a otros y otras a menudo decimos, "haz lo que tu conciencia te indique". A veces apelamos a la conciencia para avergonzar a alguien e inducirlo a hacer lo que debe: "parece mentira que no te remuerda la conciencia". Y con frecuencia indicamos nuestro desacuerdo con alguien refiriéndonos a la conciencia: "la conciencia no lo va a dejar tranquilo". Esta manera tan corriente de referirnos a la conciencia es una forma de dejarle saber a los demás que uno ha pensado seriamente lo que dice, que uno tiene su propia opinión acerca de una persona o un hecho, y que uno toma sus propias decisiones.

El que reconozcamos lo importante que es la conciencia y el papel que juega en nuestras vidas hace difícil que actuemos en contra de ella, "a pesar de lo que mi conciencia me dice", aun en circunstancias que no controlamos. Uno de los elementos principales de la opresión de las mujeres hispanas es el saber que repetidamente estamos obligadas a actuar en contra de lo que nos dicta la conciencia. Nosotras relacionamos el hacer lo que nos dicta la conciencia con el honor—lo que nos da valor como seres humanos, elemento importante de la cultura hispana. El actuar en contra de la conciencia nos deshonra y nos lleva a la destrucción personal.

Cuando las teólogas *mujeristas* examinamos el rol de "la conciencia", nos preocupa la influencia que tiene en este asunto la Iglesia Católica ya que recientemente la curia romana ha tratado de suprimir lo que ha enseñado tradicionalmente sobre la primacía de la conciencia, tratando de subordinar la conciencia personal a la obediencia a Roma en materia moral tanto como en disciplina eclesiástica. Este cambio obstruye el desarrollo de la agencia moral de mujeres hispanas, elemento central de nuestra lucha por la liberación.

En nuestros países de origen, la mayoría de las mujeres hispanas tiene poca relación con la Iglesia Católica "oficial". Pero aquí en los EE.UU. la Iglesia Católica tiene la posibilidad de ejercer mayor control sobre las hispanas por dos razones. Primero, en este país la Iglesia tiene una estructura de parroquia mucho más organizada mientras que en muchos de nuestros países de origen faltan sacerdotes y no hay una organización parroquial efectiva. Segundo, en este país la Iglesia Católica oficial tiene amplio acceso a los medios de comunicación, y las hispanas escuchamos la radio y vemos la televisión mucho más que las mujeres en nuestros países de origen. Por lo tanto, la Iglesia tiene oportunidad de ejercer mayor influencia sobre lo que pensamos y cómo actuamos. Es por eso que nuestra tarea como teólogas *mujeristas* de apoyar el desarrollo de la agencia moral de las mujeres hispanas es tan importante. Es más, nos toca a las teólogas *mujeristas* defender el derecho y la obligación que tenemos de desarrollar y obedecer nuestras conciencias, enseñanza tradicional de la Iglesia Católica.

La posición de los obispos católicos sobre la conciencia hoy día

Aunque la doctrina de la primacía de la conciencia es muy antigua, en general no es una enseñanza conocida por la mayoría de los fieles y hoy en día no es una doctrina muy respetada—en términos prácticos—por muchos en la jerarquía de la Iglesia. La jerarquía hoy día tiende a pensar en la naturaleza y función de la conciencia en relación con el rol casi exclusivo que cree tener en determinar qué es la verdad, y en la obligación que tiene como jerarquía de lograr que su perspectiva de la verdad sea aceptada por todos. Cada vez más un mayor número de obispos parece creer que la autoridad de la jerarquía es el factor decisivo en la función educativa de la Iglesia. Es más, Juan Pablo II y algunos miembros de la jerarquía han afirmado que la Biblia y la jerarquía tienen la misma función en determinar cómo actúa y lo que cree la feligresía católica. Como dijo un delegado del Vaticano no hace mucho, "no hay diferencia sustancial entre la palabra de Dios y la palabra del Papa". Esta manera de pensar amplía el dogma de la infalibilidad papal la cual se debe invocar sólo en cuestiones de fe. Esta manera de pensar no permite estar en desacuerdo con enseñanzas de la Iglesia que no son infalibles y pone a las católicas y a los católicos en un dilema: hacer lo que nos dice la conciencia o lo que dice el Vaticano.

Restricción de la libertad de conciencia

Negar la posibilidad de estar en desacuerdo con las enseñanzas no infalibles de la

Iglesia tiene como resultado disminuir la importancia y el papel de la conciencia. La insistencia por parte de la jerarquía en que hay que obedecer, y la amenaza de medidas punitivas contra quienes no lo hacen, el énfasis que los obispos ponen en saber y obedecer las leyes de la Iglesia—todo esto lleva a una "conciencia autoritaria" que impone desde afuera la moral de la persona. La "conciencia autoritaria" piensa que no hay derecho a preguntar, a criticar; el pecado principal para ella es la desobediencia. Personas con una "conciencia autoritaria" creen que deben obedecer a ciegas y se sienten culpables cuando se ven fuertes, independientes, orgullosos de quiénes son y lo que piensan. Personas con "conciencia autoritaria" creen que las personas en posiciones de autoridad son superiores a ellas.

Las personas con autoridad parecen promover la "conciencia autoritaria" creyéndose con el privilegio de dictar lo que los demás deben hacer, pensar, ser; las personas con autoridad piensan que son, no un medio, sino el fin en sí: no se ponen al servicio de la verdad sino que se ven más bien como dictando la verdad. Es posible que ésta sea la razón por la cual la jerarquía hoy día no quiere que las teólogas y los teólogos participen en la función magisterial de la Iglesia: la jerarquía no puede aceptar el ser influenciada por otros, no puede dejarse llevar por lo que otros dicen. Ésta también puede ser la razón por la cual la jerarquía hoy día parece ignorar la creencia en el *sensus fidelium,* creencia que la Iglesia ha mantenido por siglos y siglos. El *sensus fidelium* es la creencia de que los fieles, desde los obispos hasta el último miembro de la feligresía, guiados por el Espíritu Santo, no yerran en sus creencias. Es verdad que los fieles no se pueden considerar en esto aparte de la jerarquía; pero la jerarquía tampoco puede considerarse incapaz de errar sino se considera antes como parte del Pueblo de Dios, sino se ve intrínsecamente ligada al resto de los fieles.

El reverso de la "conciencia autoritaria" es la "conciencia buena", que no se entiende como algo aparte del resto de la persona, sino que le ayuda a ver que lo importante no son las normas externas sino la coherencia de la persona. Para la "conciencia buena" lo que se hace no sólo revela quién uno es, sino también lo ayuda a uno a constituirse en sujeto; lo ayuda a verse y actuar como agente moral que se auto-regula.

Desarrollo histórico de la tradición católica

Desgraciadamente desde el siglo XVI hasta la segunda mitad del siglo XX la teología moral en la Iglesia Católica se alejó de sus raíces dogmáticas y espirituales y se enfocó casi exclusivamente en educar a los confesores como si fueran jueces. Este cambio se debió en gran parte a la mentalidad de sitio que prevaleció en la Iglesia a partir de la Reforma Protestante. El Concilio de Trento en 1545 homogeneizó las enseñanzas de la Iglesia y centralizó su autoridad tratando de proteger a la Iglesia del "asedio" protestante. Fue por eso que se le dio tanta importancia a los decretos disciplinarios y que se estableció la Oficina del Santo Oficio para vigilar la ortodoxia de la fe.

Durante todos estos siglos la teología moral católica estuvo totalmente preocupada con la conciencia entendida como una función racionalista, sin ninguna función o influencia afectiva. La consciencia se consideraba en forma minimalista repitiendo o reflejando un orden objetivo, y en forma legalista obedeciendo leyes. Esto llevó a un entendimiento de la moralidad y la vida moral como algo extrínseco a la persona. Pero aun durante estos siglos, aunque a veces se trató de restarle importancia a la primacía de la conciencia, nunca llegó a negarse que uno esta obligado, por encima de todo, a hacer lo que la conciencia dicta.

Es a partir del Concilio Vaticano Segundo que la perspectiva jurídica de la conciencia ha ido cambiando. Aunque de vez en cuando todavía se habla de la conciencia como una facultad humana, hoy se entiende la conciencia mayormente como una clase de "instinto espiritual" para la preservación de la persona que surge del deseo de unidad y armonía. Esta unidad y armonía no son conceptos abstractos sino que se refieren a lo concreto, a las experiencias en las cuales el ser mismo de la persona está involucrado.

Desde la perspectiva cristiana puede decirse que la conciencia tiene una voz propia pero no una palabra propia; su palabra es la de Cristo que habla a través de la creación, la encarnación del Verbo, y la gracia divina. Los puntos de vista que se tienen—nuestros entendimientos racionales—son responsabilidad propia, pero es la voz de Dios, la gracia de Dios, lo que nos lleva a actuar de acuerdo con esos entendimientos. La conciencia, por lo tanto, no crea la verdad pero la persona sí tiene que actuar de acuerdo con lo que considera que es la verdad aunque esté equivocada.

La obligación de actuar de acuerdo a lo que dicta la conciencia va mano a mano con el hecho de que los seres humanos tenemos libre albedrío. En la teología *mujerista* vemos que el libre albedrío está encaminado a la meta de la persona que no puede ser sino su liberación/salvación. Los intentos que parece hacer la Iglesia oficial de controlar la conciencia, de limitar el sentido del *sensus fidelium* y del libre albedrío nos lleva a preguntarnos si la Iglesia institucional cree que existe para ayudar a la persona a lograr su meta o si la persona es una consideración secundaria. La Iglesia institucional es una realidad sociológica e histórica creada para la persona y no al revés—al igual que lo fue para Jesús la ley y el sábado. Es por eso que la persona puede insistir en que la Iglesia debe reconocer y respetar el derecho que tiene a seguir los dictados de su conciencia.

Para poder serle fiel a la conciencia, las fieles tenemos que tener libertad interna y externa: libertad de verdad. Cada una de las fieles tiene que tener inmunidad contra fuerzas externas, tiene que poder reclamar plenamente el privilegio de obedecer su conciencia, y tiene que poder actuar de acuerdo a lo que la conciencia le dicta "sin estorbo ni embarazo". En vez de la preocupación casi enfermiza de la jerarquía por la obediencia, las teólogas *mujeristas* creemos que la Iglesia institucional debería establecer programas de educación religiosa que nos ayuden a formar nuestras conciencias y nos eduquen acerca de los derechos y las obligaciones que tenemos las católicas y los católicos en lo que se refiere a la conciencia.

"Conciencia" en las iglesias protestantes históricas, las fundamentalistas y las pentecostales

Veinte por ciento de la población hispana en EE.UU. pertenece o va a iglesias protestantes. En general en la tradición protestante, debido al énfasis que pone en la fe en vez de en las obras, hay tendencia a explicar la conciencia desde una perspectiva teológica y no ética. En la tradición protestante el papel de la conciencia ha sido mayormente el de hacer que la gente sepa que ha pecado. Se ha enfatizado mayormente el rol de la conciencia en hacer que la persona se sienta culpable y condenada y no se le ha dado, en general, el papel de orientar a la persona: se le ha dado a la conciencia mayormente el rol de juez y no de guía. Esto se debe en gran parte a que en la teología protestante el pecado tiene poco que ver con la relación que la persona tiene con Dios debido a que la salvación la da Dios y no depende de los actos de la persona. Es por eso que en el contexto protestante usualmente se ha pensado que el discutir el papel de la conciencia pudiese llevar a un énfasis en la moralidad que pudiese desembocar en legalismo.

En el fundamentalismo, las iglesias pentecostales y las iglesias no-denominacionales, esta perspectiva protestante de la conciencia, junto con un énfasis en la disciplina y la obediencia, hacen peligrar la auto-determinación de las mujeres hispanas. Los miembros de estos tipos de iglesias obedecen lo que se les dice que es la ley porque creen que es la ley en sí misma lo que tiene autoridad, en vez de ver que la autoridad de la ley tiene que ver con el hecho de que refleja o encarna los juicios morales de la comunidad. Es importante hacer notar dos cosas sobre la mayoría de estas iglesias. Primero, sus ministros son, mayormente, hombres, y gran parte de lo que llaman la "disciplina" tiene que ver con la regulación del comportamiento de las mujeres: cómo vestirse, cómo arreglarse. Segundo, la lectura fundamentalista de la Biblia niega que existan mediaciones entre la palabra de Dios en la Biblia y la manera en que entendemos la Biblia. No se ve diferencia entre la palabra de Dios en la Biblia y la manera que interpretan los textos bíblicos aquéllos que reclaman tener autoridad. Además, lo que la Biblia dice se aplica hoy día directamente a situaciones contemporáneas totalmente ajenas al contexto histórico en que se escribieron esos textos. El resultado no es sólo una moralidad basada exclusivamente en el obedecer leyes, sino también una obediencia ciega. Todo esto lo que hace es disminuir la capacidad de las mujeres hispanas como sujetos morales.

Conocimiento moral y conscientización

El pensar en la conciencia como elemento integral de la persona lleva a poner énfasis, no en la conciencia como si fuera una facultad aislada de la persona, sino en la persona como sujeto de su propia vida, capaz de determinar y de ser responsable de sí misma y de lo que hace. La vida moral, por lo tanto, es mucho más que un obedecer leyes; y la formación de la conciencia es más que un aprender leyes. Cuando el enfoque es la persona como agente moral, las consideraciones éticas no se relegan sólo a la toma de decisiones sino que se concentran en facilitar el desarrollo de la capacidad de la persona como agente moral a través de esas decisiones. La conciencia, por lo tanto, tiene que ver con el conocimiento moral de la persona, el conocimiento de la persona como agente moral que se conoce a sí misma a través de sus propias experiencias, y del comprender, juzgar y decidir por sí misma. El conocimiento moral incluye lo que percibimos a través de los sentidos, lo cual vamos entendiendo y juzgando hasta que llega el momento en el que tenemos que tomar una decisión. Es ahí que entramos en un proceso de evaluación moral, analizamos valores, los juzgamos y entonces decidimos de acuerdo a cómo hemos juzgado. Cuando las decisiones son libres, el agente moral escoge lo que cree que debe hacer para ser coherente consigo misma.

Desde la perspectiva de la teología *mujerista,* la mejor manera de educar acerca de la moral es a través de un proceso de conscientización. En el proceso de conscientización se distinguen tres elementos: (1) reconocer la diferencia entre lo que es natural e inevitable y lo que es cultural y cambiable; (2) desenmascarar los mitos que permiten a los opresores dominar la sociedad negando las diferencias entre lo natural y lo cultural; (3) explorar las alternativas que se pueden lograr a través del proceso de liberación.

El proceso de conscientización no se da sino en la praxis, en la acción y en el hacer. La conscientización es un proceso de análisis crítico que lleva a entendimientos claves que nos ayudan a decidir cuál deberá ser la próxima acción liberadora. Nadie puede conscientizar a otra persona. Cada cual se conscientiza a sí mismo participando en el proceso de acción-reflexión-acción que revela la realidad opresora en que vivimos las mujeres hispanas. Es por eso que el tema generador principal del proceso de conscientización de las hispanas, la idea central en el proceso de acción-reflexión-acción, es el binomio sobrevivencia-liberación. Este tema expresa tanto lo que nos motiva como nuestra meta.

Vimos en las entrevistas con las mujeres hispanas lo central de este tema sobrevivencia-liberación. Para ellas lo importante es hacer todo lo posible, lo que tengan que hacer, para vivir ellas—pero sobre todo, para que vivan sus hijas e hijos. Éste es el valor central que guía sus decisiones, el que constituye el eje motriz de su conocimiento moral. Y para ellas lo que la ética llama "norma moral" no es sino la responsabilidad que sienten por lograr que sobrevivan no sólo sus familias, sino toda la comunidad. Las mujeres hispanas—las que entrevistamos para este libro, las cientos de ellas con las que hemos trabajado por años, y nosotras las teólogas *mujeristas*—sabemos que tenemos esta responsabilidad también para con nosotras mismas, que tenemos que cuidarnos, respetarnos y amarnos porque si no, ¿cómo vamos a poder tener una relación con nadie y mucho menos con Dios? Sabemos que el no cuidarnos, el no preocuparnos por sobrevivir nosotras tanto como lo hacemos por nuestras hijas, por nuestros hijos y por la comunidad en general, es el pecado que expresa y genera todo otro pecado.

EN LA DÉCADA QUE HA PASADO DESDE QUE ESCRIBÍ ESTE LIBRO, las autoridades eclesiales—y aunque pienso principalmente en las autoridades católicas romanas creo que esto también se da en las autoridades de iglesias protestantes—han continuado insistiendo en la obediencia como virtud esencial. O sea, los encargados de las iglesias han continuado pensando que la función de los feligreses es la de obedecer; ellos—sí, todavía mayormente hombres—continúan entendiendo y ejerciendo su función de "pastoreo" de tal forma que lo que promueven es una "conciencia autoritaria". Este tipo de conciencia limita e incapacita, infantilizando en vez de ayudar a que nos responsabilicemos por quiénes somos y cómo actuamos. La "conciencia autoritaria" continúa siendo una manera efectiva de controlar, dominar y oprimir.

Por eso, hoy más que nunca, desde nuestra perspectiva *mujerista*, seguimos insistiendo en la necesidad de una educación de la conciencia liberadora: de una conscientización que nos ayude a ser responsables de nosotras mismas, que nos capacite más y más para ser sujetos de nuestra propia historia—tanto personal como comunitaria. El proceso de conscientización continúa siendo, desde la perspectiva *mujerista*, un método práctico y efectivo en la lucha por la liberación de las mujeres hispanas. Hay tres elementos de este proceso que son importantes destacar. Uno es el hecho de que el proceso de conscientización nos ayuda a las mujeres hispanas a enfrentarnos a nosotras mismas: a cómo hemos internalizado "los mitos" del opresor; a cómo hemos internalizado al opresor a tal punto de convertirnos en extrañas a quiénes a menudo nos es difícil reconocer. El proceso de conscientización continúa siendo importante para las mujeres hispanas porque no nos deja detenernos ni en el presente ni en nosotras mismas. El proceso de conscientización, aunque es un proceso personal—un proceso que podemos facil-itarles a las demás pero por el cual cada una tiene que pasar voluntariamente—es un proceso que se da en comunidad y en vista a la comunidad. La consciencia es un proceso que tiene como meta explorar alternativas. ¿Cómo es el futuro por el que luchamos? ¿Cómo es el futuro que favorecemos, qué queremos? ¿Qué te-nemos que hacer, empezando con qué tenemos que hacer con nosotras mismas, para lograrlo? En este sentido, la consciencia tiene como meta el enfren-tarnos a cómo conceptualizamos la realidad y cómo nos enfrentamos a ella. El proceso de consciencia, el cual nunca termina, es parte de cómo conocemos, de cómo sabemos: conocemos la realidad sólo cuando la aprehendemos, nos responsabilizamos por ella, y la acogemos—ya sea abrazándola o luchando por cambiarla en forma concreta.

El segundo elemento del proceso de consciencia es que, al ser un pro-ceso personal pero no individualista ni privado, deja por sentado el hecho de que ser sujeto moral, ser persona madura y responsable no es algo que se logra ni se da en forma aislada. Para las mujeres hispanas, la familia—que funciona como comunidad y por lo tanto no se limita a las personas que son de nuestra propia sangre—es tan central, que entendemos la subjetividad como un aspecto intrínseco de nuestra persona pero el cual se da a partir de y en vista a los demás. La conciencia, una de las modalidades de nuestras subjetividad, una de las fun-ciones de nuestro ser que realizamos en el vivir diario y que nos ayuda a estable-cer quiénes y cómo somos, no es algo que se da a nuestro interior afectando sólo a la persona. Al contrario, la conciencia funciona desde la persona pero siempre volcada hacia fuera, haciendo que la persona evalúe constantemente lo que hace y lo que tiene que hacer en vista a cómo afecta su vida y la vida de su comunidad. El proceso de consciencia, en este sentido, deja por sentado que la subjectivi-dad y la agencia moral del ser humano se van dando en comunidad y a partir de la participación de la persona en la comunidad. La agencia moral, que no es sino el responsabilizarse por la forma de ser y de actuar, es algo personal pero no es algo ni individual ni privado.

Por último, el proceso de consciencia nos ayuda a entender cómo la agencia moral de la persona es un proceso continuo y no ocurre o se da sólo en momentos cuando hay que tomar una decisión. Vamos desarrollando el ser suje-tos de nuestra propia historia a partir de las veinte mil decisiones—de mayor o menor envergadura—que vamos tomando día a día. El proceso de consciencia-zación nos hace ver cómo lo que se decide se convierte en parte de quién la per-sona es, ayudándole o impidiéndole luchar por su liberación, por la plenitud de vida. El proceso de consciencia capacita a la persona a aplicar lo que ha apren-dido a diferentes esferas de su vida : lo que se aprende de cómo uno se enfrenta a las relaciones íntimas da cabida a entender cómo la forma en que lo tratan a una en el trabajo nos hace menospreciarnos; o el enfrentarse a un jefe abusivo ayuda a que uno descubra convicciones que lo lleven a uno a parar relaciones de pareja abusivas. El proceso de conscientización facilita el desarrollo de la persona en forma integral.

CHAPTER 6

Praxis and Lived-Experience
in *Mujerista* Theology

At the heart of all liberation theologies is precisely the struggle for the liberation of the oppressed group from which each of these theologies arises. Though at times it may not be specifically pointed out and though at times an objectifying language does creep into some writings, most liberation theologians and other liberation activists claim, or at least recognize, that liberation is a personal, self-actualizing struggle which each one must accept as one's own responsibility. Liberation is a struggle that lasts one's whole life. Personal responsibility is one of the elements at the core of the moral subject and, therefore, at the heart of moral agency. Liberation theologies insist that the poor and the oppressed must struggle consciously to be agents of our own history. They must move away from being mere objects acted upon by the oppressors and become active subjects: moral persons.

As the women who speak to the reader through the pages of chapter 4 indicate, Latinas produce practical reality as they struggle to survive. Their telling of their stories shows how their struggle to survive is a praxis: a critical reflective action. This is obvious in their decision making, which is not something they sit down to do apart from their daily struggles. Their decision making, formed within the Latino cultural ethos and sharpened by the struggle for survival, provides for them the moral wisdom they need in their everyday lives and results in a praxis that challenges and effectively changes, even if only in minute ways, the oppressive reality in which they live.

Struggle and agency, then, do not exist apart from praxis. Liberative praxis is a dominant theme in *mujerista* theology, providing a point of entry into it and into its main preoccupation: the moral agency of Latinas. This is why in this chapter I will examine the meaning of *praxis,* how it is used in *mujerista* theology, and why we consider our theological enterprise a praxis in itself.

What grounds *mujerista* theology as a praxis? It is grounded by and arises from the lived-experience of Latinas, which in turn leads to future lived-experience that enables and expresses our moral agency. We have dealt with the centrality of the lived-experience of Latinas since the beginning of this book. In the second part of this chapter we concentrate on analyzing why *mujerista* theologians insist on the lived-experience of Latinas as the source of our theology.

The collective or communal lived-experience of Latinas as oppressed people is at the heart of *mujerista* theology and leads to a preferential option for Latinas, a preferential option that constitutes the "verifying criterion" of all Christian understandings, practices, and institutions for *mujerista* theology and ethics. When this preferential option becomes the lens through which doing theology is analyzed, it becomes necessary to embrace grassroot Latinas not merely as the subject matter of *mujerista* theology and as the ones to whom we who write about *mujerista* theology are accountable. We must also embrace grassroot Latinas engaged in liberative praxis infused with their religiosity as *mujerista* theologians themselves and their liberative praxis as *mujerista* theology. We will explore this important concept in the last section of this chapter.

Praxis in *Mujerista* Theology

From the very beginning of our attempts to articulate a *mujerista* theology, the centrality of praxis has been clear. In *mujerista* theology praxis is critical reflective action based on an analysis of historical reality perceived through the lens of an option for and a commitment to the liberation of Latinas.[1] In *mujerista* theology "life is already praxis; that is why in the praxis is included, in a condensed form, all of reality."[2] For us, praxis is a political action which seeks to change the oppressive economic-sociocultural structures of society.[3] This political action is a liberative action which requires a historical project—a project that, as we have indicated in chapter 2, questions the established order while proposing its own perspective about a preferred future. Praxis, therefore, requires human agency, intentionality, and a political commitment to change the infrastructure in relationship to the suprastructures. It demands a keen awareness that *how* we go about changing the structures is a key element in what we will accomplish.[4] Praxis in *mujerista* theology is always understood as liberative praxis.

In defining praxis as critical reflective action—reflective as different from mechanical, routine action—*mujerista* theology seeks to emphasize that the reflection part does not follow action nor is it "at the service of action."[5] Both action and reflection become inseparable moments, though neither is reduced to the other. Praxis "combines reflection with action to create the human world of ideas, symbols, language, science, religion, art, and production."[6]

In *mujerista* theology liberative praxis is one of the main referents of *mujerista* anthropology. Praxis as a referent leads to an anthropology that departs from that of modern theology. Modern theology's anthropology revolves around a so-called bourgeois subject characterized by a freedom based on rationalism and individualism. In contrast, the anthropology of Latin American liberation theology (and perhaps of other liberation theologies as well) centers on the poor, on those who suffer, on those who have been ignored by history and are not only marginal but considered and treated by the power elites as superfluous population.[7]

An anthropology developed out of the lived-experience of Latinas centers on a subject who struggles to survive and who understands herself as one who struggles. A small but common indication of this is how, to the casual question "How are you?" grassroot Latinas commonly respond just as *casually, "Ahí, en la lucha,"* there, in the struggle, instead of the "Fine, thank you" which we are accustomed to hear. Of course, the centrality of struggle as a constitutive element of the everyday lives of Latinas, of Latinas' self-construction, can be understood and grasped only against a background of oppression due to specific historical injustices that are the cause of great suffering. But in listening carefully to grassroot Latinas, one finds that what locates us in life is not suffering but *la lucha* to survive.[8] To consider suffering as what locates us would mean that we understand ourselves not as a moral subject but as one acted upon by the oppressors.[9] It would mean that what is central to ourselves is consenting and accepting a life full of opprobrium. That is the opposite of what our lives are.[10]

Though we have not received much public recognition for it, Latinas are often leaders in our communities. Latinas have been always in charge of making ends meet in our families and when we have not been able to do so any longer, we have been the ones to raise our voices in protest, to push Latino men to organize and demand more. Our exclusion from the public arena has not kept us out of struggles for justice, and we have, time and again, realized that waiting for our reward in heaven will not feed our children here on this earth. Often Latinas are seen as submissive and docile, and perhaps this is why suffering is seen by some as the main referent in our self-understanding. But most of the time submission and docility are survival tactics that make it possible to find a space to "be," to fight for our families and communities and, yes, for ourselves.

If what locates Latinas is *la lucha,* then we will be seen not only as a strategic force in history but also as historical, moral subjects, aware of our own role in defining and bringing about a preferred future. Latinas have always been key actors in the history of our people. *Mujerista* theology recognizes this and moves on to enable the "irruption of history" into the lives of Latinas:

> When we speak of the irruption of history into the lives of women—and especially the theological expression of their faith—we do not mean the entrance of women into history; they have always been present. What we have in mind is something qualitatively different and new, that is, the irruption of historic consciousness into the lives of millions and millions of women, leading them to struggle by means of an active participa-

tion in different fronts from which they had previously been absent. . . . [Women have become] aware of history, entering into a broader meaning, in which women are also creators or increasingly want to be forgers of history.[11]

But we cannot understand *la lucha* as what locates the Latinas unless, as we have said above, we posit praxis as a referent for a *mujerista* anthropology. Only if Latinas as human subjects are reconceived through praxis can our everyday struggle be understood as having meaning in our lives and giving meaning to our existence, as an element of our process to become moral agents and moral subject.[12]

To grasp better what claiming praxis as a referent for *mujerista* anthropology means, we must, first of all, understand the importance of reflection in praxis. *Mujerista* theology insists on the reflective moment of praxis, for it is precisely Latinas' ability to understand and think that is often questioned and debased. Praxis must not be equated with practice. Praxis is both intellectual enterprise and action; the dichotomy between intellectual activity and physical work is a fictitious one. *Mujerista* theology has insisted that Latinas are organic intellectuals because, as Gramsci stated, "one cannot speak of non-intellectuals, because non-intellectuals do not exist. . . . There is no human activity from which every form of intellectual participation can be excluded: *homo faber* cannot be separated from *homo sapiens*."[13] We believe with Gramsci that each person who participates "in a particular conception of the world, has a conscious line of moral conduct, and therefore contributes to sustain a conception of the world or to modify it, that is, to bring into being new modes of thought."[14]

Mujerista theologians' insistence on the centrality of praxis, therefore, does not make our enterprise anti-intellectual, just as Latinas' self-construction as persons who struggle to survive does not mean that we surrender the intellectual enterprise to the dominant groups.[15] Our insistence on praxis does not put reason and intellect aside. On what grounds can oppressors claim that Latinas' style of life, a style necessary to survive, is nonrational? On the contrary, those who struggle to survive are the very ones who can question the rationality of oppressors, who themselves are not capable of understanding this basic truth: that in the long run, only what benefits all of humanity will really benefit them. Those whose daily bread is the struggle for survival are the ones who have grounds to question what is considered intelligent and reasonable by society at large.

Another reason praxis is a referent for *mujerista* anthropology is that praxis is not just any reflective action. Rather, it is reflective action grounded in community, action that depends on the changing needs of the Latino community, action that is ongoing in a community responsible for itself.[16] The sense of community pervades Latinas' liberative praxis because for us community is not a matter of where we live or of how we work, but of who we are. In our culture, to be a person one necessarily has to relate to others. Community is not something added on, but a web of relationships constitutive of who we are. This is why our use of the word *individual* is not a positive one. Commonly, when one says *ese individuo,* that individual, one is talking about someone who is selfish, who is despicable in some way or other, someone who for some reason or other is outside the Latino community. Since community, then, is also in intrinsic element of praxis, community becomes another motive for considering praxis as the main referent in a *mujerista* anthropology.[17]

Mujerista theology not only understands liberative praxis as one of its key elements but claims that the doing of *mujerista* theology is itself a praxis. We do not believe that our theological enterprise is a "second step,"[18] or a "second reality."[19] We do not see theology as the reflection part of the "dialectic circularity of praxis-reflection [which] constitutes the unity and richness of the experience."[20] We do not see our writing of *mujerista* theology as a reflection on praxis, or mostly as "an explication of what was already present in a diffuse and a-thematic way in the praxis."[21]

In claiming the doing of *mujerista* theology as a liberative praxis, as a matter of fact, we are carrying out one of the constitutive dimensions of praxis: critiquing and denouncing oppressive structures. Simply claiming that *mujerista* theology is a liberative praxis severely critiques and protests the diminishment of Latinas portrayed by the dominant culture, which does not recognize us as intellectuals capable of critical and creative thinking. This critique is precisely the motivating force behind our insistence on the reflective moment of praxis.

Second, the doing of *mujerista* theology is a liberative praxis because our enterprise has as its lens the liberation of Latinas and, therefore, it critiques oppressive structures of the dominant culture while refusing to romanticize Latino culture. We critique the oppressive understandings and practices of women inherent in Latino culture, and we refuse to keep silence in the name of "protecting" our communities against the dominant culture.

Third, *mujerista* theology is a liberative praxis because our critique extends to the attempts that are made, even by some liberation theologians, to reserve the title of "theologian" to those who are academically trained. We believe that one of the elements at work in this reservation is the lack of acceptance of the intellectual capacity of grassroot people, of poor and oppressed people, the majority of whom—as demonstrated in the Latino community—are women.

Finally, as a liberative praxis *mujerista* theology does not shrink from the responsibility of critiquing ourselves when necessary. As we did in chapter 2 above, we critique Latinas who seek to accommodate, who want to make it in this society, no matter what the cost, who work vigorously to become part of the dominant group instead of struggling to change oppressive structures. We see their attempts as an individualistic struggle betraying the sense of community which grounds us. Those of us who do make it in this society must examine how we ourselves have become part of oppressive structures, how we maintain these structures, and how our apparent "liberation" comes at the expense of others.

For us, then, doing *mujerista* theology is not a second moment, having to do only with the reflection part of praxis. For us, reflection and practice are inseparably bound in praxis, and our doing theology is a liberative praxis. This does not mean, however, that we see the doing of *mujerista* theology as the only praxis in our struggle for liberation. But admitting that it is not the only praxis does not mean that it is not a praxis and, at times, a very important one.

Our understanding of *mujerista* theology as a liberating praxis is a refusal to reduce theology to a formal, disciplinary discourse in which adequacy has to do with certain intellectual criteria formulated by those who control the cultural and academic apparatus and which are quite foreign to the day-to-day struggle of Latinas to survive.[22] *Mujeristas'* understanding of theology is indeed an attempt to deconstruct the normative, mainline, disciplinary method of theology in order to recognize that theological understandings play an important role in Latinas' daily life, where the norm is *hacer lo que se puede aunque no sea siempre lo mejor,* to do what one is able to do even if it is not always the best thing to do, in order to survive.[23]

Hacer lo que se puede para sobrevivir, to do what one has to do in order to survive, points to the importance of preferring orthopraxis to orthodoxy in *mujerista* theology.[24] For *mujerista* theologians, then, "truth is at the level of history, not in the realm of ideas."[25] We do not understand *mujerista* theology as contributing primarily to an explanation of the world or to traditional, mainline understandings of questions of ultimate meaning. For us, theology is a task, a doing; it is an attempt to change, in a radical way, oppressive structures. It aims to transform the world by making the voice of Latinas heard, by having our understandings impact what is normative in society. This is why our concern is with orthopraxis, with transformative action, with the ways in which religious understandings are at the heart of Latinas' struggle to survive; with how our struggle impacts religious understandings and practices; and with helping to enable the development of Latinas' moral agency. We believe that in the long run *mujerista* theology, understood and functioning as a liberative praxis, will contribute significantly to the creation of new constructs within new paradigms, paradigms that will always be in the process of being developed and that will remain open to the critique arising out of the lived-experience of Latinas and of other oppressed peoples.

The Lived-Experience of Latinas

For some, the phrase *lived-experience* may seem tautological, but we use it in *mujerista* theology to differentiate it from our regular, daily experience, that is, everything we do and everything that happens to us. In *mujerista* theology, lived-experience identifies those experiences in our lives about which we are intentional. It is the sum of our experience which we examine, reflect upon, deal with specifically. In so doing we make it a building block for our personal and communal struggle for liberation. Because intentionality is required in order to reflect actively on what we experience, Latinas' lived-experience is the ground for our moral development, for our consciousness-raising and conscience formation, for the discovery and development of our values. And for us Latinas, none of this can happen without an awareness of the oppression and alienation we suffer.

As we have analyzed in the first two chapters, Latinas are oppressed in our society because of our ethnicity and our sex. Most Latinas are also oppressed economically: we are poor. This means that our lived-experience is often not the same as that of other ethnic groups or even of Latino men. Even if some of our experiences are the same as others', when we reflect on those experiences we bring to that reflection understandings which are different from those of other groups. Because of cultural differences, the way we understand a situation and the motives and values that come into play as we live through it are different from those of the dominant culture, and different, too, from those of other marginalized racial/ethnic groups. Although we often conform outwardly to society's norms in order to survive, we are under great stress—as indeed would any group which is not an integral part of society—because of differences in our values and motivations. Racial/ethnic prejudices and sexism compound the stress in the lives of Latinas.

Those who are influential in society are not our models. Their reasons for success are not our reasons. In other words, we Latinas do not find our understandings and values reflected in those of society. Our values are not part of the societal norm and are not, therefore, validated by society. But our lack of participation in setting what is normative in society results in more than mere lack of validation. Not only have we been excluded from shaping and interpreting the norms as well as the principles and institutions of society according to our own experience, but those norms, principles, and societal institutions have been shaped and interpreted against us, in order to exclude and exploit us.[26]

What is worse, the very understandings and values of Latino culture and the role of women within our culture are used to justify excluding and oppressing us.[27] The cultural and androcentric bias of contemporary U.S. society not only does not allow us to participate in setting the norm but even ignores anyone who may point out our absence.[28] Therefore, in order to validate who we are and what we do, in order to keep our sanity, we have to go deep within ourselves. We have to reflect on what we do and on who we are in order to remain faithful to ourselves, in order to remain sane.

Our lived-experiences have to be the building blocks of our self-understanding and of our morality if we are not to lose ourselves in the process. We have to depend on how we understand and live the events of our daily lives. We have to consider carefully our own stories in order to bring understanding out of the chaos created in our lives by the many forces that pull us in different directions. This chaos, this uprootedness, this not-having-a-place-to-call-home— these are the main reasons why our central preoccupation in this society is and has to be survival.

The lived-experience of Latinas, which deals mainly with the struggle to survive, is not only the *locus theologicus* which situates *mujerista* theology. Our lived-experience is also the primary source of *mujerista* theology. This understanding validates our struggle and enables the development of the moral agency of Latinas. This understanding calls into question the whole issue of "objectivity." The need for a hermeneutic of suspicion regarding "objectivity" and "validity" is intrinsic to any theological enterprise arising from oppressed communities. For too long theology done by those belonging to the dominant culture, the dominant race, the dominant sex, has claimed to be objective. Those of us who belong to marginalized, oppressed groups have come to understand that what is called "objective" is simply the understanding of a given group of people who have the power to impose that understanding as normative in society. This so-called objectivity arises from the lived-experience of dominant groups of society and ignores the lived-experience of the oppressed to the point of considering it deviant.

As *mujerista* theologians we claim that even the attempt to be objective is flawed. Though we do not deny that *the truth* does or might exist, what we are insisting on is that our theological enterprise has to do with the reality Hispanic Women create and confront every day.[29] For *mujerista* theologians it is clear that theology is not so much about God as about how we understand and relate to God. And that is precisely one of the reasons for our insistence on the lived-experience of Latinas as the source of our theology. We insist on our lived-experience as central not because we think that our reality is necessarily unique. This insistence should not be understood either as an attempt to claim a clearer or better understanding of *the truth*. We do it because we believe that what needs to be done is to identify the perspective from which we are writing and to state clearly the goal of our theological discourse. This will make it possible for those who engage us to understand and to analyze what we are saying.

When we claim the lived-experience of Hispanic Women as the source of *mujerista* theology, we are making clear our subjectivity by identifying what it is that grounds us, what our starting point is, and where we get the material we work with.[30] Those who claim the Bile or church teaching as the source of their theology are glossing over the fact that the real source of their theology is *their* understanding of the Bible and of church teaching. Furthermore, theologians often ignore the fact that the Bible as well as church teaching are conditioned by the socioeconomic-political realities of the period in which both were formulated.

To use the lived-experience of Hispanic Women as the source of *mujerista* theology contributes to a reconceptualization of what is rational. Instead of thinking that only thought processes can yield rationality, we insist that lived-experience highlights the point of view that the whole mystery of existence—including what we know, conclude, and express using the senses, desires, flavor, pleasure, pain, imagination—can also contribute to and yield rational thinking and rational behavior. The totality of Latinas' lived-experience, not only our thought process, amplifies our theological language, leading it to include not only linear, logical argumentation but also prophetic denunciation, songs and poems of protest and hope, lamentations and language of consolation. And our theological language is not only a matter of written words but also of liturgical rituals, street demonstrations, and protest actions.[31]

The doing of *mujerista* theology starts by examining the lived-experience of Latinas and uses it to understand who we are, to ask questions of ultimate meaning for survival, and to answer those questions. Without this lived-experience, *mujerista* theology would have nothing to say: it could only repeat what has already been said. That is not a valid reason for any theological enterprise. Because of its source, *mujerista* theology goes beyond a reinterpretation of theological understandings. Our agenda, then, has to do with framing new questions rather than providing answers to old ones, challenging religious understandings which negate our experience rather than finding ways to relate those understandings to our lives. *Mujerista* theology is more about questioning the way theology is done than making a niche for ourselves within the structures of contemporary theology and academia.

Grassroot Latinas as *Mujerista* Theologians

Since the source of *mujerista* theology is the lived-experience of Latinas, since we believe that grassroot Latinas are organic intellectuals capable of reflection, and since *mujerista* theology is a liberative praxis, we do not hesitate to call grassroot Latinas whose religious understandings and practices are an intrinsic element of their struggle to survive *mujerista* theologians.[32] In chapter 3 we argued from a sociological perspective the need to present the actual voices of Latinas in *mujerista* theology. We also indicated that if Latinas do not speak for ourselves we run the risk of once again being objectified, of perhaps becoming subject matter for theology but not being the subjects of the process of theologizing.

If the title and role of theologian is reserved only for those with academic education and degrees, it would not be possible to claim that *mujerista* theology is a liberative praxis in which all Latinas can engage, and it would be impossible to have as its main goal the enablement of moral agency for Latinas. Though we realize that those who are not poor and oppressed—or those who are less poor and oppressed than Latinas—can stand in solidarity with us and use their theological enterprise to help us in our struggle for liberation, such theological enterprise still cannot be sufficient, for it might excuse us from doing *mujerista* theology.[33]

To insist that grassroot Latinas can be and are *mujerista* theologians is part of the process of conquering spaces to express our word and our being.[34] It points to a change in our consciousness: though we have earlier understood ourselves as struggling to survive, now we are conscious of our own causality. This sense of causality in our lives is not a mere psychological development but is also an intellectual and rational process promoting hermeneutical suspicions in all areas of our lives and leading to great creativity in the way we understand ourselves and in our day-to-day living.[35] Being conscious of the causality of our lives leads us to claim the right to speak for ourselves, for only *we* can explain how we understand ourselves and our reality.

As we have said before, *mujerista* theology as a praxis is done by the community as each one contributes to the process of doing theology according to her own gifts. At a given moment, because of a particular need, one gift may be more useful than another, but that does not make it more important. Those of us who are the "theological technicians," who generally have academic training and academic degrees, are not to be considered more fully theologians than the Latinas who lead the action component of our liberating praxis, or those who are gifted in expressing the beliefs of the community through rituals.[36] Therefore, there is no such thing as academic *mujerista* theology on one hand and grassroot *mujerista* theology on the other.[37]

Some Latin American liberation theologians have posited different levels of liberation theology: professional, pastoral, popular.[38] Though *mujerista* theologians accept that there are different kinds of "theological jobs" to be done in the community,[39] declaring that these jobs yield different kinds of discourse, have different kinds of logic, and use different kinds of methods is not congruent with our experience.[40] But we go further and question the very understandings of discourse, logic, and method that are proposed in an attempt to differentiate different levels of liberation theology. In *mujerista* theology, for example, theological discourse cannot but be organically related to practice and that does not make it any less detailed or rigorous. Nor does being detailed and rigorous mean that it is not spontaneous, for *mujerista* theology as a discourse is not something obscure. It is, rather, something *a flor de piel*—only skin-deep—which Latinas share quite readily. And when it comes to logic, can one really differentiate between a "logic of life" and a "logic of action that is specific, prophetic, propulsive"? For Latinas who struggle to survive, is not our logic of life, which is necessarily a logic of action, a logic that has to be "methodical, systematic, and dynamic"?

Finally, perhaps it is with the differences posited in method that we have the greatest problems. For *mujerista* theologians the ongoing revelation of who God is and what God is like is to be found in our struggle for survival and justice. For us, to be a Christian is to participate in this struggle, and we participate in this struggle by doing *mujerista* theology. We do not live differently as Christians from the way we live as *mujerista* theologians. We do not accept the understanding that "contemplation and practice together constitute the *first act;* theologizing is the *second* act."[41] For us, this division is artificial not only because of our understanding of the intrinsic connection between reflection and practice in praxis but also because for us the sacred is an integral part of our daily lives. This is why our operative understanding is that our doing *mujerista* theology is our way of life.

It seems to us that to insist that grassroot Latinas whose liberative praxis is informed by their religiosity are the same kind of and as fully *mujerista* theologians as those of us who are academically trained is to take seriously the preferential option for the poor and the oppressed that grounds all liberation struggles. This option is grounded in the belief that from their marginality the poor and the oppressed can see a different future, a better future for themselves, and, in the long run if not in the short one, a better future for all. The option for the poor is also grounded in what we said above about Latinas coming into a new consciousness regarding our causality in history. Although we believe we have always been "one of the most decisive dynamic elements in history,"[42] up to now this dynamism has been unspecific, part of the structural forces of society. At present, however, Latinas have moved from being "a submerged conscience" to being "an emerged or critical conscience."[43]

A preferential option for the poor cannot be paternalistic, it cannot be a "doing for them," no matter how self-sacrificing that is. How can liberation theologians claim on the one hand that the preferential option of the church for the poor entails recognizing the poor as the agents, the protagonists, of the evangelizing efforts of the church,[44] and not recognize grassroot people as theologians? How can they insist that "the exact meaning" of the preferential option for the poor is "to recognize the privileged status of the poor as the new and emerging historical subject which will carry on the Christian project in the world,"[45] while at the same time excluding them from the theological task or severely limiting their participation by creating different levels of liberation theology?

Mujerista theologians believe that the preferential option for the poor has to be more than a conceptual claim and that in order to do so it has to yield specific praxis. A key praxis it must produce is the recognition that all Latinas engaged in the struggle to survive—the struggle for liberation—are capable of speaking our own word, naming our own reality, reflecting upon and making explicit our own religious understandings and practices.

I HAVE LITTLE TO ADD TO WHAT I SAID TEN YEARS AGO about how *mujerista* theology understands praxis and about the fact that we claim *mujerista* theology to be a liberation praxis. That we understand *mujerista* theology as a liberation praxis, as action-reflection based on the religious beliefs of Latinas, helps us to press on in spite of the fact that we see little progress in our struggle for the liberation of Latinas and of our communities. Our theological work is valuable because it is a process that helps Latinas to understand the importance of each life. To claim that in doing *mujerista* theology we contribute to the liberation of Latinas counters the view that liberation struggles are things of the past that have, in general, failed. We claim that liberation is a process that lasts one's whole life. It is a process that little by little affects social structures by what we decide, what we do, how we live—according to our daily praxis.

Faced with government and dominant-class hegemonic control in the society in which we Latinas live, creating spaces for self-determination continues to be an effective way of struggling for our liberation. As long as our theological work contributes to this process, regardless of how small a contribution it makes, it will be worthwhile to do *mujerista* theology. *Mujerista* theologians continue to be committed to doing theology in a way that highlights the religious beliefs and practices of grassroot Latinas that contribute to their liberation and to society in general.

Síntesis del Capítulo 6

Praxis y Experiencias en la teología *mujerista*

Como indican las entrevistas que hicimos para este libro, las latinas producen su realidad cotidiana al luchar por sobrevivir. La manera en que viven prueba el hecho de que esa lucha es una verdadera praxis, una acción reflexiva. La lucha por la liberación, por ser agentes o sujetos morales, no se da sino en la praxis. Vimos cómo toman decisiones de acuerdo a los valores de la cultura latina y a lo que les ha enseñado la lucha por sobrevivir. Esos valores y esas luchas son lo que les da la sabiduría moral que necesitan en la vida cotidiana, en la praxis liberadora que va cambiando, casi en forma imperceptible, la realidad opresiva que vivimos.

¿Por qué la teología *mujerista* se considera praxis liberadora? Porque está centrada en la experiencia cotidiana, en la experiencia colectiva-comunitaria de las latinas como grupo oprimido, y porque es un proceso que incluye oportunidades para que las latinas reflexionen y nombren sus propias experiencias. Porque la teología *mujerista* encarna una opción preferencial por las latinas, opción que constituye el criterio central de lo que es ser cristiana. La opción preferencial es el lente a través del cual analizamos todo aspecto teológico, y esto hace necesario que las latinas sean no sólo el tema principal de la teología *mujerista,* sino también que sean consideradas ellas mismas teólogas: mujeres que reflexionan en forma crítica sobre sus creencias y prácticas religiosas.

La praxis en la teología *mujerista*

Desde el principio hemos insistido en que la teología *mujerista* es una praxis liberadora. En la teología *mujerista* entendemos praxis como la acción reflexiva basada en un análisis crítico de nuestra realidad histórica a partir de una opción por y un compromiso con la liberación de las latinas. La vida de las mujeres latinas es una praxis porque nuestro sobrevivir—teniendo en cuenta que para nosotras sobrevivir quiere decir luchar por plenitud de vida—es una acción política que busca cambiar estructuras económicas, sociales y culturales que son opresivas. Esta praxis, al ser acción política—acción que se da y repercute en la sociedad en la que vivimos—requiere un proyecto histórico que cuestione el orden presente y tenga su propia visión del futuro. La praxis, por lo tanto, requiere intencionalidad y un compromiso con el cambio tanto de la infraestructura como de la superestructura social. También requiere especial atención a la manera en que se lleva a cabo el cambio de las estructuras ya que los métodos que se usan influyen lo que se logra.

El definir la praxis como acción reflexiva la distingue de la acción rutinaria y enfatiza que la reflexión no viene después de la acción ni está al servicio de la acción. En la praxis, la acción y la reflexión son inseparables aunque no se deben confundir la una con la otra. En la praxis, la reflexión se combina con la acción para crear el mundo de ideas, símbolos, lenguaje, ciencia, religión, arte y producción.

Para comprender que la praxis es punto central de la antropología *mujerista* hay que insistir en el aspecto reflexivo de la praxis. Hemos insistido en que las latinas somos "intelectuales orgánicas" porque tenemos una concepción específica del mundo—reflexión—que lleva a una conducta moral—acción. Esta conducta moral–acción—contribuye a sostener la concepción del mundo que existe en la sociedad o la modifica introduciendo nuevas formas de pensar.

Para la teología *mujerista* la praxis liberadora es uno de los puntos de referencia principales para la elaboración de una antropología *mujerista*. Como esta praxis es parte integral de la experiencia cotidiana de las latinas, la antropología *mujerista* se centra en la mujer latina como sujeto histórico que lucha por sobrevivir y que se entiende como tal. Una pequeña pero muy común prueba de esto es que a la pregunta "¿Cómo estás?" las latinas mayormente responden, "Ahí, en la lucha". Claro está, el que la lucha por sobrevivir sea punto de referencia clave de la manera cómo las latinas nos entendemos a nosotras mismas sólo se puede comprender si se conoce específicamente la opresión que sufrimos. Es importante notar, desde la perspectiva antropológica, que para las latinas, sobre todo latinas de la base, lo que identifica sus vidas, a pesar de la opresión, no es el sufrimiento sino la lucha por sobrevivir. Si fuese el sufrimiento no nos veríamos mayormente como sujetos morales sino como objetos sobre los cuales el opresor actúa infligiéndonos dolor, y sería el aceptar y el consentir a ese dolor lo que nos daría nuestra identidad. Lo contrario es precisamente lo que es verdad.

Lo que nos identifica es la lucha. Por eso somos una fuerza estratégicamente importante en la historia; por eso somos sujetos morales conscientes del rol que tenemos en definir y hacer realidad nuestro proyecto histórico. Las latinas siempre hemos jugado un rol importantísimo en la historia de nuestros pueblos aunque la "historia oficial" haga caso omiso a esa realidad. Lo que la teología *mujerista* hace posible es la irrupción de la historia en la vida de las latinas en el sentido de ayudarnos a adquirir conciencia histórica. Esto posibilita el saber que debemos participar en esferas de la sociedad de las cuales hemos estado ausentes pero en las que podemos hacer que se oigan nuestras voces, y contribuir a crear y forjar la historia.

Otra razón por la cual la praxis liberadora es elemento central de una antropología *mujerista* es porque dicha praxis está enraizada en nuestras comunidades y sus necesidades. Comunidad para las latinas no es una experiencia fuera de nosotras sino que es parte constitutiva de quienes somos: es parte de nuestro ser personas.

Las teólogas *mujeristas* consideramos nuestro quehacer teológico una praxis liberadora ya que, al tomar como punto de partida la experiencia cotidiana de las latinas, la teología *mujerista* se convierte en una crítica y una denuncia de las estructuras que nos oprimen. Parte importante de esta crítica y denuncia tiene que ver con el hecho de que la sociedad en la que vivimos no reconoce a las latinas como intelectuales capaces de un pensar creativo. Pero la crítica que es elemento de la teología *mujerista* no es parcial—sólo hacia fuera—sino que incluye una crítica al interior de la cultura latina y aun de nosotras mismas. Esta particularidad nos lleva a estar en desacuerdo con los teólogos de la liberación que no reconocen a las personas de la base como teólogos, queriendo reservar ese título para quienes tenemos una educación académica.

El que entendamos la teología *mujerista* como una praxis liberadora, nos lleva a rehusar reducir la teología a un discurso formal y disciplinado, en el sentido de sólo considerar adecuada las ideas que se pueden encasillar en criterios intelectuales formulados por los que regulan los aparatos culturales y académicos. Para la teología *mujerista* lo "adecuado" tiene que necesariamente ver ante todo con la lucha cotidiana de las latinas por sobrevivir. La manera en que las teólogas *mujeristas* entendemos la teología sin duda lleva a "de-construir" lo normativo, lo considerado "central" en los métodos tradicionales de la teología. Este proceso de "de-construir" se da precisamente a partir de la insistencia en la experiencia cotidiana de las latinas. Por ejemplo, esto lleva a la ética *mujerista* a abrazar lo que se escucha repetidamente en la comunidad: para sobrevivir, "hacemos lo que se puede aunque no sea siempre excelente". Por eso, en nuestro quehacer teológico preferimos enfatizar la ortopraxis en vez de la ortodoxia. La verdad para nosotras se encuentra en la historia, en la experiencia de lucha diaria, no en el ámbito de las ideas. No nos preocupa si la teología *mujerista* contribuye a una "explicación" del mundo o de lo tradicional o a la manera en que se "piensa" acerca de cuestiones de significado trascendental. Para nosotras la teología es un *quehacer;* es un vivir en el mundo en vez de explicar—en forma abstracta—el mundo. Esta manera de concebir la teología requiere una lucha constante para cambiar las estructuras opresivas al igual que las formas tradicionales de entender la realidad: una lucha por transformar el mundo.

La experiencia cotidiana de las latinas

En la teología *mujerista* la frase "experiencia cotidiana" se refiere a esas experiencias que son intencionales, a la suma de las experiencias que analizamos, sobre las que reflexionamos y con las que lidiamos día a día. Es a partir de estas experiencias y en ellas que se da la lucha personal y comunitaria en contra de la opresión. Como hemos dicho ya en el capítulo 2, en esta sociedad las latinas sufrimos opresión étnica y sexista y la mayoría también sufrimos opresión económica. Esta multiplicidad de elementos en nuestra opresión lleva a una especificidad que sólo nosotras podemos apreciar y comprender por completo. Esta opresión nos lleva a menudo a vivir bajo gran presión sicológica ya que nuestras motivaciones y valores a menudo son diferentes de los de la cultura dominante. La sociedad en general no valida ni nuestros valores culturales ni a nosotras mismas. No solamente se nos excluye de darle forma a los principios y las instituciones de la sociedad en la que vivimos, sino que muchas veces dichos principios e instituciones son interpretados y usados en contra de las latinas, para excluirnos y oprimirnos.

Peor aún, los valores y las costumbres de nuestra propia cultura latina son a menudo usados en contra de nosotras. Los prejuicios étnicos y androcéntricos no sólo nos oprimen y excluyen sino que también hacen posible ignorar a las personas que hacen notar nuestra ausencia. Es por eso que para validarnos a nosotras mismas, para no volvernos locas, las latinas tenemos que reflexionar continua y profundamente, tenemos que saber por qué es que actuamos como lo hacemos. Tenemos que pensar con cuidado quiénes somos para saber hacia dónde vamos o si no, no lograremos mucho en nuestras vidas. El caos de la situación de pobreza material, social y espiritual, la falta de raíces, este no tener un lugar en el que nos podamos sentir en casa, es una preocupación constante a la que tenemos que atender continuamente para poder sobrevivir.

La experiencia cotidiana de las latinas, esta lucha diaria por sobrevivir, no sólo es el *locus theologicus,* sino también la fuente de nuestro quehacer teológico. Esto quiere decir que la teología *mujerista* valora la lucha diaria de las latinas y ayuda en el desarrollo de nuestra agencia moral. Este reconocimiento de la subjetividad de la teología *mujerista* cuestiona lo "objetivo" come base para reclamar validez. Las latinas miramos con sospecha lo que se refiere a "objetividad" y "validez". Esta sospecha es elemento de todas las teologías que surgen de comunidades oprimidas. Los miembros de estas comunidades sabemos que lo llamado "objetivo" es sencillamente la manera de ver y entender la realidad de aquéllos que tienen el poder para hacer que su punto de vista sea el normativo. Lo "objetivo" en realidad surge de la experiencia cotidiana de los grupos dominantes e ignora o clasifica como aberrante las experiencias cotidianas de los grupos minoritarios, en este caso de las latinas.

Las teólogas *mujeristas* creemos que aun pensar que se pueda ser objetivo es una equivocación. Aunque no negamos la realidad ontológica de las cosas, en lo que insistimos es que nuestro quehacer teológico tiene que ver no con esa realidad, sino con la realidad que las latinas construimos y confrontamos día a día. Para la teología *mujerista* es obvio que la teología no es tanto acerca de Dios como acerca de lo que los humanos creemos de Dios. Y una de las mayores influencias en el pensar es la experiencia vivida. Lo importante entonces, en vez de insistir en que somos objetivas, es reclamar e identificar nuestra subjetividad: dejar saber cuál es nuestra perspectiva en nuestro quehacer teológico. Y eso es precisamente lo que hacemos cuando reclamamos la experiencia cotidiana de las latinas como fuente teológica.

El usar la experiencia cotidiana de las latinas como fuente de la teología *mujerista* lleva a una reconceptualización de lo racional. En vez de pensar que sólo los procesos intelectuales producen racionalidad, la insistencia en la experiencia cotidiana hace resaltar que es la totalidad del misterio de nuestra existencia, incluyendo lo que nos enseñan y expresan los sentidos, los deseos, los placeres, las penas, la imaginación—todo—lo que contribuye a lo racional. La totalidad de la experiencia cotidiana de las latinas, no solamente nuestra manera de pensar, amplifica nuestro lenguaje teológico, llevándonos a incluir no sólo argumentos que responden a una lógica lineal, sino también denuncias proféticas, cantos y poesías de protesta y esperanza, lamentaciones y el lenguaje de la verdadera consolación. Nuestro lenguaje teológico no se circunscribe sólo a la palabra escrita sino que también incluye rituales litúrgicos, marchas y manifestaciones públicas, protestas callejeras, y una presencia persistente en los eventos y lugares de donde tratan de excluirnos.

Latinas de la base como teólogas *mujeristas*

En el capítulo 3 indicamos desde una perspectiva sociológica la necesidad de usar las voces de las latinas de la base en el quehacer teológico. Ya indicamos también que si las latinas no hablamos, otros hablarán por nosotras convirtiéndonos en objetos de su reflexión en vez de ser nosotras sujetos de nuestro pensar teológico. Si el título de "teóloga" se reservara sólo para quienes tenemos una educación formal y grados académicos, no podríamos decir que el hacer teología *mujerista* es una praxis para todas aquellas latinas que luchan por la liberación. El insistir en que las latinas de la base son teólogas *mujeristas* es parte del proceso de conquistar espacios en los cuales podemos expresar nuestra palabra y nuestro ser. Esto señala un cambio en nuestra manera de concebirnos: hasta ahora nos entendíamos como latinas luchando por sobrevivir; ahora estamos conscientes de que además de eso también somos causa de nuestra lucha, de nuestra sobrevivencia. Este sentido de ser causa no es meramente un desarrollo sicológico sino también un proceso intelectual y racional que nos lleva a aplicar la sospecha hermenéutica a todas las áreas de nuestras vidas y nos hace posible tener gran creatividad en nuestra auto-comprensión. El estar conscientes de que somos causa de nuestras propias luchas nos ayuda a reclamar el derecho que tenemos a hablar en nombre propio, ya que sólo nosotras sabemos explicar cómo es que nos entendemos y entendemos nuestra realidad.

Como la teología *mujerista* es un quehacer comunitario, no todas las teólogas *mujeristas* de una comunidad realizamos las mismas tareas teológicas. Las "teólogas técnicas", que hemos dedicado tiempo al entrenamiento académico y tenemos diplomas académicos, no somos más teólogas, por ejemplo, que las que se encargan de programar actos de protesta o de organizar rituales litúrgicos. Tampoco creemos que haya distintas categorías de teología *mujerista* que atiendan a diferentes quehaceres teológicos y usen diferentes clases de lógica. A lo que más nos oponemos es a pensar que el quehacer teológico viene después de la acción. Para las teólogas *mujeristas* ésta es una división artificial que no sólo desconoce e ignora la conexión intrínseca que hay entre la acción y la reflexión en la praxis, sino que tampoco respeta la unión que existe en la cultura latina entre lo sagrado y todo lo demás. Es por eso que para las teólogas *mujeristas* el quehacer teológico es nuestra manera de vivir, nuestra vocación.

Finalmente, el insistir en llamar a las latinas que luchan por la liberación y reflexionan sobre sus creencias religiosas y el papel que la religión tiene en esa lucha es una manera de afirmar que los pobres y los oprimidos—en su mayoría mujeres—son hoy en día el elemento dinámico decisiva de nuestra historia. En realidad, ha sido así siempre; ¡pero es ahora que los oprimidos nos hemos dado cuenta de ello! El pensar que sólo los que tenemos diplomas académicos podemos ser teólogas y teólogos de la liberación desemboca necesariamente en un paternalismo opresivo que traiciona el reclamo de nuestro quehacer teológico: la teología *mujerista* en sí es una praxis liberadora.

POCO TENGO QUE AGREGAR A LO QUE DIJE HACE diez años sobre cómo entendemos la praxis en la teología *mujerista* y sobre nuestro reclamo de que la teología *mujerista* es una praxis liberadora. El conceptualizar la teología *mujerista* como praxis liberadora, como acción-reflexión basada en las creencias religiosas de las latinas, nos ayuda a no darnos por vencidas a pesar de lo poco que parecemos avanzar en la lucha por la liberación de las latinas y de nuestras comunidades. Nuestro quehacer teológico tiene valor porque es un proceso que ayuda a las latinas a entender lo importante de la vida de cada cual. Al proveer una plataforma para las voces de las latinas, la teología *mujerista* contribuye en forma concreta a que las latinas entiendan el valor que tienen sus vidas y sus luchas por plenitud de vida. Reclamar que al hacer teología *mujerista* contribuimos a la liberación de las latinas contrarresta el sentido de que las luchas por la liberación son cosas del pasado y que mayormente han fracasado. Insistimos en que la liberación es un proceso que dura toda la vida, y que se va inscribiendo en las estructuras sociales a partir de cómo nosotras vamos decidiendo, haciendo, viviendo: a partir de nuestra praxis diaria.

Frente a la hegemonía del gobierno y la clase dominante de la sociedad en la que vivimos las latinas, el crear espacios de auto-determinación continúa siendo una forma efectiva de luchar por nuestra liberación. Mientras que nuestro quehacer teológico contribuya en algo a este proceso, la teología *mujerista* valdrá la pena, tendrá valor, y las teólogas *mujeristas* mantendremos nuestro compromiso de hacer teología en tal forma que haga resaltar cómo las creencias y prácticas religiosas de las latinas de la base son elemento liberador en sus vidas. Las teólogas *mujeristas* insistiremos en que las creencias y prácticas religiosas de las latinas son una contribución positiva a la liberación de las comunidades latinas y que tienen algo que contribuir a la sociedad en general.

CHAPTER 7

Mestizaje: Symbol of Hispanic
Women's Moral Truth-Praxis

At the beginning of this book mestizaje was examined as one of the key elements of Hispanic Women's self-understanding, an integral aspect of our racial/ethnic cultural reality. In chapter 2 we saw that there is a *mestizaje* that has to do with the mingling of sixteenth-century Spanish Catholicism and Amerindian and African religious understanding, resulting in the practices and rituals of a *religiosidad popular.* There we analyzed how this *mestizaje* has yielded a theologically rich *religiosidad popular* empowering to us in our everyday struggles. In this chapter we return to *mestizaje* in order to analyze the challenges it presents to Hispanic Women.

Many of us doing Hispanic theology understand and use *mestizaje* as a hermeneutical tool and a paradigm. As a hermeneutical tool, *mestizaje* helps us interpret the complex and rich reality of our community; as a paradigm, it is a way of representing, of talking about, who we are as a community. Some of us *mujerista* theologians, however, fear that the use of *mestizaje* in Hispanic theology may lead to a romanticizing of our culture, and of the way we understand community. In meeting with Hispanic Women throughout the U.S.A., in reflecting with them on their lived-experiences, on their struggles for self-definition and survival, it becomes obvious and important that in the elaboration of *mujerista* theology we have to insist on two things if we are not to fall into an idealization of *mestizaje.* First, there is a need for in-depth analysis not only of differences among Hispanics, but of the way we deal with differences, because if we do not embrace differences there is no possibility of *mestizaje.* Second, we acknowledge that because ethnicity is a social construct, a heuristic device that includes not only biological and cultural characteristics but also social and economic elements of the Hispanic community in the U.S.A., Hispanics have a choice: we must choose to be or not to be Hispanics, and this includes choosing *mestizaje* as a way of understanding and interpreting ourselves.

The need to *choose* to be Hispanic became obvious to me as I talked with the women the reader has heard from in this book. Though I continue to find a pattern of cultural similarities in their religious and ethical understandings and practices, it is very obvious that these similarities do not yield sameness but rather a continuum of characteristics punctuated by particularity, specificity, diversity. As

I heard them talk about themselves as Cubans, Puerto Ricans, Mexican Americans, or Mexicans—not as Hispanics—I could not help but remember my own journey from *being* exclusively Cuban to an understanding of being Cuban-Hispanic, or, as I always introduce myself in this country and abroad, as "a Cuban who lives in the U.S.A." This journey has led me to understand and appreciate that the insistence on particularity and specificity is not antithetical to *mestizaje,* but, on the contrary, is required for *mestizaje* to exist.

Another issue that has made it important for *mujeristas* to consider differences has been the need to challenge European-American feminists' way of conceptualizing all women as the same. Though many of them nowadays acknowledge this failing, the majority of their writings do not go beyond that: differences among women do not seem to impact their practice or theories. In the first part of this chapter, I want to capitalize on what we have learned from dealing with European-American feminists in order to examine differences, diversity, specificity, and particularities.[1]

The second part of the chapter contains a short discussion on the need we have as Hispanic Women to learn for our own communities much of what we have said to European-American feminists. The third part explains how we are using *mestizaje* as a symbol of *mujerista* moral truth-praxis.

Understanding and Valuing Differences

One of the easiest ways of approaching the understanding of difference in the U.S.A. is to analyze the way people react to Hispanic Women.[2] These reactions manifest the significance that difference has for the dominant culture. The way those in power—those from the dominant culture—respond in general to Hispanic Women indicates that difference is not appreciated or embraced in this culture. Difference breeds at best a competitiveness that has to end in someone's losing. And at its worst, difference breeds a destructive contempt commonly defined as racism and ethnic prejudice. As we have already examined, this destructive contempt, which results in oppression, depends on domination and works by subjugating, exploiting, and repressing.[3]

One reaction to Hispanic Women is to ignore us totally. Elsewhere I have referred to this as "invisible invisibility."[4] "Invisible invisibility" questions the very existence of Hispanic Women; it makes us question not only the value of our specificity but the very reality of it. Most of those who totally ignore us do not even know they are doing so; they are not even capable of acknowledging our presence. Their only point of reference seems to be themselves, their reality, their world, and this is often why they can insist that who they are, the way they understand reality, and the way they deal with it is what should be and is therefore normative in society. Those for whom Hispanic Women are "invisibly invisible" usually react with shock when one points out what they are doing. Their reaction is generally, "Well, I never think of you as Hispanic." And when we let them know how offensive that is, they cannot understand why we feel that way. Many of those who react to Hispanic Women this way consider themselves as people committed to doing away with group difference. To them this is what justice is about. In doing this, however, they are espousing a model of assimilation that excludes diversity and specificity and allows "norms expressing the point of view and experience of the privileged groups to appear neutral and universal," and ultimately, normative.[5]

A second kind of reaction to Hispanic Women that we experience is that of *respect*. This kind of respect is not the profound awe that makes one value and give importance to someone else. No, the "respect" we experience is the quick-nod-of-the-head-acknowledgment, the politically correct response that one gets from those in control when they do not want to take Hispanic Women seriously. This is the reaction we also get from well-meaning people of the dominant culture who believe they recognize and accept differences. Those who respond to Hispanic Women with respect are aware of the *problem* of differences but are not willing to take difference into consideration. Though they do acknowledge that there are other understandings than their own and that of the dominant culture, these well-meaning people proceed as if the only understanding is their own. They obviously fail to recognize that if they really respected Hispanic Women, their very identity and their theories and practices would have to be different.[6]

What is missing in the respect some of us Hispanic Women receive is engagement. The respect we are given does not seem to include being taken seriously. It does not allow what we say to affect the other. It does not recognize that what one says about oneself cannot ignore others and their struggles. That is precisely what engagement is all about. For engagement to happen, difference has to be recognized as an asset and not as a problem. Difference is truly an asset because those who are different

> are mirrors in which you can see yourselves as no other mirror shows you. . . . It is not that we are the only faithful mirrors, but I think we are faithful mirrors. Not that we show you as you really are; we just show you as one of the people who you are. What we reveal to you is that you are many—something that may in itself be frightening to you. But the self we reveal to you is also one that you are not eager to know for reasons that one may conjecture.[7]

For difference to be seen as a positive factor making engagement possible, the person who is different has to be allowed to be herself. Hispanic Women cannot be required to act or present ourselves first and foremost in a way intelligible to those of the dominant culture. Engagement requires that we enter into each other's worldview as much as possible and help others open up to new perspectives. If there is no willingness to enter into the world of the other, the self presented to people who are different from us is a "pretend self." We will hide our real selves in order to protect ourselves from others' projection of us. Respectful engagement requires honesty and a willingness to risk on the part of the Hispanic Women as well. But we are not called to lose ourselves in engagement; rather, we are called to grow and effectively contribute to our liberation and that of our community. For this to happen, those who are willing to engage us must embrace our difference instead of making us a reflection of who they are.

Engagement and interaction are not a matter of including Hispanic Women in the dominant culture. It is not a matter of adding us to the melting pot as a way of avoiding guilt or accusations of being either noninclusive or falsely inclusive. It is a matter of embracing the other because she is important, and not because of how much she can be used. This requires a commitment to know Hispanic Women and our struggles, and to recognize that our oppression is related to the privileges which the dominant culture enjoys.[8] Honest engagement ultimately leads to and demands that we understand that the "self requires self-conscious interaction"[9] to the point that without such interaction we cannot be our own selves.

Finally, engagement and interaction require more than applauding diversity and romanticizing it. For pluralism to be part of the construction of our everyday reality we need an analysis of power as part of our commitment. Because of the way those in power have oppressed us, Hispanic Women—as well as women in general—have been reticent to speak about power, to analyze power, and to claim power. But unless we analyze who has the power and how it is being used, unless we are willing to understand power as an intrinsic element of our struggle to be self-determining women, difference will not be embraced. Engagement and interaction will succumb to manipulation.

Having Hispanic Women around the table does not guarantee engagement and interaction. These will become a reality when Hispanic Women are not always having to adapt to the way meetings are conducted, groups are run, businesses operate, U.S. society is organized, and the public interest is administered. For engagement and interaction actually to happen, my claim as a Hispanic Woman to participate in defining what is normative must be attended to. This means that Hispanic Women will have a share of power. This, I suggest, will not happen as long as power is understood as a closed quantum instead of as a dynamic interaction that is rooted in and belongs to the community. Therefore, those who have power need to be accountable to the community. They need to understand power not as something to possess but as a dynamism to be shepherded for the good of the whole community.

Differences among Hispanic Women

What has been said about differences between Hispanic Women and persons of the dominant culture applies also to differences between Hispanic Women and Hispanic men as well as to differences between Hispanic Women and persons, women and men, of other marginalized groups. Furthermore, it also applies to differences among Hispanic Women ourselves, differences that must be analyzed and acknowledged if we are really to claim and embrace *mestizaje*.

Intrinsic to *mujerista* theology's method is not only an acceptance of differences among Hispanic Women but an insistence on pointing out such differences.[10] From the very beginning of our attempts to articulate Hispanic Women's religious understandings and practices and our conscious practice of it as a liberative praxis, *mujerista* theologians have welcomed and not just tolerated expressions of diversity. We have attempted repeatedly not to tailor the perspectives and experiences of other Hispanic Women to fit our own. This is one of the reasons we have insisted that the voices of Hispanic Women, as diverse as possible, be an integral part of our articulation of *mujerista* theology. It is also important to make clear that we have not done this in an attempt to be politically correct but because we have felt and known what our own incompleteness would be if we were to listen to and reflect theologically only with Hispanic Women in our communities who are similar to us or who agree with us.

The challenge of diversity among Hispanic Women and the role that such a diversity plays in this liberative praxis that we call *mujerista* theology is not one we feel we have resolved. Perhaps we will never resolve it. Our awareness that there is not a universal Hispanic womanness pushes us to deal more and more with particularity and specificity and to stay away from universal claims regarding Hispanic Women. While we embrace the similarities among ourselves, we understand that these similarities exist within the context of specificities and particularities, in a continuum of diversity. Our challenge always will be to recognize "the particularity and multiplicity of practices, cultural symbols, and the ways of relating," while resisting unifying them in distinct categories.[11] The attempt to set up unifying categories would result in doing to each other what the dominant culture does to us. It would result in defining those of us who do not have those similarities as totally other, and this would lead in turn to exclusion and opposition.

This is something that those of us who wield the pen, who publish books, and have access to public forums will always have to be on guard against. We must acknowledge that we do have more of an opportunity at least to set parameters about the meaning of Hispanic womanness.[12] We must indeed be constant in our efforts to see Hispanic Women as distinct persons with historical specificity and particularity. We must understand the *mestizaje* of Hispanic Women as a dynamic concept that is always welcoming diversity and, therefore, always reworking what we consider our similarities to be. In other words, the fact that we are Hispanic Women means that we share those characteristics and struggles we discussed in the first two chapters of this book instead of claiming a common nature or a given essentialness.

One of the leads we need to follow here is the understanding that in rejecting differences as substantive categories and attributes, what we are doing is welcoming our diversity as relational.[13] Therefore, what we need to do to embrace diversity is to engage each other respectfully and to integrate each other's understandings of reality into our own. We must require of each other as Hispanic Women what we require of non-Hispanic Women. To briefly restate what has been said above: we must acknowledge and live in ways that recognize that Hispanic Women from whom I am different are important in themselves, and that who I am—for better or for worse—depends on them and vice versa, and further we must elucidate the power dynamics among us.

The understanding of difference prevalent in the U.S.A. that creates minority groups, I believe, both hinders and helps Hispanic Women to recognize diversity and to embrace it as something precious. How and why does it hinder? First, the use of the term *Hispanic* in the U.S.A. by government agencies, the media, and the public at large shows that the dominant culture thinks of us as a homogeneous group. Grouping us under the label *Hispanic* also helps the dominant group in society to conceive of us and maintain us as totally other. This makes it possible to use Hispanic as a label with mostly negative connotations: it identifies a certain kind of people who are poor, uneducated, stealing jobs from Americans, who do not speak English, and so forth. Second, seeing us as a *minority* group makes the process of marginalization, oppression, and discrimination possible and viable. Third, because it ignores the variety of backgrounds and conditions of individual persons as well as the myriad of reasons why different ones of us find ourselves in the U.S.A., the term *Hispanic* makes it more difficult for us to have a positive sense of self and often leads to an internalized devaluation that is very difficult to overcome.[14] Fourth, being seen as totally *other* means that Hispanic Women are caught in a dilemma: to participate in this society means to accept and adopt an identity that is not ours, and to participate means to remember and be reminded constantly of what we are not.[15]

Being thrown together into a pile labeled Hispanic, however, can also be helpful for us in our process of self-definition and self-determination. I contend that being "other" in this society provides for us an opportunity to embrace diversity, to affirm differences, to engage each other, and to interact self-consciously. Experiencing what it means to be considered totally "other" helps us to understand and reject the dynamics of cultural imperialism. Being considered a homogeneous group in a way forces us to face up to our own prejudices: our own racism, classism, and sexism. That we are looked upon as all being the same, as a homogeneous group, can become an opportunity for us to make a conscious choice of what it does mean that we are Hispanics living in the U.S.A. as well as the role we want to have in this society. In a word, we have the opportunity of defining ourselves, of opting to be *mestizos,* opting to be *for* Hispanics, opting to be Hispanics.[16]

Hispanic Women Opting for Hispanic Women

Much has been written in the last decade about the option for the poor. Most of what has been said on this subject has to do with calling the rich, the oppressors, to conversion. I used this concept of the option for the poor in the previous chapter in a somewhat different fashion. It is my contention that option for the poor demands of us to embrace grassroot Hispanic Women not merely as the subject matter of *mujerista* theology and as the ones to whom those of us who publish writing about *mujerista* theology are accountable. It also calls us to recognize Hispanic Women who are engaged in liberative praxis because of their religious understanding as *mujerista* theologians themselves and to acknowledge their liberative praxis as doing *mujerista* theology. I now look at the option for the poor from the underside and across, instead of from the top and down. I look at the need for the poor to choose the poor, for Hispanic Women to choose Hispanicness and *mestizaje* as an expression of their option for the poor and the oppressed, an option to which I believe the poor and the oppressed are also called.

The term "preferential option for the poor" appears in the "Message to the Peoples of Latin America," written by the Latin American bishops during the 1979 Puebla Conference.[17] There the bishops took up once again the position they had taken at Medellín ten years earlier when they "adopted a clear and prophetic option expressing preference for, and solidarity with, the poor."[18] The bishops saw having a preferential option for the poor within the context of a conversion that they believe the whole church needs. This preferential option is aimed at the "integral liberation" of the poor. The bishops also made clear that this option is not an excluding option. Among the reasons the bishops give for such a preferential option is the fact that poverty dims and defiles the image and likeness of God in human beings. The bishops make explicit that the preferential option for the poor remains regardless of "the moral or personal situation in which they [the poor] find themselves."[19]

The preferential option for the poor does not rest on their being morally better, or more innocent, or purer in their motives. It exists because the poor can see and understand what the rich and privileged cannot, because power and richness are self-protective and, therefore, distort reality. The poor have no vested interest in maintaining their present situation. It is that the poor,

> pierced by suffering and full of hope, are able, in their struggles, to conceive another reality. Because the poor suffer the weight of alienation, they can conceive a hope-filled project and they can provide dynamism to a new way of organizing human life for all.[20]

These reasons for a preferential option for the poor can very well be the same reasons why we Hispanic Women should choose Hispanicness, *mestizaje*. These are the reasons we must welcome and embrace diversity. Because Hispanic Women embody a diversity of races and cultures, of socioeconomic strata and political ideologies, failure to affirm our *mestizaje* will definitely dim and defile the image and likeness of God in us. Only if we choose to be Hispanic Women within the U.S. society can we see different possibilities for our communities and for all those living here. We must choose an integrating liberation that demands changes of structures rather than participation in present oppressive structures. For us to choose *mestizaje* means that as Hispanic Women we have to be committed to making our *proyecto histórico* a reality.[21]

Hispanic Women opting for Hispanic Women entails struggling to make a reality our *proyecto histórico*.[22] To opt for Hispanic Women means, first of all, being self-identifying, risking whatever it takes to enhance our moral agency, to be agents of our own history by not allowing others to act upon us, to treat us as objects. Second, opting for Hispanic Women means that we, as Hispanic Women, engage in the difficult and painful task of getting rid of the oppressor within, of the internalized oppressor. Although we have few other models than the oppressor's, and although everything in society invites us to be like the oppressor in order to be successful, we must withstand such pressure. Becoming the image and likeness of the oppressor will only assure us of a continuation of the status quo, which necessitates that a group always be at the bottom of the social-economic-political ladder. Third, to opt for Hispanic Women means that we renounce vengeance, that we realize that our task is to work to make a reality a *proyecto histórico* that benefits not only us, but everyone. As Hispanic Women, we have a preferential option for Hispanic Women not because we are better but because, we hope, our struggle makes us see different possibilities and a reality different from the present one in which we can hardly survive.

In having a preferential option for Hispanic Women we are engaging in liberative praxis, which, as such, has to be an intentional, effective struggle against oppression. In other words, a preferential option of Hispanic Women for Hispanic Women is for us a moral imperative, a key element of our moral truth-praxis. Without such an option we cannot claim to embrace *mestizaje*. And if we do not do that, we will be betraying who we are and what we understand we should be about.

Mestizaje and Hispanic Women's Moral Truth-Praxis

For Hispanic Women *mestizaje* is not only a paradigm and a hermeneutical tool for our theological praxis, but, because it is a symbol of our communities, it also is a symbol of Hispanic Women's moral truth-praxis. In *mujerista* theology we understand *mestizaje* as happening now, being experienced now, in many different ways. By using *mestizaje*, therefore, as a symbol of our moral truth-praxis, we once again claim the experience of Hispanic Women as the source of our theology. In claiming *mestizaje* as a symbol of our moral truth-praxis we are saying that we do not believe in abstract notions of truth. We are using the binomial *truth-praxis* to indicate that we deal with our own experience in a critical way and look at it in light of the histories of our own communities and of other communities of struggle, and in light of what has been passed down to us by our forebears, particularly our mothers, our *tías,* and our *abuelitas.*[23]

Hispanic Women's communities, like all communities, are moral communities. Specific norms and behaviors based on the values of Hispanic culture are set by our communities. Communities as a whole are expected to hold specific values and to function accordingly. Each member of our communities, of course, is expected to act according to the values and norms of the community to which she belongs. In our communities, Hispanic Women are important and active moral laborers. Hispanic Women are the main transmitters of moral norms. But we do not transmit moral standards in an acritical fashion. On the contrary, as the women we have heard speaking in the pages of this book show, Hispanic Women in their daily lives are vitally involved in a process of evaluating existing moral norms of our communities, adapting them, and producing new ones in order to survive. Although most Hispanic Women might not be aware of this, their daily struggle to survive challenges the dominant culture and its moral claims, denouncing the racism / ethnic prejudice characteristic of U.S. society. And our embracing of *mestizaje* is a clear expression of this denunciation.[24]

As a symbol of our truth-praxis, then, our embracing of *mestizaje* is, first of all, a call to re-create moral standards according to our daily struggle for survival, and it is a call for social change so we can embrace diversity and live according to our own moral norms. This means that one of the characteristics of *mestizaje* as a symbol of our moral truth-praxis is that it has to be an effective praxis. That is to say, we judge our morality and our commitment to *mestizaje* by how effective we are in welcoming diversity and in engaging each other. We cannot continue to talk positively about *mestizaje* without denouncing the prejudices that exist among us as Hispanic Women and without working to make those prejudices disappear.

Another characteristic of *mestizaje* is that it is not an abstraction or something that happened in the past. *Mestizaje* is a present historical reality being elaborated in our very lives. This is why it must be affirmed and chosen repeatedly in all aspects of our lives. As a symbol of Hispanic Women's truth-praxis, *mestizaje* concretizes and makes public a fundamental option that helps define us as historical agents. It must be clear that to choose *mestizaje* means that we reject hierarchical understandings that set some over others. It also means that we reject a competitive individualism that destroys our sense of community and makes us see life as a win-lose situation.

Finally, as a symbol of Hispanic Women's moral truth-praxis, *mestizaje* is an expression of our responsibility to each other. Responsibility to others—and not for others—means that we allow other Hispanic Women to hold us accountable for who we are and what we do. To be responsible to others is to respect them for who they are and what they do while at the same time challenging them. To be responsible to others means that we welcome diversity and embrace it because we respect each other. That requires that we take each other seriously, that we engage and challenge each other to be ever more committed to the liberation of Hispanic Women.

As already explained in chapter 1, it is clear that I now use *mestizaje-mulatez* as symbol of the truth-praxis that we proclaim and which we struggle to honor in the way we live. In claiming this symbol, we recognize it as a reality defining who we are, but also pointing to what we choose to be. Hispanic women value and embrace the diversity of cultures and races among us and that make us face the ethnic/racial prejudice of the society in which we live and of our own societies of origin.

Mestizaje-mulatez makes us confront continuously the need we have to be in solidarity among ourselves and with all those who struggle for liberation. *Mestizaje-mulatez* calls us to mutuality, an intrinsic element of solidarity, without which justice cannot exist. Solidarity requires us to understand that justice happens when we start to pay attention to the requirements made of us by relationships in our lives: just relationships with other persons, with animals and nature, and with God. *Mestizaje-mulatez* helps us understand that it is precisely because of differences that we relate to each other and that we have to tend to others' needs, receiving as much as giving. *Mestizaje-mulatez* helps us to understand the dissimilarity in the way each one of us faces the differences that exist within our culture. It helps us to conceptualize liberation today as a struggle for inclusion and against exclusion. Faced with hegemonic powers that struggle to exclude the majority of the human race and our biosphere, *mestizaje-mulatez* helps us Hispanic women see the "other" that we carry within us.

In *mujerista* theology we see the need to continue to claim *mestizaje-mulatez* as symbol of our truth-praxis not only because we need to continue to struggle against ethnic prejudice/racism in the U.S.A., but also because *mestizaje-mulatez* is an essential element of our reality, of our moral values, of our culture, and, therefore, of our struggle for liberation.

Síntesis del Capítulo 7
Mestizaje: Símbolo de la Moral, la Verdad y la Praxis
de las Mujeres Hispanas

Al comienzo de este libro vimos cómo "mestizaje" es uno de los elementos principales en la realidad étnica, racial y cultural de las mujeres hispanas. En el capítulo 2 analizamos cómo mestizaje también se puede referir a la mezcla del catolicismo español del siglo XVI con las religiones africanas y amerindias que ha resultado en nuestra religiosidad popular. En este capítulo vamos a analizar los desafíos que mestizaje presenta a las mujeres hispanas.

En la teología hispana en general se usa "mestizaje" en forma paradigmática para hablar acerca de la comunidad hispana, y también como instrumento hermenéutico para ayudarnos a interpretar nuestra rica y compleja realidad. Algunas de nosotras, teólogas *mujeristas*, tememos que el uso de mestizaje en la teología hispana puede resultar en un romantizar la cultura hispana y nuestra comunidad. Al entrevistar a mujeres hispanas en diferentes partes de este país, nos dimos cuenta de que para no "idealizar" mestizaje teníamos que hacer dos cosas. Primero, tenemos que hacer un análisis profundo no sólo de las diferencias entre hispanos, sino también de cómo lidiamos con esas diferencias porque, si no abrazamos nuestras diferencias, no hay posibilidad de un verdadero mestizaje. Segundo, como la etnicidad es una construcción social que incluye no sólo características culturales y biológicas sino también elementos socioeconómicos de la comunidad hispana en los EE.UU., los hispanos y las hispanas podemos— tenemos—que escoger ser o no ser hispanas/hispanos. Tener que optar por abrazar nuestro mestizaje, y no sólo verlo como un hecho que no podemos controlar o decidir, nos ayuda en forma muy efectiva a no pensar en el mestizaje como algo ilusorio y sentimental que se refiere a las manifestaciones externas de nuestra cultura.

Escoger ser hispana fue algo que vi claramente cuando hice las entrevistas para este libro. Aunque continuamente encontré similitudes culturales en los entendimientos y las prácticas religiosas y éticas de las mujeres hispanas, es obvio que las similitudes no producen uniformidad sino un continuo de características, puntualizado por particularidad, especificidad y diversidad. Tenemos que entender que el mestizaje requiere esta diversidad.

Otra razón por la que las *mujeristas* hemos tenido que prestarle atención a las diferencias es porque hemos tenido que desafiar la manera en que las feministas euro-americanas hablan de las mujeres como si todas fuéramos idénticas. Este desatino nos ha llevado a examinar en la primera parte de este capítulo cómo es que las mujeres hispanas entienden diversidad y diferencias. En la segunda parte discutiremos qué tenemos que hacer las hispanas en cuanto a diversidad y diferencias. En la tercera parte explicaremos cómo usamos mestizaje como símbolo de nuestra verdad-praxis moral.

Entendiendo y valorizando diferencia

La manera cómo las personas del grupo dominante reaccionan ante las mujeres hispanas indica lo poco que se aprecia en esta sociedad el ser diferente. Parece que lo mejor que la diferencia engendra es una clase de competencia que termina siempre con alguien perdiendo; y lo peor que engendra es un desprecio destructivo al que nos referimos por el nombre de racismo y prejuicio étnico. Como ya hemos dicho, este desprecio destructivo es lo que lleva a la dominación que depende de y resulta en la subyugación, la explotación y la represión.

Una manera de reaccionar a la presencia de las hispanas es ignorarnos. La mayoría de las personas que nos ignoran no saben ni que lo están haciendo; es como si no fuesen capaces de aceptar nuestra presencia. Para ellas su punto de referencia es exclusivamente ellas mismas, su mundo, y es por eso que a menudo insisten en que quiénes ellas son, la manera en que entienden la realidad, y la manera cómo lidian con ella es lo que debe ser la norma en la sociedad.

Muchos de los que reaccionan en esta forma ante la presencia de las mujeres hispanas son personas que quieren eliminar diferencias, porque entienden que eso es lo que la justicia requiere. Al hacer esto, sin embargo, lo que están haciendo es abrazando la asimilación, lo cual excluye la diversidad y especificidad y permite que existan normas que sólo expresen el punto de vista y las experiencias de los grupos privilegiados, lo cual se ve como normal, universal y normativo, y a las que el resto nos tenemos que adaptar.

Una segunda reacción ante las hispanas que encontramos es el "respeto". Pero este respeto no es esa reverencia profunda que reconoce el valor y la importancia de la persona. No, el respeto que se nos tiene es ese reconocimiento superficial, la reacción políticamente correcta de quienes controlan y no nos prestan verdadera atención. Los que se comportan así saben que existe un problema en esta sociedad en cuanto a diferencias, pero no lo consideran cosa seria. Lo que le falta a este tipo de respeto es la interacción. El respeto que se nos tiene no nos toma en cuenta seriamente, no reconoce que lo que uno dice sobre uno mismo no puede ignorar a las demás y sus luchas. Para que de verdad haya interacción, lo diferente se tiene que reconocer como algo positivo; las personas diferentes a nosotras son espejos que nos reflejan de una manera distinta a cómo lo hacen las personas a las que más nos asemejamos. Las personas diferentes a nosotras no son nuestro único espejo, pero el reflejo que nos ofrecen es un reflejo fiel de quiénes somos. Estos espejos no nos reflejan en nuestra totalidad, pero sí nos muestran una de las maneras de cómo somos.

Para que la diferencia sea un factor positivo, haciendo posible la interacción, se les tiene que permitir a las personas que son diferentes, a las mujeres hispanas, ser quiénes somos y cómo somos. La interacción requiere el respeto, la honestidad y el riesgo. No estamos llamadas a disolvernos en la interacción, sino a través de ella a crecer y a contribuir en forma efectiva a nuestra liberación y a la de nuestra comunidad. La interacción no es un añadir a las mujeres hispanas a la olla—al *melting pot*—para no sentirse culpable o para evitar acusaciones de no ser inclusivo. En vez, la verdadera interacción es un abrazar a las demás porque son importantes en sí mismas y no porque las podemos usar. Esto requiere conocer a las mujeres hispanas y, nuestras luchas, y reconocer que nuestra opresión tiene una relación directa con los privilegios de los que gozan las personas de la cultura dominante.

Finalmente, la interacción requiere más que aplaudir y romantizar la diversidad. Para que la pluralidad sea parte de la construcción de nuestra vida cotidiana necesitamos analizar quién tiene poder. Si las mujeres hispanas no tienen poder, no podremos influir lo que es normativo. Y nosotras no tendremos poder mientras el poder se entienda como algo cuantitativo que se posee individualmente en vez de ver el poder como una interacción dinámica que se da en la comunidad y "pertenece" a la comunidad. Es por eso que la gente con poder tiene que rendir cuentas a la comunidad. Esas personas necesitan entender que el poder no es una posesión privada sino un dinamismo que se tiene que pastorear en vistas al bien común.

Diferencias entre las mujeres hispanas

Lo que hemos dicho acerca de las diferencias entre las hispanas y las personas de la cultura dominante también se debe aplicar a las diferencias entre las hispanas y los hispanos, entre las personas hispanas y personas de otros grupos marginados, y entre las mismas mujeres hispanas. Si no analizamos y aceptamos las diferencias que existen entre nosotras, no podemos reclamar y abrazar el mestizaje.

Un elemento intrínseco del método de la teología *mujerista* es aceptar diferencias entre las mujeres hispanas en forma consciente y decisiva. Es por eso que hemos insistido en incluir las voces de las hispanas en nuestro quehacer teológico: para respetar la diversidad que representan. Hemos hecho esto porque sentimos y sabemos que estaríamos incompletas si sólo escucháramos e incluyéramos en nuestra teología a hispanas que fueran como nosotras o que estuviesen de acuerdo con nosotras.

La diversidad entre las mujeres hispanas y el papel que esa diversidad tiene en este proceso liberador que llamamos teología *mujerista* continúa siendo un desafío. El estar conscientes de que no existe una sola clase de mujer hispana nos lleva más y más a reconocer y a señalar particularidades y a alejarnos de dictámenes universales acerca de las hispanas. Al abrazar las similitudes que existen entre nosotras, entendemos que estas similitudes se dan en un contexto en el cual lo específico y lo particular forman un continuo de diversidad. El desafío siempre consistirá en reconocer las particularidades y multiplicidad de prácticas, símbolos culturales y maneras de relacionarnos, resistiendo el deseo de unificarlos en categorías discretas. El insistir en establecer categorías que homogenizan las particularidades y diferencias sería hacer lo mismo que la cultura dominante hace con nosotras. El resultado sería que las que no comparten las similitudes serían consideradas personas ajenas, y esto llevaría a excluirlas.

También rechazamos ver las diferencias como atributos ya que entendemos la diversidad como algo relacional. Lo que tenemos que hacer para abrazar la diversidad es establecer una interacción respetuosa y tratar de integrar en nuestra manera de ser la manera en que otros entienden y lidian con la realidad.

Pero la manera en que esta sociedad entiende las diferencias es muy distinta y lleva a que existan los llamados "grupos minoritarios". Yo creo que esto obstaculiza pero también ayuda a que las mujeres hispanas reconozcamos y aceptemos la diversidad como algo precioso. ¿Cómo obstaculiza? Primero, el que se refieran a todas con la etiqueta "hispanas" ayuda al grupo dominante a vernos como totalmente ajenas a él. Esto lleva a que lo "hispano" tenga connotaciones mayormente negativas: somos pobres, sin educación, robamos los empleos a los americanos, no hablamos inglés, etcétera. Segundo, el vernos como grupo minoritario hace posible marginarnos, oprimirnos y discriminar contra nosotras. Tercero, el que se nos reduzca a una sola clase de personas llamadas hispanas nos hace difícil el tener un sentido positivo de nosotras mismas y a menudo nos lleva a internalizar la forma en que nos devalúa la clase dominante. Cuarto, el ser clasificadas como "otras" nos causa un dilema: participar en esta sociedad quiere decir aceptar y adoptar una identidad que no es la nuestra, cosa que, a la vez, nos hace recordar constantemente que no somos de la sociedad en la que estamos tratando de participar.

¿Cómo nos ayuda? Yo creo que el que se nos considere personas "ajenas", "otras", nos hace enfrentarnos a la posibilidad de abrazar la diversidad, afirmar las diferencias, tomar en cuenta a las demás e interactuar con ellas conscientes de las diferencias que existen. Experimentar lo que es ser considerada totalmente "ajena" y "otra" nos ayuda a entender las formas en que el imperialismo cultural nos oprime y nos lleva a rechazarlo. El ser visto como un grupo homogéneo nos hace enfrentarnos con nuestros propios prejuicios: nuestro racismo, clasismo y sexismo. El que se nos vea a todas las hispanas como si no existieran diferencias y particularidades entre nosotras puede darnos la oportunidad de hacer una opción consciente: nos da la oportunidad de definirnos a nosotras mismas, de subrayar el mestizaje de nuestra cultura, de escoger el ser hispanas y el optar siempre por las hispanas.

Mujeres hispanas optando por mujeres hispanas

Se ha escrito mucho en los últimos diez años acerca de la opción por los pobres. La mayor parte de lo que se ha dicho tiene que ver con llamar a los ricos, a los opresores, a que se conviertan. Ya he insistido en que las que son pobres y las oprimidas también tienen que abrazar la opción por los pobres. Si examinamos la opción por los pobres no de arriba para abajo sino desde abajo y horizontalmente, ¿qué vemos? Lo que vemos es la necesidad que tienen los pobres de optar por los pobres, las mujeres hispanas de optar por la hispanidad con el mestizaje como elemento intrínseco. Uno de los resultados en el quehacer teológico, por ejemplo, es valorizar a las hispanas en tal forma que seamos no sólo el tema de la teología *mujerista* sino también nos reconozcamos capaces de hacer teología, de ser teólogas *mujeristas*.

Las mujeres hispanas reunimos una gran diversidad de razas y culturas, de ideologías políticas y posiciones socioeconómicas. Si no afirmamos nuestro mestizaje en esta sociedad, profanamos y obscurecemos la imagen y semejanza de Dios que hay en nosotras. Si no afirmamos nuestro mestizaje de culturas, perspectivas políticas y económico-sociales, y razas no podremos implantar nuestro proyecto histórico: no podremos luchar por la liberación. Es obvio que mestizaje para la teología *mujerista* quiere decir más que mezcla de razas; "mestizaje" es la integración de la diversidad que existe entre las hispanas como elemento de nuestra lucha por la liberación.

El optar por las mujeres hispanas quiere decir, primero, que tenemos que ser auto-determinantes, y tomar todo riesgo necesario para fortalecer nuestra agencia moral, siendo sujetos de nuestra propia historia, oponiéndonos a que se nos trate como si fuéramos objetos. Segundo, el optar por las mujeres hispanas quiere decir que tenemos que librarnos del opresor que hemos internalizado. Aunque tenemos pocos modelos más allá de nuestros opresores y aunque todo en la sociedad nos invita a imitar a los opresores, si queremos "salir adelante", tenemos que resistir esa tentación. Ser la imagen y semejanza del opresor sólo asegura que las cosas continuarán como están: que siempre habrá un grupo oprimido, un grupo en el último peldaño de la escala sociopolítico-económica. Tercero, el optar por las mujeres hispanas implica que renunciemos a la venganza, que nos demos cuenta de que lo que tenemos que hacer es luchar por implantar nuestro proyecto histórico, el cual nos beneficia no sólo a nosotras sino a toda nuestra sociedad.

Mestizaje: símbolo de nuestra verdad-praxis moral

El mestizaje puede ser símbolo de nuestra verdad-praxis moral porque es símbolo de la comunidad hispana. En la teología *mujerista* reconocemos que hay un nuevo mestizaje que se está llevando a cabo de muchas maneras diferentes hoy en día en esta sociedad. Por lo tanto, al usar el mestizaje como símbolo de nuestra verdad-praxis reclamamos una vez más que la fuente de la teología *mujerista* es la experiencia de las mujeres hispanas. Usamos el binomio verdad-praxis para indicar que lidiamos con nuestra experiencia en forma crítica, a la luz de las historias de nuestras comunidades y de otras comunidades de lucha, y tomando en consideración lo que nos han legado nuestros antepasados: en especial nuestras madres, abuelitas, tías y madrinas.

Al igual que cualquiera otra comunidad, las comunidades de mujeres hispanas son comunidades morales. Nuestras comunidades tienen normas y maneras de actuar específicas basadas en los valores de nuestra cultura y se espera que los miembros de nuestras comunidades las observen. En nuestras comunidades las mujeres hispanas somos "trabajadoras morales" muy importantes. Somos las mujeres hispanas las que transmitimos las normas morales, pero no las transmitimos en forma a-crítica. Al contrario, como han demostrado las mujeres cuyas voces hemos escuchado en estas páginas, las mujeres hispanas en su vivir cotidiano están involucradas en forma vital en el proceso de evaluar las normas morales de nuestras comunidades, en adaptarlas y en producir nuevas normas que nos ayuden en nuestra lucha por sobrevivir. Aunque muchas no se den cuenta de esto, la lucha cotidiana de las mujeres hispanas por sobrevivir es un reto a la cultura dominante y a sus normas morales. Esa lucha es una denuncia del racismo-prejuicio étnico que caracteriza la sociedad de los EE.UU. y nuestro abrazar el mestizaje es una clara expresión de esta denuncia.

Como símbolo de nuestra verdad-praxis el mestizaje nos llama, en primer lugar, a crear normas morales a partir de nuestra lucha por sobrevivir. Pero no se crean normas morales en el aire sino al ir implementando los cambios necesarios para poder abrazar la diversidad y vivir de acuerdo a nuestros propios valores morales. Esto lleva a que el mestizaje sea en sí una praxis efectiva. O sea, tenemos que juzgar nuestra moralidad y nuestro compromiso con el mestizaje de acuerdo a cuán efectivo es en ayudarnos a denunciar los prejuicios que existen entre las mujeres hispanas y lo poco que hacemos para que esos prejuicios desaparezcan. No podemos continuar elogiando el mestizaje sin abrazar nuestra diversidad.

El mestizaje no es una idea abstracta o algo que sucedió en el pasado. El mestizaje es una realidad presente que elaboramos día a día en nuestras vidas. Como símbolo de la verdad-praxis de las mujeres hispanas, el mestizaje concretiza y da a conocer nuestra opción fundamental por nosotras mismas, lo que nos ayuda a definirnos como sujetos históricos. Tenemos que entender claramente que el optar por el mestizaje significa rechazar una mentalidad jerárquica que nos pone a unos por arriba de los otros. También quiere decir que rechazamos el sentido de competencia individualista que destruye el sentido de comunidad y nos hace ver la vida como una contienda en la que se gana o se pierde.

Finalmente, como símbolo de la verdad-praxis de las mujeres hispanas, el mestizaje es una expresión de nuestra responsabilidad para con las demás. Somos responsables *para* con los demás y no *por* los demás. Ésta es la razón por la cual les pedimos a otras mujeres hispanas que nos hagan rendir cuentas por quiénes somos y lo que hacemos; esto quiere decir que respetamos a las demás pero que las desafiamos a ser mejores; quiere decir que aceptamos la diversidad porque nos respetamos las unas a las otras. El ser responsable para con los demás requiere que nos tomemos en serio las unas a las otras y que nos desafiemos a estar más y más comprometidas con la liberación de las mujeres hispanas.

Dado lo que ya he explicado en los apuntes del capítulo 1, hoy en día uso mestizaje-mulatez como símbolo de la verdad-praxis que proclamamos y luchamos por vivir como *mujeristas*. Al reclamar mestizaje-mulatez como símbolo reconocemos que es una realidad que se da en quiénes somos, pero que también apunta a lo que debemos escoger ser: mujeres hispanas que apreciamos y abrazamos la diversidad que existe entre nosotras, la multiplicidad de culturas y razas que forman nuestra cultura, y que nos hace enfrentarnos al prejuicio étnico/racial de la sociedad en la que vivimos y de nuestras sociedades de origen.

Mestizaje-mulatez como símbolo de nuestra verdad-praxis nos sitúa continuamente frente a la necesidad que tenemos de solidaridad entre nosotras y con todas las personas que luchan por la liberación. Mestizaje-multatez nos llama a la mutualidad que es elemento intrínseco de la solidaridad, sin la cual no puede existir la justicia. La solidaridad requiere que entendamos que la justicia no se da sino a partir de los requisitos que nos imponen las relaciones en nuestras vidas: relaciones justas entre los seres humanos, relaciones con los animales y la naturaleza, y relaciones con Dios. Mestizaje-mulatez nos ayuda a entender que es precisamente a partir de las diferencias que uno se relaciona y que tenemos que atender las necesidades de con quienes nos relacionamos tanto recibiendo como dando. Mestizaje-mulatez nos ayuda a entender las diferencias que abrigamos en nuestras personas y en nuestra cultura y nos hace ver que tenemos que conceptualizar liberación hoy en día como inclusión y luchar en contra de la exclusión. Ante fuerzas hegemónicas que luchan por dejar fuera a la mayor parte de la raza humana y a la naturaleza, mestizaje-mulatez nos ayuda a las mujeres hispanas a ver que llevamos a la "otra" en nosotras.

Por esta razón, en la teología *mujerista* vemos la necesidad de reclamar mestizaje-mulatez como símbolo de nuestra verdad-praxis no sólo porque para sobrevivir tenemos que luchar contra el racismo/prejuicio racial de la sociedad en que vivimos las mujeres hispanas. Reclamamos mestizaje-mulatez como símbolo de nuestra verdad-praxis porque es parte esencial de nuestra realidad, es elemento central de nuestros valores morales, de nuestra cultura, y, por lo tanto, de nuestra lucha por la liberación.

NOTES

Preface

1. Two reasons compel me not to use the usual word employed by English Bibles, *kingdom*. First, it is obviously a sexist word that presumes that God is male. Second, the concept of kingdom in our world today is both hierarchical and elitist. The same reasons hold for not using *reign*. The word *kin-dom* makes it clear that when the fullness of God becomes a day-to-day reality in the world at large, we will all be sisters and brothers—kin to each other. This terminology was suggested to me by Georgenne Wilson, O.S.F.

Prefacio

1. "Familia de Dios" es la frase que uso para traducir *kin-dom of God,* siguiendo el pensamiento de Georgenne Wilson, OSF. No uso la frase tradicional "reino de Dios", por dos razones. Aunque la palabra "reino" en español no necesariamente se refiere a un monarca masculino, sí es una referencia a una institución jerárquica y elitista. Prefiero, por lo tanto, usar "familia de Dios," que señala la relación de familia que debe existir entre nosotras y nosotros, con todo lo que eso significa en las culturas hispanas, para que pueda hacerse realidad la presencia de Dios en la vida cotidiana.

Mujerista Theology at the Beginning of the Twenty-first Century

1. This is a word I heard used by Jasmine Zine, a Muslim feminist, in a presentation at the American Academy of Religion, in Toronto, Canada, November 2002. She uses this word to make clear that the dominant groups are the ones that turn us ethnic/racial groups into "minority" groups by not allowing us to have power in order to be able to control how we participate in society.

2. Mario C. Casalla, "El Cuarteto de Jerusalén—Sobre la justicia y sus avatares históricos," in *Márgenes de la Justicia*, ed. Mario C. Casalla (Buenos Aires: Grupo Editor Altamira, 2000), 238 and 262 (note 11).

3. Franz Hinkelammert, *Crítica a la razón utópica* (Costa Rica: Editorial D.E.I., 1984), 240; cited in Enrique Dussel, *Ética de la liberación—en la edad de la globalización y de la exclusión* (Madrid: Editorial Trotta, 1998), 262.

4. Hugo Assmann, "Por una sociedad donde quepan todos," in *Por una sociedad donde quepan todos,* ed. José Duque (Costa Rica: Editorial D.E.I., 1996), 387.

5. Dussel, 618. Single quotation marks and italics are from the original text.

6. See ibid., 622.

7. See Ivone Gebara, *Longing for Running Water—Ecofemnism and Liberation* (Minneapolis: Fortress Press, 1999), 71-99. Also see her most recent book, *Out of the Depths—Women's Experience of Evil and Salvation* (Minneapolis: Fortress Press, 2002), 133–144.

8. This is a way of saying in a clearer and more precise way what we have been saying all along, that liberation cannot be attained at the expense of anyone else, and that we want to work to bring about radical change in society and not just work to participate in present-day structures.

9. Franz Hinkelammert, "Una sociedad en la que todos quepan: de la impotencia de la omnipotencia," in Duque, 364.

10. Ibid.

11. David Harvey, *Spaces of Hope* (Berkeley: University of California Press, 2000), 234.

12. It has been said, without offering any proof, that I learned this word when I worked in Peru. This is not true. It has been said, without offering any proof, that the word *mujerista* refers to an essentialist, invalid understanding. This is not true. Only once did I use the word *mujerismo,* and when it was pointed out that it could be read as an essentialist term, I accepted the critique and never again have used it. It has been said, without offering any proof, that *mujerista* theology is not valid because it does not arise from a popular

movement. I have never claimed that it arises from a movement but have always presented *mujerista* theology as a school of thought that is rooted in the thinking and doing of grassroot *Latinas*.

Teología *Mujerista* al Comienzo del Siglo 21

1. Palabra que le escuché a Jasmine Zine, una feminista musulmana, en su presentación en American Academy of Religion, en Toronto, Canada en noviembre de 2002. Ella usa esta palabra para dejar por sentado que los grupos dominantes nos convierten a los grupos étnico-raciales que no tienen poder en grupos "minoritarios" para así poder controlar mejor nuestra participación en la sociedad.

2. Mario C. Casalla, "El Cuarteto de Jerusalén—Sobre la justicia y sus avatares históricos", en *Márgenes de la Justicia*, ed. Mario C. Casalla (Buenos Aires: Grupo Editor Altamira, 2000), 238 y 262 (cita #11).

3. Franz Hinkelammert, *Crítica a la razón utópica* (Costa Rica: Editorial DEI, 1984), 240; citado en Enrique Dussel, *Ética de la liberación—en la edad de la globalización y de la exclusion* (Madrid: Editorial Trotta, 1998), 262.

4. Hugo Assmann, "Por una sociedad donde quepan todos", en *Por una sociedad donde quepan todos,* ed. José Duque (Costa Rica: Editorial DEI, 1996), 387.

5. La cita completa lee así: "La vida humana tiene la racionalidad como constitutivo intrínseco (porque 'humana') y el ejercicio intersubjetivo y veritativo de la racionalidad es una exigencia de la propia vida: es una 'astucia' de la vida. La vida humana nunca es 'lo otro' que la razón, sino que es la condición absoluta material intrínseca de la racionalidad. Por esto se exige, entonces, no poner la razón sobre la vida.... Defendemos entonces que la vida humana es fuente de toda racionalidad, y que la racionalidad material tiene como criterio y última 'referencia' de verdad y como condición absoluta de su posibilidad a la vida humana." Duseel, 618.

6. Ver ibid., 622.

7. Ver Ivone Gebara, *Longing for Running Water—Ecofemnism and Liberation* (Minneapolis: Fortress Press, 1999), 71–99; también ver su libro más reciente, *Out of the Depths—Women's Experience of Evil and Salvation* (Minneapolis: Fortress Press, 2002), 133–144.

8. Ésta es una manera más clara y precisa de decir que lo hemos venido diciendo, que la liberación no se logra a expensas de otras u otros, y de que queremos y trabajamos por cambios radicales y no meramente para lograr participar en las estructuras que existen.

9. Franz Hinkelammert, "Una sociedad en la que todos quepan: de la impotencia de la omnipotencia", en Duque, 364.

10. Ibid.

11. David Harvey, *Spaces of Hope* (Berkeley: University of California Press, 2000), 234.

12. Se ha dicho, sin ofrecer ninguna prueba, que esta palabra la conocía de cuando trabajé en el Perú. No es cierto. Se ha dicho, sin ofrecer prueba alguna, que la palabra *mujerista* se refiere a una visión esencialista inválida. No es cierto. Una sóla vez usé la palabra *mujerismo* y cuando se me hizo notar que se podía leer como esencialista, acepté la crítica y no la he vuelto a usar. Se ha dicho, sin ofrecer prueba, que la teología *mujerista* no es válida porque no surge de un movimiento. Nunca he dicho que surge de un movimiento sino que siempre la he presentado como una escuela de pensamiento que tiene como fuente el pensar y el hacer de mujeres hispanas/latinas de la base.

Introduction

1. Initially I was not able to locate one of the women, Adela. She had moved and nobody in the community knew where she was. Eventually she got in contact with me and I was able to visit with her. But by then I had already interviewed Esperanza and what she shared with me was so rich that I could not but include it. I also include the material from the interview with Caridad. The circumstances in her life seemed to me to be so different from those of the others that I felt that her understandings would greatly enrich this work.

2. I was delighted to find one other person who insists that she is concerned with ethics in order to enable moral agency. See Sarah Lucia Hoagland, *Lesbian Ethics* (Palo Alto, Calif.: Institute of Lesbian Studies, 1989), 1–23.

3. Some now are proposing that we use "Hispanic American." See Fernando Segovia, "Introduction," *Listening 27,* no. 1 (winter 1992): 3–6.

4. Of course, it is important to point out that a significant number of Mexican Americans refer to themselves as "chicanas," many from New Mexico call themselves "Spanish-Americans," and some simply refer to themselves as "mejicanas." To understand the differences implied in each of these terms see Earl Shorris, *Latinos—A Biography of the People* (New York: W. W. Norton & Company, 1992), chap. 7.

5. Ada María Isasi-Díaz, "Toward an Understanding of *Feminismo Hispano* in the U.S.A.," in *Women's Consciousness, Women's Conscience,* ed. Barbara H. Andolsen, Christine E. Gudorf, and Mary D. Pellauer (New York: Winston, 1985), 51–61.

6. Ada María Isasi-Díaz, "A Hispanic Garden in a Foreign Land," in *Inheriting Our Mothers' Gardens,* ed. Letty Russell, Kwok Pui Lan, Ada María Isasi-Díaz, and Katie Cannon (Philadelphia: Westminster Press, 1988), 91–106.

7. Ada María Isasi-Díaz et al., "Roundtable: Who We Are and What We Are About," *Journal of Feminist Studies in Religion* 8, no. 1 (spring 1992): 105–25.

8. Charles E. Curran, *Directions in Fundamental Moral Theology* (Notre Dame: University of Notre Dame Press, 1985), 221–22.

CHAPTER 1: Hispanic Ethnicity and Social Locality in *Mujerista* Theology

1. For amplification of this understanding of ethnicity see Mary C. Waters, *Ethnic Options—Choosing Identities in America* (Los Angeles: University of California Press, 1990). Also see Candace Nelson and Marta Tienda, "The Structuring of Hispanic Ethnicity: Historical and Contemporary Perspectives," in *Ethnicity and Race in the U.S.A.—Toward the Twenty-First Century,* ed. Richard D. Alba (London: Henley Routledge & Kegan Paul, 1985).

2. See Fernando Segovia, "Two Places and No Place on Which to Stand: Mixture and Otherness in Hispanic American Theology," *Listening 27,* no. 1 (winter 1992): 27–33. Segovia uses the term "Hispanic American" precisely to include both ethnic and sociopolitical traits of our social location. I prefer including both traits under the single terms Hispanic or Latina/o.

3. Joan Moore and Harry Pachón, *Hispanics in the United States* (Englewood Cliffs, N.J.: Prentice-Hall, 1985), 1.

4. More on this concept later in this chapter.

5. Moore and Pachón, 182. See also, Alma M. García, "The Development of Chicana Feminist Discourse, 1970–1980" *Gender and Society* 3, no. 2 (June 1989): 217–38.

6. Moore and Pachón, 31. Puerto Ricans do not pay federal income tax but do pay income tax to the government of the island.

7. Ibid.

8. Though the term Cuban-American is beginning to be used mainly in political circles, it is not a term used by the community in most instances. Even Cubans born in the U.S.A. usually explain that they were born here of Cuban parents, and do not call themselves Cuban-Americans.

9. Close to one-third of all businesses in Miami and 40 percent of the industry are Cuban-owned. Twenty percent of the banks are controlled by Cubans: sixteen out of sixty-two bank presidents and 250 vice presidents are Cubans. In the Miami area, 75 percent of the construction workforce is Cuban. Other Cuban strongholds are in the areas of textiles, food, cigars, and trade with Latin America. See Nelson and Tienda, 59.

10. Moore and Pachón, 46.

11. Virgilio Elizondo makes extensive use of these two terms. See Virgilio Elizondo, *Galilean Journey— The Mexican American Promise* (Maryknoll, N.Y.: Orbis Books, 1983), 7–18. For an overall exposition of the importance of *mestizaje* in the development of Hispanic theologies, see John P. Rossing, "*Mestizaje* and Marginality: A Hispanic American Theology," *Theology Today* 44, no. 3 (October 1988): 293–304.

12. The poem by Lourdes Casals I have used as a preamble for this book expresses this idea, which for those of us who live it is a very strong sentiment, a reality.

13. José Vasconcelos, *La Raza Cósmica,* 11th ed., Colección Austral (Mexico City: Espasa-Calpé Mexicana, 1948), 25.

14. I believe a positive understanding of *mestizaje,* though somewhat different from ours, will emerge out of the structures of the "commonwealth" of nations, politically and/or economically, that an increasing number of nations in different continents are adopting. However, at present the terrible ethnic wars in what was the U.S.S.R., in Eastern Europe, and in different parts of Africa and Asia, as well as the racism/ethnic prejudice of so-called hate groups in the U.S.A. and other parts of the world, certainly indicate that much needs to be overcome before a healthy sense of *mestizaje* can emerge the world over.

15. Juan Carlos Scannone, "Teología cultural popular y discernimiento," in *Cultura popular y filosofía de la liberación* (Buenos Aires: Fernando García Cambeiro, 1975), 253–54.

16. The term "anthropological poverty" is found in "Doing Theology in a Divided World: Final Statement of the Sixth EATWOT Conference," in *Doing Theology in a Divided World,* ed. Virginia Fabella and Sergio Torres (Maryknoll, N.Y.: Orbis Books, 1985), 185. Paul Tillich discussed "being" and "not being" in *Systematic Theology* (Chicago: University of Chicago Press, 1951), 1, 44.

17. Cornel West, "Marxist Theory and the Specificity of Afro-American Oppression," in *Marxism and the Interpretation of Culture,* ed. Carry Nelson and Lawrence Grossberg (Chicago: University of Chicago Press, 1988), especially note 15.

18. Teresa L. Amott and Julie A. Matthaei, *Race, Gender & Work* (Boston: South End, 1991), 11.

19. Ibid., 13.

20. Rosemary Radford Ruether, "A Feminist Perspective," in *Doing Theology in a Divided World,* ed. Fabella and Torres, 70; see also Deborah K. King, "Multiple Jeopardy, Multiple Consciousness: The Context of a Black Feminist Ideology," in *Feminist Theory in Practice and Process,* ed. Micheline R. Malson, Jean F. O'Barr, Sara Westphal-Wihl, and Mary Wyer (Chicago: University of Chicago Press, 1989), 75–105.

21. Much of this thinking was based on the concept that Richard Lovejoy called "the Great Chain of Being." This was a plan and structure of the world in which there existed an infinite number of links arranged in "hierarchical order from the meagerest kind of existents, which barely escape non-existence, through 'every possible' grade . . . to the highest possible kind of creature, between which and the Absolute Being the disparity was assumed to be infinite." Of course, European whites were placed at the top of this hierarchy and the greater the physical differences from them, the lower was the person in this chain of being. Richard Lovejoy, *The Great Chain of Being* (Cambridge: Harvard University Press, 1936), 59.

22. Amott and Matthaei, 17.

23. Ibid.

24. See Rudolfo Acuña, *Occupied America: A History of Chicanos* (New York: Harper and Row, 1988), 395; María González, Victoria L. Barrera, Peter Guarnaccia, and Stephen L. Schensul, " 'La Operación': An Analysis of Sterilization in a Puerto Rican Community in Connecticut," in *Work, Family, and Health: Latina Women in Transition,* ed. Ruth E. Zambrana (Bronx, N.Y.: Hispanic Research Center, Fordham University, 1982), 50.

25. See Paulo Agirrebaltzategi, *Configuración ecclesial de las culturas* (Bilbao, Spain: Universidad de Deusto, 1976), 61–62.

26. Ibid., 364. See also Juan Luis Segundo, *The Liberation of Theology* (Maryknoll, N.Y.: Orbis Books, 1982), 185–86.

27. For a concise but important discussion of Hispanic Women's critique of our culture see García, "The Development of Chicana Feminist Discourse."

28. Amott and Matthaei, 5.

29. Ibid., 24.

30. Franz J. Hinkelammert, "La Crisis del socialismo y el tercer mundo," *Pasos* 30 (July–August 1990): 1–6. See also Pablo Richard, "La Teología de la liberación en la nueva coyuntura," *Pasos* 34 (March–April 1991): 1–8.

31. See below, chap. 6, where this theme is pursued further.

32. Bruce C. Birch and Larry L. Rasmussen, *Bible and Ethics in the Christian Life* (Minneapolis: Augsburg Fortress, 1989), 78–79. See also Ada María Isasi-Díaz and Yolanda Tarango, *Hispanic Women: Prophetic Voice in the Church* (Minneapolis: Fortress Press, 1992), 77–79.

33. See below, chap. 6.

34. For the importance of the socioeconomic reality of women in theology and ethics see Pamela K. Brubaker, "Rendering the Invisible: Methodological Constraints on Economic Ethics in Relation to Women's Impoverishment," Ph.D. diss., Union Theological Seminary, New York, 1989.

35. U.S. Bureau of the Census, *Poverty in the United States: 1990*, P-60, no. 175. "The government includes a person or family among the poor if their income falls below an officially designated *poverty line* or *threshold,* which varies according to family size. In 1985 the poverty line for a family of four was $10,990; for a single person between the ages of 15 and 64, it was $5,590. Every year these thresholds are adjusted for inflation." Taken from The Center for Popular Economics, *A Field Guide to the U.S. Economy* (New York: Pantheon Books, 1987), sec. T.10. These thresholds are criticized by the poor and their advocates as unrealistic. What the government says it costs to have a roof over one's head and heat in winter, enough food to eat, clothes to wear, and minimal medical attention, is inadequate for it does not take into consideration things like child care, time wasted in using government-sponsored programs, and lack of full-time jobs for women. The government's understanding also reduces "living" to "barely living" and thus creates a standard of living for the poor far below that of those who own property and have access to the benefits of being a citizen of one of the richest countries of the world.

36. *Poverty: 1990.*

37. U.S. Bureau of the Census, Current Population Reports, Series P-20, no. 455, *The Hispanic Population in the United States: March, 1991* (Washington, D.C.: U.S. Government Printing Office, 1991), 8.

38. "In 2000 the poverty line for a family of 4 with one child was $18,052; for a single person between the ages of 18 and 64 it was $8,959." U.S. Bureau Census, *Poverty in the United States: 2000* (Washington, D.C.: U.S. Government Printing Office, 2001), 5.

39. U.S. Bureau of the Census, Current Population Reports, Series P-20, no. 535, *The Hispanic Population in the United States: March 2000* (Washington, D.C.: U.S. Government Printing Office, 2001), 6; *Poverty: 2000,* Table A, p. 2.

40. *The Hispanic Population: 2000,* Table 14.1.

41. U.S. Department of Labor, Bureau of Labor Statistics. Data derived from the Current Population Survey, February 1992. African American and white teen unemployment is seasonally adjusted, but Hispanic youth unemployment is not because of too small a sample; therefore, these figures are not strictly comparable.

42. U.S. Bureau of Labor Statistics, "Employment Status of the Civilian Noninstitutional Population by Sex, Age, Race, and Hispanic Origin, 2001," in *Employment and Earnings* (Washington, D.C.: U.S. Government Printing Office, 2002), 170.

43. *Poverty: 1990.*

44. *The Hispanic Population: March 2000,* Table 14.1.

45. U.S. Department of Commerce, Bureau of the Census, CB91-288, September 26, 1991.

46. *The Hispanic Population: March 2000,* Table 1.

47. *Poverty: 2000,* Table A-1.

48. *The Hispanic Population: March 2000,* Table 15.1

49. Moore and Pachón, 64.

50. *Hispanic Population: 2000,* Table 6.1.

51. Ibid.

52. *A Field Guide,* sect.4.15.

53. U.S. Department of Commerce, Bureau of the Census, SB-3-89.

54. "Internet Table 1, Detailed Living Arrangements of Children by Race and Hispanic Origin," U.S. Bureau of the Census, April 13, 2001, June 24, 2002 <http://www.census.gov/population/socdemo/child/ p70-74/tab01.pdf>.

55. *Poverty: 1990.*

56. "Table F1, Family Households, by Type, Age of Own Children, Age of Family Members, and Age, Race and Hispanic Origin of Householder, March 1999," in *America's Families and Living Arrangements, March 2000,* U.S. Bureau of the Census, June 29, 2001, June 30, 2002 <http://www.census.gov/population/socdemo/hh-fam/p20-537/1999/tabF1.pdf>.

57. Deborah J. Carter and Reginald Wilson, *Eighth Annual Status Report on Minorities in Higher Education* (Washington, D.C.: American Council on Education Publications Department, December 1989), 1; *Hispanic Population: 2000*, Tables 7.2 and 7.3.

58. "2000–2001: Eighteenth Annual Status Report on Minorities in Higher Education," American Council on Education, Office of Minorities in Higher Education, May 16, 2002, June 25, 2002, <http://www.acenet.edu/programs/omhe/status-report/>.

59. William B. Johnson, *Workforce 2000: Work and Workers for the 21st Century* (Indianapolis: Hudson Institute, 1987), Tables 3-8, 3-7.

60. Ibid.

61. Moore and Pachón, 103.

62. This is also true of Central and South American women. Ibid., 104.

63. *The Hispanic Population: March 2000*, Table 11.3.

64. I am making a distinction between women having privilege and women profiting from the privilege of their husbands and/or fathers. Also, this is intended to help us understand not only the diversity among Hispanic Women, but also the differences between Hispanic Women and women of the controlling race and ethnic origin.

65. Richard, "La Teología de la liberación," 5. For an explanation of the understanding of culture we use in *mujerista* theology, see Isasi-Díaz and Tarango, *Hispanic Women*, 71–73. Since writing *Hispanic Women* we have come to understand that our adaptation of one of Niebuhr's models regarding Christ and culture results in a symbiosis of culture and Christianity that does not resonate with the religious understanding and practices of Protestant, evangelical, and Pentecostal Hispanic Women. However, we still understand *mujerista* theology to be cultural theology because it is a liberative praxis that happens within Hispanic culture and the religious understandings and practices of Hispanic Women are intrinsic to the definition of Hispanic culture.

CHAPTER 2: Popular Religiosity, Spanish, and *Proyecto Histórico*

1. José Míguez Bonino, *Doing Theology in a Revolutionary Situation* (Philadelphia: Fortress Press, 1975), 38–39. Chapter 3 of this book is perhaps the most detailed description of the meaning of *proyecto histórico* by a Latin American liberation theologian. *Mujerista* theology appropriates this term critically according to our lived-experience.

2. Audrey Lorde, "Poems Are Not Luxuries," *Chrysalis* 3 (1977): 8.

3. See Gustavo Gutiérrez, *A Theology of Liberation.* (Maryknoll, N.Y.: Orbis Books, 1988), xxxix, 83–91. See also Gustavo Gutiérrez, *The Truth Shall Make You Free* (Maryknoll, N.Y.: Orbis Books, 1990), 14–16, 116–21.

4. Gutiérrez, *Theology of Liberation,* 94.

5. Using Paulo Freire, Gutiérrez sees the relationship of what he calls "utopia" to historical reality as appearing under two aspects: denunciation and annunciation. See ibid., 136–40.

6. This is why we avoid using the terms "minority" or "marginalized." These labels communicate the way the dominant group sees us and not the way we see ourselves; they imply that what we want is to participate in present structures that are oppressive. We see ourselves as a group that has a significant contribution to make precisely because we demand radical change of oppressive structures.

7. See "Larry Rasmussen," *Christianity and Crisis,* October 22, 1990.

8. For the effectiveness of this understanding of struggling to build a preferred future see Renny Golden, *The Hour of the Poor, The Hour of Women* (New York: Crossroad, 1991).

9. We have appropriated Gutiérrez's understanding of the three levels or aspects of the process of liberation. The specifics of each of these aspects arise from our lived-experience as Latinas.

10. Gutiérrez refers to the "Chalcedonian Principle," and uses the Chalcedonian language regarding the two natures of the one person Jesus, in order to clarify the distinctiveness and intrinsic unity of the three aspects of liberation. In this, *mujerista* theology follows Gutiérrez quite closely. The distinctiveness of Latinas' struggle, however, will come in the "content" of each of the three aspects of the process of liberation. See Gutiérrez, *The Truth Shall Make You Free,* 120–4.

11. Following the venerable tradition referred to in Acts 1:26, we cast lots to decide the order in which we would deal with these three aspects of liberation! We know some will try to see in the order we use a certain priority of importance or relevance. That is indeed not our intention.

12. The only reason a *balsero,* a young man who escaped from Cuba in a makeshift raft, could give me for risking his life in such a way was the lack of *libertad* he experienced in Cuba. I assumed that for him, influenced by U.S. propaganda, *libertad* had to do with accessibility to consumer goods, with a better material life. But I was wrong. For him *libertad* had to do with self-determination, with wanting something different and being able to work toward making it a reality. Whether I agree or disagree with his assessment of the present Cuban situation, his understanding of *libertad* and his willingness to risk his life for it have helped me to understand what I and other Latinas mean by *libertad.*

13. Cf. Gutiérrez, *The Truth Shall Make You Free,* 132–34.

14. Since psychology is not my field of expertise, my attempt here is only to describe apathy and fear and to locate them in reference to the historical situation Latinas face.

15. This fear is compounded by the fact that seeing ourselves as different from the status quo is an intrinsic element of what it means for us to be Latina.

16. The best proof of this mind-set is the name of the U.S. government program for Puerto Rico in the middle decades of the twentieth century: "Operation Bootstrap." The Puerto Ricans understood very clearly the American expression that was behind that title and they responded painfully and cleverly, "How do you expect us to lift ourselves by our bootstraps when we do not even have boots!"

17. I use the word "God" here not to refer to one divine being but rather as a collective noun that embraces God, the saints, dead ones whom we love, manifestations of the Virgin (not always the same as manifestations of Mary, the mother of Jesus), Jesus (not very similar to the Jesus of the Gospels), Amerindian and African gods, and so forth.

18 To the accusation that this places us in the neoorthodox ranks, we answer that Latinas have not been part of the "modern experiment"; that the kind of belief in the divine that for the enlightened, scientific mind signifies a lack of autonomous, critical, rational thought is for us a concrete experience that we use as a key element in the struggle for liberation. See Christine Gudorf, "Liberation Theology's Use of Scripture—A Response to First World Critics," *Interpretation—a Journal of Bible and Theology* (January 1987): 12–13.

19. Ada María Isasi-Díaz and Yolanda Tarango, *Hispanic Women: Prophetic Voice in the Church* (Minneapolis: Fortress Press, 1992), 90.

20. Guitérrez, *Theology of Liberation,* 24.

21. Though indeed we have much to learn from the Base Ecclesial Communities that are at the heart of the Latin American liberation struggle, our *comunidades de fe* have to develop their own characteristics based on our lived-experiences and needs. For a concise articulation of what Base Ecclesial Communities are and the role they play in Latin America, see Pablo Richard, "The Church of the Poor in the Decade of the 90s," *LADOC* 21 (November/December 1990): 11–29.

22. See John Stuart Mill, *Utilitarianism* (New York: Bobbs-Merrill, 1957).

23. See also Acts 4:35.

24. For an excellent short analysis of six main justice theories see Karen Lebacqz, *Six Theories of Justice* (Minneapolis: Augsburg, 1986).

25. For a more comprehensive analysis of the meaning of solidarity see Ada María Isasi-Díaz, "Solidarity: Love of Neighbor in the 1980s," in *Lift Every Voice—Constructing Christian Theologies from the Underside,* ed. Susan Brooks Thistlethwaite and Mary Potter Engels (San Francisco: Harper and Row, 1990).

26. José Míguez Bonino, "Nuevas tendencias en teología," *Pasos* 9 (1987): 22.

27. Fernando Romero, "Sentido práctico y flexibilidad popular," *Páginas* 111 (October 1991): 43. See also Arthur F. McGovern, *Liberation Theology and Its Critics* (Maryknoll, N.Y.: Orbis Books, 1990), 177–212.

28. For an amplification of this theme see Isasi-Díaz, "Solidarity," 37.

29. Teresa L. Amott and Julie A. Matthaei, *Race, Gender & Work* (Boston: South End, 1991), 346–48.

30. Michael Parenti, *Power and the Powerless* (New York: St. Martin's Press, 1978), 226.

31. Romero, "Sentido práctico," 45–47.

32. Isasi-Díaz and Tarango, *Hispanic Women,* 77–80, 109–10; see below, chap. 6.

33. We set the basis for this section in chap. 3 of ibid.

34. Though popular religiosity among Latinas is suffused with Catholic rituals and understandings, there begins to be a Protestant perspective regarding popular religiosity. See Tito Paredes, "Popular Religiosity: A Protestant Perspective" *Missiology* 20, no. 2 (April 1992): 205–20; see also Juan Sepúlveda, "Pentecostalism as Popular Religiosity," *International Review of Mission* 78 (January 1989): 80–88.

35. Juan José Huitrado-Rizo, MCCJ, "Hispanic Popular Religiosity: The Expression of a People Coming to Life," *New Theology Review* 3, no. 4 (November 1990): 43–54.

36. Gutiérrez, *Theology of Liberation,* 13.

37. Clifford Geertz, *The Interpretation of Culture* (New York: Basic Books, 1973), 90.

38. Robert J. Schreiter, *Constructing Local Theologies* (Maryknoll, N.Y.: Orbis Books, 1985), 87–88.

39. Luis N. Rivera Pagán, *Evangelización y violencia—la conquista de América* (San Juan, Puerto Rico: Editorial Cemi, 1991), 1.

40. Ibid., 14–21. Rivera Pagán carefully explains how the discovery was accompanied by the juridical act of taking possession.

41. This definition of enculturation is found in Paulo Agirrebaltzategi, *Configuración ecclesial de las culturas* (Bilbao, España: Universidad de Deusto, 1976), 82. The author explains the three terms "acculturation," "enculturation," and "culturization" on pp. 81–82. He indicates that what has become cultural expression is what is transcultural or transcendent. It also means the form in which culturally the Gospel message is realized in the church. I use the term here in a narrower sense to mean simply that which has become a cultural expression.

42. Juan Luis Segundo, *The Liberation of Theology* (Maryknoll, N.Y.: Orbis Books, 1982), 185. Though it is true that an increasing number of Latinas are participating in denominations and churches that give great importance to the Bible, the majority of Latinas still relate to the Catholic church and do not use the Bible often. *Mujerista* theologians are concerned with the way the Bible is imposed on Latinas by some churches since it is done in a way that often threatens rather than enhances our moral agency.

43. The same is often true of sermons we hear on Sundays. Imaginative interpretations are not considered "good theology" when Latinas do it, but it is all right when priests and/or pastors do it.

44. Sixto J. García and Orlando Espín are doing very exciting work on developing a Hispanic-American theology using popular religiosity as its key element. In 1987 and 1988 they gave workshops at the Catholic Theological Society of America Conferences. Only synopses of the papers they presented there have been published. See Orlando Espín and Sixto García, "Hispanic-American Theology," *Catholic Theological Society of America Proceedings* 42 (1987): 114–19, and "The Sources of Hispanic Theology," *Catholic Theological Society of America Proceedings* 43 (1988): 122–25. In 1989 they gave a full presentation that has been published. See García and Espín, "'Lilies of the Field,'" *Catholic Theological Society of America Proceedings* 44 (1989): 70–90.

45. Espín and García, "Toward a Hispanic-American Theology," unpublished notes of workshop presented at the *Catholic Theological Society of America* (1987): 6–7. All quotations from Espín and García's presentation at the CTSA conferences in 1987 and 1988 will be from unpublished notes the authors passed out, which are much more complete than the published synopses.

46. Sacramentals in the Roman Catholic tradition are things or actions—candles, processions—used as reminders of God's effective presence in the world. The laity has access to the use of sacramentals without having to depend on the priests.

47. Manuel M. Marzal, "La religiosidad popular en el Perú," in *Panorama de la teología latinoamericana,* I, ed. Equipo Seladoc (Salamanca: Ediciones Sígueme, 1975), 28–29. These are adaptations of elements presented by Marzal that I have translated in such a way as to exclude the judgmental tone of his analysis, which I believe limits the value of popular religiosity.

48. See Segundo Galilea, "The Theology of Liberation and the Place of 'Folk Religion,'" in *What Is Religion?: An Inquiry for Christian Theology,* ed. Mircea Eliade and David W. Tracy, *Concilium* 136 (Edinburgh: T. & T. Clark, 1980), 43.

49. Ibid., 44.

50. Michael R. Candelaria, *Popular Religion and Liberation* (Albany: State University of New York Press, 1990), 13.

51. Ibid., 43.

52. Espín and García, "Sources of Hispanic Theology," unpublished notes of workshop presented at the Catholic Theological Society of America (1988): 4.

53. García and Espín, "Lilies of the Field," 72.

54. María Pilar Aquino, *Nuestro Clamor por la Vida* (San Jose, Costa Rica: Editorial D.E.I., 1992), 218–22.

55. See Isasi-Díaz and Tarango, *Hispanic Women,* 67, where we indicate that popular religiosity could offer needed correctives to some of the religious understandings of "official" Christianity.

56. Ibid., 14–26. See also II Consulta Ecuménica de Pastoral Indígena, *Aporte de los pueblos indígenas de América Latina a la teología cristiana* (Quito, Ecuador, 1986). Espín and García, "Toward a Hispanic," *American Theology,* 4. Jaime R. Vidal, "Popular Religion among the Hispanics in the General Area of the Archdiocese of Newark," in *Presencia Nueva* (Newark: Office of Research and Planning, Archdiocese of Newark 1988), 250–54.

57. Espín and García, "Toward a Hispanic-American Theology," 17. On this point Espín and García contradict themselves. In spite of the assertion they make here, they make only one reference to Amerindian and African religions and not in a very positive light. They place the Amerindian and African religious elements operative in popular religiosity in what they call a "second constellation" with which they seem to deal only insofar as it goes hand in hand with the "first constellation," which they call "popular Catholicism." See pp. 4–6.

58. Tom F. Driver, *Christ in a Changing World* (New York: Crossroad, 1981), 32–81.

59. See Isasi-Díaz and Tarango, *Hispanic Women,* 13–55.

60. John F. Baldovin, S.J., "The Liturgical Year: Calendar for a Just Community," in *Liturgy and Spirituality in Context,* ed. Eleanor Bernstein, C.S.J. (Collegeville, Minn.: The Liturgical Press, 1990), 104.

61. Compare the difference in interpretation and explanation of Guadalupe between Elizondo and Lafaye. See Virgilio Elizondo, *La morenita* (Liguori, Mo.: Liguori Publications, 1981), and J. Lafaye, *Quetzalcoatl et Guadalupe* (Paris: Gallimard, 1974).

62. One of my earliest memories has to do with fulfilling a promise my father had made to Our Lady of Charity, the title under which Mary is patroness of Cuba. During World War II my father tried to produce glucose from yucca starch. As a chemical engineer he knew that this could be done, but the process is an industrial secret and he had to start from scratch. To be sure he would succeed, he promised Our Lady of Charity a visit to her sanctuary by the whole family if she would help him, enlighten him in his research. He was able to get glucose from yucca starch, something needed and, therefore, profitable during the war. It was not until a few years later that he was able to keep the promise. We traveled over twelve hours by car and then walked up the hill on the top of which the sanctuary sits. Thus we all honored the divine intervention in the life of my family. I was about seven years old at that time.

63. This is exactly what my grandmother always said!

64. A few years ago I arrived at the very southern tip of Manhattan for a 7 P.M. meeting. I could not find the building where we were to meet, so I decided to park my car and find someone who could help me. Since there are no homes in that area, at that hour of the evening it is not unusual to see not a single soul. Finally I saw a man who was emptying trash cans in the back entrance of one of the huge office buildings. I approached him a little apprehensively and asked him for directions. Apologetically, he started in a very broken English to tell me he did not understand me. I stopped him by repeating the question in Spanish. His eyes lit up, he squared his shoulders, and told me he did not know where that building was. He then looked into my eyes and said, *"Venga aca, used es cubana?"* (Come listen here, are you Cuban?). When I told him I was, he became all the more helpful. Talking to me as you do to an old friend, he let me know that the doorman around the corner was also Cuban and that he surely knew the answer to my question. Without thinking much, because he spoke Spanish and was a Cuban, I put aside all the cautions I should have been taking and asked him if he thought my car was safe there. *"No hay problema, no hay problema"* (No problem, no problem). I smiled broadly, thanked him, and went to get directions from the Cuban doorman, who I was sure would help me because I was his *compatriota* (compatriot), and he did!

65. I am not claiming that there is not racism in our culture, and certainly in our countries of origin, skin color, though dealt with in a different way from the way it is operative in the U.S.A., plays a role in societal stratification.

66. Vidal, "Popular Religion among the Hispanics," 257.

67. Ibid.

68. See Eldin Villafañe, "The Socio-Cultural Matrix of Intergenerational Dynamics: An Agenda for the 90s," *Apuntes* 12, no. 1 (spring 1992): 13–20.

69. Juan González, *Harvest of Empire—A History of Latinos in America* (New York: Viking Penguin, 2000), 208.

70. Ibid., 213.

71. All of the statistics regarding the use of Spanish are taken from Yankelovich Partners, Inc., *2000 Hispanic Monitor Study* (Norwalk, Conn., 2000). Yankelovich is the leading authority on consumer behavior. I am most grateful to Mr. Simon Kaplan, who works for this research firm, for providing me with and helping me to interpret the information included here.

72. Joshua A. Fishman, "Language Maintenance," in *Harvard Encyclopedia of Ethnic Groups,* ed. Stephan Thernstrom (Cambridge: The Belknap Press of Harvard University Press, 1980), 631.

73. Ibid., 636.

74. Nelson and Tienda, "The Structuring of Hispanic Ethnicity: Historical and Contemporary Perspectives," in *Ethnicity and Race in the U.S.A.—Toward the Twenty-First Century,* ed. Richard D. Alba (London: Henley Routledge & Kegan Paul, 1985), 53.

CHAPTER 3: *Mujerista* Theology's Methods

1. Ruth Behar, "Rage and Redemption: Reading the Life Story of a Mexican Marketing Woman," *Feminist Studies* 16, no. 2 (summer 1990): 229.

2. Ibid., 230.

3. Ibid., 231.

4. See Harold Garfinkel, *Studies in Ethnomethodology* (Cambridge, England: Polity Press, 1984), 1–115. See also Thomas Dale Watts, "Ethnomethodology: A Consideration of Theory and Research," *Cornell Journal of Social Relations* 9, no. 1 (spring 1973): 99–115.

5. Jerome Kirk and Marc L. Miller, *Reliability and Validity in Qualitative Research,* Qualitative Research Methods 1 (Beverly Hills, Calif.: Sage Publications, 1988), 9.

6. Ibid., 12.

7. George W. Noblit and R. Dwight Hare, *Meta-Ethnography: Synthesizing Qualitative Studies,* Qualitative Research Methods 11 (Beverly Hills, Calif.: Sage Publications, 1988), 12.

8. Ibid.

9. James P. Spradley, *You Owe Yourself a Drunk—An Ethnography of Urban Nomads* (Boston: Little, Brown and Company, 1970), 7.

10. James P. Spradley, *The Ethnographic Interview* (New York: Holt, Rinehart and Winston, 1979), 4.

11. Ethnographic interviews are only one of the tools used by *mujerista* theology. Observation, studies of traditional religious understandings and beliefs, studies in comparative religions—all of these are also tools used by *mujerista* theology.

12. I am referring here to the research done for this book and the one we did for the book Ada María Isasi-Díaz and Yolanda Tarango, *Hispanic Women: Prophetic Voice in the Church* (Minneapolis: Fortress Press, 1992).

13. I never ask the Latinas I interview if they are Roman Catholic. However, that is my own faith tradition and the church in which I have worked in different ways for many years. Also, most of the women I have worked with in articulating a *mujerista* theology are Roman Catholic. On the other hand, most of my work in the decade of the 1980s was in ecumenical settings. This allowed me to come in contact with and learn from Hispanic Women who belong to Protestant denominations and also to Pentecostal churches.

14. I have used the basic understanding of ethnography presented by Spradley and adapted it according to the values I hold as a *mujerista* theologian. See Spradley, *The Ethnographic Interview,* 3–16.

15. Though basically following the understandings and techniques explained in the works quoted in this section, I have also adapted meta-ethnography according to values I hold as a *mujerista* theologian.

16. Noblit and Hare, *Meta-Ethnography,* 16.

17. An emic approach is one that deals with various elements of a culture as they are related to each other rather than describing them in reference to a general classification decided in advance, outside the culture. The "emic" approach can best be understood in reference to the "etic" approach, which is a generalized approach working to fit the different elements of a culture into general categories claiming to apply to all cultures. See *Oxford English Dictionary,* 2d ed., s.v. "emic" and "etic."

18. Noblit and Hare, *Meta-Ethnography,* 28–29. To avoid confusion, I will use quotation marks around the word "translation" when it refers to the process just identified.

19. This is the name given to them by Freire. See Paulo Freire, *La educación como práctica de la libertad* (Madrid: Siglo Veintiuno de España Editores, S.A., 1976), 108–13.

20. Ibid., 109.

21. Ibid., 62–-64.

22. Professional theologian is one of the kinds of Hispanic Women theologians that *mujerista* theology recognizes, takes into consideration, enables, and welcomes. *Mujerista* theology also welcomes the grassroot Hispanic Woman theologian who does theology in the simple sharing of what happens in day-to-day life, who is gifted in analyzing and expressing the beliefs which ground her religious practices. A third "kind" of *mujerista* theologian includes those Hispanic Women who have some training in religious studies: catechists, pastoral workers, and ordained Hispanic Women in Protestant churches.

23. Paulo Freire, *Cultural Action for Freedom* (Cambridge: Harvard Educational Review, 1970), 45.

24. Ibid., 52.

25. This has happened to me repeatedly with the women I interviewed. I knew most of them before and I have continued to be their friend. Two of those whom I met for the first time during the research for the book have kept in contact with me, and we too have become friends.

26. Elizabeth Jameson, "Introduction," in *Insider/Outsider Relationships with Informants,* Working Paper No. 13 (University of Arizona, Southwest Institute for Research on Women, 1982), 3.

27. Elizabeth Jameson, "May and Me," in *Insider/Outsider Relationships with Informants,* Working Paper No. 13 (University of Arizona: Southwest Institute for Research on Women, 1982), 11.

28. Linda Light and Nancy Kleiber, "Interactive Research in a Feminist Setting: The Vancouver Women's Health Collective," in *Anthropologists at Home in North America* (Cambridge: Cambridge University Press, 1981), 167–84. The authors report that the informants they dealt with demanded that they share their research notes!

29. Ada María Isasi-Díaz, "Solidarity: Love of Neighbor in the 1980s," in *Lift Every Voice: Constructing Christian Theologies from the Underside,* ed. Susan Brooks Thistlethwaite and Mary Potter Engel (San Francisco: Harper and Row, 1990), 31–40.

30. Following Gramsci, I believe that action has a reflective quality. This assertion is very important for Hispanics because U.S. society tends to disregard our intellectual ability due to a certain lack of formal education. Following Gramsci, I claim that Hispanic Women are organic thinkers and that *mujerista* theology, which is based on "the principles and problems raised by . . . their practical activity," is organic theology. See Antonio Gramsci, *Prison Notebooks,* ed. and trans. Quintin Hoare and Geoffrey Nowell Smith (New York: International Publishers, 1975), 6, 330.

31. As Rosaldo said, "What is needed . . . is not so much data as questions." M. Z. Rosaldo, "The Use and Abuse of Anthropology: Reflections on Feminism and Cross-Cultural Understanding," *Signs* 5 (spring 1980): 390.

32. See Virgilio Elizondo, *Galiean Journey: The Mexican American Promise* (Maryknoll, N.Y.: Orbis Books, 1983).

33. The first person I ever heard give this expression the interpretation I present here was Barbara Zanotti, who together with me and four other women participated in a dialogue with United States bishops on the issue of the ordination of women in the Roman Catholic Church at the beginning of the 1980s.

34. Liz Stanley and Sue Wise, *Breaking Out: Feminist Consciousness and Feminist Research* (London: Routledge

& Kegan Paul, 1983), 154. Also Janet Silman, "In Search of a Liberative Methodology," unpublished paper, May 7, 1988.

35. José Míguez Bonino, "Nuevas Tendencias en Teología," *Pasos* 9 (1987): 22.

36. These interviews, together with the information gathered when we did the research for *Hispanic Women,* plus my own experience as a Latina, plus my observation of other Hispanic Women during many years, provide the information about Latinas' experience that is the source of this study.

37. With the women I did not know very well, I asked two questions used by Gilligan: "How would you describe yourself to yourself?" "If you had to describe the person you are in a way that you yourself would know it was you, what would you say?" Carol Gilligan, *In a Different Voice* (Cambridge: Harvard University Press, 1982), 33. Gilligan does not present in toto the protocol she used in her research. Her questions are scattered throughout the text.

38. After the first couple of interviews, I realized there was no point in asking the women whether they considered the decisions they had taken to be moral or immoral, good or bad. What I did mostly was to ask them, "What comes to your mind when you hear the words moral or immoral?"

39. John B. Williamson, David A. Karp, and John R. Dalphin, *The Research Craft* (Boston and Toronto: Little, Brown and Company, 1977), 165.

40. Ibid., 168–75.

41. Ibid., 168.

42. Ibid., 171.

43. Ibid.

CHAPTER 4: In Their Own Words

1. Alysius Pieris, "Place of Non-Christian Religions," in *Irruption of the Third World,* ed. Virginia Fabella and Sergio Torres (Maryknoll, N.Y.: Orbis Books, 1983), 134.

2. Spanglish is the result of constant switching between English and Spanish. Spanglish also has "new" words resulting from mixing parts of Spanish words with parts of English words. For example, the Spanish ending added to the root of verbs of the first conjugation to form the present participle is *ando.* Latinos, especially those of us coming from the Caribbean, will take a verb, for example, "to rain," and add the Spanish verb ending. The result is "rainando." Finally, Spanglish uses a lot of transliteration instead of translation.

3. *Mexicano* is what Mexican Americans who have little formal education call the Spanish they speak. *Mexicano* is indeed Spanish with a heavy dose of colloquialisms, mistakes in grammar and pronunciation, and a fair amount of transliteration.

4. See the last section in this chapter for an explanation of generative themes.

5. Some of the names used for the women are not their real names, as most of them requested.

6. See Ada María Isasi-Díaz and Yolanda Tarango, *Hispanic Women: Prophet Voice in the Church* (Minneapolis: Fortress Press, 1992), 24.

7. Neither Julieta nor Caridad participated in the weekend reflections that we did to collect material for the book *Hispanic Women.* I am introducing them here at greater length than the others in order to provide information about them that is available about the others in the book *Hispanic Women.* I include Julieta's understandings and perspectives because I believe that being on welfare gives her insights and understandings that are important for this study given the socioeconomic reality of the majority of Latinas.

8. She did not avail herself of the opportunity to get her immigration papers during the recent "amnesty programs" because she was told that if she did, they would cut off her welfare check. This kind of disinformation and misinformation about this program and many others is rampant in the community.

9. I decided to interview Julieta when I thought I could not get in touch with Adela. Personally, I was moved by her story and by Julieta as a person in a very special way.

10. I include Caridad's understandings and perspectives because, having had no religious upbringing, her input provides different and important insights for this study.

11. This way of referring to the U.S.A. by Cubans and other Latinos indicates the "space" that we place between ourselves and this country even if we are U.S. citizens. At present she is trying to find time to go

to religious instruction so she can then receive First Communion and Confirmation.

12. It is indicative how much Roman Catholicism is/was a part of Marta's life that she here uses the Latin expression, not the Spanish!

13. The use of the word *criatura* in Spanish is very different from the one in English. We use it to refer to a defenseless child, an innocent child.

14. The literal translation of this phrase is "A very strong epoch, very strong, very strong."

15. This is what I remember the movie *Sophie's Choice* to be about. Most of the time I shared more details from the movie with the women, how this was the choice a woman had to make when arriving at a concentration camp. I insisted on the fact that there was no way she could get around deciding. I also shared with them the outcome, how she gave up her daughter to be killed and never really knew if her son survived, and how she really became crazy even if she did survive the concentration camp. See Allan Pakula, dir., *Sophie's Choice* with Meryl Streep (Hollywood: Universal Pictures, 1982).

16. One of the typical dishes of Puerto Rico, *pasteles* are made of grated plantains, yautia, and pieces of meat or chicken. All of this is wrapped in plantain leaves and boiled until solid. It is a dish requiring much work and that is why it is prepared only for special occasions.

17. To appreciate the impact of Caridad's long silences as part of her response to this question, you have to keep in mind the quickness of her style, how well she knows what she thinks, and how lightning fast she speaks. Her silence stunned me!

18. Inez had a government-related job that combined advocacy and service.

19. Because of space, I am giving here only the main reasons for two other key decisions in Inez's life.

20. At the beginning of our conversation Adela described herself as an *aventurera,* an adventurer.

21. In the company in which Lupe works, the whole board votes for the CEO and those interested in the position lobby actively for endorsement by the board members. The board members are also lobbied by the consumers.

22. People knew that the person who would most probably get the job this time around would take it for only a short time because of his age. So "the next opportunity" to apply for the CEO position was not so far away.

23. The company had made it known that in order to make this an open search it would not give serious consideration to an insider. So the few from within the company who applied for the position had to start by leaving their jobs.

24. I think Olivia meant that they would do what the majority decided, but she did say what is written here.

25. Margarita has a very positive attitude toward life and it did not surprise me that she could not think of any serious or difficult decision she had made in her life. In the previous interview I had done with her, it was hard for her to think of the best thing that had ever happened to her because so many good things had occurred in her life. And when it came to talk about the worst thing that had happened she could not think of any except not being able to go back to Cuba to see her dying mother. See Isasi-Díaz and Tarango, *Hispanic Women,* 88–90.

26. I do not think the written word, no matter how gifted the writer, could ever convey the absolute matter-of-factness and the decisiveness of the analytical account Caridad shared with me.

27. Their discomfort in talking about the process of decision making as something separate from their moral being reaffirms the understanding that process and content simply cannot be separated, that the process affects the content and the content should be part of determining the process.

28. This was no small wedding. It was going to take place at the cathedral of the archdiocese with the cardinal officiating. Inez had taken a loan of several thousand dollars to cover all the expenses.

29. For reasons María has not explained to me fully, her mother gave her to a cousin to rear and, as a result, María did not see much of her mother. María has found this very difficult to live with and she says laughingly that she has overcompensated by loving her children to excess.

30. See pp. 70–72.

31. And, again, in order to be sure that this exercise does not result in just the viewpoint of the writer, the reader can check to see whether these themes are found in the accounts. The writer also takes the

responsibility of having at least a few of the women read the materials to see whether they are true to their understandings and perspectives.

32. Caridad's quickness of reasoning and action reminds me of what Aquinas calls *solertia,* an easy and prompt response to sudden and unexpected situations, a certain nimbleness and adroitness in reaction to new situations. *Solertia* seems to build on habitus, which leads one to know from within, as through a disposition that one has, instead of from without, as one usually knows an object. See Daniel Maguire, *The Moral Choice* (New York: Doubleday & Co., 1978), 281–308, 375–76.

CHAPTER 5: Conscience, Conscientization, and Moral Agency in *Mujerista* Theology

1. I mention here just a few cases in different parts of the world which substantiates this statement. Starting with the U.S.A., which probably has the largest number of incidents, those best known are: Charles E. Curran, Agnes Mary Mansour, Liz Morancy, Arlene Violet, Ardith Platte, the Vatican 24+1, Mary Ann Sorrentino, Geraldine Ferraro, Mario Cuomo, and so forth. In Latin America: Leonardo Boff, the Cardenal brothers, Miguel D'Escoto, Gustavo Gutiérrez, Bishop Pedro Casaldaliga, and so forth. In Europe: Edward Schillebeeckx, Hans Küng, and so forth.

2. I am neither proposing nor endorsing the legitimacy of all dissent from what the Roman Catholic Church calls noninfallible teaching. My concern is with how the corrosion of this principle impinges negatively on primacy of conscience and the development of moral agency.

3. Magisterium has to do with the teaching authority of the church. Since the bishops, with the pope—the bishop of Rome who is "first among equals"—usually are the ones to voice such teachings, the word has come to refer to them. However, as explained later in this chapter, theologians and the faithful in the church do play a part in the magisterium of the church.

4. John Paul II, "Truth in the Magisterium," *The Pope Speaks* 34, no. 2 (July/August 1989): 99.

5. Ibid.

6. I am grateful to Ann Patrick Ware for sharing this insight with me.

7. According to the *National Catholic Reporter* for July 25, 1985, this was said by Archbishop Vincenzo Fagiolo, the papal delegate to the general chapter of the Franciscans in Assisi, when he asked them to meditate on a letter from the pope; quoted in Anne E. Patrick, "Conscience and Community: Catholic Moral Theology Today," The Warren Lecture Series in Catholic Studies (Tulsa, Okla.: University of Tulsa, February 13, 1989).

8. This dogma teaches that when the pope purposefully speaks officially in matters of faith, he cannot err. Noninfallible teaching is all other teachings of the pope or of the hierarchy of the church—teachings that Catholics are taught to consider seriously but which we know do not obligate us.

9. Timothy O'Connell, *Principles for a Catholic Morality* (New York: Seabury, 1978), 95.

10. Ibid., 96.

11. Charles E. Curran, *Faithful Dissent* (Kansas City, Mo.: Sheed & Ward, 1986), 47.

12. Erich Fromm, "Conscience," in *Moral Principles of Action,* ed. Ruth Nanda Anshen, Science of Culture Series, 6 (New York: Harper and Row, 1952), 179.

13. Ibid.

14. "Blind" obedience is used here not only in the popular sense of obeying no matter at what cost, but also in the sense of an obedience that demands not only complying because a superior says so but also requiring the person to believe that what the superior says is right, and therefore one must comply. It is a concept geared, I believe, to circumvent the accusation that religious and church superiors are promoting the development of "authoritarian" conscience.

15. Fromm, "Conscience," 182.

16. *The Dogmatic Constitution on the Church,* n. 12. For an English translation of the Vatican II documents see Watler M. Abbott, ed. *The Documents of Vatican II* (New York: Guild, 1966), 29.

17. Ibid. The text here is from St. Augustine, *Liber de Praedestinatione Sanctorum,* 14, 27, in *Patrologia Latina,* ed. J. B. Migne (Paris: J. B. Migne, 1841), 44:980. About ten years ago, I participated in a panel discussion on dissent with Charles E. Curran and an archbishop of the Roman Catholic Church. The archbishop and I

reached an impasse exactly on this point. He insisted that the *sensus fidelium* did not mean that the faithful could disagree with the hierarchy even in noninfallible matters like the ordination of women, which was the subject of this panel. I insisted on asking him for his understanding of what it did mean but he would only assert what it did not mean. I remember asking whether the hierarchy was not part of the People of God. When he said it was, I then argued that the *sensus fidelium* did not provide space for the hierarchy to disagree with what was a generalized belief among the laity and a significant segment of the hierarchy. Curran tried bravely, though unsuccessfully, to break the impasse. This episode taught me firsthand much of what I argue here.

18. Fromm, "Conscience," 183.

19 Charles E. Curran, *Directions in Fundamental Moral Theology* (Notre Dame, Ind.: Notre Dame University Press, 1985), 232.

20. Ibid., 221-22.

21. This brief explanation is based on the monumental work by Bernard Cooke, *Ministry to Word and Sacraments* (Philadelphia: Fortress Press, 1977), 133–53, 464–94, 591–613 passim.

22. Curran, *Directions,* 153.

23. Ibid., 226.

24. Bernard Häring, *The Law of Christ* (Westminster, Md.: The Newman Press, 1966), 135.

25. Ibid., 142.

26. Ronald Preston, "Conscience," in *Dictionary of Christian Ethics,* ed. James E. Childress and John Macquarrie (Philadelphia: Westminster, 1986), 116.

27. Häring, *Law of Christ,* 143.

28. Daniel Maguire, *The Moral Choice* (New York: Doubleday & Co., 1979), 371.

29. Häring, *Law of Christ,* 135.

30. Ibid., 147. Given Haring's use of natural law in his understanding of conscience, it may be helpful here to keep in mind that "the Catholic tradition in moral theology has insisted that its moral teaching is based primarily on natural law and not primarily on faith or the Scripture. The natural law is understood to be human reason reflecting on human nature. Even those teachings which have some basis in Scripture . . . were also said to be based on natural law" (Curran, *Faithful Dissent,* 61).

31. Ibid., Haring, *Law of Christ,* 147.

32. Ibid., 148.

33. Thomas Aquinas, *Summa Theologiae, Pars Prima Secondae,* question 19, article 5.

34. Ibid., question 6, article 8.

35. Eric D'Arcy, *Conscience and Its Right to Freedom* (New York: Sheed & Ward, 1961), 205. The argument presented in this paragraph is based on D'Arcy, 190–272.

36. Curran, *Faithful Dissent,* 52–62. It would be too long here to develop fully the issue of dissent from noninfallible teaching in the church. Curran's book is certainly an excellent resource on this matter.

37. Abbott, *Documents of Vatican II,* 49.

38. Joseph A. Komonchak, "Ordinary Papal Magisterium and Religious Assent," in *Readings in Moral Theology #3: The Magisterium and Morality,* ed. Charles E. Curran and Richard A. McCormick, S.J. (New York: Paulist Press, 1982), 67–90 passim.

39. Charles E. Curran, *Moral Theology: A Continuing Journey* (Notre Dame, Ind.: University of Notre Dame Press, 1982), 4. See also Curran, *Faithful Dissent,* 57–58.

40. Bernard Cooke, *Ministry to Word and Sacraments* (Philadelphia: Fortress Press, 1976), 195–97.

41. Curran, *Moral Theology,* 4. See also, Joseph A. Komonchak, "Humanae Vitae and Its Reception: Ecclesiological Reflections," *Theological Studies* 39 (June 1978): 229–30.

42. Ibid., 5.

43. Ibid.

44. Ibid., 7. Here Curran quotes from an address to Catholic academics given by John Paul II in 1979 during his visit to the U.S.A. "It is the right of the faithful not to be troubled by theories and hypotheses that they are not expert in judging or that are easily simplified or manipulated by public opinion."

45. Ibid.

46. See Preston, "Conscience," 116–18. See also Walter Conn, *Conscience: Development and Self-Transcendence* (Birmingham, Ala.: Religious Education Press, 1981), 18.

47. James M. Gustafson, *Protestant and Roman Catholic Ethics* (Chicago: University of Chicago Press, 1978), 10.

48. Ibid., 11.

49. Ibid., 10.

50. I am greatly indebted for these understandings and insights to the Reverend Nicanor González, D.Min., presbyter of the Hispanic District of the Assemblies of God of the South Bronx. See Nicanor González, "Hacia una teología de acción y reflexión Pentecostal hispana" (D.Min. diss., New York Theological Seminary, 1991). Regarding the authority of the minister or pastor see Eldin Villafañe, *The Liberating Spirit* (Lanham, Md.: University Press of America, 1992), 128.

51. I strongly disagree with the attempt of Villafañe throughout his book to find value in Hispanic male chauvinism. See Villafañe, *The Liberating Spirit,* 14–15, 118–19, 130–31.

52. Ibid., 205–6, including note 31.

53. Ada María Isasi-Díaz, "The Bible and *Mujerista* Theology," in *Lift Every Voice: Constructing Christian Theologies from the Underside,* ed. Susan Brooks Thistlethwaite and Mary Potter Engle (San Francisco: Harper & Row, 1990): 261–69.

54. For a somewhat different way of connecting conscience and conscientization see Antonio Moser and Bernardino Leers, *Moral Theology* (Maryknoll, N.Y.: Orbis Books, 1990), 112–27.

55. Curran, *Directions in Fundamental Moral Theology,* 233.

56. This concept of moral consciousness was developed by Bernard Lonergan. I have used the work of both Curran and of Conn to guide me through Lonergan's exposition. The three books in which Lonergan deals with this concept are included in the bibliography.

57. Conn, *Conscience,* 121–24.

58. Ibid., 133.

59. Ibid., 138.

60. Dennis P. McCann, "Conscientization," in *The Westminster Dictionary of Christian Ethics,* ed. James F. Childress and John Macquarris (Philadelphia: Westminter, 1986), 120.

61. Paulo Freire, "Education, Liberation and the Church," *Religious Education* 79 (fall 1984): 527–8.

62. Anne Hope and Sally Timmel, *Training for Transformation,* Book 1 (Zimbabwe: Mambo Press, 1984), 40.

63. Following Curran's lead in *Directions in Fundamental Moral Theology,* 240–43, my starting place for this analysis of moral consciousness was Bernard Lonergan, *Method in Theology* (New York: Herder and Herder, 1972), 103–5. I have changed his schema significantly to reflect what I have learned from the Hispanic Women whose voices are presented in this work. See also Carol Gilligan, *In a Different Voice* (Cambridge: Harvard University Press, 1982), 160.

64. See Juan Luis Segundo, *The Liberation of Theology* (Maryknoll: Orbis Books, 1982), 7-9.

65. Curran, *Directions,* 246.

66. In the term "tenets of Catholicism," I include the doctrine and dogmas of the Roman Catholic Church as well as accepting the teaching authority of the church in its broadest sense and not exclusively to mean the hierarchical magisterium.

67. This explanation of the process of conscientization, though my own, borrows terminology used by Curran, *Directions in Fundamental Moral Theology,* 244–50.

CHAPTER 6: Praxis and Lived-Experience in Mujerista Theology

1. Ada María Isasi-Díaz and Yolanda Tarango, *Hispanic Women: Prophetic Voice in the Church* (Minneapolis: Fortress Press, 1992), 1.

2. Leonardo Boff, "¿Qué es hacer teología desde América Latinas?" in *Liberación y cautiverio.* Encuentro Latinoamericano de Teología (Mexico City, 1975), 144.

3. Political here is used not in the sense of partisan politics nor having to do directly with holding governmental positions. Political here refers to the activity we carry out in society that seeks to influence soci-

ety, that has consequences for society at large.

4. Xosé Miguélez, *La Teología de la liberación y su método* (Barcelona: Editorial Herder, 1976), 49.

5. José Míguez Bonino, *Doing Theology in a Revolutionary Situation* (Philadelphia: Fortress Press, 1975), 72.

6. Denis E. Collins, *Paulo Freire: His Life, Works, and Thought* (New York: Paulsit Press, 1977), 49.

7. Rebecca Chopp, *The Praxis of Suffering* (Maryknoll, N.Y.: Orbis Books, 1986), 121–26.

8. As a *mujerista* theologian I want to stay within the boundaries of this specific theological enterprise, but I do believe "struggle" is what locates all oppressed people. I believe that even—or maybe precisely—in the worst of conditions, what makes a human being maintain her humanity until her last breath is her capacity to struggle to live.

9. Here I am arriving at a different conclusion from that of several Latin American liberation theologians, of Rebecca Chopp in *The Praxis of Suffering*, and of Hispanic theologians, Roberto Goizueta, "*Nosotros: Toward a U.S. Hispanic Anthropology,*" *Listening* 27, no. 1 (winter 1992): 55–69, and Samuel Solivan, "Orthopathos: Interlocutor between Orthodoxy and Praxis," *Andover Newton Review* 1, no. 2 (winter 1990): 19–25.

10. María Pilar Aquino, *Nuestro Clamor por la Vida* (San José, Costa Rica: Editorial D.E.I., 1992), 37.

11. Ivone Gebara, "Women Doing Theology in Latin America," in *Through Her Eyes*, ed. Elsa Tamez (Maryknoll, N.Y.: Orbis Books, 1989), 43. I find parts of this translation, like most translations, lacking in preciseness, somewhat distorting what the original version says. Though I have made use of the book in English, I have referred to the Spanish version often, in itself a translation of Gebara's Portuguese.

12. Cf. Chopp, *The Praxis of Suffering*, 122.

13. Antonio Gramsci, *Prison Notebooks*, ed. and trans. Quintin Hoare and Geoffrey Nowell Smith (New York: International Publishers, 1975).

14. Ibid.

15. See Roberto Goizueta, "Presidential Address," *ACHTUS Newsletter* (a publication of the Academy of Catholic Hispanic Theologians of the United States, 1050 N. Clark, El Paso, TX 79905), 2, no. 1 (winter 1990): 4–6.

16. Chopp, *The Praxis of Suffering*, 122–23.

17. For an insightful view of the role of the Hispanic view of community in articulating a Hispanic anthropology see Goizueta, "*Nosotros,*" 55–69.

18. Gustavo Gutiérrez, *A Theology of Liberation* (Maryknoll, N.Y.: Orbis Books, 1988), 9.

19. Leonardo Boff, "Qué es hacer teología," 143.

20. Ibid., 144.

21. Ibid.

22. We are not denying the need for consistency and coherence as part of moral and theological criteria, but the way they are understood has to take into consideration, for example, the practicality and flexibility of Latinas' everyday life which is essential for their survival. Mainline intellectuals often consider practicality and flexibility to be incoherent because of what they consider inconsistencies and contradictions.

23. Pedro A. Sandín-Fremaint, "Domesticating the Theology of Liberation: A Deconstructive Reading of Clodovis Boff's *Theology and Praxis,*" *Apuntes* 7, no. 2 (spring 1987): 27–41.

24. In this we follow the lead of Latin American liberation theology and other liberation theologies. See Gutiérrez, *A Theology of Liberation*, 8; and Juan Luis Segundo, "Two Theologies," *Journal of Theology for South Africa* 52 (1985): 321–27.

25. Míguez Bonino, *Doing Theology in a Revolutionary Situation*, 81.

26. Cf. Rosemary Radford Ruether, "Feminist Interpretation: A Method of Correlation," in *Feminist Interpretation of the Bible,* ed. Letty Russell (Philadelphia: Westminster, 1985), 112.

27. This is also true within Latino culture, in the Latino communities.

28. Ruether, "Feminist Interpretation," 113.

29. Sheila Greeve Davaney, "The Limits of the Appeal to Women's Experience," in *Shaping New Vision: Gender and Values in American Culture,* ed. Clarissa W. Atkinson, Constance H. Buchanan, and Margaret R. Miles (Ann Arbor: U.M.I. Research Press, 1987), 41–49.

30. The bibliographical references in our work point to other sources, secondary ones, of our theology.

31. Cf. the interview of Ivone Gebara in Elsa Tamex, *Teólogos de la liberación hablan sobre la mujer* (San José, Costa Rica: Editorial D.E.I., 1986), 121–22.

32. In Isasi-Díaz and Tarango, *Hispanic Women*, 104–9, we called those of us who facilitate the theological process, gather the wisdom of the Latinas, and do the writing "theological technicians," and we outlined the task of these technicians. Since the first edition of our book, published in 1988, this is one of the points that has been most debated and opposed. This is why we felt it important to expand this understanding here.

33. This was already dealt with in much greater detail in chap. 3 when we talked about the issue of the theologian as insider or outsider.

34. Gebara, "Women Doing Theology," 44.

35. Aquino, *Nuestro Clamor*, 58–62.

36. Isasi-Díaz and Tarango, *Hispanic Women*, 104–10. We owe much in helping us to understand and formulate what we believe in this regard to Carlos Abesamis, "Doing Theological Reflection in a Philippine Context," in *The Emergent Gospel* (Maryknoll, N.Y.: Orbis Books, 1978), 112–23.

37. See Gustavo Gutiérrez, "Reflections from a Latin American Perspective," in *Irruption of the Third World*, ed. Virginia Fabella and Sergio Torres (Maryknoll, N.Y.: Orbis Books, 1983), 224–31. Here Gutiérrez struggles with this differentiation and we believe tends to affirm it because of understanding theology as a "second act," which in our opinion separates action from reflection.

38. Leonardo Boff and Clodovis Boff, *Introducing Liberation Theology* (Maryknoll, N.Y.: Orbis Books, 1987), 11–21.

39. See Isasi-Díaz and Tarango, *Hispanic Women*, 104–5, for examples of possible jobs. See also Ivone Gebara's interview in *Teólogos de la liberación hablan sobre la mujer*, 1986), 12–125. A synthesis of what she says there is included in Gebara, "Women Doing Theology."

40. We also question the other five elements that the Boff brothers indicate as being different in the three levels of liberation theology that they posit. We concentrate here on these three because they are the ones that most contradict *mujerista* theology's understandings and practices.

41. Gutiérrez, "Reflections," 226.

42. Marciano Vidal García, "La Preferencia por el pobre, criterio moral," *Studia Moralia* 20 (1982): 284.

43. Ibid. Vidal here is using some of the terminology of Paulo Freire. I do not think this is the place to verify this irruption of history into Latinas' lives. Vidal verifies this in regard to the poor in Latin America in a way that we believe we can apply to Latinas. The same is true of Gutiérrez's arguments in this regard in *The Power of the Poor in History* (Maryknoll, N.Y.: Orbis Books, 1984), especially chaps. 4 and 7.

44. Vidal, "La Preferencia," 290.

45. Leonardo Boff, *Church: Charism and Power* (New York: Crossroad, 1986), 9.

CHAPTER 7: *Mestizaje*

1. I will use these four words interchangeably in this chapter because I think they throw light on the issue here discussed from different sides, thus giving a richness to the discussion that it would lack if I used only one of these terms.

2. Of course, by doing this I am focusing on Hispanic Women, on how we experience the way people relate to us. The complexities of difference for theories of feminism as well as for the politics of feminism are dealt with at length in Elizabeth V. Spelman, *Inessential Woman* (Boston: Beacon Press, 1988). Also important is the work of María Lugones. See María C. Lugones and Elizabeth V. Spelman, "Have We Got a Theory for You! Feminist Theory, Cultural Imperialism, and the Demand for the 'Woman's Voice,'" *Women's Studies International Forum* 6, no. 6 (1983): 573–81; María C. Lugones, "On the Logic of Pluralist Feminism," in *Feminist Ethics*, ed. Claudia Card (Lawrence: University Press of Kansas, 1991), 35–44; María C. Lugones, "Playfulness, 'World'-Travelling, and Loving Perception," in *Hypatia* 2, no. 2 (summer 1987): 3–19.

3. See above, chapter 1, pp. 6–7.

4. Ada María Isasi-Díaz, "Toward an Understanding of *Feminismo Hispano*," in *Women's Consciousness, Women's Conscience*, ed. Barbara Hilkert Andolsen, Christine Gudorf, and Mary D. Pellauer (Minneapolis: Winston-Seabury, 1985), 51–61.

5. Iris Marion Young, *Justice and the Politics of Difference* (Princeton, N.J.: Princeton University Press, 1990), 165.

6. María Lugones, "On the Logic of Pluralist Feminism," 35–44.

7. Ibid., 41–42.

8. I am here referring mostly to how people of the dominant culture relate to Hispanic Women. But of course we also have to deal with difference among communities of struggle. Much of the same dynamics are operative, and we unfortunately tend to see the other and her struggles in view of ours instead of respecting each other's specificity and building together a "new heaven and a new earth."

9. Lugones, "On the Logic of Pluralist Feminism," 43.

10. For example, see above the analysis of what the women whose voices we present in this book said in chapter 4. The section of that chapter titled, "Latinas' Understanding of Themselves," which starts on p. 133, points out not only the similarities but also the differences.

11. Young, *Justice and Politics of Difference,* 169.

12. See Spelman, *Inessential Woman,* 159.

13. Ibid., 171.

14. Suzanne Oboler, "The Politics of Labeling—Latino/a Cultural Identities of Self and Other," *Latin American Perspectives* issue 74, vol. 19, no. 4 (fall 1992): 18–36. This is of course most obvious in the identity crisis suffered by Hispanic youth.

15. Young, *Justice and the Politics of Difference,* 165.

16. Oboler rightly indicates that this option is a political decision that includes a social-justice advocacy stance. Oboler, "The Politics of Labeling," 29–92.

17. Third General Conference of Latin American Bishops, *Puebla—Evangelization at Present and in the Future of Latin America* (Washington, D.C.: National Conference of Catholic Bishops Secretariat, Committee for the Church in Latin America, 1979).

18. Ibid., 178.

19. Ibid.

20. José Míguez Bonino, "Nuevas Tendencias en Teología," *Pasos 9* (1987) (Departmento Ecuménico de Investigaciones, San José, Costa Rica, 1987): 22.

21. I hope this paragraph makes it clear that I have amplified significantly the meaning of *mestizaje.* Originally referring to the mixing of Spanish and Amerindian blood, I use *mestizaje* to mean and embrace of all sorts of diversity among Hispanics as an intrinsic element of our struggle for liberation.

22. See chapter 2.

23. See the interpretation Susan B. Thistlethwaite has given to my words and her own elaboration of truth in action in her book *Sex, Race and God* (New York: Crossroad, 1989), 24–26.

24. For a most insightful exposition of moral labor and women's role in it, see Janet R. Jakobsen, "The Gendered Division of Moral Labor and the Possibilities for a Responsible Feminist Ethic," unpublished dissertation, Emory University, 1992.

BIBLIOGRAPHY

I. Hispanics in the United States

Abalos, David. *Latinos in the United States:The Sacred and the Political*. Notre Dame, Ind.: University of Notre Dame Press, 1986.

Anzaldúa, Gloria, and Cherríe Moraga. *This Bridge Called My Back: Writings by Radical Women of Color*. Watertown, Maine: Persephone Press, 1981.

Archdiocese of New York, Office of Pastoral Research. *Hispanics in New York: Religious, Cultural, and Social Experiences*. New York: Archdiocese of New York, 1980.

Carlson, Marifran. *Feminismo*. Chicago: Chicago Publishers, 1988.

Carter, Deborah J., and Reginald Wilson. *Eighth Annual Status Report on Minorities in Higher Education*. Washington, D.C.: American Council on Education, Publication Department, December 1989.

Conferencia Episcopal Cubana. *Documento Final e Instrucción Pastoral de Los Obispos*. Rome: Tipografía Don Bosco, 1986.

Consulta del Proyecto Hispano: Teología en las Américas. "Documento Final." New York: Theology in the Americas, 1979.

Cortes, Carlos, ed. *Protestantism and Latinos in the U.S.* New York: Arno Press, 1980.

Deck, Allan Figueroa. *The Second Wave*. New York: Paulist Press, 1989.

———, ed. *Frontiers of Hispanic Theology in the United States*. Maryknoll, N.Y.: Orbis Books, 1992.

Díaz, Rey. "La liberación hispana en U.S.A." *Apuntes* 9, no. 1 (spring 1989): 13–19.

Elizondo, Virgilio. *Galilean Journey—The Mexican American Promise*. Maryknoll, N.Y.: Orbis Books, 1983.

———. *La Morenita*. Liguori, Mo.: Liguori Publications, 1981.

Elsasser, Nan, Kyle MacKenzie, and Yvonne Tixier y Vigil, eds. *Las Mujeres: Conversations from a Hispanic Community*. Old Westbury, N.Y.: Feminist Press, 1980.

Espín, Orlando O., and Sixto J. García. "Sources of Hispanic Theology." Notes handed out at a workshop conducted at the Catholic Theological Society of America, Toronto, 1988.

———. "Toward a Hispanic-American Theology." Notes handed out at a workshop conducted at the Catholic Theological Society of America Convention, Philadelphia, 1987.

Espinoza, Marco A. "Pastoral Care of Hispanic Families in the United States: Socio-Cultural, Psychological, and Religious Considerations." D.Min. diss., New York, Union Theological Seminary, 1982.

Extension. Chicago: The Catholic Church Extension Society of the United States of America (July 1985).

Fitzpatrick, Joseph P. "The Hispanic Poor in a Middle-Class Church." *America*, July 2, 1988.

———. *Hispanoamericanos y la iglesia en el Nordeste*. New York: Centro de Pastoral Hispana para el Nordeste, 1977.

Galilea, Segundo. *Religiosidad popular y pastoral hispano-americana*. New York: Centro Católico de Pastoral para Hispanos del Nordeste, 1981.

García, Alma M. "The Development of Chicana Feminist Discourse, 1970–1980." *Gender and Society* 3, no. 2 (June 1989): 217–38.

García, Sixto J., and Orlando Espín. " 'Lilies of the Field': A Hispanic Theology of Providence and Human Responsibility." *Catholic Theological Society of America Proceedings* 44 (1989): 70–90.

Goizueta, Roberto. *"Nosotros:* Toward a U.S. Hispanic Anthropology." *Listening* 27, no. 1 (winter 1992): 55–69.

———. *We Are a People!* Minneapolis: Fortress Press, 1993.

Gómez, Alma, Cherríe Moraga, and Mariana Romo Carmona, eds. *Cuentos: Stories by Latinas*. New York: Kitchen Table, Women of Color Press, 1983.

González, Justo L., *Mañana: Christian Theology from a Hispanic Perspective*. Nashville, Tenn.: Abingdon, 1990.

———. *The Theological Education of Hispanics*. New York: Fund for Theological Education, 1988.

———, ed. *Voces: Voices from the Hispanic Church*. Nashville, Tenn.: Abingdon, 1992.

González, Nicanor. "Hacia una theología de acción y reflexión Pentecostal hispana." D.Min. diss., New York Theological Seminary, 1991.

González, Roberto O., and Michael La Velle. *The Hispanic Catholic in the United States: A Socio-Cultural and Religious Profile.* New York: Northeast Catholic Pastoral Center for Hispanics, 1985.

Guerrero, Andrés. *A Chicano Theology.* Maryknoll, N.Y.: Orbis Books, 1987.

Hawkins, Wayne R. "Hispanic and Anglo Christians: A Model of Shared Life." *Pacific Theological Review* 19, no. 2 (winter 1986): 39–42.

Huitrado-Rizo, Juan José, MCCJ. "Hispanic Popular Religiosity: The Expression of a People Coming to Life." *New Theology Review* 3, no. 4 (November 1990): 43–54.

Information Systems Development. *The Chicana Feminist.* Austin, Tex., 1977.

Isasi-Díaz, Ada María. "The Bible and *Mujerista* Theology." In *Lift Every Voice: Constructing Christian Theologies from the Underside,* edited by Susan Brooks Thistlethwaite and Mary Potter Engel, 261–69. San Francisco: Harper and Row, 1990.

———. "A Hispanic Garden in a Foreign Land." In *Inheriting Our Mothers' Gardens,"* edited by Letty M. Russell, Kwok Pui Lan, Ada María Isasi-Díaz, and Katie Geneva Cannon, 91–106. Philadelphia: Westminster, 1988.

———. "La mujer hispana: voz profética en la iglesia de los Estados Unidos." *Informes de Pro Mundi Vita, América Latina* 28 (1982).

———. "*Mujeristas:* A Name of Our Own." In *The Future of Liberation Theology,* edited by Marc H. Ellis and Otto Maduro (Maryknoll, N.Y.: Orbis Books, 1989): 410–19.

———. "A New Mestizaje/Mulatez: Reconceptualizing Difference." In *A Dream Unfinished—Theological Reflections on America from the Margins,* Eleazar Fernández and Fernando Segovia, eds., 203–19. Maryknoll, N.Y.: Orbis Books, 2001.

———. "Solidarity: Love of Neighbor in the 1980s." In *Lift Every Voice: Constructing Christian Theologies from the Underside,* edited by Susan Brooks Thistlethwaite and Mary Potter Engel, 31–40. San Francisco: Harper and Row, 1990.

———. "Toward an Understanding of *Feminismo Hispano* in the U.S.A." In *Women's Consciousness, Women's Conscience,* edited by Barbara Hilkert Andolsen, Christine E. Gudorf, and Mary D. Pellauer, 51–61. Minneapolis: Winston Press, 1985.

———. "¡Viva La Diferencia!" *Journal of Feminist Studies in Religion* 8, no. 2 (fall 1992): 98–102.

Isasi-Díaz, Ada María, Elena Olazagasti-Segovia, Sandra Mangual-Rodríguez, María Antonietta Berriozábal, Daisy L. Machado, Lourdes Arguelles, and Raven-Anne Rivero. "*Mujeristas:* Who We Are and What We Are About." *Journal of Feminist Studies in Religion* 8, no. 1 (spring 1992): 105–25.

Isasi-Díaz, Ada María, and Yolanda Tarango, *Hispanic Women: Prophetic Voice in the Church.* San Francisco: Harper and Row, 1988. Reprint, Minneapolis: Fortress Press, 1992.

Lachaga, José María de. *El Pueblo Hispano en U.S.A.: minorías étnicas y la iglesia católica.* Bilbao: Desclée de Brouwer, 1982.

Lucas, Isidro. *The Browning of America.* Chicago: Fides/Claretian, 1981.

Lafaye, J. *Quetzalcoatl et Guadalupe.* Paris: Gallimard, 1974.

Lara-Braud, Jorge. "Hispanic Ministry: Fidelity to Christ." *Pacific Theological Review* 19, no. 2 (winter 1986): 5–14.

Lugones, María. "*Hablando Cara a Cara*/Speaking Face to Face." In *Making Face, Making Soul—Haciendo Caras,* edited by Gloria Anzaldúa, 46–54. San Francisco: An Aunt Lute Foundation Book, 1990.

———. "On the Logic of Pluralist Feminism." In *Feminist Ethics,* edited by Claudia Card, 35–44. Lawrence: University Press of Kansas, 1991.

———. "Playfulness, 'World'-Travelling, and Loving Perception." *Hypatia* 2, no. 2 (summer 1987): 3–19.

Lugones, María, and Elizabeth V. Spelman. "Have We Got a Theory for You! Feminist Theory, Cultural Imperialism, and the Demand for the 'Woman's Voice.'" *Women's Studies International Forum* 6, no. 6 (1983): 573–81.

Martínez, Jill. "In Search of an Inclusive Community." *Apuntes* 9, no. 1 (spring 1989): 3–9.

Mirande, Alfredo. *La Chicana.* Chicago: University of Chicago Press, 1979.

_____. *The Chicano Experience: An Alternative Perspective*. Notre Dame, Ind.: University of Notre Dame Press, 1985.

Montoya, Alex D. *Hispanic Ministry in North America*. Grand Rapids, Mich.: Zondervan Publishing, 1987.

Moore, Joan, and Harry Pachón. *Hispanics in the United States*. Englewood Cliffs, N.J.: Prentice-Hall, 1985.

Mosqueda, Lawrence J. *Chicanos, Catholicism, and Political Ideology*. Lanham, Md.: University Press of America, 1986.

New *Catholic World*. New York: Paulist Press, July/August 1980.

Nieto, Leo D. "Toward a Chicano Liberation Theology." In *Liberation Theologies in North America and Europe*, Mission Trends, no. 4, edited by Gerald H. Anderson and Thomas F. Stransky, 277–82. New York: Paulist Press, 1979.

Oboler, Suzanne. "The Politics of Labeling—Latino/a Cultural Identities of Self and Other." *Latin American Perspectives* issue 74, 19, no. 4 (fall 1992): 18–36.

Ponce, Frank. "Los católicos hispanos en los Estados Unidos." *Informes de Pro Mundi Vita, América Latina* 23 (1981).

Recinos, Harold J. *Hear the Cry! Latino Pastor Challenges the Church*. Louisville, Ky.: Westminster/John Knox Press, 1989.

"Recovery Fails Latinos." *Dollars and Sense*, November 1989.

Rodríguez, Richard. *Hunger of Memory*. New York: Bantam, 1982.

Romero, C. Gilbert. "On Choosing a Symbol System for a Hispanic Theology." *Apuntes* 1, no. 4 (1981): 16–20.

Rosado, Caleb. "Thoughts on a Puerto Rican Theology of Community." *Apuntes* 9, no. 1 (spring 1989): 10–12.

Rossing, John P. "*Mestizaje* and Marginality: A Hispanic-American Theology." *Theology Today* 45 (October 1988): 293–304.

Sandín-Fremaint, Pedro A. "Hacia una teología feminista puertorriqueña." *Apuntes* 4, no. 2 (1984): 27–37.

Sandoval, Moisés. "A Four-Part Series on Hispanic Catholics." Washington, D.C.: National Catholic News Service, July 1985.

_____. "Hispanic Challenges to the Church." Washington, D.C.: Secretariat of Hispanic Affairs, 1978.

_____, ed. *Fronteras: A History of the Latin American Church in the U.S.A. since 1513*. San Antonio: The Mexican American Cultural Center, 1983.

_____, ed. *The Mexican American Experience in the Church*. New York: William H. Sadlier, 1983.

Secretariat for Hispanic Affairs, National Conference of Catholic Bishops/United States Catholic Conference. *Proceedings of the II Encuentro Nacional Hispano de Pastoral*. Washington, D.C.: Secretariat for Hispanic Affairs/USCC, 1978.

Segovia, Fernando. "Two Places and No Place on Which to Stand: Mixture and Otherness in Hispanic American Theology." *Listening* 27, no. 2 (winter 1992): 26–40.

Segunda Consulta Ecuménica de Pastoral Indígena. In *Aporte de los pueblos indígenas de América Latina a la Teología Cristiana*. Quito, Ecuador, 1986.

Sepúlveda, Juan. "Pentecostalism as Popular Religiosity." *International Review of Mission* 78 (January 1989): 80–88.

Solivan, Samuel. "Orthopathos: Interlocutor between Orthodoxy and Praxis." *Andover Newton Review* 1, no. 2 (winter 1990): 19–25.

Sosa, Juan J. "Religiosidad popular y sincretismo religioso: santería y espiritualismo." *Documentación Sureste*, no. 4 (March 1983):

Stevens Arroyo, Antonio, ed. *Prophets Denied Honor*. Maryknoll, N.Y.: Orbis Books, 1980.

Tafolla, Carmen. *To Split a Human: Mitos, Machos y la Mujer Chicana*. San Antonio, Tex.: Mexican American Cultural Center, 1985.

Vasconcelos, José. *La Raza Cósmica*. 11th ed. Colección Austral. Mexico City: Espasa-Calpe Mexicana, 1948.

Vázquez, Edmundo E. "Toward a Multicultural Church: A Future for the Presbyterian Church in the Southwest." *Pacific Theological Review* 19, no. 2 (winter 1986): 15–23.

Vidal, Jaime. "Popular Religion among the Hispanics in the General Area of the Archdiocese of Newark." In *Presencia Nueva*, edited by Office of Research and Planning, 241–347. Newark: Office of Research and Planning, 1988.

Villafañe, Eldin. *The Liberating Spirit.* Lanham, Md.: University Press of America, 1992.

Weyr, Thomas. *Hispanic U.S.A.: Breaking the Melting Pot.* New York: Harper and Row, 1988.

Yankelovich, Skelly & White. *Spanish U.S.A.—A Study of the Hispanic Market in the United States.* New York: Yankelovich, Skelly & White, 1981.

Zavala Martínez, Iris. "*En la lucha:* Economic and Socioemotional Struggles of Puerto Rican Women in the United States." In *For Crying Out Loud,* edited by Rochelle Lefkowitz and Ann Withorn, 111–24. New York: Pilgrim Press, 1986.

II. Latin America

Aldunate, J. "Poder político, ciencia económica y moral." *Moralia* 4, no. 1–2 (1982): 83–100.

Alves, Rubem. "Thoughts on a Program for Ethics." *Union Seminary Quarterly Review* 26 (1970): 43–58.

Anjos, M. F. dos, ed. *Articulacão da teologia moral na América Latina.* Teologia Moral na América Latina, 2. Aparecida, São Paulo: Editora Santuario, 1987.

_____. *Temas Latino-Americanos de Etica.* Teologia Moral na América Latina, 3. Aparecida, São Paulo: Editora Santuario, 1987.

Aquino, Pilar. *Nuestro Clamor por la Vida.* San José, Costa Rica: Editorial D.E.I., 1992.

Arriaga, P. "Los pobres ante la moral cristiana." *Christus* 39 (1974): 33–40.

Assmann, Hugo. "Por una sociedad donde quepan todos." In *Por una sociedad donde quepan todos,* ed. José Duque, 379–391. Costa Rica: Editorial D.E.I., 1996.

Boff, Clodovis. "The Poor of Latin America and Their New Ways of Liberation." In *Changing Values and Virtues,* edited by Dietmar Mieth and Jacques Pohier, 33–44. Concilium 191. Edinburgh: T. & T. Clark, 1987.

_____. "The Social Teaching of the Church and the Theology of Liberation: Opposing Social Practices?" In *Christian Ethics: Uniformity, Universality, Pluralism,* edited by Jacques Pohier and Dietmar Mieth, 17–22. Concilium 150. New York: Seabury, 1981.

_____. *Theology and Praxis.* Maryknoll, N.Y.: Orbis Books, 1987.

Boff, Leonardo. *Church: Charism and Power.* New York: Crossroad, 1986.

_____. "Método teológico. Problemática actual en Europa y en América Latina: Epistemología y Análisis." In *Liberación y cautiverio,* 566–68. Mexico City, 1975.

_____. "¿Qué es hacer teología desde América Latina?" In *Liberación y cautiverio,* Encuento Latinamericano de Teología, 129–54. Mexico City:, 1975.

_____. *Salvation and Liberation.* Maryknoll, N.Y.: Orbis Books, 1984.

_____. *When Theology Listens to the Poor.* San Francisco: Harper and Row, 1988.

Boff, Leonardo, and Clodovis Boff. *Introducing Liberation Theology.* Maryknoll, N.Y.: Orbis Books, 1987.

_____. *Liberation Theology.* San Francisco: Harper and Row, 1986.

Bonnin, E., ed. *Espiritualidad y liberación en América Latina.* San José: Costa Rica: 1982.

Candelaria, R. Michael. *Popular Religion and Liberation.* Albany: State University of New York Press, 1990.

Carreras de Bastos, Laura. *Feminismo Cristiano: Conferencia.* Montevideo, 1907.

Casalla, Mario C. "El Cuarteto de Jerusalén—Sobre la justicia y sus avatares históricos." In *Márgenes de la Justicia,* ed. Mario C. Casalla, 227–65. Buenos Aires: Grupo Editor Altamira, 2000.

Castro Rocha, Patricia. *Jesús liberador de la mujer, la sociedad y el mundo.* Managua, Nicaragua: Departamento de Publicaciones del Centro Inter-Eclesial de Estudios Teológicos y Sociales, 1987.

Cavalcanti, Tereza. "Produzindo Teologia No Feminino Plural." *Perspectiva Teológica* 20, no. 52 (September/December 1988): 359–70.

Chao, X. "Da autonomia a libertasão. Tres etapas do pensamiento etico." *Encrucilhada* 8 (1984): 316–27.

II Consulta Ecuménica de Pastoral Indígena. In *Aporte de los Pueblos Indígenos de América Latina a la Teología Cristiana.* Ecuador, Documento de Circulación Interna, 1986.

Crespo Garduno, Joaquín. "Métodos y condicionamientos de la teología moral latinoamericana." *Humanidades Anuario* 4 (1976): 151–58.

DeZan, Julio D. "Para una filosofía de la cultura y una filosofía política nacional." In *Cultura popular y filosofía de la liberación,* 89–139. Buenos Aires: Fernando García Cambeiro, 1975.

Dussel, Enrique. *Ética de la liberación – en la edad de la globalización y de la exclusión.* Madrid: Editorial Trotta, 1998.

――――. "One Ethics and Many Moralities?" In *Christian Ethics: Uniformity, Universality, Pluralism,* edited by Jacques Pohier and Dietmra Mieth, 54–61. Concilium 150. Edinburgh: T. & T. Clark, 1981.

――――. *Para una ética de la liberación latinoamericana.* Tomo I. Buenos Aires: Siglo Ventiuno Argentina Editores, 1973.

――――. *Philosophy of Liberation.* Maryknoll, N.Y.: Orbis Books, 1985.

――――. *Ethics and Community.* Maryknoll, N.Y.: Orbis Books, 1988.

――――. "An Ethics of Liberation: Fundamental Hypotheses." In *The Ethics of Liberation—The Liberation of Ethics,* edited by Dietmar Mieth and Jacques Pohier, 54–63. Concilium 172. Edinburgh: T. & T. Clark, 1984.

――――. *Ethics and the Theology of Liberation.* Maryknoll, N.Y.: Orbis Books, 1978.

Echegaray, Hugo. *La Práctica de Jesús.* Lima, Perú: 1980.

Encuentro Latinoamericano de teología. *Liberación y cautiverio.* Mexico City:, 1975.

Fabella, Virginia, and Mercy Oduyoye, eds. *With Passion and Compassion.* Maryknoll, N.Y.: Orbis Books, 1988.

Ferre, Alberto Methol. "Itinerario de la Praxis." *Víspera* 29 (November 1972): 40–44.

Foster, Theodora Carroll. *Women, Religion and Development in Third World Countries.* New York: Praeger Publishers, 1983.

Frei Betto. "The Church, Ideology and Popular Culture." *Barricada Internacional,* July 1989.

Galilea, Segundo. *Religiosidad Popular y Pastoral.* Madrid: Ediciones Cristiandad, 1979.

García, Ismael. *Justice in Latin American Liberation Theology.* Atlanta, Ga.: John Knox Press, 1987.

Gebara, Ivone. *Longing for Running Water—Ecofemnism and Liberation.* Minneapolis: Fortress Press, 1999.

――――. "Option for the Poor as an Option for the Poor Woman." In *Women, Work and Poverty,* edited by Elisabeth Schüssler Fiorenza and Anne Carr, 110–17.

――――. *Out of The Depths—Women's Experience of Evil and Salvation.* Minneapolis: Fortress Press, 2002.

Gibellini, Rossino. *The Liberation Theology Debate.* London: SCM, 1987.

Giménez, Gilberto. "De la doctrina social de la Iglesia a la ética de liberación." In *Panorama de la Teología,* 2:45–62. Equipo Seladoc. Salamanca: Ediciones Sígueme, 1975.

Goizueta, Roberto. *Liberation, Method and Dialogue: Enrique Dussel and North American Theological Discourse.* Atlanta, Ga.: Scholars Press, 1988.

Golden, Renny. *The Hour of the Poor, The Hour of Women.* New York: Crossroad, 1991.

González, L. J. *Etica latinoamericana.* 2d ed. Bogotá: 1983.

González, Martínez, José Luis. "La ética popular y su autonomía relativa." *Allpanchis* 20, no. 31 (Primer Semestre 1988): 125–62.

――――. "Teología de la liberación y religiosidad popular." *Páginas* 7, no. 49–50 (November–December 1982): 4–13.

Grupo de Investigación "Teología de la Praxis." *Sólo los cristianos militantes pueden ser teólogos de la liberación.* Documento no. 9 (1977): 4–32 y Documento no. 10 (1977): 3–37.

Gutiérrez, Gustavo. *El Dios de la vida.* Lima, Peru: Departamento de Teología, Pontificia Universidad Católica del Perú, 1983.

――――. *On Job.* Maryknoll, N.Y.: Orbis Books, 1987.

――――. *The Power of the Poor in History.* Maryknoll, N.Y.: Orbis Books, 1983.

――――. *Sobre el trajabo humano.* Lima, Peru: Centro de Estudios y Publicaciones, 1982.

――――. *A Theology of Liberation.* Maryknoll, N.Y.: Orbis Books, 1988.

――――. *La verdad los hará libres.* Lima, Peru: Centro de Estudios y Publicaciones, 1986.

――――. *We Drink from Our Own Wells.* Maryknoll, N.Y.: Orbis Books, 1984.

Hinkelammert, Franz J. "La Crisis del Socialismo y el Tercer Mundo." *Pasos* 30 (July–August 1990): 1–6.

――――. *Crítica a la razón utópica.* San José, Costa Rica: Editorial D.E.I., 1984.

――――. "Una sociedad en la que todos quepan: de la impotencia de la omnipotencia." In *Por una sociedad donde quepan todos,* ed. José Duque, 379–91. San José, Costa Rica: Editorial D.E.I., 1996.

Idígoras, J. L. *Vocabulario teológico para América Latina*. São Paulo: Ediciones Paulinas, 1983.

Junges, José Roque. "Moral especial: Princípio Organizativo das Suas Diferentes Areas e Conteudos." *Perspectiva Teológica* 20, no. 52 (September/December 1988): 371–77.

Koh, Jae Sik. "A Comparison of Walter George Muelder's Christian Social Ethics of the Responsible Society and José Míguez Bonino's Liberation Ethics." Ph.D. diss., Northwestern University 1979.

Lepargneur, François Huber. *Demografia, etica e igreja*. São Paulo: Editora Ática, 1983.

Lora, Carmen, Cecilia Barnechea, and Fryne Santisteban. *Mujer: víctima de opresión; portadora de liberación*. Lima, Peru: Instituto Bartolomé de las Casas, 1985.

Lozano, Itziar, and Maruja Gonzáles. *Feminismo y Movimiento Popular*. Cuadernos para la Mujer. Serie: Pensamiento y Luchas, no. 8 (Mexico City:), October 1986.

Manzanera, Miguel. *Teología, salvación y liberación en la obra de Gustavo Gutiérrez*. Bilbao: Universidad de Deusto, 1978.

Marzal, Manuel. "Evangelio y mitos populares. ¿Es posible una iglesia indígena en el Perú?" In *Panorama de la teología latinoamericana*, 2:143–60. Equipo Seladoc. Salamanca: Ediciones Sígueme, 1975.

―――. "La religiosidad popular en el Perú." *Panorama de la teología latinoamericana*, 1:27–42. Equipo Seladoc. Salamanca: Ediciones Sígueme, 1975.

Melano Couch, Beatriz. "Estudio bíblico: el reino de Dios y la ética." *Cuadernos de Teología* 7, no. 3 (1986): 177–96.

Mieth, Dietmar. "Autonomy or Liberation—Two Paradigms of Christian Ethics?" In *Ethics of Liberation— The Liberation of Ethics*, edited by Dietmar Mieth and Jacques Pohier, 87–93. Concilium 172. Edinburgh: T. & T. Clark, 1984.

Miguelez, Xosé. *La Teología de la liberación y su método*. Barcelona: Herder, 1976.

Míguez Bonino, José. *Doing Theology in a Revolutionary Siuation*. Philadelphia: Fortress Press, 1975.

―――. "Historical Praxis and Christian Identity." In *Frontiers of Theology in Latin America*, edited by Rosino Gibellini, 260–83. Maryknoll, N.Y.: Orbis Books, 1979.

―――. "Nuevas Tendencias en Teología." *Pasos* 9 (1987): 18–23.

―――. *Toward a Christian Political Ethics*. Philadelphia: Fortress Press, 1983.

Mino G., Cecilia. "Algunas reflexiones sobre pedagogía de género y cotidianidad." *Tejiendo Nuestra Red*, 1, no. 1 (October 1988): 10–15.

Mirandad, A. A. de. *Moral, consciência e pecado*. São Paulo: 1983.

Misfud, Tony. *Moral de discernimiento*. Vol. 1. *Hacia una moral liberadora. Ensayo de una teología moral fundamental desde América Latina*. Santiago de Chile: CUIDE, 1983.

―――. "El tema ético en Puebla: vision panorámica." *Moralia* 4, no. 1–2 (1982): 115–33.

Moreno Rejón, Francisco. "Bibliografía latinoamericana sobre moral fundamental (1984–1986)." *Moralia* 9 (1987): 157–64.

―――. "Información bibliografía sobre la moral fundamental desde América Latina." *Moralia* 7 (1985): 213–31.

―――. "Perspectivas para una ética de la liberación." *Moralia* 4 (1982): 135–50.

―――. *Salvar la vida de los pobres*. Lima, Peru: Centro de Estudio y Publicaciones, 1986.

―――. "Seeking the Kingdom and Its Justice: The Development of the Ethic of Liberation." In *The Ethics of Liberation—The Liberation of Ethics*, edited by Dietmar Mieth and Jacques Pohier, 35–41. Concilium 172. Edinburgh: T. & T. Clark, 1984.

―――. *Teología moral desde los pobres. La moral en la reflexión teológica desde América Latina*. Madrid: PS Editorial, 1986.

―――. "La teología moral en América Latina a partir de Medellín." *Páginas* 92 (August 1988): 29–38.

Moser, Antonio. "Ciencias sociales y teología moral." *Páginas* 94 (December 1988): 75–99.

―――. "Como se faz teologia moral no Brasil hoje." *Revista Eclesiástica Brasileira* 44 (1984): 242–64.

―――. "The Representation of God in the Ethics of Liberation." In *The Ethics of Liberation—The Liberation of Ethics*, edited by Dietmar Mieth and Jacques Pohier, 42–47. Concilium 172. Edinburgh: T. & T. Clark, 1984.

Moser, Antonio, and Bernardino Leers. *Moral Theology*. Maryknoll, N.Y.: Orbis Books, 1990.

Mujeres Para el Diálogo. *Mujer Latinamericana—Iglesia y Teología.* Mexico City: 1981.

Munera, Alberto. "Conciencia moral y pecado." *Teología Xaveriana* 35 (1985): 157–85.

Myscofski, Carole A. "Women's Religious Roles in Brazil: A History of Limitations." *Journal of Feminist Studies in Religion* 1, no. 2 (fall 1985): 43–57.

Paredes, Tito. "Popular Religiosity: A Protestant Perspective." *Missiology* 20, no. 2 (April 1992): 205–20.

Parker, C. "Popular Religion in Latin America." *Popular Religions.* Pro Mundi Vita Studies (November 1988): 18–26.

Pixley, Jorge, ed. *La mujer en la construcción de la iglesia.* San José, Costa Rica: Editorial D.E.I., 1986.

Portugal, Ana María, and Amparo Claro. "Virgin and Martyr." *Conscience* (July/August 1988).

Pravera, Kate E. "The Primacy of Orthopraxis: Theological Method in the Nicaraguan Church of the Poor." Ph.D. diss., Garrett-Northwestern University, 1984.

Quade, Quentin, ed. *The Pope and Revolution.* Washington, D.C.: Ethics and Public Policy Center, 1982.

Richard, Pablo. "La ética como espiritualidad liberadora en la realidad ecclesial de América Latina." *Moralia* 4, 1–2 (1982): 101–14.

————. "La Teología de la Liberación en la Vueva Coyuntura." *Pasos* 34 (March/April 1991): 1–8.

Rivera Pagán, Luis N. *Evangelización y Violencia—La Conquista de América.* San Juan, Puerto Rico: Editorial Cemi, 1991.

Ruiz García, Samuel. "Condicionamientos eclesiales de la reflexión teológica en América Latina." In *Liberación y cautiverio,* 83–89. Mexico City, 1975.

Scannone, Juan Carlos. "Dios desde las víctimas." In *Márgenes de la Justicia,* ed. Mario C. Casalla, 287–307. Buenos Aires: Grupo Editor Altamira, 2000.

————. *Teología de la liberación y pruxis popular.* Salamanca: Ediciones Sígueme, 1976.

————. "Trascendencia, praxis liberadora y lenguaje. Hacia una filosofía de la religion postmoderna y latinoamericana situada." In *Panorama de la teología latinoamericana,* 2:83–115. Equipo Seladoc. Salamanca: Ediciones Sígueme, 1975.

Segundo, Juan Luis. "Condicionamientos actuales de la reflexión teológica en Latinoamerica." In *Liberación y cautiverio,* 91–101. Mexico City, 1975.

————. *The Liberation of Theology.* Maryknoll, N.Y.: Orbis Books, 1982.

————. *Teología de la liberación.* Madrid: Ediciones Cristiandad, 1985.

————. "Two Theologies of Liberation." *Journal of Theology for South Africa* no. 52 (1985): 321–27.

Sepúlveda, Juan. "Pentecostalism as Popular Religiosity." *International Review of Mission* 78 (January 1989): 80–88.

Snoek, C. J. "La teología moral en el Brasil de hoy." *Moralia* 4, 1–2 (1982): 67–81.

Tamez, Elsa, ed. *Against Machismo.* Oak Park, Ill.: Meyer Stone, 1987.

————, ed. *El rostro femenino de la iglesia.* San José, Costa Rica: Editorial D.E.I., 1986.

————, ed. *Teólogos de la liberación hablan sobre la mujer.* San José, Costa Rica: Editorial D.E.I., 1986.

————, ed. *Through Her Eyes.* Maryknoll, N.Y.: Orbis Books, 1989.

Torre, Julio de la. "Movimientos de liberación y liberación cristiana." *Moralia* 4, 3 (1982): 265–73.

Trapasso, Rose Dominic. "Poverty, Gender and Justice in Peru." *Christianity and Crisis,* February 6, 1989.

"Una ética liberadora." *Misión Abierta* 4 (1985): 11–112.

Valentín, Dora. "El Cristianismo y la Mujer." *Heraldo Cristiano* 24, nos. 11–12 (1979): 2–9.

Vidal García, Marciano. "Is Morality Based on Autonomy Compatible with the Ethics of Liberation? In *The Ethics of Liberation—The Liberation of Ethics,* edited by Dietmar Mieth and Jacques Pohier, 80–86. Concilium 172. Edinburgh: T. & T. Clark, 1984.

————. "La preferencias por el pobre, criterio de moral." *Studia Moralia* 20 (1982): 277–306.

————. "Teología de la liberación y ética social cristiana." *Studia Moralia* 15 (1977): 207–18.

III. Feminism

Alcoff, Linda. "The Problem of Speaking for Others." In *Feminist Nightmares—Women At Odds*, eds., Susan Ostron Weisser and Jennifer Fleischner, 285–309. New York: New York University Press, 1994.

———. "Cultural Feminism versus Post-Structuralism: The Identity Crisis in Feminist Theory." In *Feminist Theory in Practice and Process*, ed. Micheline R. Malson, Jean F. O'Barr, Sarah Westphal-Wihl, and Mary Wyer, 295–326. Chicago: University of Chicago Press, 1989.

Amott, Teresa L., and Julie Matthaei. *Race, Gender and Work*. Boston: South End Press, 1991.

Andolsen, Barbara Hilkert, Christine E. Gudorf, and Mary D. Pellauer, eds. *Women's Consciousness, Women's Conscience*. San Francisco: Harper and Row, 1985.

Beneria, Lourdes, and Gita Sen. "Class and Gender Inequalities and Women's Role in Economic Development—Theoretical and Practical Implications." *Feminist Studies* 8, no. 1 (spring 1982): 157–76.

Benhabib, Seyla. "The Generalized and the Concrete Other: The Kohlberg-Gilligan Controversy." In *Feminism as Critique*, edited by Sylvia Benhabib and Drucilla Cornell, 77–95. Minneapolis: University of Minnesota Press, 1987.

Bettenhausen, Elizabeth. "The Concept of Justice and a Feminist Lutheran Social Ethics." *The Annual of the Society of Christian Ethics* (1986): 163–82.

———. "Three Dimensions of Conviction and Conflict in Morality." *Nexus* 23, no. 2 (summer 1980):

Brubaker, Pamela K. "The Pauperization of Women: A Proposal for Feminist Ethical Theory." Presentation at the American Academy of Religion. Chicago, November 20, 1988.

———. "Rendering the Invisible Visible: Methodological Constraints on Economic Ethics in Relation to Women's Impoverishment." Ph.D. diss., Union Theological Seminary, New York, 1989.

Bunch, Charlotte. *Passionate Politics*. New York: St. Martin's Press, 1987.

Card, Claudia. *Virtues and Moral Luck*. Series 1, Institute for Legal Studies, Working Papers. Madison: University of Wisconsin-Madison, Law School, November 1985.

Carr, Anne E. "Is a Christian Feminist Theology Possible?" *Theological Studies* 43, no. 2 (June 1982): 279–97.

———. *Transforming Grace: Christian Tradition and Women's Experience*. San Francisco: Harper and Row, 1988.

Cheatham, Annie, and Mary Clare Powell. *This Way Daybreak Comes: Women's Values and the Future*. Philadelphia: New Society Publishers, 1986.

Chopp, Rebecca. *The Praxis of Suffering*. Maryknoll, N.Y.: Orbis Books, 1986.

Christ, Carol P. *Diving Deep and Surfacing*. Boston: Beacon Press, 1980.

Christ, Carol P., Ellen M. Umansky, and Anne Carr. "What Are the Sources of My Theology?" *Journal of Feminist Studies in Religion* 1, no. 1 (spring 1985): 119–32.

Chung, Hyun Kyung. "Opium of the Seed for Revolution? Shamanism: Women Centered Popular Religiosity in Korea." Paper given at the Ecumenical Association of Third World Theologians, New Delhi, December 1–5, 1987.

———. *Struggle to be the Sun Again—Introducing Asian Women's Theology*. Maryknoll, N.Y.: Orbis Books, 1990.

Code, Lorraine, Sheila Mullett, and Christine Overall. *Feminist Perspectives: Philosophical Essays on Methods and Morals*. Toronto: University of Toronto Press, 1988.

Culpepper, Emily Erwin. "New Tools for Theology: Writings by Women of Color." *Journal of Feminist Studies in Religion* 4, no. 2 (fall 1988): 39–50.

———. "Philosophia: Feminist Methodology for Constructing a Female Train of Thought." *Journal of Feminist Studies in Religion* 3, no. 2 (fall 1987): 7–16.

Daly, Mary. *Gyn/Ecology—The Metaethics of Radical Feminism*. Boston: Beacon Press, 1978.

Donovan, Josephine. *Feminist Theory*. New York: Frederick Ungar Publishing Co., 1985.

Farley, Margaret A. "Feminist Ethics." In *Dictionary of Christian Ethics*, edited by James E. Childress and John Macquarrie, Philadelphia: Westminster, 1986.

———. "Feminist Ethics in the Christian Ethics Curriculum." *Horizons* 11 (fall 1984): 361–72.

———. "Moral Imperatives for the Ordination of Women." In *Women and Catholic Priesthood: An Expanded Vision*, edited by Anne Marie Gardiner, 35–51. New York: Paulist Press, 1976.

_____. *Personal Commitments.* San Francisco: Harper and Row, 1988.

Fiorenza, Elisabeth Schüssler. *In Memory of Her.* New York: Crossroad, 1983.

_____. "The Will to Choose or to Reject: Continuing Our Critical Work." In *Feminist Interpretation of the Bible,* edited by Letty M. Russell, 124–36. Philadelphia: Westminster, 1985.

Fiorenza, Elisabeth Schüssler, Karen McCarthy Brown, Anne Llewellyn Barstow, Cheryl Townsend Gilkes, and Mary E. Hunt. "On Feminist Methodology." *Journal of Feminist Studies in Religion* 1, no. 2 (fall 1985): 73–88.

Gilligan, Carol. *In a Different Voice: Psychological Theory and Women's Development.* Cambridge: Harvard Univ. Press, 1982.

_____. "Remapping the Moral Domain: New Images of the Self in Relationship." In *Reconstructing Individualism,* edited by Thomas C. Heller, Morton Sosna, and David E. Wellbery, 237–351. Stanford, Calif.: Stanford University Press, 1986.

Gilligan, Carol, Janie Victoria Ward, and Jill McLean, with Betty Bardige. *Mapping the Moral Domain.* Cambridge: Harvard University Press, 1989.

Grimshaw, Jean. *Philosophy and Feminist Thinking.* Minneapolis: University of Minnesota Press, 1986.

Haney, Eleanor Humes. "What Is Feminist Ethics?" *Journal of Religious Ethics* 8, no. 1 (1980): 115–24.

Harrison, Beverly W. "A Feminist Perspective on Moral Responsibility." *Conscience,* winter 1984/1985.

_____. *Making the Connections.* Boston: Beacon Press, 1985.

_____. *Our Right to Choose.* Boston: Beacon Press, 1983.

Hartsock, Nancy. *Money, Sex and Power.* Boston: Northeastern University Press, 1983.

Heyward, Isabel Carter. *Our Passion for Justice.* New York: Pilgrim Press, 1984.

_____. *The Redemption of God.* University Press of America, 1982.

_____. *Speaking of Christ.* New York: Pilgrim Press, 1989.

_____. *Touching Our Strength.* San Francisco: Harper and Row, 1989.

Hoagland, Sarah Lucia. *Lesbian Ethics: Toward New Value.* Palo Alto, Calif.: Institute of Lesbian Studies, 1988.

Hunt, Mary E. "Beyond the Academy Gates." *Center for Women and Religion Journal* 3, no. 1 (1983): 7–16.

_____. "Feminist Liberation Theology: The Development of Method in Construction." Ph.D. diss., Graduate Theological Union, Berkeley, California, 1980.

Hunter College Women's Studies Collective. *Women's Realities, Women's Choices.* New York: Oxford University Press, 1983.

Jay, Nancy. "Sacrifice as Remedy for Having Been Born of Woman." In *Immaculate and Powerful,* edited by Clarissa W. Atkinson, Constance H. Buchanan, and Margaret R. Miles, 283–309. Boston: Beacon Press, 1985.

Kittay, Eva Feder, and Diana T. Meyers, eds. *Women and Moral Theory.* Totowa, N.J.: Rowman & Littlefield, 1987.

Morstein, Petra von. "A Message from Cassandra." In *Feminist Perspectives,* edited by Lorraine Code, Sheila Mullett, and Christine Overall, 46–63. Toronto: University of Toronto Press, 1988.

Mullett, Sheila. "Shifting Perspective: A New Approach to Ethics." In *Feminist Perspectives,* edited by Lorraine Code, Sheila Mullett, and Christine Overall, 109–26. Toronto: University of Toronto Press, 1988.

Nelson, Lou. "What's So Feminist about Feminist Ethics?" *Canadian Journal of Feminist Ethics* 2, no. 1 (spring 1987): 29–34.

Nicholson, Linda. "Women, Morality, and History." *Social Research* 50, no. 3 (autumn 1983): 514–36.

Noddings, Nell. *Caring: A Feminine Approach to Ethics and Moral Education.* Berkeley: University of California Press, 1984.

O'Connor, June. "On Doing Religious Ethics." *Journal of Religious Education* (1979): 81–96.

Parsons, Kathryn Pyne. "Moral Revolution." In *The Prism of Sex,* edited by Julia A. Sherman and Evelyn Torton Beck, 189–227. Madison: University of Wisconsin Press, 1979.

Patrick, Anne E. "Conscience and Community: Catholic Moral Theology Today." The Warren Lecture Series in Catholic Studies. University of Tulsa, February 13, 1989.

_____. "Narrative and the Social Dynamics of Virtue." In *Changing Values and Virtues,* edited by Ditmar Mieth and Jacques Pohier, 69–80. Concilium 191. Edinburgh: T & T Clark, 1987.

Plaskow, Judith. *Sex, Sin, and Grace*. New Haven: Yale University Press, 1975.

Raymond, Janice. *A Passion for Friends*. Boston: Beacon Press, 1986.

Reineke, Martha J. "The Politics of Difference: A Critique of Carol Gilligan." *Canadian Journal of Feminist Ethics* 2, no. 1 (spring 1987): 3–20.

Robb, Carol. "A Framework for Feminist Ethics." *Journal of Religious Ethics* 9, no. 1 (spring 1980): 48–68.

Ruether, Rosemary Radford. "Feminist Interpretation: A Method of Correlation." In *Feminist Interpretation of the Bible*, edited by Letty M. Russell, 111–24. Philadelphia: Westminster, 1985.

_____. "A Feminist Perspective." In *Doing Theology in a Divided World*, edited by Virginia Fabella and Sergio Torres, 65–71. Maryknoll, N.Y.: Orbis Books, 1985.

_____. *New Woman / New Earth: Sexist Ideologies and Human Liberation*. New York: Seabury, 1985.

Russell, Letty M. "Authority and the Challenge of Feminist Interpretation." In *Feminist Interpretation of the Bible*, edited by Letty M. Russell, 137–46. Philadelphia: Westminster, 1985.

_____. *Human Liberation in a Feminist Perspective*. Philadelphia: Westminster, 1984.

Schaef, Anne Wilson. *Woman's Reality: An Emerging Female System in the White Male Society*. Minneapolis: Winston, 1981.

Sherif, Carolyn Wood. "Bias in Psychology." In *The Prism of Sex*, edited by Julia A. Sherman and Evelyn Torton Beck, 93–133. Madison: University of Wisconsin Press, 1979.

Smith, Dorothy E. *The Everyday World as Problematic—A Feminist Sociology*. Toronto: University of Toronto Press, 1987.

_____. "A Sociology for Women." In *The Prism of Sex*, edited by Julia A. Sherman and Evelyn Torton Beck, 135–87. Madison: University of Wisconsin Press, 1979.

Smith, Ruth. "Moral Transcendence and Moral Space in the Historical Experiences of Women." *Journal of Feminist Studies in Religion* 4, no. 2 (fall 1988): 21–37.

_____. "Morality and Perceptions of Society: The Limits of Self-Interest." *Journal for the Scientific Study of Religion* 26 (fall 1987): 279–93.

Spelman, Elizabeth V. *Inessential Woman*. Boston: Beacon Press, 1988.

Vaughn, Judy. *Sociality, Ethics, and Social Change*. Boston: University Press of America, 1983.

Welch, Sharon D. "A Genealogy of the Logic of Deterrence: Habermas, Foucault and a Feminist Ethic of Risk." *Union Seminary Quarterly Review* 41, no. 2 (1987): 1–12.

IV. Womanism

Cannon, Katie Geneva. *Black Womanist Ethics*. Atlanta, Ga.: Scholars Press, 1988.

_____. "Hitting a Straight Lick with a Crooked Stick: The Womanist Dilemma in the Development of a Black Liberation Ethic." In *The Annual of the Society of Christian Ethics*, edited by D. Yeager (1987): 100–112.

_____. "Resources for a Constructive Ethic in the Life and Work of Zora Neale Hurston." *Journal of Feminist Studies in Religion* 1, no. 1 (spring 1985): 37–54.

Grant, Jacquelyn. *White Women's Christ and Black Women's Jesus: Feminist Christology and Womanist Response*. Atlanta: Scholars Press, 1989.

Hooks, Bell. *Feminist Theory: From Margin to Center*. Boston: South End Press, 1974.

_____. *Talking Back*. Boston: South End Press, 1989.

Stack, Carol B. *All Our Kin: Strategies for Survival in a Black Community*. New York: Harper and Row, 1975.

Walker, Alice. *In Search of Our Mothers' Gardens: Womanist Prose*. San Diego: Harcourt Brace Jovanovich, 1983.

Weems, Renita. *Just a Sister Away: A Womanist Vision of Women's Relatonships in the Bible*. San Diego: Lura Media, 1988.

Williams, Delores. "Black Women's Literature and the Task of Feminist Theology." In *Immaculate and Powerful*, edited by Clarissa W. Atkinson, Constance H. Buchanan, and Margaret R. Miles, 88–110. Boston: Beacon Press, 1985.

_____. "Rumbling and Rambling with Sustenance." *Probe* (September/October 1988).

_____. "Theological and Ethical Themes *Christianity and Crisis* Ought to Address." Unpublished presentation at the Advisory Board of *Christianity and Crisis*, September 25, 1987.

_____."Womanist Theology: Black Women's Voices." *Christianity and Crisis,* March 2, 1987.

_____. "Women's Oppression and Life-Line Politics in Black Women's Religious Narratives." *Journal of Feminist Studies in Religion* 1, no. 2 (fall 1985): 59–72.

V. Sociological Method

Behar, Ruth. "Rage and Redemption: Reading the Life Story of a Mexican Marketing Woman." *Feminist Studies* 16, 2 (summer 1990): 223–58.

Bureau of Rural Workers. *Rural Women Selected Coconut and Sugar-Tenanted Farms.* Philippines: Ministry of Labor and Employment, 1986.

Cannon, Lyn Weber, Elizabeth Higginbotham, and Marianne L. A. Leung. "Race and Class Bias in Qualitative Research on Women." *Gender and Society* 2, no. 4 (December 1988): 449–62.

de Certeau, Michel. *Heterologies: Discourse on the Other.* Minneapolis: University of Minnesota Press, 1986.

Geertz, Clifford. *The Interpretation of Culture.* New York: Basic Books, 1973.

Garfinkel, Harold. *Studies in Ethnomethodology.* Cambridge: Polity Press, 1984.

Gorden, Deborah. "The Politics of Feminist Ethnography: On Women Representing Other Women." Unpublished manuscript.

Griffen, Joyce. "Inside and Outside: The Moebius Strip of Oral History." Paper presented at the Conference "Methodologies and Strategies for Women's Oral History in the Rocky Mountains/Southwest," Denver, Colorado, November 13–14, 1981. Tucson, Ariz.: Southwest Institute for Research on Women, 1982.

Jameson, Elizabeth. "May and Me: Relationships with Informants and the Community." Paper presented at the Conference "Methodologies and Strategies for Women's Oral History in the Rocky Mountains/Southwest," Denver, Colorado, November 13–14, 1981. Tucson, Ariz.: Southwest Institute for Research on Women, 1982.

Kirk, Jerome, and Marc L. Miller. *Reliability and Validity in Qualitative Research.* Beverly Hills, Calif.: Sage Publications, 1986.

Light, Linda, and Nancy Kleiber. "Interactive Research in a Feminist Setting: The Vancouver Women's Health Collective. In *Anthropologies at Home in North America,* 167–84. Cambridge: Harvard University Press, 1981.

Miller, Delbert C. *Handbook of Research Design and Social Measurement.* New York: Longman, 1983.

Noblit, George W., and R. Dwight Hare. *Meta-Ethnography: Synthesizing Qualitative Studies.* Beverly Hills, Calif.: Sage Publications, 1988.

Riessman, Catherine Kohler. "When Gender Is Not Enough: Women Interviewing Women." *Gender and Society* 1, no. 2 (June 1987): 172–207.

Silman, Janet. "In Search of Liberation Methodology." Unpublished paper, May 7, 1985.

Spradley, James R. *The Ethnographic Interview.* New York: Holt, Rinehart & Winston, 1979.

_____. *You Owe Yourself a Drunk.* Boston: Little, Brown & Co., 1970.

Stanley, Liz, and Sue Wise. *Breaking Out: Feminist Consciousness and Feminist Research.* London: Routledge & Kegan Paul, 1983.

Watts, Dale. "Ethnomethodology: A Consideration of Theory and Research." *Cornell Journal of Social Relations* 9.1 (spring 1973): 99–115.

Williamson, John B., David A. Karp, and John R. Dalphin. *The Research Craft.* Boston and Toronto: Little, Brown & Co., 1977.

Zavella, Patricia. "Recording Chicana Life Histories: Refining the Insider's Perspective." Paper presented at the Conference "Methodologies and Strategies for Women's Oral History in the Rocky Mountains/Southwest," Denver, Colorado, November 13–14, 1981. Tucson, Ariz.: Southwest Institute for Research on Women, 1982.

VI. Additional Resources

Agirrebaltzategi, Paulo. *Configuración eclesial de las culturas*. Bilbao: Universidad de Deusto, 1976.

Amirtham, Samuel, and John S. Pobee. *Theology by the People*. Geneva: World Council of Churches, 1986.

Birch, Bruce C., and Larry L. Rasmussen. *Bible and Ethics in the Christian Life*. Rev. ed. Minneapolis: Fortress Press, 1989.

Centre "Cultures and Religions." *Effective Inculturation and Ethnic Identity*. Rome: Pontifical Gregorian University, 1987.

Clark, David. *The Liberation of the Church: The Role of Basic Christian Groups in a New Re-formation*. Birmingham (West Midlands): National Centre for Christian Communities and Networks, 1984.

Collins, Denis E. *Paulo Freire: His Life, Works, and Thought*. New York: Paulist Press, 1977.

Cone, James. *A Black Theology of Liberation*. New York: Lippincott, 1970.

Conn, Walter. *Conscience: Development and Self-Transcendence*. Birmingham, Ala.: Religious Education Press, 1981.

Cooke, Bernard. *Ministry to Word and Sacraments*. Philadelphia: Fortress Press, 1976.

Costa, Ruy O., ed. *One Faith, Many Cultures: Inculturation, Indigenization, and Contextualization*. Maryknoll, N.Y.: Orbis Books, 1988.

Curran, Charles E. *Directions in Catholic Social Ethics*. Notre Dame, Ind.: University of Notre Dame Press, 1985.

_____. *Directions in Fundamental Moral Theology*. Notre Dame, Ind.: University of Notre Dame Press, 1985.

_____. *Faithful Dissent*. Kansas City: Sheed and Ward, 1986.

_____. *Moral Theology, A Continuing Journey*. Notre Dame, Ind.: University of Notre Dame Press, 1982.

_____. *Themes in Fundamental Moral Theology*. Notre Dame, Ind.: University of Notre Dame Press, 1977.

Curran, Charles, and Richard McCormick. *Readings in Moral Theology No. 6: Dissent in the Church*. New York: Paulist Press, 1988.

_____. *Readings in Moral Theology No. 5: Official Catholic Social Teaching*. New York: Paulist Press, 1986.

_____. *Readings in Moral Theology No. 4: The Use of Scripture in Moral Theology*. New York: Paulist Press, 1984.

D'Arcy, Eric. *Conscience and Its Right to Freedom*. New York: Sheed and Ward, 1961.

"Declaration on Religious Freedom." In *The Documents of Vatican II*, edited by Walter M. Abbott, S.J., 14–101. New York: America Press, 1966.

Dehavenon, Mary Lou. "Cultural Anthropology and the Values of Community, Diversity, Poverty, Femininity, Peace, and Change in the United States in 1984." Lecture delivered at the Leadership Conference of Women Religious, Kansas City, Mo., August 1984.

"Dogmatic Constitution on the Church." *The Documents of Vatican II*, edited by Walter M. Abbott, S.J., 14–101. New York: America Press, 1966.

Driver, Tom R. *Christ in a Changing World*. New York: Crossroad, 1981.

Ellwood, Robert S. *Religion and Spiritual Groups in Modern America*. Englewood Cliffs, N.J.: Prentice-Hall, 1973.

Emmet, Dorothy. "Ethical Systems and Social Structures." In *International Encyclopedia of the Social Sciences*, edited by David L. Sills. New York: Macmillan and Free Press, 1968.

_____. *The Moral Prism*. New York: St. Martin's Press, 1979.

Fabella, Virginia. *Asia's Struggle for Humanity*. Maryknoll, N.Y.: Orbis Books, 1980.

Fabella, Virginia, and Sergio Torres, eds. *Doing Theology in a Divided World*. Maryknoll, N.Y.: Orbis Books, 1985.

_____. eds. *Irruption of the Third World*. Maryknoll, N.Y.: Orbis Books, 1983.

Fishman, Joshua A. "Language Maintenance." In *Harvard Encyclopedia of Ethnic Groups*, edited by Stephan Thernstrom, 629–38. Cambridge: The Belknap Press of Harvard University, 1980.

Franklin, Robert Michael. "An Ethic of Hope: The Moral Thought of Martin Luther King, Jr." *Union Seminary Quarterly Review* 40, no. 4 (1986): 41–51.

Freire, Paulo. *Cultural Action for Freedom*. Cambridge, Mass.: Harvard Education Review, 1970.

_____. *La Educación como práctica de la libertad*. Madrid: Siglo Ventiuno de España Editores, 1976.

_____. "Education, Liberation and the Church." *Religious Education* 79 (fall 1984): 527–28.

_____. *The Politics of Education: Culture, Power and Liberation*. Hadley: Bergin & Garvey, 1985.

Fromm, Erich. "Conscience." In *Moral Principles of Action: Man's Ethical Imperative*, edited by Ruth Nanda Anshen, 176–98. New York: Harper and Row, 1952.

Gottwald, Norman. *The Bible and Liberation*. Maryknoll, N.Y.: Orbis Books, 1983.

Gramsci, Antonio. *Prison Notebooks*. Edited and translated by Quintin Hoare and Geoffrey Nowell Smith. New York: International Publishers, 1975.

Green, James W. *Cultural Awareness in the Human Services*. New York: Prentice-Hall, 1982.

Gustafson, James M. *Theology and Ethics*. Oxford: Blackwell, 1981.

Haring, Bernard. *The Law of Christ*. Westminster, Md.: The Newman Press, 1966.

_____. "La teología moral después del Vaticano II y la contribución de América Latina." *Páginas* 97 (June 1989): 95–111.

Harrod, Howard L. *The Human Center: Moral Agency in the Social World*. Philadelphia: Fortress Press, 1981.

Hauerwas, Stanley. *A Community of Character*. Notre Dame, Ind.: University of Notre Dame Press, 1981.

Harvey, David. *Spaces of Hope*. Berkeley: University of California Press, 2000.

Herkovits, Melville J. *Cultural Relativism: Perspectives in Cultural Pluralism*. New York: Vintage Books, 1973.

Holland, Joe, and Peter Henriot. *Social Analysis: Linking Faith and Justice*. Maryknoll, N.Y.: Orbis Books, 1983.

Hope, Anne, and Sally Timmel. *Training for Transformation*. Zimbabwe: Mambo Press, 1984.

Johnston, William B. *Workforce 2000: Work and Workers for the 21st Century*. Indianapolis, Ind.: Hudson Institute, 1987.

Jones, Major J. *Christian Ethics for Black Theology*. Nashville, Tenn.: Abingdon Press, 1975.

Kammer, Charles, *Ethics and Liberation*. Maryknoll, N.Y.: Orbis Books, 1988.

Kelly, Matthew. "St. Thomas and the Moral Agent." *The Thomist* 46 (April 1982): 307–12.

Komonchak, Joseph. "Moral Pluralism and the Unity of the Church." In *Christian Ethics: Uniformity, Universality, Pluralism,* edited by Jacques Pohier and Dietmar Mieth, 89–94. Concilium 150. New York: Seabury, 1981.

_____. "Ordinary Papal Magisterium and Religious Assent." In *Readings in Moral Theology No. 3: The Magisterium and Morality,* edited by Charles E. Curran and Richard A. McCormick, 67-90. New York: Paulist Press, 1982.

Lebacqz, Karen. *Six Theories of Justice*. Minneapolis: Augsburg Press, 1986.

Lafaye, J. *Quetzalcoatl et Guadalupe*. Paris: Gallimard, 1974.

Langan, John, S.J. "Roman Catholic Theological Anthropology as a Basis for Human Rights." Paper presented at the 24th Annual Meeting of the Society of Christian Ethics. Indianapolis, Ind., 14–16 January 1983.

Linton, Ralph. "Universal Ethical Principles: An Anthropological View." In *Moral Principles of Action: Man's Ethical Imperative,* edited by Ruth Nanada Anshen, 645–60. New York: Harper and Row, 1952.

Lonergan, Bernard J. F. *Insight: A Study of Human Understanding*. New York: Philosophical Library, 1970.

_____. *Method in Theology*. New York: Herder and Herder, 1972.

_____. *The Subject*. Milwaukee, Wis.: Marquette University Press, 1968.

McCann, Dennis. *Christian Realism and Liberation Theology*. Maryknoll, N.Y.: Orbis Books, 1981.

_____. "Conscientization." In *The Westminster Dictionary of Christian Ethics,* edited by James F. Childress and John Macquarrie. Philadelphia: Westminster, 1986.

Macmurray, J. *The Self as Agent*. London: Faber and Faber, 1957.

Maguire, Daniel C. "The Feminization of God and Ethics." *Christianity and Crisis,* March 15, 1982.

_____. *The Moral Choice*. New York: Doubleday & Co., 1979.

Mahoney, John. "The Spirit and Moral Discernment in Aquinas." *Heythrop Journal* 13 (1972): 291–94.

McErlane, M. J. "El tratamiento de la moral católica actual. Acercamiento a la teología moral de Ch. E. Curran." *Moralia* 4, no. 4 (1982): 421–38.

McGovern, Arthur F. *Liberation Theology and Its Critics*. Maryknoll, N.Y.: Orbis Books, 1990.

Morgan, John H. "The Concept of 'Meaning' in Religion and Culture: A Dialogue between Theology and Anthropology." In *Understanding Religion and Culture*, edited by John H. Morgan. Washington, D.C.: University of America, 1979.

Mueller, J. J. *What Are They Saying about Theological Method?* New York: Paulist Press, 1984.

Murray, John Courtney, ed. *Freedom and Man*. New York: P. L. Kennedy, 1965.

Mveng, Engelbert. "A Cultural Perspective." In *Doing Theology in a Divided World*, edited by Virginia Fabella and Sergio Torres, 72–75. Maryknoll, N.Y.: Orbis Books, 1985.

Neal, Maria Augusta. *The Just Demands of the Poor: Essays in Socio-Theology*. New York: Paulist Press, 1987.

Nelson, Paul. *Narrative and Morality: A Theological Inquiry*. University Park: Pennsylvania State University Press, 1987.

Niebuhr, H. Richard. *Christ and Culture*. New York: Harper and Row, 1951.

————. *The Responsible Self*. New York: Harper and Row, 1963.

O'Connell, Timothy. *Principles for a Catholic Morality*. New York: Seabury, 1978.

Oglesby, Enoch Hammond. *Ethics and Theology from the Other Side: Sounds of Moral Struggle*. Washington, D.C.: University Press of America, 1979.

Ogletree, Thomas W. *The Use of the Bible in Christian Ethics*. Philadelphia: Fortress Press, 1983.

Paris, Peter. "The Task of Religious Social Ethics in the Light of Black Theology." In *Liberation and Ethics*, edited by Charles Amjad-Ali and W. Alvin Pitcher, 135–43. Chicago: Center for the Scientific Study of Religion, 1985.

Parker, C. "Popular Religion in Latin America." *Popular Religions*. Pro Mundi Vita Studies (November 1988): 18–26.

Pfeifer, Michael. "Thoughts on Freedom, Conscience and Obedience." *Conscience* (July/August 1987).

Pieris, Aloysius. "Place of Non-Christian Religions." In *Irruption of the Third World*, edited by Virginia Fabella and Sergio Torres, 113–39. Maryknoll, N.Y.: Orbis Books, 1983.

Piper, Otto A. *Christian Ethics*. London: Thomas Nelson & Sons, 1970.

Preston, Ronald. "Conscience." In *The Westminster Dictionary of Christian Ethics*, edited by James E. Childress and John Macquarrie, 116–18. Philadelphia: Westminster, 1986.

Proudfoot, Wayne. *The Pope and Revolution*. Washington, D.C.: Ethics and Public Policy Center, 1982.

————. *Religious Experience*. Berkeley: University of California Press, 1985.

Rahner, Karl. *Concern for the Church*. 2, *Theological Investigations*. New York: Crossroad, 1981.

————. *Grace in Freedom*. New York: Herder and Herder, 1969.

————. *Theological Investigations*. Vol. 6. Baltimore: Helicon Press, 1969.

Rasmussen, Larry. "New Dynamics in Theology." *Christianity and Crisis*, May 16, 1988.

Reich, Alice Higman. "Ethnicity as a Cultural System." In *Understanding Religion and Culture*, edited by John H. Morgan. Washington, D.C.: University Press of America, 1979.

Rosaldo, M. Z. "The Use and Abuse of Anthropology: Reflections on Feminist and Cross-Cultural Understanding." *Signs* 5, no. 3 (spring 1980): 389–417.

Sano, Roy I. "Ethnic Liberation Theology: Neo-Orthodoxy Reshaped or Replaced?" In *Liberation Theologies in North America and Europe*, edited by Gerald H. Anderson and Thomas F. Stransky. Mission Trends, 4, 247–58. New York: Paulist Press, 1979.

Sassen, Saskia. *Globalization and Its Discontents*. New York: New Press, 1998.

Scheman, Naomi. "Individualism and the Objects of Psychology." In *Discovering Reality*, edited by Sandra Harding and Merrill B. Hintikka. Dordrecht, Holland: D. Reidel Publishing Co., 1983.

Schneewind, J. B. "The Use of Autonomy in Ethical Theory." In *Reconstructing Individualism*, edited by Thomas C. Heller, Morton Sosna, David E. Wellbery, 64–75. Palo Alto, Calif.: Stanford University Press, 1986.

Schreiter, Robert J. *Constructing Local Theologies*. Maryknoll, N.Y.: Orbis Books, 1985.

Smith, Erwin. *The Ethics of Martin Luther King, Jr.* Lewiston, N.Y.: Edwin Mellen Press, 1981.

Spaeth, Robert L. *The Church and a Catholic's Conscience*. Minneapolis: Winston, 1985.

Sprio, M.E., and Roy D'Andrade. "A Cross-Cultural Study of Some Supernatural Beliefs." *American Anthropologist* 60 (1958):

Third General Conference of Latin American Bishops. *Evangelization at Present and in the Future of Latin America.* Washington, D.C.: National Conference of Catholic Bishops, 1979.

Tillich, Paul. *Systematic Theology.* Vol. 1. Chicago: University of Chicago Press, 1951.

Tracy, David. *Blessed Rage for Order.* New York: Seabury, 1978.

U.S. Bishops' Committee for Social Development and World Peace. "Beyond the Melting Pot: Cultural Pluralism in the United States." *Origins* 10, no. 31 (January 15, 1981):

Verhey, Allen. *The Great Reversal: Ethics and the New Testament.* Grand Rapids, Mich.: Eerdmans, 1984.

Vidal, Marciano. *El Discernimiento ético.* Madrid: Ediciones Cristiandad, 1980.

West, Charles. "Culture, Power and Ideology in Third World Theologies." *Missiology* 12, no. 4 (October 1984): 405–20.

West, Cornel. "Marxist Theory and the Specificity of Afro-American Oppression." In *Marxism and the Interpretation of Culture,* edited by Carry Nelson and Lawrence Grossberg. Chicago: University of Chicago Press, 1988.

_____. *Prophetic Fragments.* Grand Rapids, Mich.: Erdmans, 1988.

_____. *Prophesy Deliverance!* Philadelphia: Westminster, 1982.

Young, Iris Marion. *Justice and the Politics of Difference.* Princeton, N.J.: Princeton University Press, 1990.

INDEX

CPSIA information can be obtained
at www.ICGtesting.com
Printed in the USA
LVHW101624301222
736215LV00001B/9

9 780800 635992